THE CHRONICLES OF BARSETSHIRE • VOLUM
TROLLOPE

General Books LLC™, Memphis, USA, 2012. ISBN: 9781150714665.

❦ ❦ ❦ ❦ ❦ ❦ ❦ ❦

E CHRONICLES OF BARSETSHIRE IN EIGHT VOLUMES
VOL. II.
LONDON: PRINTED BY J. S. VIRTUE AND CO., 'IMITED, CITY ROAD
" I think, Mrs. Proudie. that under all the circumstances." etc. AND BARCTT ESTER TOWERS *in* ANTHONY TftOLLOPE IN TWO VOLUMES
VOL. II.
LONDON CHAPMAN AND HALL, Limited
CONTENTS OF VOL. II.
BAECHESTEK TOWERS.
(Ctmtinued.)

CHAPTER XIX.
PAGK
Barchester By Moonlight 3
CHAPTER XX.
Ms. Ababin IS
CHAPTER XXI.
St. Ewold's Parsonage 28
CHAPTER XXII.
The Thornes Of Ullathornb 40
CHAPTER XXHI.
Mr. Ababin Reads Himself In At St. Ewold's 54
CHAPTER XXIV.
Mr. Slope Manages Matters Very Cleverly At PunniNonALE.. 64
CHAPTER XXV.
PAGB
Fourteen Arguments In Favour Of Mr. Quiverful's Claims.. 76
CHAPTER XXVI.
Mrs. Proudie Wrestles And Gets A Fall 85
CHAPTER XXVII.
A Love Scene 97
CHAPTER XXVIII.
Mrs. Bold Is Entertained By Dr. And Mrs. Grantly At Plumstead. 113
CHAPTER XXIX.
A Serious Interview 128
CHAPTER XXX.
Another Love Scene 137
CHAPTER XXXI.
The Bishop's Library 151
CHAPTER XXXII.

A New Candidate For Ecclesiastical Honours..... 157
CHAPTER XXXIH.
Mrs. Proudie Victrix 173
CHAPTER XXXIV.
Oxford—The Master And Tutor Of Laz Rus 185
CHAPTER XXXVII.
The Signora Neroni, The Countess De Courcy, And Mrs. Prmjdib
MEET EACH OTHER AT Ullathorne 218
CHAPTER XXXVIII.
The Bishop Breakfasts, And The Dean Dies 230
CHAPTER XXXIX.
The Dooxaloftb And The Greenacres 243
CHAPTER XL.
Ullathorne Sports.—Act. II..... 253
CHAPTER XLI.
Mrs. Bold Confides Hee Sorrow To Her Friend Miss Stanhope. 263
CHAPTER XLII.
Ullathorne Sports.—Act III 272
CHAPTER XLIII.
Mr. And Mrs. Quiverful Are Made Happy. Mr. Slope Is Encouraged By The Press 287
CHAPTER XLIV.
Mrs. Bold At Home SCI
CHAPTER XLV.
TAQB
The Stanhopes At Home 311
CHAPTER XLVI.
Mi. Slope's Parting Interview With The Signorv.... 322
CHAPTER XLYII.
The Dean Elect 331
CHAPTER XLVIII.
Miss Thorne Shows Her Talent At Match-making....341
CHAPTER XLIX.
The Belzebub Colt 353
CHAPTER L.
The Archdeacon Is Satisfied With The State Op Affairs... 360
CHAPTER LI.
Mr. Slope Bids Farewell To The Palace And Its Inhabitants.. 368

CHAPTER LII.

The New Dean Takes Possession Of The Deanery, And The New

Warden Of The Hospital 376

CHAPTER LIII.

Conclusion 885

BARCHESTER TOWERS (Continued) VOL. II.

B BARCHESTER TOWERS.

CHAPTER XIX. BARCHESTER BY MOON-LIGHT.

Thebe was much cause for grief and occasional perturbation of spirits in the Stanhope family, but yet they rarely seemed to be grieved or to be disturbed. It was the peculiar gift of each of them that each was able to bear his or her own burden without complaint, and perhaps without sympathy. They habitually looked on the sunny side of the wall, if there was a gleam on either side for them to look at; and, if there was none, they endured the shade with an indifference which, if not stoical, answered the end at which the Stoics aimed. Old Stanhope could not but feel that he had illperformed his duties as a father and a clergyman; and could hardly look forward to his own death without grief at the position in which he would leave his family. His income for many years had been as high as 3000?. a year, and yet they had among them no other provision than their mother's fortune of 10,000?. He had not only spent his income, but was in debt. Yet with all this, he seldom showed much outward sign of trouble.

It was the same with the mother. If she added little to the pleasures of her children she detracted still less. She neither grumbled at her lot, nor spoke much of her past or future sufferings. As long as she had a maid to adjust her dress, and had those dresses well made, nature with her was satisfied. It was the same with the children. Charlotte never rebuked her father with the prospect of their future poverty, nor did it seem to grieve her that she was becoming an old maid so quickly; her temper was rarely ruined, and, if we might judge by her appearance, she was always happy. The Signora was not so sweet-tempered, but she possessed much enduring courage; she seldom complained,—never, in-deed, to her family. Though she had a cause for affliction which would have utterly broken down the heart of most women as beautiful as she and as devoid of all religious support, yet, she bore her suffering in silence, or alluded to it only to elicit the sympathy and stimulate the admiration of the men with whom she flirted. As to Bertie, one would have imagined from the sound of his voice and the gleam of his eye that he had not a sorrow nor a care in the world. Nor had he. He was incapable of anticipating to-morrow's griefs. The prospect of future want no more disturbed his appetite than does that of the butcher's knife disturb the appetite of the sheep.

Such was the usual tenour of their way; but there were rare exceptions. Occasionally the father would allow an angry glance to fall from his eye, and the lion would send forth a low dangerous roar as though he meditated some deed of blood. Occasionally also Madame Neroni would become bitter against mankind, more than usually antagonistic to the world's decencies, and would seem as though she was about to break from her moorings and allow herself to be carried forth by the tide of her feelings to utter ruin and shipwreck. She, however, like the rest of them, had no real feelings,—could feel no true passion. In that was her security. Before she resolved on any contemplated escapade she would make a small calculation, and then would at last conclude that the Stanhope villa or even Barchester close was better than the world at large.

They were most irregular in their hours. The father was generally the earliest in the breakfast-parlour, and Charlotte would soon follow and give him his coffee; but the others breakfasted anywhere, anyhow, and at any time. On the morning after the archdeacon's futile visit to the palace Dr. Stanhope came down stairs with an ominously dark look about his eyebrows; his white locks were rougher than usual, and he breathed thickly and loudly as he took his seat in his arm-chair. He had open letters in his hand, and when Charlotte came into the room he was still reading them. She went up and kissed him as was her wont, but he hardly noticed her as she did so, and she knew at once that something was the matter.

"What's the meaning of that?" said he, throwing over the table a letter with a Milan post-mark. Charlotte was a little frightened as she took it up, but her mind was relieved when she saw that it was merely the bill of their Italian milliner. The sum total was certainly large, but not so large as to create an important row.

"It's for our clothes, papa, for six months before we came here. The three of us can't dress for nothing, you know. "

"Nothing, indeed!" said he, looking at the figures, which in Milanese denominations were certainly monstrous.

"The man should have sent it to me," said Charlotte.

"I wish he had with all my heart,—if you would have paid it. I see enough in it to know that three quarters of it are for Hadeline."

"She has little else to amuse her, sir," said Charlotte, with true good nature.

"And I suppose he has nothing else to amuse him," said the doctor, throwing over another letter to his daughter. It was from some member of the family of Sidonia, and politely requested the father to pay a small trifle of 700?., being the amount of a bill discounted in favour of Mr. Ethelbert Stanhope, and now overdue for a period of nine months. Charlotte read the letter, slowly folded it up, and put it under the edge of the tea-tray. "I suppose he has nothing to amuse him but discounting bills with Jews. Does he think I 'll pay that?"

"I am sure he thinks no such thing," said she.

"And who does he think will pay it?"

"As far as honesty goes I suppose it won't much matter if it is never paid," said she. "I dare say he got very little of it."

"I suppose it won't much matter either," said the father, "if h«5 goes to prison and rots there. It seems to me that that's the other alternative."

Dr. Stanhope spoke of the custom of his youth. But his daughter, though she had lived so long abroad, was much more completely versed in the ways of the English world. "If the man arrests him," said she, "he must go through the court."

It is thus, thou great family of Sidonia,—it is thus that we Gentiles treat thee, when, in our extremest need, thou and thine have aided us with mountains of gold as big as lions,—and occasionally with wine-warrants and orders for dozens of dressingcases.

"What, and become an insolvent?" said the doctor. "He's that already," said Charlotte, wishing always to get over a difficulty.

"What a condition," said the doctor, "for the son of a clergyman of the Church of England!"

"I don't see why clergymen's.sons should pay their debts more than other young men," said Charlotte.

"He's had as much from me since he left school as is held sufficient for the eldest son of any nobleman," said the angry father.

"Well, sir," said Charlotte; "give him another chance."

"What!" said the doctor, do you mean that I am to pay that Jew?"

"Oh no! I wouldn't pay him. He must take his chance; and if the worst comes to the worst, Bertie must go abroad. But I want you to be civil to Bertie, and let him remain here as long as we stop. He has a plan in his head that may put him on his feet after all."

"Has he any plan for following up his profession?"

"Oh, he'll do that too; but that must follow. He's thinking of getting married."

Just at that moment the door opened, and Bertie came in whistling. The doctor immediately devoted himself to his egg, and allowed Bertie to whistle himself round to his sister's side without noticing him.

Charlotte gave a sign to him with her eye, first glancing at her father, and then at the letter, the corner of which peeped out from under the tea-tray. Bertie saw and understood, and with the quiet motion of a cat abstracted the letter and made himself acquainted with its con-

tents. The doctor, however, had seen him, deep as he appeared to be inersed in his egg-shell, and said in his harshest voice, "Well, sir, do you know that gentleman?"

"Yes, sir," said Bertie. "I have a sort of acquaintance with him, but none that can justify him in troubling you. If you will allow me, sir, I will answer this."

"At any rate I sha'n't, said the father, and then he added, after a pause. "Is it true, sir, that you owe the man 700?.?"

"Well," said Bertie, "I think I should be inclined to dispute the amount, if I were in a condition to pay him such of it as I really do owe him."

"Has he your bill for 700?.?" said the father, speaking very loudly and very angrily.

"I believe he has," said Bertie?" but all the money I ever got from him was 150?."

"And what became of the 550?.?"

"Why, sir, the commission was 100?. or so, and I took the remainder in paving-stones and rocking-horses."

"Paving-stones and rocking-horses!" said the doctor. "Where are they?"

"Oh, sir, I suppose they are in London somewhere;—but I'll inquire if you wish for them."

"He's an idiot," said the doctor, "and it's sheer folly to waste more money on him. Nothing can save him from ruin. " So saying, the unhappy father walked out of the room.

"Would the governor like to have the paving-stones?" said Bertie to his sister.

"I '11 tell you what," said she, "if you don't take care you will find yourself loose upon the world without even a house over your head. You don't know him as well as I do. He's very angry."

Bertie stroked his big beard, sipped his tea, chatted over his misfortunes in a half comic, half serious tone, and ended by promising his sister that he would do his very best to make himself agreeable to the widow Bold. Then Charlotte followed her father to his own room, and softened down his wrath, and persuaded him to say nothing more about the Jew bill discounter, at any rate for a few weeks. He even went so far as to say he would pay the 700?., or at any rate set-

tle the bill, if he saw a certainty of his son's securing for himself anything like a decent provision in life. Nothing was said openly between them about poor Eleanor; but the father and the daughter understood each other.

They all met together in the drawing-room at nine o'clock, in perfect good humour with each other; and about that hour Mrs. Bold was announced. She had never been in the house before, though she had of course called; and now she felt it strange to find herself there in her usual evening dress, entering the drawingroom of these strangers in this friendly unceremonious way, as though she had known them all her life. But in three minutes they made her at home. Charlotte tripped down stairs and took her bonnet from her, and Bertie came to relieve her from her shawl, and the Signora smiled on her as she could smile when she chose to be gracious, and the old doctor shook hands with her in a kind benedictory manner that went to her heart at once and made her feel that he must be a good man.

She had not been seated for above five minutes when the door again opened, and Mr. Slope was announced. She felt rather surprised, because she was told that nobody was to be there, and it was very evident from the manner of some of them, that Mr. Slope was unexpected. But still there was not much in it. In such invitations a bachelor or two more or less are always spoken of as nobodies, and there-was no reason why Mr Slope should not drink tea at Dr. Stanhope's as well as Eleanor herself. He, however, was very much surprised and not very much gratified at finding that his own embryo spouse made one of the party. He had come there to gratify himself by gazing on Madame Neroni's beauty, and listening to and returning her flattery; and though he had not owned as much to himself, he still felt that if he spent the evening as he had intended to do, he might probably not thereby advance his suit with Mrs. Bold.

The Signora, who had no idea of a rival, received Mr. Slope with her usual marks of distinction. As he took her hand she made some confidential communication to him in a low voice, declaring that she had a plan to communicate to him after tea, and was evidently prepared to go on with her work of reducing the chaplain to a state of captivity. Poor Mr. Slope was rather beside himself. He thought that Eleanor could not but have learnt from his demeanour that he was an admirer of her own, and he had also flattered himself that the idea was not unacceptable to her. What would she think of him if he now devoted himself to a married woman!

But Eleanor was not inclined to be severe in her criticisms on him in this respect, and felt no annoyance of any kind, when she found herself seated between Bertie and Charlotte Stanhope. She had no suspicion of Mr. Slope's intentions; she had no suspicion even of the suspicion of other people; but still she felt well pleased not to have Mr. Slope too near to her.

And she was not ill-pleased to have Bertie Stanhope near her. It was rarely indeed that he failed to make an agreeable impression on strangers. With a bishop indeed who thought much of his own dignity it was possible that he might fail, but hardly with a young and pretty woman. He possessed the tact of becoming instantly intimate with women without giving rise to any fear of impertinence. He had about him somewhat of the propensities of a tame cat. It seemed quite natural that he should be petted, caressed, and treated with familiar good nature, and that in return he should purr, and be sleek and graceful, and above all never show his claws. Like other tame cats, however, he had his claws, and sometimes made them dangerous.

When tea was over Charlotte went to the open window and declared loudly that the full harvest moon was much too beautiful to be disregarded, and called them all to look at it. To tell the truth, there was but one there who cared much about the moon's beauty, and that one was not Charlotte; but she knew how valuable an aid to her purpose the chaste goddess might become, and could easily create a little enthusiasm for the purpose of the moment. Eleanor and Bertie were soon with her. The doctor was now quiet in his arm-chair, and Mrs. Stanhope in hers, both prepared for slumber.

"Are you a Whewellite or a Brewsterite, or a t'othermanite, Mrs. Bold?" said Charlotte, who knew a little about everything, and had read about a third of each of the books to which she alluded.

"Oh!" said Eleanor; "I have not read any of the books, but I feel sure that there is one man in the moon at least, if not more."

"You don't believe in the pulpy gelatinous matter?" said Bertie.

"I heard about that," said Eleanor; "and I really think it's almost wicked to talk in such a manner. How can we argue about God's power in the other stars from the laws which he has given for our rule in this one?"

"How indeed!" said Bertie. ""Why shouldn't there be a race of salamanders in Venus? and even if there be nothing but fish in Jupiter, why shouldn't the fish thfere be as wide awake as the men and women here?"

"That would be saying very little for them," said Charlotte. "I am for Dr. Whewell myself; for I do not think that men and women are worth being repeated in such countless worlds. There may be souls in other stars, but I doubt their having any bodies attached to them. But come, Mrs. Bold, let us put our bonnets on and walk round the close. If we are to discuss sidereal questions, we shall do so much better under the towers of the cathedral, than stuck in this narrow window."

Mrs. Bold made no objection, and a party was made to walk out. Charlotte Stanhope well knew the rule as to three being no company, and she had therefore to induce her sister to allow Mr. Slope to accompany them.

"Come, Mr. Slope," she said; "I'm sure you'll join us. We shall be in again in a quarter of an hour, Madeline."

Madeline read in her eye all that she had to say, knew her object, and as she had to depend on her sister for so many of her amusements, she felt that she must yield. It was hard to be left alone while others of her own age walked out to feel the soft influence of the bright night, but it would be harder still to be without the sort of sanction which Charlotte gave to all her flirtations and intrigues. Charlotte's eye told her that she must give up just at present for the good of the family, and so Madeline obeyed.

But Charlotte's eyes said nothing of the sort to Mr. Slope. He had no objection at all to the *tete-d-tete* with the Signora, which the departure of the other three would allow him, and gently whispered to her, "I shall not leave you alone."

"Oh, yes," said she; "go,—pray go, pray go, for my sake. Do not think that I am so selfish. It is understood that nobody is kept within for me. You will understand this too when you know me better. Pray join them, Mr. Slope, but when you come in speak to me for five minutes before you leave us."

Mr. Slope understood that he was to go, and he therefore joined the party in the hall. He would have had no objection at all to this arrangement, if he could have secured Mrs. Bold's arm; but this of course was out of the question. Indeed, his fate was very soon settled, for no sooner had he reached the hall-door than Miss Stanhope put her hand within his arm, and Bertie walked off with Eleanor just as naturally as though she were already his own property.

And so they sauntered forth. First they walked round the close, According to their avowed intent; then they went under the old arched gateway below St Cuthbert's little church, and then they turned behind the grounds of the bishop's palace, and so on till they came to the bridge just at the edge of the town, from which passers-by can look down into the gardens of Hiram's Hospital; and here Charlotte and Mr. Slope, who were in advance, stopped till the other two came up to them. Mr. Slope knew that the gableends and old brick chimneys which stood up so prettily in the moonlight, were those of Mr. Harding's late abode, and would not have stopped on such a spot, in such company, if he could have avoided it; but Miss Stanhope would not take the hint which he tried to give.

"This is a very pretty place, Mrs. Bold," said Charlotte; "by far the prettiest place near Barchester. I wonder your father gave it up."

It was a very pretty place, and now by the deceitful light of the moon looked twice larger, twice prettier, twice more antiquely picturesque than it would have done in truth-telling daylight. Who does not know the air of complex multiplicity and the mysterious interesting grace which the moon always lends to old gabled buildings half surrounded, as was the hospital, by fine trees! As seen from the bridge on the night of which we are speaking, Mr. Harding's late abode did look very'lovely; and though Eleanor did not grieve at her father's having left it, she felt at the moment an intense wish that he might be allowed to return.

"He is going to return to it almost immediately, is he not?" asked Bertie.

Eleanor made no immediate reply. Many such a question passes unanswered, without the notice of the questioner; but such was not now the case. They all remained silent as though expecting her to reply, and after a moment or two, Charlotte said, "I believe it is settled that Mr. Harding returns to the hospital, is it not?"

"I don't think anything about it is settled yet," said Eleanor.

"But it must be a matter of course," said Bertie; "that is, if your father wishes it; who else on earth could hold it after what has occurred?"

Eleanor quietly made her companion understand that the matter was one which she could not discuss in the present company, and then they passed on. Charlotte said she would go a short way up the hill out of the town so as to look back upon the towers of the cathedral, and as Eleanor lent upon Bertie's arm for assistance in the walk, she told him how the matter stood between her father and the bishop.

"And, he," said Bertie, pointing on to Mr. Slope; "what part does he take in it?"

Eleanor explained how Mr. Slope had

at first endeavoured to tyrannise over her father, but how he had lately come round, and done all he could to talk the bishop over in Mr. Harding's favour. "But my father," said she, "is hardly inclined to trust him. They all say he is so arrogant to the old clergymen of the city."

"Take my word for it," said Bertie, "your father is right. If I am not very much mistaken, that man is both arrogant and false."

They strolled up to the top of the hill, and then returned through the fields by a footpath which leads by a small wooden bridge, or rather a plank with a rustic rail to it, over the river to the other side of the cathedral from that at which they had started. They had thus walked round the bishop's grounds, through which the river runs, and round the cathedral and adjacent fields, and it was past eleven before they reached the doctor's door.

"It is very late," said Eleanor; it will be a shame to disturb your mother again at such an hour."

"Oh," said Charlotte, laughing, "you won't disturb mamma; I dare say she is in bed by this time, and Madeline would be furious if you did not come in and see her. Come, Bertie, take Mrs. Bold's bonnet from her."

They went up stairs, and found the Signora alone, reading. She looked somewhat sad and melancholy, but not more so perhaps than was sufficient to excite additional interest in the bosom of Mr. Slope; and she was soon deep in whispered intercourse with that happy gentleman who was allowed to find a resting-place on her sofa. The Signora had a way of whispering that was peculiarly her own, and was exactly the reverse of that which prevails among great tragedians. The great tragedian hisses out a positive whisper, made with bated breath, and produced by inarticulated tongue-formed sounds, but yet he is audible through the whole house. The Signora however used no hisses, and produced all her words in a clear silver tone, but they could only be heard by the ear into which they were poured.

Charlotte hurried and skurried about

the room hither and thither, doing, or pretending to do many things; and then saying something about seeing her mother, ran up stairs. Eleanor was thus left alone with Bertie, and she hardly felt an hour fly by her. To give Bertie his due credit, he could not have played his cards better. He did not make love to her, nor sigh, nor look languishing; but he was amusing and familiar, yet respectful; and when he left Eleanor at her own door at one o'clock, which he did by the bye with the assistance of the now jealous Slope, she thought that he was one of the most agreeable men, and the Stanhopes decidedly the most agreeable family, that she had ever met.

CHAPTER XX. MR. ARABIN.

The Rev. Francis Arabin, fellow of Lazarus, late professor of poetry at Oxford, and present vicar of St. Ewold in the diocese of Barchester, must now be introduced personally to the reader. And as he will fill a conspicuous place in this, and perhaps another, volume, it is desirable that he should be made to stand before the reader's eye by the aid of such portraiture as the author is able to produce.

It is to be regretted that no mental method of daguerreotype or photography has yet been discovered by which the characters of men can be reduced to writing and put into grammatical language with an unerring precision of truthful description. How often does the novelist feel, ay, and the historian also and the biographer, that he has conceived within his mind and accurately depicted on the tablet of his brain the full character and personage of a man, and that nevertheless, when he flies to pen and ink to perpetuate the portrait, his words forsake, elude, disappoint, and play the deuce with him, till at the end of a dozen pages the man described has no more resemblance to the man conceived than the sign-board at the corner of the street has to the Duke of Cambridge?

And yet such mechanical descriptive skill would hardly give more satisfaction to the reader than the skill of the photographer does to the anxious mother desirous to possess an absolute duplicate of her beloved child. The likeness is indeed true; but it is a dull, dead, unfeeling, inauspicious likeness. The face is indeed there, and those looking at it will know at once whose image it is; but the owner of the face will not be proud of the resemblance.

There is no royal road to learning; no short cut to the acquirement of any valuable art. Let photographers and daguerreotypers do what they will, and improve as they may with further skill on that which skill has already done, they will never achieve a portrait of the human face divine-Let biographers, novelists, and the rest of us groan as we may under the burdens which we so often feel too heavy for our shoulders, we must either bear them up like men, or own ourselves too weak for the work we have undertaken. There is no way of writing well and also of writing easily.

Labor omnia vincit improbus. Such should be the chosen motto of every labourer, and it may be that labour, if adequately enduring, may suffice at last to produce even some not untrue resemblance of the Rev. Francis Arabin.

Of his doings in the world, and of the sort of fame which he has achieved, enough has been already said. It has also been said that he is forty years of age, and still unmarried. He was the younger son of a country gentleman of small fortune in the north of England. At an early age he went to Winchester, and was intended by his father for New College; but though studious as a boy, he was not studious within the prescribed limits; and at the age of eighteen he left school with a character for talent, but without a scholarship. All that he had obtained, over and above the advantage of his character, was a gold medal for English verse, and hence was derived a strong presumption on the part of his friends that he was destined to add another name to the imperishable list of English poets.

From Winchester he went to Oxford and was entered as a commoner at BaUiol. Here his special career very soon commenced. He utterly eschewed the society of fast men, gave no wine parties, kept no horses, rowed no boats,

joined no rows, and was the pride of his college tutor. Such at least was his career till he had taken his little go; and then he commenced a course of action which, though not less creditable to himself as a man, was hardly so much to the taste of the tutor. He became a member of a vigorous debating society, and rendered himself remarkable there for humorous energy. Though always in earnest, yet his earnestness was always droll. To be true iu his ideas, unanswerable in his syllogisms, and just in his aspirations was not enough for him. He had failed, failed in his own opinion as well as that of others when others came to know him, if he could not reduce the arguments of his opponents to an absurdity, and conquer both by wit and reason. To say that his object was ever to raise a laugh, would be most untrue. He hated such common and unnecessary evidence of satisfaction on the part of his hearers. A joke that required to be laughed at was, with him, not worth uttering. He could appreciate by a keener sense than that of his ears the success of his wit, and would see in the eyes of his auditory whether or no he was understood and appreciated.

He had been a religious lad before he left school. That is, he had addicted himself to a party in religion, and having done so had received that' benefit which most men do who become partisans in such a cause. We are much too apt to look at schism in our church as an unmitigated evil. Moderate schism, if there may be such a thing, at any rate calls attention to the subject, draws in supporters who would otherwise have been inattentive to the matter, and teaches men to think upon religion. How great an amount of good of this description has followed that movement in the Church of England which commenced with tho publication of Froude's Remains!

As a boy young Arabin took up the cudgels on the side of the Tractarians, and at Oxford he sat for a while at the feet of the great Newman. To this cause he lent all his faculties. For it he concocted verses, for it he made speeches, for it he scintillated the brightest sparks

of his quiet wit. For it he ate and drank and dressed, and had his being. In due process of time he took his degree, and wrote himself B.A., but he did not do so with any remarkable amount of academical eclat. He had occupied himself

Vol. 11. o too much with high church matters, and the polemics, politics, anu outward demonstrations usually concurrent with high churchmanship, to devote himself with sufficient vigour to the acquisition of a double first. He was not a double first, nor even a first class man; but he revenged himself on the university by putting firsts and double firsts out of fashion for the year, and laughing down a species of pedantry which at the age of twenty-three leaves no room in a man's mind for graver subjects than conic sections or Greek accents.

Greek accents, however, and conic sections were esteemed necessaries at Balliol, and there was no admittance there for Mr. Arabin within the list of its fellows. Lazarus, however, the richest and most comfortable abode of Oxford dons, opened its bosom to the young champion of a church militant. Mr. Arabin was ordained, and became a fellow soon after taking his degree, and shortly after that was chosen professor of poetry.

And now came the moment of his great danger. After many mental struggles, and an agony of doubt which may be well surmised, the great prophet of the Tractarians confessed himself a Roman Catholic. Mr. Newman left the Church of England and with him carried away a waverer. He did not carry with him Mr. Arabin, but the escape which that gentleman had was a very narrow one. He left Oxford for a while that he might meditate in complete peace on the step which appeared to him to be all but unavoidable, and shut himself up in a little village on the seashore of ono of our remotest counties, that he might learn by communing with his own soul whether or no he could with a safe conscience remain within the pale of his mother church.

Things would have gone badly with him there had he been left entirely to himself. Every thing was against him.

All his worldly interests required him to remain a Protestant; and he looked on his worldly interests as a legion of foes, to get the better of whom was a point of extremest honour. In his then state of ecstatic agony such a conquest would have cost him little; he could easily have thrown away all his livelihood; but it cost him much to get over the idea that by choosing the Church of England he should be open in his own mind to the charge that he had been led to such a choice by unworthy motives. Then his heart was against him. He loved with a strong and eager love the man who had hitherto been his guide, and yearned to follow his footsteps. His tastes were against him. The ceremonies and pomps of the Church of Rome, their august feasts and solemn fasts, invited his imagination and pleased his eye. His flesh was against him. How great an aid would it be to a poor, weak, wavering man to be constrained to high moral duties, self-denial, obedience, and chastity by laws which were certain in their enactments, and not to be broken without loud, palpable, unmistakable sin! Then his faith was against him. He required to believe so much; panted so eagerly to give signs of his belief; deemed it so insufficient to wash himself simply in the waters of Jordan. Some great deed, such as that of forsaking everything for a true church, had for him allurements almost past withstanding.

Mr. Arabin was at this time a very young man, and when he left Oxford for his far retreat was much too confident in his powers of fence, and too apt to look down on the ordinary sense of ordinary people, to expect aid in the battle that he had to fight from any chance inhabitants of the spot which he had selected. But Providence was good to him; and there, in that all but desolate place, on the storm-beat shore of that distant sea, he met one who gradually calmed his mind, quieted his imagination, and taught him something of a Christian's duty. When Mr. Arabin left Oxford, he was inclined to look upon the rural clergymen of most English parishes almost with contempt. It was his ambition, should he remain within the fold of their

church, to do somewhat towards redeeming and rectifying their inferiority, and to assist in infusing energy and faith into the hearts of Christian ministers, who were, as he thought, too often satisfied to go through life without much show of either.

And yet it was from such a one that Mr. Arabin in his extremest need received that aid which he so much required. It was from the poor curate of a small Cornish parish that he first learnt to know that the highest laws for the governance of a Christian's duty must act from within and not from without; that no man can become a serviceable servant solely by obedience to written edicts; and that the safety which he was about to seek within the gates of Rome was no other than the selfish freedom from personal danger which the bad soldier attempts to gain who counterfeits illness on the eve of battle.

Mr. Arabin returned to Oxford a humbler but a better and a happier man; and from that time forth he put his shoulder to the wheel as a clergyman of the Church for which he had been educated. The intercourse of those among whom he familiarly lived kept him staunch to the principles of that system of the Church to which he had always belonged. Since his severance from Mr. Newman, no one had had so strong an influence over him as the head of his college. During the time of his expected apostasy Dr. Gwynne had not felt much predisposition in favour of the young fellow. Though a High Churchman himself within moderate limits, Dr. Gwynne felt no sympathy with men who could not satisfy their faiths with the Thirty-nine Articles. He regarded the enthusiasm of such as Newman as a state of mind more nearly allied to madness than to religion; and when he saw it evinced by very young men, was inclined to attribute a good deal of it to vanity. Dr. Gwynne himself, though a religious man, was also a thoroughly practical man of the world, and he regarded with no favourable eye the tenets of any one who looked on the two things as incompatible. When he found that Mr. Arabin was a half Roman, he

began to regret all he had done towards bestowing a fellowship on so unworthy a recipient; and when again he learnt that Mr. Arabin would probably complete his journey to Rome he regarded with some satisfaction the fact that in such case the fellowship would be again vacant.

When, however, Mr. Arabin returned and confessed himself a confirmed Protestant, the master of Lazarus again opened his arms to him, and gradually he became the pet of the college. For some little time he was saturnine, silent, and unwilling to take any prominent part in university broils; but gradually his mind recovered, or rather made, its tone, and he became known as a man always ready at a moment's notice to take up the cudgels in opposition to anything that savoured of an evangelical bearing. He was great in sermons, great on platforms, great at after dinner conversations, and always pleasant as well as great. He took delight in elections, served on committees, opposed tooth and nail all projects of university reform, and talked jovially over his glass of port of the ruin to be anticipated by the Church, and of the sacrilege daily committed by the Whigs. The ordeal through which he had gone, in resisting the blandishments of the lady of Rome, had certainly done much towards strengthening of his character. Although in small and outward matters he was selfconfident enough, nevertheless in things affecting the inner man he aimed at a humility of spirit which would never have been attractive to him but for that visit to the coast of Cornwall. This visit he now repeated every year.

Such is an interior view of Mr. Arabin at the time when he accepted the living of St. Ewold. Exteriorly, he was not a remarkable person. He was above the middle height, well made, and very active. His hair, which had been jet black, was now tinged with gray, but his face bore no sign of years. It would perhaps be wrong to say that he was handsome, but his face was, nevertheless, pleasant to look upon. The cheek bones were rather too high for beauty, and the formation of the forehead too massive and heavy. But the eyes, nose, and mouth were perfect. There was a continual play of lambent fire about his eyes, which gave promise of either pathos or humour whenever he essayed to speak, and that promise was rarely broken. There was a gentle play about his mouth which declared that his wit never descended to sarcasm, and that there was no ill-nature in his repartee.

Mr. Arabin was a popular man among women, but more so as a general than a special favourite. Living as a fellow at Oxford, marriage with him had been out of the question, and it may be doubted whether he had ever allowed his heart to be touched. Though belonging to a church in which celibacy is not the required lot of its ministers, he had come to regard himself as one of those clergymen to whom to be a bachelor is almost a necessity. He had never looked for parochial duty, and his career at Oxford was utterly incompatible with such domestic joys as a wife and nursery. He looked on women, therefore, in the same light that one sees them regarded by many Romish priests. He liked to have near him that which was pretty and amusing, but women generally were little more to him than children. He talked to them without putting out all his powers, and listened to them without any idea that what he should hear from them could either actuate his conduct or influence his opinion.

Such was Mr Arabin, the new vicar of St. Ewold, who is going to stay with the Grantlys, at Plumstead Episcopi.

Mr. Arabin reached Plumstead the day before Mr. Harding and Eleanor, and the Grantly family were thus enabled to make his acquaintance and discuss his qualifications before the arrival of the other guests. Griselda was surprised to find that he looked so young; but she told Florinda her younger sister, when they had retired for the night, that he did not talk at all like a young man: and she decided, with the authority that seventeen has over sixteen, that he was not at all nice, although his eyes were lovely. As usual, sixteen simplicity acceded to the dictum of seventeen in such a matter, and said that he certainly was

not nice. They then branched off on the relative merits of other clerical bachelors in the vicinity, and both determined without any feeling of jealousy between them that a certain Rev. Augustus Green was by many degrees the most estimable of the lot. The gentleman in question had certainly much in his favour. Having a comfortable allowance from his father, he could devote the whole proceeds of his curacy to violet gloves and unexceptionable neck ties. Having thus fixedly resolved that the new comer had nothing about him to shake the pre-eminence of the exalted Green, the two girls went to sleep in each other's arms, contented with themselves and the world.

Mrs. Grantly at first sight came to much the same conclusion about her husband's favourite as her daughters had done, though, in seeking to measure his relative value, she tiid not compare him to Mr. Green; indeed, she made no comparison by name between him and any one else; but she remarked to her husband that one person's swans were very often another person's geese,—thereby clearly showing that Mr. Arabin had not yet proved his qualifications in swanhood to her satisfaction.

"Well, Susan," said he, rather offended at hearing his friend spoken of so disrespectfully, "if you take Mr. Arabin for a goose, I cannot say that I think very highly of your discrimination."

"A goose! No, of course, he's not a goose. I've no doubt he's a very clever man. But you're so matter-of-fact, archdeacon, when it suits your purpose, that one can't trust oneself to any faÇon de parler. I've no doubt Mr. Arabin is a very valuable man,—at Oxford, and that he'll be a good vicar at St. Ewold. All I mean is, that having passed one evening with him, I don't find him to be absolutely a paragon. In the first place, if I am not mistaken, he is a little inclined to be conceited."

"Of all the men that I know intimately," said the archdeacon, "Arabin is, in my opinion, the most free from any taint of selfconceit. His fault is that he's too diffident."

"Perhaps so," said the lady; "only I

must own I did not find it out this evening."

Nothing further was said about him. Dr. Grantly thought that his wife was abusing Mr. Arabin merely because he had praised him; and Mrs. Grantly knew that it was useless arguing for or against any person in favour of or in opposition to whom the archdeacon had already pronounced a strong opinion.

In truth they were both right. Mr. Arabin was a diffident man in social intercourse with those whom he did not intimately know. When placed in situations which it was his business to fill, and discussing matters with which it was his duty to be conversant, Mr. Arabin was from habit brazen-faced enough. When standing on a platform in Exeter Hall, no man would be less mazed than he by the eyes of the crowd before him,—for such was the work which his profession had called on him to perform; but he shrank from a strong expression of opinion in general society, and his doing so not uncommonly made it appear that he considered the company not worth the trouble of his energy. He was averse to dictate when the place did not seem to him to justify dictation; and as those subjects on which people wished to hear him speak were such as he was accustomed to treat with decision, he generally shunned the traps there were laid to allure him into discussion, and, by doing so, not unfrequently subjected himself to such charges as those brought against him by Mrs. Grantly.

Mr. Arabin, as he sat at his open window, enjoying the delicious moonlight and gazing at the gray towers of the church which stood almost within the rectory grounds, little dreamed that he was the subject of so many friendly or unfriendly criticisms. Considering how much we are all given to discuss the characters of others, and discuss them often not in the strictest spirit of charity, it is singular how little we are inclined to think that others can speak ill-naturedly of us, and how angry and hurt we are when proof reaches us that they have done so. It is hardly too much to say that we all of us occasionally speak of our dearest friends in a manner in which those dearest friends would very little like to hear themselves mentioned; and that we nevertheless expect that our dearest friends shall invariably speak of us as though they were blind to all our faults, but keenly alive to every shade of our virtues.

It did not occur to Mr. Arabin that he was spoken of at all. It seemed to him, when he compared himself with his host, that he was a person of so little consequence to any that he was worth no one's words or thoughts. He was utterly alone in the world as regarded domestic ties and those inner familiar relations which are hardly possible between others than husbands and wives, parents and children, or brothers and sisters. He had often discussed with himself the necessity of such bonds for a man's happiness in this world, and had generally satisfied himself with the answer that happiness in this world is not a necessity. Herein he deceived himself, or rather tried to do so. He, like others, yearned for the enjoyment of whatever he saw enjoyable; and though he attempted, with the modern stoicism of so many Christians, to make himself believe that joy and sorrow were matters which here should he held as perfectly indifferent, these things were not indifferent to him. He was tired of his Oxford rooms and his college life. He regarded the wife and children of his friend with something like envy; he all but coveted the pleasant drawing-room, with its pretty windows opening on to lawns and flower-beds, the apparel of the comfortable house, and—above all, —the air of home which encompassed it all.

It will be said that no time can have been so fitted for such desires on his part as this, when he had just possessed himself of a country parish, of a living among fields and gardens, of a house which a wife would grace. It is true there was a difference between the opulence of Plumstead and the modest economy of St. Ewold. But surely Mr. Arabin was not a man to sigh after wealth! Of all men, his friends would have unanimously declared he was the last to do so. But how little our friends know us! In his period of stoical rejection of this world's happiness, he had cast from him as utter dross all anxiety as to fortune. He had, as it were, proclaimed himself to be indifferent to promotion, and those who chiefly admired his talents, and would mainly have exerted themselves to secure to them their deserved reward, had taken him at his word. And now, if the truth must out, he felt himself disappointed,—disappointed not by them but by himself. The daydream of his youth was over, and at the age of forty he felt that he was not fit to work in the spirit of an apostle. IIe had mistaken himself, and learned his mistake when it was past remedy. He had professed himself indifferent to mitres and diaconal residences, to rich livings and pleasant glebes, and now he had to own to himself that he was sighing for the good things of other men on whom in his pride he had ventured to look down.

Not for wealth, in its vulgar sense, had he ever sighed; not for the enjoyment of rich things had he ever longed. But for the allotted share of wordly bliss, which a wife, and children, and happy home could give him, for that usual amount of comfort which he had ventured to reject as unnecessary for him, he did now feel that he would have been wiser to have searched.

He knew that his talents, his position, and his friends would have won for him promotion, had he put himself in the way of winning it. Instead of doing so, he had allowed himself to be persuaded to accept a living which would give him an income of some 300?. a year, should he, by marrying, throw up his fellowship. Such, at the age of forty, was the worldly result of labour which the world had chosen to regard as successful. The world also thought that Mr. Arabin was, in his own estimation, sufficiently paid. Alas! alas! the world was mistaken; and Mr. Arabin was beginning to ascertain that such was the case.

And here, may I beg the reader not to be hard in his judgment upon this man. Is not the state at which he has arrived the natural result of efforts to reach that which is not the condition of humanity? Is not modern stoicism, built though it be on Christianity, as great an outrage on human nature as was the stoicism of the ancients? The philosophy of Zeno was built on true laws, but on true laws misunderstood, and therefore misapplied. It is the same with our Stoics here, who would teach us that wealth and worldly comfort and happiness on earth are not worth the search. Alas, for a doctrine which can find no believing pupils and no true teachers!

The case of Mr. Arabin was the more singular as he belonged to a branch of the Church of England well inclined to regard its temporalities with avowed favour, and had habitually lived with men who were accustomed to much worldly comfort. But such was his idiosyncrasy, that these very facts had produced within him, in early life, a state of mind that was not natural to him. He was content to be a High Churchman, if he could be so on principles of his own, and could strike out a course showing a marked difference from those with whom he consorted. He was ready to be a partisan as long as he was allowed to have a course of action and of thought unlike that of his party. His party had indulged him—and he began to feel that his party was right and himself wTong just when such a conviction was too late to be of service to him. He discovered, when such discovery was no longer serviceable, that it would have been worth his while to have worked for the usual pay assigned to work in this world, and have earned a wife and children, with a carriage for them to sit in; to have earned a pleasant dining-room, in which his friends could drink his wine, and the power of walking up the high street of his country town, with the knowledge that all its tradesmen would have gladly welcomed him within their doors. Other men arrived at those convictions in their start in life, and so worked up to them. To him they had come when they were too late to be of use.

It has been said that Mr. Arabin was a man of pleasantry; and it may be thought that such a state of mind as that described, would be antagonistic to humour. But surely such is not the case.

"Wit is the outward mental casing of the man, and has no more to do with the inner mind of thoughts and feelings than have the rich brocaded garments of the priest at the altar with the asceticism of the anchorite below them, whose skin is tormented with sackcloth, and whose body is half flayed with rods. Nay, will not such a one often rejoice more than any other in the rich show of his outward apparel? Will it not be food for his pride to feel that he groans inwardly, while he shines outwardly? So it is with the mental efforts which men make. Those which they show forth daily to the world are often the opposites of the inner workings of the spirit.

In the archdeacon's drawing-room Mr. Arabin had sparkled with his usual unaffected brilliancy, but when he retired to his bed-room, he sat there sad, at his open window, repining within himself that he also had no wife, no bairns, no soft sward of lawn duly mown for him to lie on, no herd of attendant curates, no bowings from the banker's clerks, no rich rectory. That apostleship that he had thought of had evaded his grasp, and he was now only vicar of St. Ewold's, with a taste for a mitre. Truly he had fallen between two stools.

CHAPTER XXI. ST. Ewold's Pabsonage.

When Mr Harding and Mrs. Bold reached the rectory on the following morning the archdeacon and his friend were at St. Ewold's. They had gone over that the new vicar might inspect his church, and be introduced to the squire, and were not expected back before dinner. Mr. Harding rambled out by himself, and strolled, as was his wont at Plumstead, about the lawn and round the church; and as he did so, the two sisters naturally fell into conversation about Barchester.

There was not much sisterly confidence between them. Mrs. Grantly was ten years older than Eleanor, and had been married while Eleanor was yet a child. They had never, therefore, poured into each other's ears their hopes and loves; and now that one was a wife and the other a widow, it was not probable that they would begin to do so. They lived too much asunder to be able to

fall into that kind of intercourse which makes confidence between sisters almost a necessity; and, moreover, that which is so easy at eighteen is often very difficult at twenty-eight. Mrs. Grantly knew this, and did not, therefore, expect confidence from her sister; and yet she longed to ask her whether in real truth Mr. Slope was agreeable to her.

It was by no means difficult to turn the conversation to Mr. Slope. That gentleman had become so famous at Barchester, had so much to do with all clergymen connected with the city, and was so specially concerned in the affairs of Mr. Harding, that it would have been odd if Mr. Harding's daughters had not talked about him. Mrs. Grantly was soon abusing him, which she did with her whole heart; and Mrs. Bold was nearly as eager to defend him. She positively disliked the man, would have been delighted to learn that he had taken himself off so that she should never see him again, had indeed almost a fear of him, and yet she constantly found herself taking his part. The abuse of other people, and abuse of a kind that she felt to be unjust, imposed this necessity on her, and at last made Mr. Slope's defence an habitual course of argument with her.

From Mr. Slope the conversation turned to the Stanhopes, and Mrs. Grantly was listening with some interest to Eleanor's account of the family, when it dropped out that Mr. Slope made one of the party.

"What!" said the lady of the rectory, "was Mr. Slope there too?"

Eleanor merely replied that such had been the case.

'' Why, Eleanor, he must be very fond of you, I think. He seems to follow you everywhere."

Even this did not open Eleanor's eyes. She merely laughed, and said that she imagined Mr. Slope found other attraction at Dr. Stanhope's. And so they parted. Mrs. Grantly felt quite convinced that the odious match would take place; and Mrs. Bold as convinced that that unfortunate chaplain, disagreeable as he must be allowed to be, was more sinned against than sinning.

The archdeacon of course heard before dinner that Eleanor had remained the day before in Barchester with the view of meeting Mr. Slope, and that she had so met him. He remembered how she had positively stated that there were to be no guests at the Stanhopes, and he did not hesitate to accuse her of deceit. Moreover, the fact, or rather presumed fact, of her being deceitful on such a matter, spoke but too plainly in evidence against her as to her imputed crime of receiving Mr. Slope as a lover.

"I am afraid that anything we can do will be too late," said the archdeacon. "I own I am fairly surprised. I never liked your sister's taste with regard to men; but still I did not give her credit for;ugh!"

"And so soon, too," said Mrs. Grantly, who thought more, perhaps, of her sister's indecorum in having a lover before she had put off her weeds, than her bad taste in having such a lover as Mr. Slope.

"Well, my dear, I shall be sorry to be harsh, or to do anything that can hurt your father; but, positively, neither that man nor his wife shall come within my doors."

Mrs. Grantly sighed, and then attempted to console herself and her lord by remarking that, after all, the thing was not accomplished yet. Now that Eleanor was at Plumstead much might be done to wean her from her fatal passion. Poor Eleanor!

The evening passed off without anything to make it remarkable. Mr. Arabin discussed the parish of St. Ewold with the archdeacon, and Mrs. Grantly and Mr. Harding, who knew the personages of the parish, joined in. Eleanor also knew them, but she said little. Mr. Arabin did not apparently take much notice of her, and she was not in a humour to receive at that time with any special grace any special favourite of her brother-in-law. Her first idea on reaching her bed-room was that a much pleasanter family party might be met at Dr. Stanhope's than at the rectory. She began to think that she was getting tired of clergymen and their respectable humdrum wearisome mode of living, and that, after all, people in the outer world, who had lived in Italy, London, or elsewhere, need not necessarily be regarded as atrocious and abominable. The Stanhopes, she had thought, were a giddy, thoughtless, extravagant set of people; but she had seen nothing wrong about them, and had, on the other hand, found that they thoroughly knew how to make their house agreeable. It was a thousand pities, she thought, that the archdeacon should not have a little of the same savoir vivre. Mr. Arabin, as we have said, did not apparently take much notice of her; but yet he did not go to bed without feeling that he had been in company with a very pretty woman; and as is the case with most bachelors, and some married men, regarded the prospect of his month's visit at Plumstead in a pleasanter light, when he learnt that a very pretty woman was to share it with him.

Before they all retired it was settled that the whole party should drive over on the following day to inspect the parsonage at St. Ewold. The three clergymen were to discuss dilapidations, and the two ladies were to lend their assistance in suggesting such changes as might be necessary for a bachelor's abode. Accordingly, soon after breakfast, the carriage was at the door. There was only room for four inside, and the archdeacon got upon the box. Eleanor found herself opposite to Mr. Arabin, and was, therefore, in a manner forced into conversation with him. They were soon on comfortable terms together; and had she thought about it, she would have thought that, in spite of his black cloth, Mr. Arabin would not have been a bad addition to the Stanhope family party.

Now that the archdeacon was away, they could all trifle. Mr. Harding began by telling them in the most innocent manner imaginable an old legend about Mr. Arabin's new parish. There was, he said, in days of yore, an illustrious priestess of St. Ewold, famed through the whole country for curing all manner of diseases. She had a well, as all priestesses have ever had, which well was extant to this day, and shared in the minds

of many of the people the sanctity which belonged to the consecrated ground of the parish church. Mr. Arabin declared that he should look on such tenets on the part of his parishioners as anything but orthodox. And Mrs. Grantly replied that she so entirely disagreed with him as to think that no parish was in a proper state that had not its priestess as well as its priest. "The duties are never well done," said she, "unless they are so divided."

"I suppose, papa," said Eleanor, "that in the olden times the priestess bore all the sway herself. Mr. Arabin, perhaps, thinks that such might be too much the case now if a sacred lady were admitted within the parish."

"I think, at any rate," said he, "that it is safer to run no such risk. No priestly pride has ever exceeded that of sacerdotal females. A very lowly curate I might, perhaps, essay to rule; but a curatess would be sure to get the better of me."

"There are certainly examples of such accidents happening," said Mrs. Grantly. "They do say that there is a priestess at Barchester who is very imperious in all things touching the altar. Perhaps the fear of such a fate as that is before your eyes."

When they were joined by the archdeacon on the gravel before the vicarage they descended again to grave dulness. Not that Archdeacon Grantly was a dull man; but his frolic humours were of a cumbrous kind; and his wit,—when he was witty, did not generally extend itself to his auditory. On the present occasion he was soon making speeches about wounded roofs and walls, which he declared to be in want of some surgeon's art. There was not a partition that he did not tap, nor a block of chimneys that he did not narrowly examine; all water-pipes, flues, cisterns, and sewertf underwent an investigation; and he even descended, in the care of his friend, so far as to bore sundry boards in the floors with a bradawl.

Mr. Arabin accompanied him through the rooms, trying to look wise in such domestic matters, and the other three also followed. Mrs. Grantly

showed that she had not herself been priestess of a parish twenty years for nothing, and examined the bells and window panes in a very knowing way.

"You will, at any rate, have a beautiful prospect out of your own window, if this is to be your private sanctum," said Eleanor. She was standing at the lattice of a little room up stairs, from which the view certainly was very lovely. It was from the back of the vicarage, and there was nothing to interrupt the eye between the house and the glorious gray pile of the cathedral. The intermediate ground, however, was beautifully studded with timber. In the immediate foreground ran the little river which afterwards skirted the city; and, just to the right of the cathedral, the pointed gables and chimneys of Hiram's Hospital peeped out of the elms which encompass it.

"Yes," said he, joining her. "I shall have a beautifully complete view of my adversaries. I shall sit down before the hostile town, and fire away at them at a very pleasant distance. I shall just be able to lodge a shot in the hospital, should the enemy ever get possession of it; and as for the palace, I have it within full range."

"I never saw anything like you clergymen," said Eleanor; "you are always thinking of fighting each other."

"Either that," said he, "or else supporting each other. The pity is that we cannot do the one without the other. But are we not here to fight? Is not ours a church militant? What is all our work but fighting, and hard fighting, if it be well done?

"But not with each other."

"That's as it may be. The same complaint which you make of me for battling with another clergyman of our own church, the Mohammedan would make against me for battling with the error of a priest of Home. Yet, surely, you would not be inclined to say that I should be wrong to do battle with such as him. A pagan, too, with his multiplicity of gods, would think it equally odd that the Christian and the Mohammedan should disagree."

"Ah! but you wage your wars about

trifles so bitterly."

"Wars about trifles," said he, "are always bitter, especially among neighbours. When the differences are great, and the parties comparative strangers, men quarrel with courtesy. What combatants are ever so eager as two brothers?"

"But do not such contentions bring scandal on the church?"

"More scandal would fall on tho church if there were no such contentions. We have but one way to avoid them,—that of acknowledging a common head of our church, whose word on all points of doctrine shall be authoritative. Such a termination of our difficulties is alluring enough. It has charms which are irresistible to many, and all but irrositible, I own, to me."

"You speak now of the Church of Borne?" said Eleanor.

"No," said he, "not necessarily of the Church of Borne; but of a church with a head. Had it pleased God to vouchsafe to us such a church our path would have been easy. But easy paths have not been thought good for us." He paused and stood silent for a while, thinking of the time when he had so nearly sacrificed all he had, his powers of mind, his free agency, the fresh running waters of

Vol. n. n his mind's fountain, his very inner self, for an easy path in which no fighting would be needed; and then he continued;—"What you say is partly true; our contentions do bring on us some scandal. The outer world, though it constantly reviles us for our human infirmities, and throws in our teeth the fact that being clergymen we are still no more than men, demands of us that we should do our work with godlike perfection. There is nothing godlike about us. We differ from each other with the acerbity common to man,—we triumph over each other with human frailty—we allow differences on subjects of divine origin to produce among us antipathies and enmities which are anything but divine. This is all true. But what would you have in place of it? There is no infallible head for a church on earth. This dream of believing man has been tried, and we see in Italy and in Spain

what has come of it. Grant that there are and have been no bickerings within the pale of the Pope!s Church. Such an assumption would be utterly untrue, but let us grant it; and then let us say which church has incurred the heavier scandals."

There was a quiet earnestness about Mr. Arabin, as he half acknowledged and half defended himself from the charge brought against him, which surprised Eleanor. She had been used all her life to listen to clerical discussion; but the points at issue between the disputants had so seldom been of more than temporal significance as to have left on her mind no feeling of reverence for such subjects. There had always been a hard worldly leaven of the love either of income or of power in the strains she had heard. There had been no panting for the truth; no aspirations after religious purity. It had always been taken for granted by those around her that they were indubitably right, that there was no ground for doubt, that the hard uphill work of ascertaining what the duty of a clergyman should be had been already accomplished in full; and that what remained for an active militant parson to do, was to hold his own against all comers. Her father, it is true, was an exception to this; but then he was so essentially antimilitant in all things, that she classed him in her own mind apart from all others. She had never argued the matter within herself, or considered whether this common tone was or was not faulty; but she was sick of it without knowing that she was so. And now she found to her surprise and not without a certain pleasurable excitement, that this new comer among them spoke in a manner very different from that to which she was accustomed.

"It is so easy to condemn," said he, continuing the thread of his thoughts. "I know no life that must be so delicious as that of a writer for newspapers, or a leading member of the opposition,—to thunder forth accusations against men in power; show up the worst side of everything that is produced; to pick holes in every coat; to be indignant, sarcastic, jocose, moral, or supercilious; to

damn with faint praise, or. crush with open calumny! What can be so easy as this when the critic has to be responsible for nothing? You condemn what I do. But put yourself in my position and do the reverse, and then see if I cannot condemn you."

"Oh! Mr. Arabin, I do not condemn you."

"Pardon me, you do, Mrs. Bold;— you as one of the world. You are now the opposition member; you are now composing your leading article, and well and bitterly you do it. 'Let dogs delight to bark and bite;' you fitly begin with an elegant quotation; 'but if we are to have a church at all, in heaven's name let the pastors who preside over it keep their hands from each other's throats. Lawyers can live without befouling each other's names: Doctors do not fight duels. "Why is it that clergymen alone should indulge themselves in such unrestrained liberty of abuse against each other?' And so you go on reviling us for our ungodly quarrels, our sectarian propensities, and scandalous differences. It will, however, give you no trouble to write another article next week in which we, or some of us, shall be twitted with an unseemly apathy in matters of our vocation. It will not fall on you to reconcile the discrepancy. Your readers will never ask you how the poor parson is to be urgent in season and out of season, and yet never come in contact with men who think widely differently from him. You, when you condemn this foreign treaty, or that official arrangement, will have to incur no blame for the graver faults of any different measure. It is so easy to condemn; and so pleasant too,—for eulogy charms no listeners as detraction does."

Eleanor only half followed him in his raillery, but she caught his meaning. "I know I ought to apologise for presuming to criticise you," she said; "but I was thinking with sorrow of the ill-will that has lately come among us at Barchester, and I spoke more freely than I should have done."

"Peace on earth and good-will among men, are, like heaven, promises for the future;" said he, following rather his own thoughts than hers. "When that prophecy is accomplished, there will no longer be any need for clergymen."

Here they were interrupted by the archdeacon, whose voice was heard from the cellar shouting to the vicar. "Arabin, Arabin,"— and then turning to his wife, who was apparently at his elbow— '' where has he gone to? This cellar is perfectly abominable. It would be murder to put a bottle of wine into it till it has been loofed, walled, and floored. How on earth old Goodenough ever got on with it, I cannot guess. But then Goodenough never had a glass of wine that any man could drink."

"What is it, archdeacon?" said the new vicar, running down stairs, and leaving Eleanor above to her meditations.

"This cellar must be roofed, walled, and floored," repeated the archdeacon. "Now mind what I say, and don't let the architect persuade you that it will do. Half of these fellows know nothing about wine. This place as it is now would be damp and cold in winter, and hot and muggy in summer. I wouldn't give a straw for the best wine that ever was vinted, after it had lain here a couple of years."

Mr. Arabin assented, and promised that the cellar should be reconstructed according to the archdeacon's receipt.

"And, Arabin, look here; was such an attempt at a kitchen grate ever seen?"

"The grate is really very bad," said Mrs. Grantly; "I am sure the priestess won't approve of it, when she is brought home to the scene of her future duties. Really, Mr. Arabin, no priestess aecustomed to such an excellent veil as that above could put up with such a grate as this."

"If there must be a priestess at St. Ewold's at all, Mrs. Grantly, I think we will leave her to her well, and not call down her divine wrath on any of the imperfections rising from our human poverty. However, I own I am amenable to the attractions of a well-cooked dinner, and the grate shall certainly be r hanged."

By this time the archdeacon had again ascended, and was now in the dining-room. "Arabin," said he, speaking in his usual loud clear voice, and with that tone of dictation which was so common to him; "you must positively alter this dining-room; that is, remodel it altogether; look here, it is just sixteen feet by fifteen; did anybody ever hear of a dining-room of such proportions!" And the archdeacon stepped the room longways and cross-ways with ponderous steps, as though a certain amount of ecclesiastical dignity could be imparted even to such an occupation as that by the manner of doing it. "Barely sixteen; you may call it a square."

"It would do very well for a round table," suggested the exwarden.

Now there was something peculiarly unorthodox in the archdeacon's estimation in the idea of a round table. He had always been accustomed to a goodly board of decent length, comfortably elongating itself according to the number of the guests, nearly black with perpetual rubbing, and as bright as a mirror. Now round dinner tables are generally of oak, or else of such new construction as not to have acquired the peculiar hue which was so pleasing to him. He connected them with what he called the nasty new fangled method of leaving a cloth on the table, as though to warn people that they were not to sit long. In his eyes there was something democratic and parvenue in a round table. He imagined that dissenters and calico-printers chiefly used them, and perhaps a few literary lions more conspicuous for their wit than their gentility. He was a little flurried at the idea of such an article being introduced into the diocese by a protege of his own, and at the instigation of his father-in-law.

"A round dinner-table," said he, with some heat, "is the most abominable article of furniture that ever was invented. I hope that Arabin has more taste than to allow such a thing in his house."

Poor Mr. Harding felt himself completely snubbed, and of course said nothing further; but Mr. Arabin who had yielded submissively in the small matters of the cellar and kitchen grate, found himself obliged to oppose reforms which might be of a nature too expensive for his pocket. "But it seems to me, archdeacon, that I can't very well lengthen the room without pulling down the wall, and if I pull down the wall, I must build it up again. Then if I throw out a bow on this side, I must do the same on the other. Then if I do it for the ground floor, I must carry it up to the floor above. That will be putting a new front to the house, and will cost, I suppose, a couple of hundred pounds. The ecclesiastical commissioners will hardly assist me when they hear that my grievance consists in having a dining room only sixteen feet long."

The archdeacon proceeded to explain that nothing would be easier than adding six feet to the front of the dining-room, without touching any other room in the house. Such irregularities of construction in small country houses were, he said, rather graceful than otherwise, and he offered to pay for the whole thing out of his own pocket if it cost more than forty pounds. Mr. Arabin, however, was firm, and, although the archdeacon fussed and fumed about it, would not give way.

Forty pounds, he said, was a matter of serious moment to him, and his friends, if under such circumstances they would be goodnatured enough to come to him at all, must put up with the misery of a square room. He was willing to compromise matters by disclaiming any intention of having a round table.

"But," said Mrs. Grantly, "what if the priestess insists on having both the rooms enlarged?"

"The priestess in that case must do it for herself, Mrs. Grantly."

"I have no doubt she will be well able to do so," replied the lady;—" to do that and many more wonderful things. I am quite sure that the priestess of St. Ewold, when she does come, won't come empty-handed."

Mr. Arabin, however, did not appear well inclined to enter into speculative expenses on such a chance as this, and therefore, any material alterations in the house, the cost of which could not fairly be made to lie at the door either of the ecclesiastical commissioners or of the estate of the late incumbent, were tabooed. With this essential exception, the archdeacon ordered, suggested, and carried all points before him in a manner very much to his own satisfaction. A close observer, had there been one there, might have seen that his wife had been quite as useful in the matter as himself. No one knew better than Mrs. Grantly the appurtenances necessary to a comfortable house. She did not, however, think it necessary to lay claim to any of the glory which her lord and master was so ready to appropriate as his own.

Having gone through their work effectually and systematically, the party returned to Tlumstead well satisfied with their expedition.

THE THORNES OF UXLATHOIINE.

On the following Sunday Mr. Arabin was to read himself in at his new church. It was agreed at the rectory that the archdeacon should go over with him and assist at the reading-desk, and that Mr. Harding should take the archdeacon's duty at Plumstead Church. Mrs. Grantly had her school and her buns to attend to, and professed that she could not be spared; but Mrs. Bold was to accompany them. It was further agreed also, that they would lunch at the squire's house, and return home after the afternoon service.

Wilfred Thorne, Esq., of Ullathorne, was the squire of St. Ewold's; or rather the squire of Ullathorne; for the domain of the modern landlord was of wider notoriety than the fame of the ancient saint. He was a fair specimen of what that race has come to in our days, which a century ago was, as we are told, fairly represented by Squire Western. If that representation be a true one, few classes of men can have made faster strides in improvement. Mr. Thorne, however, was a man possessed of quite a sufficient number of foibles to lay him open to much ridicule. He was still a bachelor, being about fifty, and was not a little proud of his person. When living at home at "Ullathorne there was not much room for such pride, and there therefore he always looked like a gentleman, and like that which he certainly was, the first man in his parish. But during the

month or six weeks which he annually spent in London, he tried so hard to look bike a great man there also, which he certainly was not, that he was put down as a fool by many at his club. He was a man of considerable literary attainment in a certain way and on certain subjects. His favourite authors were Montaigne and Burton, and he knew more perhaps than any other man in his own county, and the next to it, of the English essayists of the two last centuries. He possessed complete sets of the "Idler," the "Spectator," the " Tatler," the "Guardian/' and the "Rambler;" and would discourse by hours together on the superiority of such publications to anything which has since been produced in our Edinburghs and Quarterlies. He was a great proficient in all questions of genealogy, and knew enough of almost every gentleman's family in England to say of what blood and lineage were descended all those who had any claim to be considered as possessors of any such luxuries. Eor blood and lineage he himself had a most profound respect. He counted back his own ancestors to some period long antecedent to the Conquest; and could tell you, if you would listen to him, how it had come to pass that they, like Cedric the Saxon, had been permitted to hold their own among the Norman barons. It was not, according to his showing, on account of any weak complaisance on the part of his family towards their Norman neighbours. Some Ealfried of Ullathorne once fortified his own castle, and held out, not only that, but the then existing cathedral of Barchester also, against one Geoffrey De Burgh, in the time of King John; and Mr. Thorne possessed the whole history of the siege written on vellum, and illuminated in a most costly manner. It little signified that no one could read the writing, as, had that been possible, no one could have understood the language. Mr. Thorne could, however, give you all the particulars in good English, and had no objection to do so.

It would be unjust to say that he looked down on men whosefamilies were of recent date. He did not do so.

He frequently consorted with such, and had chosen many of his friends from among them. But he looked on them as great millionaires are apt to look on those who have small incomes; as men who have Sophocles at their fingers' ends regard those who know nothing of Greek. They might doubtless be good sort of people, entitled to much praise for virtue, very admirable for talent, highly respectable in every way;—but they were without the one great good gift. Such was Mr. Thome's way of thinking on this matter; nothing could atone for the loss of good blood; nothing could neutralise its good effects. Pew indeed were now possessed of it, but the possession was en that account the more precious. It was very pleasant to hear Mr. Thorne descant on this matter. Were you in your ignorance to surmise that such a one was of a good family because the head of his family was a baronet of an old date, he would open his eyes with a delightful look of affected surprise, and modestly remind you that baronetcies only dated from James I. He would gently sigh if you spoke of the blood of the Fitzgeralds and De Burghs; would hardly allow the claims of the Howards and Lowthers; and has before now alluded to the Talbots as a family who had hardly yet achieved the full honours of a pedigree.

In speaking once of a wide spread race whose name had received the honours of three coronets, scions from which sat for various constituencies, some one of whose members had been in almost every cabinet formed during the present century, a brilliant race such as there are few in England, Mr. Thorne had called them all "dirt." He had not intended any disrespect to these men. He admired them in many senses, and allowed them their privileges without envy. He had merely meant to express his feeling that the streams which ran through their veins were not yet purified by time to that perfection, had not become so genuine an ichor, as to be worthy of being called blood in the genealogical sense.

When Mr. Arabin was first introduced to him Mr. Thorne had immediately suggested that he was one of the Arabins of Uphill.Stanton. Mr. Arabin replied that he was a very distant relative of the family alluded to. To this Mr. Thorne surmised that the relationship could not be very distant. Mr. Arabin assured him that it was so distant that the families knew nothing of each other. Mr. Thorne laughed his gentle laugh at this, and told Mr. Arabin chat there was now existing no branch of his family separated from the parent stock at an earlier date than the reign of Elizabeth; and that therefore Mr. Arabia could not call himself distant. Mr. Arabin himself was quite clearly an Arabin of Uphill Stanton.

"But," said the vicar, "Uphill Stanton has been sold to the De Greys, and has been in their hands for fifty years."

"And when it has been there one hundred and fifty, if it unluckily remain there so long," said Mr. Thome, "your descendants will not be a whit the less entitled to describe themselves as being of the family of Uphill Stanton. Thank God, no De Grey can buy that;—and, thank God,—no Arabin, and no Thorne, can sell it.

In politics Mr. Thorne was an unflinching conservative. He looked on those fifty-three Trojans, who, as Mr. Dod tells us, censured free trade in November, 1852, as the only patriots left among the public men of England. When that terrible crisis of free trade had arrived, when the repeal of the corn laws was carried by those very men whom Mr. Thorne had hitherto regarded as the only possible saviours of his country, he was for a time paralysed. His country was lost; but that was comparatively a small thing. Other countries had flourished and fallen, and the human race still went on improving under God's providence. But now all trust in human fate must for ever be at an end. Not only must ruin come, but it must come through the apostasy of those who had been regarded as the truest of true believers. Politics in England, as a pursuit for gentlemen, must be at an end. Had Mr. Thorne been trodden under foot by a Whig, he could have borne it as a Tory and a martyr; but to be so ut-

terly thrown over and deceived by those he had so earnestly supported, so thoroughly trusted, was more than he could endure and live. He therefore ceased to live as a politician, and refused to hold any converse with the world at large on the state of the country.

Such were Mr. Thome's impressions for the first two or three years after Sir Eobert Peel's apostasy; but by degrees his temper, as did that of others, cooled down. He began once more to move about, to frequent the bench and the market, and to be seen at dinners, shoulder to shoulder with some of those who had so cruelly betrayed him. It was a necessity for him to live, and that plan of his for avoiding the world did not answer. He, however, and others around him who still maintained the same staunch principles of protection,—men like himself, who were too true to flinch at the cry of a mob,—had their own way of consoling themselves. They were, and felt themselves to be, the only true depositaries left of certain Eleusinian mysteries, of certain deep and wondrous services of worship by which alone the gods could be rightly approached. To them and them only was it now given to know these things, and to perpetuate them, if that might still be done, by the careful and secret education of their children.

We have read how private and peculiar forms of worship have been carried on from age to age in families, which to the outer world have apparently adhered to the services of some ordinary church. And so by degrees it was with Mr. Thome. He learnt at length to listen calmly while protection was talked of as a thing dead, although he knew within himself that it was still quick with a mystic life. Nor was he without a certain pleasure that such knowledge though given to him should be debarred from the multitude. He became accustomed to hear, even among country gentlemen, that free trade was after all not so bad, and to hear this without dispute, although conscious within himself that everything good in England had gone with his old palladium. He had within him something of the f eeling of Cato,

who gloried that he could kill himself because Romans were no longer worthy of their name. Mr. Thorne had no thought of killing himself, being a Christian, and still possessing his 4000?. a year; but the feeling was not on that account the less comfortable.

Mr. Thorne was a sportsman, and had been active though not outrageous in his sports. Previous to the great downfall of politics in his county he had supported the hunt by every means in his power. He had preserved game till no goose or turkey could show a tail in the parish of St. Ewold's. He had planted gorse covets with more care than oaks and larches. He had been more anxious for the comfort of his foxes than of his ewes and lambs. No meet had been more popular than Ullathorne; no man's stables had been more liberally open to the horses of distant men than Mr. Thome's; no man had said more, written more, or done more to keep the club up. The theory of protection could expand itself so thoroughly in the practices of a county hunt! But when the great ruin came; when the noble master of the Barsetshire hounds supported the recreant minister in the House of Lords, and basely surrendered his truth, his manhood, his friends, and his honour for the hope of a garter, then Mr. Thorne gave up the hunt. He did not cut his covers, for that would not have been the act of a gentleman. He did not Trill his foxes, for that according to his light would have been murder. He did not say that his coverts should not be drawn, or his earths stopped, for that would have been illegal according to the by-laws prevailing among country gentlemen. But he absented himself from home on the occasion of every meet at Ullathorne, left the coverts to their fate, and could not be persuaded to take his pink coat out of the press, or his hunters out of his stable. This lasted for two years, and then by degrees he came round. He first appeared at a neighbouring meet on a pony, dressed in his shooting coat, as though he had trotted in by accident; then he walked up one morning on foot to see his favourite gorse drawn, and when his groom brought his mare out by chance he did not refuse to mount her. He was next persuaded, by one of the immortal fifty-three, to bring his hunting materials over to the other side of the county, and take a fortnight with the hounds there; and so gradually he returned to his old life. But in hunting as in other things he was only supported by an inward feeling of mystic superiority to those with whom he shared the common breath of outer life.

Mr. Thorne did not live in solitude at Ullathorne. He had a sister, who was ten years older than himself, and who participated in his prejudices and feelings so strongly, that she was a living caricature of all his foibles. She would not open a modern quaiterly, did not choose to see a magazine in her drawing-room, and would not have polluted her fingers with a shred of the "Times" for any consideration. She spoke of Addison, Swift, and Steele. as though they were still living, regarded De Foe as the best known novelist of his country, and thought of Fielding as a young but meritorious novice in the fields of romance. In poetry, she was familiar with names as late as Dryden, and had once been seduced into reading the "Rape of the Lock;" but she regarded Spenser as the purest type of her country's literature in this line. Genealogy was her favourite insanity. Those things which are the pride of most genealogists were to her contemptible. Arms and mottoes set her beside herself. Ealfried of Ullathorne had wanted no motto to assist him in cleaving to the brisket Geoffrey De Burgh; and Ealfried's great grandfather, the gigantic Ullafrid, had required no other arms than those which nature gave him to hurl from the top of his own castle a cousin of the base invading Norman. To her all modern English names were equally insignificant. Hengist, Horsa, and such like, had for her ears the only true savour of nobility. She was not contented unless she could go beyond the Saxons; and would certainly have christened her children, had she had children, by the names of the ancient Britons. In some respects she was not unlike Scott's Ulrica, and had she been given to cursing, she would certainly have done so in the names of Mista, Skogula, and Zernebock. Not having submitted to the embraces of any polluting Norman, as poor Ulrica had done, and having assisted no parricide, the milk of human kindness was not curdled in her bosom. She never cursed, therefore,—but blessed rather. This, however, she did in a strange uncouth Saxon manner that would have been unintelligible to any peasants but her own.

As a politician Miss Thorne had been so thoroughly disgusted with public life by base deeds long antecedent to the Corn Law question, that that had but little moved her. In her estimation her brother had been a fast young man, hurried away by a too ardent temperament into democratic tendencies. Now happily he was brought to sounder views by seeing the iniquity of the world. She had not yet reconciled herself to the Reform Bill, and still groaned in spirit over the defalcations of the Duke as touching the Catholio Emancipation. If asked whom she thought the Queen should take as her counsellor, she would probably have named Lord Eldon; and when reminded that that venerable man was no longer present in the flesh to assist us, she would probably have answered with a sigh that none now could help us but the dead.

In religion Miss Thorne was a pure Druidess. We would not have it understood by that, that she did actually in these latter days assist at any human sacrifices, or that she was in fact hostile to the Church of Christ. She had adopted the Christian religion as a milder form of the worship of her ancestors, and always appealed to her doing so as evidence that she had no prejudices against reform when it could be shown that reform was salutary. This reform was the most modern of any to which she had as yet acceded, it being presumed that British ladies had given up their paint and taken to some sort of petticoats before the days of St Augustine. That further feminine step in advance which combines paint and petticoats together had not found a votary in Miss Thorne.

But she was a Druidess in this, that she regretted she knew not what in the usages and practices of her Church. She sometimes talked and constantly thought of good things gone by, though she had but the faintest idea of what those good things had been. She imagined that a purity had existed which was now gone; that a piety had adorned our pastors and a simple docility our people, for which it may be feared history gave her but little true warrant. She was accustomed to speak of Cranmer as though he had been the "firmest and most simple-minded of martyrs, and of Elizabeth as though the pure Protestant faith of her people had been the one anxiety of her life. It would have been cruel to undeceive her, had it been possible; but it would have been impossible to make her believe that the one was a time-serving priest, willing to go any length to keep his place, and that the other was in heart a papist, with this sole proviso, that she should be her own pope.

And so Miss Thorne went on sighing and regretting, looking back to the divine right of kings as the ruling axiom of a golden age, and cherishing, low down in the bottom of her heart of hearts, a dear unmentioned wish for the restoration of some exiled Stuart. Who would deny her the luxury of her sighs, or the sweetness of her soft regrets!

In her person and her dress she was perfect, and well she knew her own perfection. She was a small elegantly made old woman, with a face from which the glow of her youth had not departed without leaving some streaks of a roseate hue. She was proud of her colour, proud of her grey hair which she wore in short crisp curls peering out all around her face from the dainty white lace cap. To think of all the money that she spent in lace used to break the heart of poor Mrs. Quiverful with her seven daughters. She was proud of her teeth, which were still white and numerous, proud of her bright cheery eye, proud of her short jaunty step, and very proud of the neat, precise, small feet with which those steps were taken. She was proud also, ay, very proud, of the rich brocaded silk in which it was her custom to ruffle through her drawing-room.

We know what was the custom of the lady of Branksome.

"Nine-and-twenty knights of fame
Hung their shields in Branksome Hall."

The lady of Ullathorne was not so martial in her habits, but hardly less costly. She might have boasted that nine-and-twenty silken skirts might have been produced in her chamber, each fit to stand alone. The nine-and-twenty shields of the Scottish heroes were less independent, and hardly more potent to withstand any attack that might be made on them. Miss Thorne when fully dressed might be said to have been aimed cap-a-pie, and she was always fully dressed, as far as was ever known to mortal man.

For all this rich attire Miss Thorne was not indebted to the generosity of her brother. She had a very comfortable independence of her own, which she divided among juvenile relatives, the milliters, and the poor, giving much the largest share to the latter. It may be imagined, therefore, that with all her little follies she was not unpopular. All her follies have, we believe, been told. Her virtues were too numerous to describe, and not sufficiently interesting to deserve description.

While we are on the subject of the Thornes one word must be said of the house they lived in. It was not a large house, nor a fine house, nor perhaps to modern ideas a very commodious house; but by those who love the peculiar colour and peculiar ornaments of genuine Tudor architecture it was considered a perfect gem. We beg to own ourselves among the number, and therefore take this opportunity to express our surprise that so little is known by English men and women of the beauties of English architecture. The ruins of the Colosseum, the Campanile at Florence, St. Mark's, Cologne, the Bourse and Notre Dame, are with our tourists as familiar as household words; but they know nothing of the glories of Wiltshire, Dorsetshire, and Somersetshire. Nay, we much question whether many noted travellers, men who have pitched their tents perhaps under Mount' Sinai,

are not still ignorant that there are glories in Wiltshire, Dorsetshire, and Somersetshire. We beg that they will go and see.

Mr. Thorne's house was called Ullathorne Court, and was properly so called; for the house itself formed two sides of a quadrangle, which was completed on the other two sides by a wall about twenty feet high. This wall was built of cut stone, rudely cut indeed, and now much worn, but of a beautiful rich tawny yellow colour, the effect of that stonecrop of minute growth which it had taken three centuries to produce. The top of this wall was ornamented by huge round stone balls of the same colour as the wall itself. Entrance into the court was had through a pair of iron gates, so massive that no one could comfortably open or close them, consequently they were rarely disturbed. From the gateway two paths led obliquely across the court; that to the left reaching the hall-door, which was in the corner made by the angle of the house, and that to the right leading to the back entrance, which was at the further end of the longer portion of the building.

With those who are now adepts in contriving house accommodation it will militate much against Ullathorne Court that no carriage could be brought to the hall-door. If you enter Ullathorne at all, you must do so, fair reader, on foot, or at least in a voi. n. E bath-chair. No vehicle drawn by horses ever comes within that iron gate. But this is nothing to the next horror that will encounter you. On entering the front door, which you do by no very grand portal, you find yourself immediately in the dining-groom! What,—no hall? exclaims my luxurious friend, accustomed to all the comfortable appurtenances of modern life. Yes, kind sir; a noble hall, if you will but observe it; a true old English hall of excellent dimensions for a country gentleman's family; but, if you please, no dining-parlour.

Both Mr. and Miss Thorne were proud of this peculiarity of their dwelling, though the brother was once all but tempted by his friends to alter

it. They delighted in the knowledge that they, like Cedric, positively dined in their true hall, even though they so dined tete-a-tete. But though they had never owned, they had felt and endeavoured to remedy the discomfort of such an arrangement. A huge screen partitioned off the front door and a portion of the hall, and from the angle so screened off a second door led into a passage, which ran along the larger side of the house next to the courtyard. Either my reader or I must be a bad hand at topography, if it be not clear that the great hall forms the ground-floor of the smaller portion of the mansion, that which was to your left as you entered the iron gate, and that it occupies the whole of this wing of the building. It must be equally clear that it looks out on a trim mown lawn, through three quadrangular windows with stone mullions, each window divided into a larger portion at the bottom, and a smaller portion at the top, and each portion again divided into five by perpendicular stone supporters. There may be windows which give a better light than such as these, and it may be, as my utilitarian friend observes, that the giving of light is the desired object of a window. I will not argue the point with him. Indeed I cannot. But I shall not the less die in the assured conviction that no sort or description of window is capable of imparting half so much happiness to mankind as that which had been adopted at Ullathorne Court. What— not an oriel? says Miss Diana de Midellage. No, Miss Diana; not even an oriel, beautiful as is an oriel window. It has not about it so perfect a feeling of quiet English homely comfort. Let oriel windows grace a college, or the half public mansion of a potent peer; but for the sitting room of quiet country ladies, of ordinary homely folk, nothing can equal the square mullioned windows of the Tudor architects.

The hall was hung round with family female insipidities by Lely, and unprepossessing male Thornes in red coats by Kneller; each Thorne having been let into a panel in the wainscoting, in the proper manner. At the further end of the room was a huge fire-place, which afforded much ground of difference between the brother and sister. An antiquated grate that would hold about a hundredweight of coal had been stuck on to the hearth, by Mr. Thorne's father. This hearth had of course been intended for the consumption of wood fagots, and the iron dogs for the purpose were still standing, though half buried in the masonry of the grate. Miss Thorne was very anxious to revert to the dogs. The dear good old creature was always glad to revert to anything, and had she been systematically indulged, would doubtless in time have reflected that fingers were made before forks, and have reverted accordingly. But in the affairs of the fire-place Mr. Thorne would not revert. Country gentlemen around him, all had comfortable grates in their dining-rooms. He was not exactly the man to have suggested a modem usage; but he was not so far prejudiced as to banish those which his father had prepared for his use. Mr. Thorne had, indeed, once suggested that with very little contrivance the front door might have been so altered, as to open at least into the passage; but on hearing this, his sister Monica,—such was Miss Thorne's name,—had been taken ill, and had remaincd so for a week. Before she came down stairs she received a pledge from her brother that the entrance should never be changed in her lifetime.

At the end of the hall opposite to the fire-place a door led into the drawing-room, which was of equal size, and lighted with precisely similar windows. But yet the aspect of the room was very different. It was papered, and the ceiling, which in the hall showed the old rafters, was whitened and finished with a modern cornice. Miss Thorne's drawing-room, or, as she always called it, withdrawing-room, was a beautiful apartment. The windows opened on to the full extent of the lovely trim garden; immediately before the windows were plots of flowers in stiff, stately, stubborn little beds, each bed surrounded by a stone coping of its own; beyond, there was a low parapet wall, on which stood urns and images, fawns, nymphs, satyrs, and a whole tribe of Pan's fol-

lowers; and then again, beyond that, a beautiful lawn sloped away to a sunk fence which divided the garden from the park. Mr. Thorne's study was at the end of the drawing-room, and beyond that were the kitchen and the offices. Doors opened into both Miss Thorne's withdrawing-room and Mr. Thorne's sanctum from the passage above alluded to; which, as it came to the latter room, widened itself so as to make space for the huge black oak stairs, which led to the upper regions.

Such was the interior of Ullathorne Court. But having thus described it, perhaps somewhat too tediously, we beg to say that it is not the interior to which we wish to call the English tourist's attention, though we advise him to lose no legitimate opportunity of becoming acquainted with it in a friendly manner. It is the outside of Ullathorne that is so lovely. Let the tourist get admission at least into the garden, and fling himself on that soft sward just opposite to the exterior angle of the house. He will there get the double frontage, and enjoy that which is so lovely,—the expanse of architectural beauty without the formal dulness of one long line.

It is the colour of Ullathorne that is so remarkable. It is all of that delicious tawny hue which no stone can give, unless it has on it the vegetable richness of centuries. Strike the wall with your hand, and you will think that the stone has on it no covering, but rub it carefully, and you will find that the colour comes off upon your finger. No colourist that ever yet worked from a palette has been able to come up to this rich colouring of years crowding themselves on years.

Ullathorne is a high building for a country house, for it possesse3 three stories; and in each story, the windows are of the same sort as that described, though varying in size, and varying also in their lines athwart the house. Those of the ground floor are all uniform in size and position. But those above are irregular both in size and place, and this irregularity gives a bizarre and not unpicturesque appearance to the building. Along the top, on every side, runs a low

parapet, which nearly hides the roof, and at the comers are more figures of fawns and satyrs.

Such is Ullathorne House. But we must say one word of the approach to it, which shall include all the description which we mean to give of the church also. The picturesque old church of St. Ewold's stands immediately opposite to the iron gates which open into the court, and is all but surrounded by the branches of the lime trees, which form the avenue leading up to the house from both sides. This avenue is magnificent, but it would lose much of its value in the eyes of many proprietors, by the fact that the road through it is not private property. It is a public lane between hedge rows, with a broad grass margin on each side of the road, from which the lime trees spring. Ullathorne Court, therefore, does not stand absolutely surrounded by its own grounds, though Mr. Thorne is owner of all the adjacent land. This, however, is the source of very little annoyance to him. Men, when they are acquiring property, think much of such tilings, but they who live where their ancestors have lived for years, do not feel the misfortune. It never occurred either to Mr. or Miss Thorne that they were not sufficiently private, because the world at large might, if it so wished, walk or drive by their iron gates. That part of the world which availed itself of the privilege was however very small.

Such a year or two since were the Thornes of Ullathorne. Such, *we* believe, are the inhabitants of many an English country home. May it be long before their number diminishes.

CHAPTER XXm. MB. ARABIN READS HIMSELF IN AT ST. Ewolt/s.

On the Sunday morning the archdeacon with his sister-in-law and Mr. Arabin drove over to Ullathorne, as had been arranged. On their way thither the new vicar declared himself to be considerably disturbed in his mind at the idea of thus facing his parishioners for the first time. He had, he said, been always subject to mauvaise honte and an annoying degree of bashfulness, which often unfitted him for any work of a novel description; and now he felt this so strongly that he feared he should acquit himself badly in St. Ewold's reading-desk. He knew, he said, that those sharp little eyes of Miss Thome would be on him, and that they would not approve. All this the archdeacon greatly ridiculed. He himself knew not, and bad never known, what it was to be shy. He could not conceive that Miss Thome, surrounded as she would be by the peasants of Ullathorne and a few of the poorer inhabitants of the suburbs of Barchester, could in any way affect the composure of a man well accustomed to address the learned congregation of St. Mary's at Oxford, and he laughed accordingly at the idea of Mr. Arabin's modesty.

Thereupon Mr. Arabin commenced to subtilise. The change, he said, from St. Mary's to St. Ewold's was quite as powerful on the spirits as would be that from St. Ewold's to St. Mary's. Would not a peer who, by chance of fortune, might suddenly be driven to herd among navvies be as afraid of the jeers of his companions, as would any navvy suddenly exalted to a seat among the peers? Whereupon the archdeacon declared with a loud laugh that he would tell Miss Thorpe that her new minister had likened her to a navvy. Eleanor, however, pronounced such a conclusion to be unfair. A comparison might be very just in its proportions which did not at all assimilate the things compared. But Mr. Arabin went on subtilising, regarding neither the archdeacon's raillery nor Eleanor's defence. A young lady, he said, would execute with most perfect self-possession a difficult piece of music in a room crowded with strangers, who would not be able to express herself in intelligible language, even on any ordinary subject and among her most intimate friends, if she were required to do so standing on a box somewhat elevated among them. It was all an affair of education, and he at forty found it difficult to educate himself anew.

Eleanor dissented on the matter of the box; and averred she could speak very well about dresses, or babies, or legs of mutton from any box, provided it were big enough for her to stand upon without fear, even though all her friends were listening to her. The archdeacon was sure she would not be able to say a word; but this proved nothing in favour of Mr. Arabin. Mr. Arabin said that he would try the question out with Mrs. Bold, and get her on a box some day when the rectory might be full of visitors. To this Eleanor assented, making condition that the visitors should be of their own set,—and the archdeacon cogitated in his mind, whether by such a condition it was intended that Mr. Slope should be included, resolving also that, if so, the trial would certainly never take place in the rectory drawing-room at Plumstead.

So arguing, they drove up to the iron gates of Ullathorne Court.

Mr. and Miss Thorne were standing ready dressed for church in the hall, and greeted their clerical visitors with cordiality. The archdeacon was an old favourite. He was a clergyman of the old school, and this recommended him to the lady. He had always been an opponent of free trade as long as free trade was an open question; and now that it was no longer so, he, being a clergyman, had not been obliged, like most of his lay Tory companions, to read his recantation. He could therefore be regarded as a supporter of the immaculate fifty-three, and was on this account a favourito with Mr. Thorne. The little bell was tinkling, and the rural population of the parish were standing about the lane, leaning on the church stile and against the walls of the old court, anxious to get a look at their new minister as he passed from the house to the rectory. The archdeacon's servant had already preceded them thither with the vestments.

They all went forth together; and when the ladies passed into the church the three gentlemen tarried a moment in the lane that Mr. Thorne might name to the vicar with some kind of one-sided introduction, the most leading among his parishioners.

"Here are our churchwardens, Mr. Arabin; Farmer Greenacre and Mr. Stiles. Mr. Stiles has the mill as you go into Barchester; and very good churchwardens they are."

"Not very severe, I hope," said Mr. Arabin. The two ecclesiastical officers touched their hats, and each made a leg in the approved rural fashion, assuring the vicar that they were very glad to have the honour of seeing him, and adding that the weather was very good for the harvest. Mr. Stiles being a man somewhat versed in town life, had an impression of his own dignity, and did not quite like leaving his pastor under the erroneous idea that he being a churchwarden kept the children in order during church time. 'Twas thus he understood Mr. Arabin's allusion to his severity, and hastened to put matters right by observing that "Sexton Clodheve looked to the younguns, and perhaps sometimes there may be a thought too much stick going on during sermon. " Mr. Arabin's bright eye twinkled as he caught that of the archdeacon's; and he smiled to himself as he observed how ignorant his officers were of the nature of their authority, and of the surveillance which it was their duty to keep even over himself.

Mr. Arabin read the lessons and preached. It was enough to put a man a little out, let him have been ever so used to pulpit reading, to see the knowing way in which the farmers cocked their ears, and set about a mental criticism as to whether their new minister did or did not fall short of the excellence of him who had lately departed from them. A mental and silent criticism it was for the existing moment, but soon to be made public among the elders of St. Ewold's over the green graves of their children and forefathers. The excellence, however, of poor old Mr. Goodenough had not been wonderful, and there were few there who did not deem that Mr. Arabin did his work sufficiently well, in spite of the slightly nervous affection which at first impeded him, and which nearly drove the archdeacon beside himself.

But the sermon was the thing to try the man. It often surprises us that very young men can muster courage to preach for the first time to a strange congregation. Men who are as yet but little more than boys, who have but just left, what indeed we may not call a school, but a seminary intended for their tuition as scholars, whose thoughts have been mostly of boating, cricketing, and wine parties, ascend a rostrum high above the heads of the submissive crowd, not that they may read God's word to those below, but that they may preach their own word for the edification of their hearers! It seems strange to us that they are not stricken dumb by the new and awful solemnity of their position. How am I, just turned twenty-three, who have never yet passed ten thoughtful days since the power of thought first came to me, how am I to instruct these greybeards, who with the weary thinking of so many years have approached so near the grave? Can I teach them their duty? Can I explain to them that which I so imperfectly understand, that which years of study may have made so plain to them? Has my newly acquired privilege, as one of God's ministers, imparted to me as yet any fitness for the wonderful work of a preacher?

It must be supposed that such ideas do occur to young clergymen, and yet they overcome, apparently with ease, this difficulty which to us appears to be all but insurmountable. We have never been subjected in the way of ordination to the power of a bishop's hands. It may be that there is in them something that sustains the spirit and banishes the natural modesty of youth. But for ourselves we must own that the deep affection which Dominie Sampson felt for his young pupils has not more endeared him to us than the bashful spirit which sent him mute and inglorious from the pulpit when he rose there with the futile attempt to preach God's gospel.

There is a rule in our church which forbids the younger order of our clergymen to perform a certain portion of the service. The absolution must be read by a minister in priest's orders. If there be no such minister present, the congregation can have the benefit of no absolution but that which each may succeed in administering to himself. The rule may be a good one, though the necessity for it hardly comes home to the general un-

derstanding. But this forbearance on the part of youth would be much more appreciated if it were extended likewise to sermons. The only danger would be that congregations would be too anxious to prevent their young clergymen from advancing themselves in the ranks of the ministry. Clergymen who could not preach would be such blessings that they would be bribed to adhere to their incompetence.

Mr. Arabin, however, had not the modesty of youth to impede him, and he succeeded with his sermon even better than with the lessons. He took for his text two verses out of the second epistle of St. John, "Whosoever transgresseth, and abideth not in the doctrine of Christ, hath not God. He that abideth in the doctrine of Christ he hath both the Father and Son. If there come any unto you and bring not this doctrine, receive him not into your house, neither bid him God speed." He told them that the house of theirs to which he alluded was this their church in which he now addressed them for the first time; that their most welcome and proper manner of bidding him God speed would be their patient obedience to his teaching of the gospel; but that he could put forward no claim to such conduct on their part unless he taught them the great Christian doctrine of works and faith combined. On this he enlarged, but not very amply, and after twenty minutes succeeded in sending his new friends home to their baked mutton and pudding well pleased with their new minister.

Then came the lunch at Ullathorne. As soon as they were in the hall Miss Thorne took Mr. Arabin's hand, and assured him that she received him into her housed into the temple, she said, in which she worshipped, and bade him God speed with all her heart. Mr. Arabin was touched, and squeezed the spinster's hand without uttering a word in reply. Then Mr. Thorne expressed a hope that Mr. Arabin found the church easy to fill, and Mr. Arabin having repUed that he had no doubt he should do so as soon as he had learnt to pitch his voice to the building, they all sat down to the good things before them.

Miss Thorne took special care of Mrs. Bold. Eleanor still wore her widow's weeds, and therefore had about her that air of grave and sad maternity which is the lot of recent widows. This opened the soft heart of Miss Thorne, and made her look on her young guest as though too much could not be done for her. She heaped chicken and ham upon her plate, and poured out for her a full bumper of port wine. When Eleanor, who was not sorry to get it, had drunk a little of it, Miss Thorne at once essayed to fill it again. To this Eleanor objected, but in vain. Miss Thorne winked and nodded and whispered, saying that it was the proper thing and must be done, and that she knew all about it; and so she desired Mrs. Bold to drink it up, and not mind any body.

"It is your duty, you know, to support yourself," she said into the ear of the young mother; "there's more than yourself depending on it; " and thus she coshered up Eleanor with cold fowl and port wine. How it is that poor men's wives, who have no cold fowl and port wine on which to be coshered up, nurse their children without difficulty, whereas the wives of rich men, who eat and drink everything that is good, cannot do so, we will for the present leave to the doctors and the mothers to settle between them.

And then Miss Thorne was great about teeth. Little Johnny Bold had been troubled for the last few days with his first incipient masticator, and, with that freemasonry which exists among ladies, Miss Thorne became aware of the fact before Eleanor had half finished her wing. The old lady prescribed at once a receipt which had been much in vogue in the young days of her grandmother, and warned Eleanor with solemn voice against the fallacies of modern medicine.

"Take his coral, my dear," said she, "and rub it well with carrot-juice; rub it till the juice dries on it, and then give it him to play with"

"But he hasn't got a coral," said Eleanor.

"Not got a coral!" said Miss Thorne, with almost angry vehemence. "Not got a coral! How can you expect that he should cut his teeth? Have you got Daffy's Elixir?"

Eleanor explained that she had not. It had not been ordered by Mr. Berechild, the Barchester doctor whom she employed; and then the young mother mentioned some shockingly modern succedaneum, which Mr. Eerechild's new lights had taught him to recommend.

Miss Thorne looked awfully severe. "Take care, my dear," said she, "that the man knows what he's about; take care he doesn't destroy your little boy. But,"—and she softened into sorrow as she said it, and spoke more in pity than in anger,— "but I don't know who there is in Barchester now that you can trust. Poor dear old Doctor Bump well, indeed"

"Why, Miss Thorne, he died when I was a little girl."

"Yes, my dear, he did; and an unfortunate day it was for Barchester. As to those young men that have come up since," —Mr. Eerechild, by the bye, was quite as old as Miss Thorne herself,—"one doesn't know where they came from or who they are, or whether they know anything about their business or not."

"I think there are very clever men in Barchester," said Eleanor.

"Perhaps there may be; only I don't know them; and it's admitted on all sides that medical men arn't now what they used to be. They used to be talented, observing, educated men. But now any whipper-snapper out of an apothecary's shop can call himself a doctor. I believe no kind of education is now thought necessary." Eleanor was herself the widow of a medical man, and felt a little inclined to resent all these hard sayings. But Miss Thorne was so essentially good-natured that it was impossible to resent anything she said. She therefore sipped her wine and finished hei chicken. "At any rate, my dear, don't forget the carrot-juice, and by all means get him a coral at once. My grandmother Thorne had the best teeth in the county, and carried them to the grave with her at eighty. I have heard

her say it was all the carrot-juice. She couldn't bear the Barchester doctors. Even poor old Dr. Bumpwell didn't please her." It clearly never occurred to Miss Thorne that some fifty years ago Dr. Bumpwell was only a rising man, and therefore as much in need of character in the eyes of the then ladies of Ullathorne, as the present doctors were in her own.

The archdeacon made a very good lunch, and talked to his host about turnip-drillers and new machines for reaping; while the host, thinking it only polite to attend to a stranger, and fearing that perhaps he might not care about turnip crops on a Sunday, mooted all manner of ecclesiastical subjects. "I never saw a heavier lot of wheat, Thorne, than you've got in that field beyond the copse. I suppose that's guano," said the archdeacon.

"Yes, guano. I get it from Bristol myself. You'll find you often have a tolerable congregation of Barchester people out here, Mr. Arabin. They are very fond of St. Ewold's, particularly of an afternoon, when the weather is not too hot for the walk."

"I am under an obligation to them for staying away to-day, at any rate," said the vicar. "The congregation can never be too small for a maiden sermon."

"I got a ton and a half at Bradley's in High Street," said the archdeacon, "and it was a complete take in. I don't believe there was five hundred-weight of guano in it."

"That Bradley never has anything good," said Miss Thorne, who had just caught the name during her whisperings with Eleanor. "And such a nice shop as there used to be in that very house before he came. Wilfred, don't you remember what good things old Ambleoff used to have?"

"There have been three men since Ambleoff's time," said the archdeacon, "and each as bad as the other. But who gets it for you at Bristol, Thorne?"

"I ran up myself this year and bought it out of the ship. I am afraid as the evenings get shorter, Mr. Arabin, you'll find the reading desk too dark. I must send a fellow with an axe and make him

lop off some of those branches."

Mr. Arabin declared that the morning light at any rate was perfect, and deprecated any interference with the lime trees. And they they took a stroll out among the trim parterres, and Mr. Arabin explained to Mrs. Bold the difference between a naiad and a dryad, and dilated on vases and the shapes of urns. Miss Thorne busied herself among her pansies; and her brother, finding it quite impracticable to give anything of a peculiarly Sunday tone to the conversation, abandoned the attempt, and had it out with the archdeacon about the Bristol guano.

At three o'clock they again went into church; and now Mr. Arabin read the service and the archdeacon preached. Nearly the same congregation was present, with some adventurous pedestrians from the city, who had not thought the heat of the mid-day August sun too great to deter them. The archdeacon took his text from the Epistle to Philemon. "I beseech thee for my son Onesimus, whom I have begotten in my bonds." From such a text it may be imagined the kind of sermon which Dr. Grantly preached, and on the TFhole it was neither dull, nor bad, nor out of place.

He told them that it had become his duty to look about for a pastor for them, to supply the place of one who had been long among them; and that in this manner he regarded as a son him whom he had selected, as St. Paul had regarded the young disciple whom he sent forth. Then he took a little merit to himself for having studiously provided the best man he could without reference to patronage or favour; but he did not say that the best man according to his views was he who was best able to subdue Mr. Slope, and make that gentleman's situation in Barchester too hot to be comfortable. As to the bonds, they had consisted in the exceeding struggle which he had made to get a good clergyman for them. He deprecated any comparison between himself and St. Paul, but said that he was entitled to beseech them for their good will towards Mr. Arabin, in the same manner that the apostle had besought Philemon and his household with regard to Onesimus.

The archdeacon's sermon, text, blessing and all, was concluded within the half hour. Then they shook hands with their Ullathorue friends, and returned to Plumstead. 'Twas thus that Mr. Arabin read himself in at St. Ewold's.

CHAPTER XXIV. MR. SLOPE MANAGES MATTERS VERY CLEVERLY AT FUDDING-DALE.

The next two weeks passed pleasantly enough at Plumstead. Tlio whole party there assembled seemed to get on well together. 1 Eleanor made the house agreeable, and the archdeacon and Mrs. Grantly seemed to have forgotten her iniquity as regarded Mr. Slope. Mr. Harding had his violoncello and played to them while his daughters accompanied him. Johnny Bold, by the help either of Mr. Eerechild or else by that of his coral and carrot-juice, got through his teething troubles. There had been gaieties too of all sorts. They had dined at Ullathorne, and the Thornes had dined at the Rectory. Eleanor had been duly put to stand on her box, and in that position had found herself quite unable to express her opinion on the merits of flounces, such having been the subject given to try her elocution. Mr. Arabin had of course been much in his own parish, looking to the doings at his vicarage, calling on his parishioners, and taking on himself the duties of his new calling. But still he had been every evening at Plumstead, and Mrs. Grantly was partly willing to agree with her husband that he was a pleasant inmate in a house.

They had also been at a dinner party at Dr. Stanhope's, of which Mr. Arabin had made one. He also, moth-like, burnt his wings in the flames of the Signora's candle. Mrs. Bold, too, had been there, and had felt somewhat displeased with the taste,—want of. taste she called it,—shown by Mr. Arabin in paying so much attention to Madame Neroni. It was as infallible that Madeline 7 should displease and irritate the women, as that she should charm / and captivate the men. The one result followed naturally on the other. It was quite true that Mr.

Arabin had been charmed. He thought her a very clever and a very handsome woman; he thought also that her peculiar affliction entitled her to the sympathy of all. He had never, he said, met so much suffering joined to such perfect beauty and so clear a mind. 'Twas thus he spoke of the Signora coming home in the archdeacon's carriage; and Eleanor by no means liked to hear the praise. It was, however, exceedingly unjust of her to be angry with Mr. Arabin, as she had herself spent a very pleasant evening with Bertie Stanhope, who had taken her down to dinner, and had not left her side for one moment after the gentlemen came out of the dining-room. It was unfair that she should amuse herself with Bertie and yet begrudge her new friend his license of amusing himself with Bertie's sister. And yet she did so. She was half angry with him in the carriage, and said something about meretricious manners. Mr. Arabin did not understand the ways of women very well, or else he might have flattered himself that Eleanor was in love with him.

But Eleanor was not in love with him. How many shades there are between love and indifference, and how little the graduated scale is understood! She had now been nearly three weeks in the same house with Mr. Arabin, and had received much of his attention, and listened daily to his conversation. He had usually devoted at least some portion of his evening to her exclusively. At Dr. Stanhope's he had devoted himself exclusively to another. It does not require that a woman should be in love to be irritated at this. It does not require that she should even acknowledge to herself that it is unpleasant to her. Eleanor had no such selfknowledge. She thought in her own heart that it was only on Mr. Arabin's account that she regretted that he could condescend to be amused by the Signora. "I thought he had more mind," she said to herself, as she sat watching her baby's cradle on her return from the party. "After all, I believe Mr. Stanhope is the pleasanter man of the two." Alas for the memory of poor John Bold! Eleanor was not in love with Bertie Stanhope, nor was VOL. II. *v* she in

love with Mr. Arabia. But her devotion to her late husband was fast fading, when she could revolve in her mind, over the cradle of his infant, the faults and failings of other aspirants to her favour.

Will any one blame my heroine for this? Let him or her rather thank God for all His goodness.

Eleanor, in truth, was not in love. Neither was Mr. Arabin. Neither indeed was Bertie Stanhope, though he had already found occasion to say nearly as much as that he was. The widow's cap had prevented him from making a positive declaration, when otherwise he would have considered himself entitled to do so on a third or fourth interview. It was, after all but a small cap now, and had but little of the weeping-willow left in its construction. It is singular how these emblems of grief fade away by unseen gradations. Each pretends to be the counterpart of the forerunner, and yet the last little bit of crimped white crape that sits so jauntily on the back of the head, is as dissimilar to the first huge mountain of woe which disfigured the face of the weeper, as the state of the Hindoo is to the jointure of the English dowager.

But let it be clearly understood that Eleanor was in love with no one, and that no one was in love with Eleanor. Under these circumstances her anger against Mr. Arabin did not last long, and before two days were over they were both as good friends as ever. She could not but like him, for every hour spent in his company was spent pleasantly. And yet she could not quite like him, for there was always apparent in his conversation a certain feeling on his part that he hardly thought it worth his while to be in earnest. It was almost as though he were playing with a child. She knew well enough that he was in truth a sober thoughtful man, who in some matters and on some occasions could endure an agony of earnestness. And yet to her he was always gently playful. Could she have seen his brow once clouded she might have learnt to love him.

So things went on. at Plumstead, and on the whole not unpleasantly, till a huge storm darkened the horizon, and came down upon the inhabitants of the rectory with all the fury of a waterspout. It was astonishing how in a few minutes the whole face of the heavens was changed. The party broke up from breakfast in perfect harmony; but fierce passions had arisen before the evening, which did not admit of their sitting at the same board for dinner. To explain this, it will be necessary to go back a little.

It will be remembered that the bishop expressed to Mr. Slope in his dressing-room his determination that Mr. Quiverful should be confirmed in his appointment to the hospital, and that his lordship requested Mr. Slope to communicate this decision to the archdeacon. It will also be remembered that the archdeacon had indignantly declined seeing Mr. Slope, and had instead, written a strong letter to the bishop, in which he all but demanded the situation of warden for Mr. Harding. To this letter the archdeacon received an immediate formal reply from Mr. Slope, in which it was stated, that the bishop had received and would give his best consideration to the archdeacon's letter.

The archdeacon felt himself somewhat checkmated by this reply. What could he do with a man who would neither see him, nor argue with him by letter, and who had undoubtedly the power of appointing any clergyman he pleased? He had consulted with Mr. Arabin, who had suggested the propriety of calling in the aid of the master of Lazarus. "If," said he, "you and Dr. Gwynne formally declare your intention of waiting upon the bishop, the bishop will not dare to refuse to see you; and if two such men as you see him together, you will probably not leave him without carrying your point."

The archdeacon did not quite like admitting the necessity of his being backed by the master of Lazarus before he could obtain admission into the episcopal palace of Barchester; but still he felt that the advice was good and he resolved to take it. He wrote again to the bishop, expressing a hope that nothing further would be done in the matter

of the hospital, till the consideration promised by his lordship had been given, and then sent off a warm. appeal to his friend the master, imploring him to come to Plumhtead and assist in driving the bishop into compliance. The master had rejoined, raising some difficulty, but not declining; and the archdeacon had again pressed his point, insisting on the necessity for immediate action. Dr. Gwynne unfortunately had the gout, and could therefore name no immediate day, but still agreed to come, if it should be finally found necessary. So the matter stood, as regarded the party at Plumstead.

But Mr. Harding had another friend fight'ng his battle for him, quite as powerful as the master of Lazarus, and this was Mr. Slope. Though the bishop had so pertinaciously insisted on giving way to his wife in the matter of the hospital, Mr. Slope did not think it necessary to abandon his object. He had, he thought, daily more and more reason to imagine that the widow would receive his overtures favourably, and he could not but feel that Mr. Harding at the hospital, and placed there by his means, would be more likely to receive him as a son-in-law, than Mr. Harding growling in opposition and disappointment under the archdeacon's wing at Plumstead. Moreover, to give Mr. Slope due credit, he was 'actuated by greater motives even than these. He wanted a wife, /and he wanted money, but he wanted power more than either. He had fully realised the fact that he must come to blows with. Mrs. Proudie. He had no desire to remain in Barchester as her chaplain. Sooner than do so, he would risk the loss of his whole connection with the diocese. What! was he to feel within him the possession of no ordinary talents; was he to know himself to be courageous, firm, and, in matters where his conscience did not interfere, unscrupulous; and yet be contented to be the working factotum of a woman-prelate? Mr. Slope had higher ideas of his own destiny. Either he or Mrs. Proudie must go to the wall; and now had come the time when he would try which it should be.

The bishop had declared that Mr. Quiverful should be the new warden. As Mr. Slope went down stairs prepared to see the archdeacon if necessary, but fully satisfied that no such necessity would arise, he declared to himself that Mr. Harding should be warden. With the object of carrying this point he rode over to Puddingdale, and had a further interview with the worthy expectant of clerical good things. Mr. Quiverful was on the whole a worthy man. The impossible task of bringing up as ladies and gentlemen fourteen children on an income which was insufficient to give them with decency the common necessaries of life, had had an effect upon him not beneficial either to his spirit, or his keen sense of honour. Who can boast that he woidd have supported such a burden with a different result? Mr. Quiverful was an honest, pains-taking, drudging man; anxious, indeed, for bread and meat, anxious for means to quiet his butcher and cover with returning smiles the now sour countenance of the baker's wife, but anxious also to be right with his own conscience. He was not careful, as another might be who sat on an easier worldly seat, to stand well with those around him, to shun a breath which might sully his name, or a rumour which might affect his honour. He could not afford such niceties of conduct, such moral luxuries. It must suffice for him to be ordinarily honest according to the ordinary honesty of the world's ways, and to let men's tongues wag as they would.

He had felt that his brother clergymen, men whom he had known for the last twenty years, looked coldly on him from the first moment that he had shown himself willing to sit at the feet of Mr. Slope. He had seen that their looks grew colder still when it had become bruited about that he was to be the bishop's new warden at Hiram's hospital. This was painful enough; but it was the cross which he was doomed to bear. He thought of his wife, whose last new silk dress was six years in wear. He thought of all his young flock, whom he could hardly take to church with him on Sundays, for there were not decent shoes and stockings for them all to wear. He thought of the well-worn sleeves of his own black coat, and of the stern face of the draper from whom he would fain ask for cloth to make another, did he not know that the credit would be refused him. Then he thought of the comfortable house in Barchester, of the comfortable income, of his boys sent to school, of his girls with books in their hands instead of darning needles, of his wife's face again covered with smiles, and of his daily board again covered with plenty. He thought of these things; and do thou also, reader, think of them, and then wonder, if thou canst, that Mr. Slope had appeared to him to possess all those good gifts which could grace a bishop's chaplain. "How beautiful upon the mountains are the feet of him that bringeth good tidings."

Why, moreover, should the Barchester clergy have looked coldly on Mr. Quiverful? Had they not all shown that they regarded with complacency the loaves and fishes of their mother church? Had they not all, by some hook or crook, done better for themselves than he had done? They were not burdened as he was burdened. Dr. Grantly had five children, and nearly as many thousands a year on which to feed them. It was very well for him to turn up his nose at a new bishop who could do nothing for him, and a chaplain who was beneath his notice; but it was cruel in a man so circumstanced to set the world against the father of fourteen children because he was anxious to obtain for them an honourable support! He, Mr. Quiverful, had not asked for the wardenship. He had not even accepted it till he had been assured that Mr. Harding had refused it. How hard then that he should be blamed for doing that which not to have done would have argued a most insane imprudence?

Thus in this matter of the hospital poor Mr. Quiverful had his trials; and he had also his consolations. On the whole the consolations were the more vivid of the two. The stern draper heard of the coming promotion, and the wealth of his warehouse was at Mr. Quiverful's disposal. Coming events cast their shad-ows before, and the coming event of Mr. Quiverful's transference to Barchester produced a delicious shadow in the shape of a new outfit for Mrs. Quiverful and her three elder daughters. Such consolations come home to the heart of a man, and quite home to the heart of a woman. Whatever the husband might feel, the wife cared nothing for frowns of dean, archdeacon, or prebendary. To her the outsides and insides of her husband and fourteen children were everything. In her bosom every other ambition had been swallowed up in that maternal ambition of seeing them and him and herself duly clad and properly fed. It had come to that with her that life had now no other purpose. She recked nothing of the imaginary rights of others. She had no patience with her husband when he declared to her that he could not accept the hospital unless he knew that Mr. Harding had refused it. Her husband had no right to be Quixotic at the expense of fourteen children. The narrow escape of throwing away his good fortune which her lord had had, almost paralysed her. Now, indeed, they had received the full promise not only from Mr. Slope, but also from Mrs. Proudie. Now, indeed, they might reck-on with safety on their good fortune. But what if all had been lost? What if her fourteen bairns had been resteeped to the hips in poverty by the morbid sentimentality of their father? Mrs. Quiverful was just at present a happy woman, but yet it nearly took her breath away when she thought of the risk they had run.

"I don't know what your father means when he talks so much of what is due to Mr. Harding," she said to her eldest daughter. "Hoes he think that Mr. Harding would give him 450?. a year out of fine feeling? And what signifies it whom he offends, as long as he gets the place? He does not expect anything better. It passes me to think how your father can be so soft while everybody around him is so griping."

Thus, while the outer world was ac-cusing Mr. Quiverful of rapacity for promotion and of disregard to his hon-our, the inner world of his own house-hold was falling foul of him, with equal vehemence, for his willingness to (sac-rifice their interest to a false feeling of sentimental pride. It is astonishing how much difference the point of view makes in the aspect of all that we look at!

Such were the feelings of the differ-ent members of the family at Tulding-dale on the occasion of Mr. Slope's sec-ond visit. Mrs. Quiverful, as soon as she saw his horse coming up the avenue from the vicarage gate, hastily packed up her huge basket of needlework, and hurried herself and her daughter out of the room in which she was sitting with her husband. "It's Mr. Slope," she said. "He's come to settle with you about the hospital. I do hope we shall now be able to move at once." And she hastened to bid the maid of all work go to the door, so that the welcome grea. man might not be kept waiting.

Mr. Slope thus found Mr. Quiverful alone. Mrs. Quiverful went off to her kitchen and back settlements with anx-ious beating heart, almost dreading that there might be some slip between the cup of her happiness and the hp of her fruition, but yet comforting herself with the reflection that after what had taken place, any such slip could hardly be possible.

Mr. Slope was all smiles as he shook his brother clergyman's hand, and said that he had ridden over because he thought it right at once to put Mr. Quiv-erful in possession of the facts of the matter regarding the wardenship of the hospital. As he spoke, the poor expec-tant husband and father saw at a glance that his brilliant hopes were to be dashed to the ground, and that his visi-tor was now there for the purpose of un-saying what on his former visit he had said. There was something in the tone of the voice, something in the glance of the eye, which told the tale. Mr. Quiverful knew it all at once. He maintained his self-possession, however, smiled with a slight unmeaning smile, and merely said that he was obliged to Mr. Slope for the trouble he was taking.

"It has been a troublesome matter from first to last," said Mr. Slope; "and the bishop has hardly known how to act. Between ourselves;—but mind this of course must go no further, Mr. Quiverful." Mr. Quiverful said that of course it should not. "The truth is, that poor Mr. Harding has hardly known his own mind. You remember our last conversation, no doubt."

Mr. Quiverful assured him that he remembered it very well indeed.

'' You will remember that I told you that Mr. Harding had refused to return to the hospital."

Mr. Quiverful declared that nothing could be more distinct on his memory. "And acting on this refusal I suggested that you should take the hospital," continued Mr. Slope.

"I understood you to say that the bishop had authorised you to offer it to me."

"Did I? Did I go so far as that? Well, perhaps it may be; that in my anxiety in your-behalf I did commit myself further than I should have done. So far as my own memory serves me I don't think I did go quite so far as that. But I own I was very anxious that you should get it; and I may have said more than was quite prudent."

"But," said Mr. Quiverful, in his deep anxiety to prove his case, "my wife received as distinct a promise from Mrs. Proudie as one human being could give to another."

Mr. Slope smiled, and gently shook his head. He meant that smile for a pleasant smile, but it was diabolical in the eyes of the man he was speaking to. "Mrs. Proudie!" he said. "If we are to go to what passes between the ladies in these matters we shall really be in a nest of troubles from which we shall never extricate ourselves. Mrs. Proudie is a most excellent lady, kind-hearted, charitable, pious, and in every way estimable. But, my dear Mr Quiverful, the patronage of the diocese is not in her hands."

Mr. Quiverful for a moment sat panic-stricken and silent. "Am I to understand, then, that I have received no promise?" he said, as soon as he had sufficiently collected his thoughts.

"If you will allow me I will tell you exactly how the matter rests. You cer-

tainly did receive a promise conditional on Mr. Harding's refusal. I am sure you will do me the justice to remember that you yourself declared that you could accept the appointment on no other condition than the knowledge that Mr. Harding had declined it."

"Yes," said Mr. Quiverful; "I did say that, certainly."

"Well; it now appears that he did not refuse it."

"But surely you told me, and repeated it more than once, that he had done so in your own hearing."

"So I understood him. But it seems I was in error. But don't for a moment, Mr. Quiverful, suppose that I mean to throw you over. No! Having held out my hand to a man in your position, with your large family and pressing claims, I am not now going to draw it back again. I only want you to act with me fairly and honestly."

"Whatever I do, I shall endeavour at any rate to act fairly," said the poor man, feeling that he had to fall back for support on the spirit of martyrdom within him.

"I am sure you will," said the other. "I am sure you have no wish to obtain possession of an income which belongs by right to another. No man knows better than you do Mr. Harding's history, or can better appreciate his character. Mr. Harding is very desirous of returning to his old position, and the bishop feels that he is at the present moment somewhat hampered—though of course he is not bound by the conversation which took place on the matter between you and me."

"Well!" said Mr. Quiverful, dreadfully doubtful as to what his conduct under such circumstances should be, and fruitlessly striving to harden his nerves with some of that instinct of self-preservation which made his wife so bold.

"The wardenship of this little hospital is not the only thing in the bishop's gift, Mr. Quiverful, nor is it by many degrees the best. And his lordship is not the man to forget any one whom he has once marked with approval. If you would allow me to advise you as a friend"

"Indeed I shall be most grateful to

you," said the poor vicar of Pudding-dale.

"I should advise you to withdraw from any opposition to Mr. Harding's claims. If you persist in your demand, I do not think you will ultimately succeed. Mr. Harding has all but a positive right to the place. But if you will allow me to inform the bishop that you decline to stand in Mr. Harding's way, I think I may promise you,—though, by the bye, it must not be taken as a formal promise,—that the bishop will not allow you to be a poorer man than you would have been had you become warden."

Mr. Quiverful sat in his arm chair silent, gazing at vacancy. What was he to say? All this that came from Mr. Slope was so true. Mr. Harding had a right to the hospital. The bishop had a great many good things to give away. Both the bishop and Mr. Slope would be excellent friends and terrible enemies to a man in his position. And then he had no proof of any promise. He could not force the bishop to appoint him.

"Well, Mr. Quiverful, what do you say about it?"

"Oh, of course, whatever you think fit, Mr. Slope. It's a great disappointment, a very great disappointment. I won't deny that I am a very poor man, Mr. Slope."

"In the end, Mr. Quiverful, you will find that it will have been better for you. " The interview ended in Mr. Slope receiving a full renunciation from Mr. Quiverful of any claim he might have to the appointment in question. It was only given verbally and without witnesses;—but then the original promise was made in the same way.

Mr. Slope again assured him that he should not be forgotten, and then rode back to Barchester, satisfied that he would now be able to mould the bishop to his wishes.

CHAPTER XXV. FOURTEEN ARGUMENTS IN FAVOUR OF MR. QUIVERFUL'S CLAIMS.

We have most of us heard of the terrible anger of a lioness when, surrounded by her cubs, she guards her prey. Few of us wish to disturb the mother of a litter of puppies when mouthing a bone in the midst of her young family. Medea and her children are famihar to us, and so is the grief of Constance. Mrs. Quiverful, when she first heard from her husband the news which he had to impart, felt within her bosom all the rage of a lioness, the rapacity of the hound, the fury of the tragic queen, and the deep despair of the bereaved mother.

Doubting, but yet hardly fearing, what might have been the tenor of Mr. Slope's discourse, she rushed back to her husband as soon as the front door was closed behind the visitor. It was well for Mr. Slope that he so escaped. The anger of such a woman, at such a moment, would have cowed even him. As a general rule, it is highly desirable that ladies should keep their temper. A woman when she storms always makes herself ugly, and usually ridiculous also. There is nothing so odious to man as a virago. Though Theseus loved an Amazon, he showed his love but roughly; and from the time of Theseus downward, no man ever wished to have his wife' remarkable rather for forward prowess than retiring gentleness. A low voice " is an excellent thing in woman."

Such may be laid down as a very general rule; and few women should allow themselves to deviate from it, and then only on rare occasions. But if there be a time when a woman may let her hair to the winds, when she may loose her arms and scream out trumpettongued to the ears of men, it is when nature calls out within hei not for her own wants, but for the wants of those whom her womb has bome, whom her breasts have suckled, for those who look to her for their daily bread as naturally as man looks to his Creator.

There was nothing poetic in the nature of Mrs. Quiverful. She was neither a Medea nor a Constance. When angry, she spoke out her anger in plain words, and in a tone which might have been modulated with advantage. But she did so, at any rate, without affectation. Now, without knowing it, she rose to a tragic vein.

"Well, my dear; we are not to have it?" Such were the words with which her ears were greeted when she entered the parlour, still hot from the kitchen fire. And the face of her husband spoke even more plainly than his words;—

"E'en such a man, so faint, so spiritless,
So dull, so dead in look, so woe-begone,
Drew Priam's curtain in the dead of night."

"What!" said she,—and Mrs. Siddons could not have put more passion into a single syllable,—"What! not have it? Who says so?" And she sat opposite to her husband, with her elbows on the table, her hands clasped together, and her coarse, solid, but once handsome face stretched over it towards him.

She sat as silent as death while he told his story, and very dreadful to him her silence was. He told it very lamely and badly, but still in such a manner that she soon understood the whole of it.

"And so you have resigned it?" said she.

"I have had no opportunity of accepting it," he replied. "I had no witnesses to Mr. Slope's offer, even if that offer would bind the bishop. It was better for me, on the whole, to keep on good terms with such men than to fight for what I should never get!"

"Witnesses!" she screamed, rising quickly to her feet and walking up and down the room. "Do clergymen require witnesses to their words? He made the promise in the bishop's name, and if it is to be broken I'll know the reason why. Did he not positively say that the bishop had sent him to offer you the place?"

"Ho did, my dear. But that is now nothing to the purpose."

"It is everything to the purpose, Mr. Quiverful. Witnesses indeed! and then to talk of your honour being questioned, because you wish to provide for fourteen children. It is everything to the purpose; and so they shall know, if I scream it into their ears from the town cross of Barchester."

"You forget, Letitia, that the bishop has so many things in his gift. We must wait a little longer. That is all."

"Wait! Shall we feed the children by waiting. Will waiting put George, and Tom, and Sam, out into the world? Will it enable my poor girls to give up some of their drudgery? Will waiting make Bessy and Jane fit even to be governesses? Will waiting pay for the things we got in Barchester last week?"

"It is all we can do, my dear. The disappointment is as much to me as to you; and yet, God knows, I feel it more for your sake than my own."

Mrs. Quiverful was looking full into her husband's face, and saw a small hot tear appear on each of those furrowed cheeks. This was too much for her woman's heart. He also had risen, and was standing with his back to the empty grate. She rushed towards him, and seizing him in her arms, sobbed aloud upon his bosom. "You are too good, too soft, too yielding," she said at last. "These men, when they want you, they use you like a cat's-paw; and when they want you no longer, they throw you aside like an old shoe. This is twice they have treated you so."

"In one way this will be all for the better," argued he. "It will make the bishop feel that he is bound to do something for me."

"At any rate he shall hear of it," said the lady, again reverting to her more angry mood. '' At any rate he shall hear of it, and that loudly. And so shall she. She little knows Letitia Quiverful, if she thinks I will sit down quietly with the loss after all that passed between us at the palace. If there's any feeling within her, I'll make her ashamed of herself." And she paced the room again, stamping the floor as she went with her fat heavy foot. "Good heavens! what a heart she must have within her to treat in such a way as this the father of fourteen unprovided children!"

Mr. Quiverful preceeded to explain that he didn't think that Mrs. Proudie had had anything to do with it.

"Don't tell me," said Mrs. Quiverful. "I know more about it than that. Doesn't all the world know that Mrs. Proudie is bishop of Barchester, and that Mr. Slope is merely her creature? Wasn't it she that made me the promise, just as though the thing was in her own particular gift? I tell you, it was that woman who sent him over here to-day because, for some reason of her own, she wants to go back from her word."

"My dear, you're wrong."

"Now, Q., don't be so soft," she continued. "Take my word for it, the bishop knows no more about it than Jemima does." Jemima was the two-year-old. "And if you'll take my advice, you'll lose no time in going over and seeing him yourself."

Soft, however, as Mr. Quiverful might be, he would not allow himself to be talked out of his opinion on this occasion, and proceeded with much minuteness to explain to his wifo the tone in which Mr. Slope had spoken of Mrs. Proudie's interference in diocesan matters. As he did so, a new idea gradually instilled itself into the matron's head, and a new course of conduct presented itself to her judgment. What if, after all, Mrs. Proudie knew nothing of this visit of Mr. Slope's? In that case might it not be possible that that lady would still be staunch to her in this matter, still stand her friend, and, perhaps, possibly carry her through in opposition to Mr. Slope? Mrs. Quiverful said nothing as this vague.hope occurred to her, but listened with more than ordinary patience to what her husband had to say. While he was still explaining that in all probability the world was wrong in its estimation of Mrs. Proudie's power and authority, she had fully made up her mind as to her course of action. She did not, however, proclaim her intention. She shook her head ominously as he continued his narration; and when he had completed she rose to go, merely observing that it was cruel, cruel treatment. She then asked him if he would mind waiting for a late dinner instead of dining at their usual hour of three, and having received from him a concession on this point, she proceeded to carry her purpose into execution.

She determined that she would at once go to the palace, that she would do so, if possible, before Mrs. Proudie could have had an interview with Mr. Slope; and that she would be either submissive piteous and pathetic, or else indignant violent and exacting, according to the manner in which she was received.

She was quite confident in her own power. Strengthened as she was by the pressing wants of fourteen children, she felt that she could make her way through legions of episcopal servants, and force herself, if need be, into the presence of the lady who had so wronged her. She had no shame about it, no mauvaise honte, no dread of archdeacons. She would, as she declared to her husband, make her wail heard in the market-place if she did not get redress and justice. It might be very well for an unmarried young curate to be shamefaced in such matters; it might be all right that a snug rector, really in want of nothing, but still looking for better preferment, should carry on his affairs decently under the rose. But Mrs. Quiverful, with fourteen children, had given over being shamefaced, and, in some things, had given over being decent. If it were intended that she should be ill used in the manner proposed by Mr. Slope it should not be done under the rose. All the world should know of it.

In her present mood Mrs. Quiverful was not over careful about her attire. She tied her bonnet under her chin, threw her shawl over her shoulders, armed herself with the old family cotton umbrella, and started for Barchester. A journey to the palace waa not quite so easy a thing for Mrs. Quiverful as for our friend at Plumstead. Plumstead is nine miles from Barchester, and Puddingdale is but four. But the archdeacon could order round his brougham, and his high-trotting fast bay gelding would take him into the city within the hour. There was no brougham in the coachhouse of Puddingdale Vicarage, no bay horse in the stables. There was no method of locomotion for its inhabitants but that which nature has assigned to man.

Mrs. Quiverful was a broad heavy woman, not young, nor given to walking. In her kitchen, and in the family dormitories, she was active enough; but her pace and gait were not adapted for the road. A walk into Barchester and back in the middle of an August day would be to her a terrible task, if not

altogether impracticable. There was living in the parish, about half a mile from the vicarage on the road to the city, a decent, kindly farmer, well to do as regards this world, and so far mindful of the next that he attended his parish church with decent regularity. To him Mrs. Quiverful had before now appealed in some of her more pressing family troubles, and had not appealed in vain. At his door she now presented herself, and, having explained to his wife that most urgent business required her to go at once to Barchester, begged that Farmer Subsoil would take her thither in his tax-cart. The farmer did not reject her plan; and, as soon as Prince could be got into his collar, they started on their journey.

Mrs. Quiverful did not mention the purpose of her business, nor did the farmer alloy his kindness by any unseemly questions. She merely begged to be put down at the bridge going into the city, and to be taken up again at the same place in the course of two hours. The farmer promised to be punctual to his appointment, and the lady, supported by her umbrella, took the short cut to the close, and in a few minutes was at the bishop's door.

Hitherto she had felt no dread with regard to the coming interview. She had felt nothing but an indignant longing to pour forth her claims, and declare her wrongs, if those claims were not fully admitted. But now the difficulty of her situation touched her a little. She had been at the palace once before, but then she went to give grateful thanks. Those who have thanks to return for favours received find easy admittance to the halls of the great. Such is not always the case with men, or even with women, who have favours to beg. Still less easy is access for those who demand the fulfilment of promises already made.

Vol. u. a

Mrs. Quiverful had not been slow to learn the ways of the world. She knew all this, and she knew also that her cotton umbrella and all but ragged shawl would not command respect in the eyes of the palatial servants. If she were too humble, she knew well that she would never succeed. To overcome by imperious overbearing with such a shawl as hers upon her shoulders, and such a bonnet on her head, would have required a personal bearing very superior to that with which nature had endowed her. Of this also Mrs. Quiverful was aware. She must make it known that she was the wife of a gentleman and a clergyman, and must yet condescend to conciliate.

The poor lady knew but one way to overcome these difficulties at the very threshold of her enterprise, and to this she resorted. Low as were the domestic funds at Puddingdale, she still retained possession of half-a-crown, and this she sacrificed to the avarice of Mrs. Proudie's metropolitan sesquipedalian serving-man. She was, she said, Mrs. Quiverful of Puddingdale, the wife of the Rev. Mr. Quiverful. She wished to see Mrs. Proudie. It was indeed quite indispensable that she should see Mrs. Proudie. James Fitzplush looked worse than dubious, did not know whether his lady were out, or engaged, or in her bedroom;—thought it most probable she was subject to one of these or to some other cause that would make her invisible; but Mrs. Quiverful could sit down in the waiting-room while inquiry was being made of Mrs. Proudie's maid.

"Look here, my man," said Mrs. Quiverful; "I must see hor;" and she put her card and half-a-crown,—think of it, my reader, think of it; her last half-crown,—into the man's hand, and sat herself down on a chair in the waiting-room.

Whether the bribe carried the day, or whether the bishop's wife really chose to see the vicar's wife, it boots not now to inquire. The man returned, and begging Mrs. Quiverful to follow him, ushered her into the presence of the mistress of the diocese.

Mrs. Quiverful at once saw that her patroness was in a smiling humour. Triumph sat throned upon her brow, and all the joys of dominion hovered about her curls. Her lord had that morning contested with her a great point He had received an invitation to spend a couple of days with the archbishop. His soul

longed for the gratification. Not a word, however, in his grace's note alluded to the fact of his being a married man; and, if he went at all, he must go alone. This necessity would have presented no insurmountable bar to the visit, or have militated much against the pleasure, had he been able to go without any reference to Mrs. Proudie. But this he could not do. He could not order his portmanteau to be packed, and start with his own man, merely telling the lady of his heart that he would probably be back on Saturday. There are men,—may we not rather say monsters r —who do such things; and there are wives,—may we not rather say slaves?—who put up with such usage. But Doctor and Mrs. Proudie were not among the number.

The bishop, with some beating about the bush, made the lady understand that he very much wished to go. The lady, without any beating about the bush, made the bishop understand that she wouldn't hear of it. It would be useless here to repeat the arguments that were used on each side, and needless to record the result. Those who are married will understand very well how the battle was lost and won; and those who are single will never understand it till they learn the lesson which experience alone can give. When Mrs. Quiverful was shown into Mrs. Proudie's room, that lady had only returned a few minutes from her lord. But before she left him she had seen the answer to the archbishop's note written and sealed. No wonder that her face was wreathed with smiles as she received Mrs. Quiverful.

She instantly spoke of the subject which was so near the heart of her visitor. "Well, Mrs. Quiverful," said she, "is it decided yet when you are to move into Barchester?"

"That woman," as she had an hour or two since been called, became instantly re-endowed with all the graces that can adorn a bishop's wife. Mrs. Quiverful immediately saw that her business was to be piteous, and that nothing was to be gained by indignation;—nothing, indeed, unless she could be indignant in company with her patroness.

"Oh, Mrs. Proudie," she began, "I

fear we are not to move to Barchester at all."

"Why not?" said that lady sharply, dropping at a moment's v notice her smiles and condescension, and turning with her sharp

I quick way to business which she saw at a glance was important..

I And then Mrs. Quiverful told her tale. As she progressed in the history of her wrongs she perceived that the heavier she leant 1 upon Mr. Slope the blacker became Mrs. Proudie's brow, but that such blackness was not injurious to her own cause. When Mr. Slope was at Puddingdale vicarage that morning she had regarded him as the creature of the lady-bishop. Now she perceived that they were enemies She admitted her mistake to herself without sny pain or humiliation. She had but one feeling, and that was confined to her family. She cared little how she twisted and turned among these new comers at the bishop's palace so long as she could twist her husband into the warden's house. She cared not which was her friend or which was her enemy, if only she could get this preferment which she so sorely wanted.

She told her tale, and Mrs. Proudie listened to it almost in silence. She told how Mr. Slope had cozened her husband into resigning his claim, and had declared that it was the bishop's will that none but Mr. Harding should be warden. Mrs. Proudie's brow became blacker and blacker. At last she started from her chair, and begging Mrs. Quiverful to sit and wait for her return, marched out of the room.

"Oh, Mrs. Proudie, it's for fourteen children,—for fourteen children." Such was the burden that fell on her ear as she closed 'the door behind her.

OHAPTEE XXVI. MRS. PROUDIE WRESTLES AND GETS A FALL.

It was hardly an hour since Mrs. Proudie had left her husband's apartment victorious, and yet so indomitable was her courage that she now returned thither panting for another combat. She was greatly angry with what she thought was his duplicity. He had so clearly given her a promise on this matter of the hospital. He had been already so absolutely vanquished on that point. Mrs. Proudie began to feel that if every affair was to be thus discussed and battled about twice and even thrice, the work of the diocese would be too much even for her.

Without knocking at the door she walked quickly into her husband's room, and found him seated at his office table, with Mr. Slope opposite to him. Between his fingers was the very note which he had written to the archbishop in her presence, and it was open! Yes, he had absolutely violated the seal which had been made sacred by her approval. They were sitting in deep conclave, and it was too clear that the purport of the archbishop's invitation had been absolutely canvassed again, after it had been already debated and decided on in obedience to her behests! Mr. Slope rose from his chair, and bowed slightly. The two opposing spirits looked each other fully in the face, and they knew that they were looking each at an enemy.

"What is this, bishop, about Mr. Quiverful?" said she, coming to the end of the table and standing there.

Mr. Slope did not allow the bishop to answer, but replied himself. "I have been out to Puddingdale this morning, ma'am, and have seen Mr. Quiverful. Mr. Quiverful has abandoned his claim to the hospital, because he is now aware that Mr. Harding is desirous to fill his old place. Under these circumstances I have strongly advised his lordship to nominate Mr. Harding."

"Mr. Quiverful has not abandoned anything," said the lady, with a very imperious voice. "His lordship's word has been pledged to him, and it must be respected."

The bishop still remained silent. He was anxiously desirous of making his old enemy bite the dust beneath his feet. His new ally had told him that nothing was more easy for him than to do so. The ally was there now at his elbow to help him, and yet his courage failed him. It is so hard to conquer when the prestige of former victories is all against one. It is so hard for the cock who has once been beaten out of his yard to resume his courage and again take a proud place upon a dunghill.

"Perhaps I ought not to interfere," said Mr. Slope, "but yet."

"Certainly you ought not," said the infuriated dame.

"But yet," continued Mr. Slope, not regarding the interruption, "I have thought it my imperative duty to recommend the bishop not to slight Mr. Harding's claims."

"Mr. Harding should have known his own mind," said the lady.

"If Mr. Harding be not replaced at the hospital his lordship will have to encounter much ill will, not only in the diocese, but in the world at large. Besides, taking a higher ground, his lordship, as I understand, feels it to be his duty to gratify, in this matter, so very worthy a man and so good a clergyman as Mr. Harding."

"And what is to become of the Sabbath-day school, and of the Sunday services in the hospital?" said Mrs. Proudie, with something very nearly approaching to a sneer on her face.

"I understand that Mr. Harding makes no objection to the Sabbath-day school," said Mr. Slope. "And as to the hospital services, that matter will be best discussed after his appointment. If he has any permanent objection, then, I fear, the matter must rest."

"You have a very easy conscience in such matters, Mr. Slope," said she.

"I should not have an easy conscience," he rejoined, "but a conscience very far from being easy, if anything said or done by me should lead the bishop to act unadvisedly in this matter. It is clear that in the interview I had with Mr. Harding, I misunderstood him"

"And it is equally clear that you have misunderstood Mr. Quiverful," said she, now at the top of her wrath. "What business have you at all with these interviews? Who desired you to go to Mr. Quiverful this morning? Who commissioned' you to manage this affair? Will you answer me, sir? Who sent you to Mr. Quiverful this morning?"

There was a dead pause in the room. Mr. Slope had risen from his chair, and was standing with his hand on the back of it, looking at first very solemn and now very black. Mrs. Proudie was standing as she had at first placed herself, at the end of the table, and as she interrogated her foe she struck her hand upon it with almost more than feminine vigour. The bishop was sitting in his easy chair twiddling his thumbs, turning his eyes now to his wife, and now to his chaplain, as each took up the cudgels. How comfortable it would be if they could fight it out between them without the necessity of any interference on his part; fight it out so that one should kill the other utterly, as far as diocesan life was concerned, so that he, the bishop, might know clearly by whom it behoved him to be led. There would be the comfort of quiet in either case; but if the bishop had a wish as to which might prove the victor, that wish was certainly not antagonistic to Mr. Slope.

"Better the d you know than the d you don't know," is an old saying, and perhaps a true one; but the bishop had not yet realised the truth of it.

"Will you answer me, sir?" she repeated. "Who instructed you to call on Mr. Quiverful this morning?" There was another pause. "Do you intend to answer me, sir?"

"I think, Mrs. Proudie, that under all the circumstances it will be better for me not to answer such a question," said Mr. Slope. Mr. Slope had many tones in his voice, all duly under his command; among them was a sanctified low tone, and a sanctified loud tone; a-id he now used the former.

"Did any one send you, sir?"

"Mrs. Proudie," said Mr. Slope, "I am quite aware how much I owe to your kindness. I am aware also what is due by courtesy from a gentleman to a lady. But there are higher considerations than either of those, and I hope I shall be forgiven if I now allow myself to be actuated solely by them. My duty in this matter is to his lordship, and I can. admit of no questioning but from him. He has approved of what I have done, and you must excuse me if I say, that having that approval and my own, I want none other."

What horrid words were these which greeted the ear of Mrs. Proudie? The matter was indeed too clear. There was premeditated mutiny in the camp. Not only had ill-conditioned minds become insubordinate by the fruition of a little power, but sedition had been overtly taught and preached. The bishop had not yet been twelve months in his chair, and rebellion had already reared her hideous head within the palace. Anarchy and misrule would quickly follow unless she took immediate and strong measures to put down the conspiracy which she had detected.

"Mr. Slope," she said, with slow and dignified voice, differing much from that which she had hitherto used, "Mr. Slope, I will trouble you, if you please, to leave the apartment. I wish to speak to my lord alone."

Mr. Slope also felt that everything depended on the present interview. Should the bishop now be repetticoated his thraldom would be complete and for ever. The present moment was peculiarly propitious for rebellion. The bishop had clearly committed himself by breaking the seal of the answer to the archbishop. He had therefore fear to influence him. Mr. Slope had told him that no consideration ought to induce him to refuse the archbishop's invitation. He had therefore hope to influence him. He had accepted Mr. Quiverful's resignation, and therefore dreaded having to renew that matter with his wife. He had been screwed up to the pitch of asserting a will of his own, and might possibly be carried on till by an absolute success he should have been taught how possible it was to succeed. Now was the moment for victory or rout. It was now that Mr. Slope must make himself master of the diocese, or else resign his place and begin his search for fortune again. He saw all this plainly. After what had taken place any compromise between him and the lady was impossible. Let him once leave the room at her bidding, and leave the bishop in her hands, and he might at once pack up his portmanteau and bid adieu to episcopal honours, Mrs. Bold, and the Signora Neroni.

And yet it was not so easy to keep his ground when he was bidden by a lady to go; or to continue to make a third in a party between a husband and wife when the wife expressed a wish for a tete-a-tete with her husband.

"Mr. Slope," she repeated, "I wish to be alone with my lord."

'' His lordship has summoned me on a most important diocesan business," said Mr. Slope, glancing with uneasy eye at Dr. Proudie. He felt that he must trust something to the bishop, and yet that trust was so woefully ill-placed. '' My leaving him at the present moment is, I fear impossible."

"Do you bandy words with me, you ungrateful man?" said she. "My lord, will you do me the favour to beg Mr. Slope to leave the room?" My lord scratched his head, but for the moment said nothing. This was as much as Mr. Slope expected from him, and was on the whole, for him, an active exercise of marital rights. "My lord," said the lady, "is Mr. Slope to leave this room, or ami?"

Here Mrs. Proudie made a false step. She should not have alluded to the possibility of retreat on her part. She should not have expressed the idea that her order for Mr. Slope's expulsion could be treated otherwise than by immediate obedience. In answer to such a question the bishop naturally said in his own mind, that as it was necessary that one should leave the room, perhaps it might be as well that Mrs. Proudie did so. He did say so in his own mind, but externally he again scratched his head and again twiddled his thumbs.

Mrs. Proudie was boiling over with wrath. Alas, alas! could she but have kept her temper as her enemy did, she would have conquered as she had ever conquered. But divine anger got the better of her, as it had done of other heroines, and she fell.

"My lord," said she, "am I to be vouchsafed an answer or am I not?"

At last he broke his deep silence and proclaimed himself a Slopeite. "Why, my dear," said he, "Mr. Slope and I are very busy."

That was all. There was nothing more necessary. He had gone to the battlefield, stood the dust and heat of the day, encountered the fury of the foe, and won the victory. How easy is success to those who will only be true to themselves!

Mr. Slope saw at once the full amount of his gain, and turned on the vanquished lady a look of triumph which she never forgot and never forgave. Here he waiTwrbng He should have looked humbly at her, and with meek entreating eye have deprecated her anger. He should have said by his glance that he asked pardon for his success, and that he hoped forgiveness for the stand which he had been forced to make in the cause of duty. So might he perchance have somewhat mollified that imperious bosom, and prepared the way for future terms. But Mr. Slope meant to rule without terms. Ah, forgetful, inexperienced man! Can you cause that little trembling victim to be divorced from the woman that possesses him? Can you provide that they shall be separated at bed and board? Is he not flesh of her flesh and bone of her bone, and must he not so continue? It is very well now for you to stand your ground, and triumph as she is driven ignominiously from the room; but can you be present when those curtains are drawn, when that awful helmet of proof has been tied beneath the chin, when the small remnants of the bishop's prowess shall be cowed by the tassel above his head? Can you then intrude yourself when the wife wishes " to speak to my lord alone?"

But for the moment Mr. Slope's triumph was complete; for Mrs. Proudie without further parley left the room, and did not forget to shut the door after her. Then followed a close conference between the new allies, in which was said much which it astonished Mr. Slope to say and the bishop to hear. And yet the one said it and the other heard it without ill will. There was no mincing of matters now. The chaplain plainly told the bishop that the world gave him credit for being under the governance of his wife; that his credit and character in the diocese were suffering; that he would surely get himself into hot water if he allowed Mrs. Proudie to interfere in matters which were not suitable for a woman's powers; and in fact that he would become contemptible if he did not throw off the yoke under which he groaned. The bishop at first hummed and hawed, and affected to deny the truth of what was said. But his denial was not stout and quickly broke down. He soon admitted by silence his state of vassalage, and pledged himself, with Mr. Slope's assistance, to change his courses. Mr. Slope also did not make out a bad case for himself. He explained how it grieved him to run counter to a lady who had always been his patroness, who had befriended him in so many ways, who had, in fact, recommended him to the bishop's notice; but, as he stated, his duty was now imperative; he held a situation of peculiar confidence and was immediately and especially attached to the bishop's person. In such a situation his conscience required that he should regard solely the bishop's interests, and therefore he had ventured to speak out.

The bishop took this for what it was worth and Mr. Slope only intended that he should do so. It gilded the pill which Mr. Slope had to administer, and which the bishop thought would be less bitter than that other pill which he had so long been taking.

"My lord," had his immediate reward, like a good child. He was instructed to write and at once did write another note to the archbishop accepting his grace's invitation. This note Mr. Slope, more prudent than the lady, himself took away and posted with his own hands. Thus he made sure that this act of self-jurisdiction should be as nearly as possible a fait accompli. He begged, and coaxed, and threatened the bishop with a view of making him also write at once to Mr. Harding; but the bishop, though temporarily emancipated from his wife, was not yet enthralled to Mr. Slope. He said, and probably said truly, that such an offer must be made in some official form; that he was not yet prepared to sign the form; and that he should prefer seeing Mr. Harding before he did so.

Mr. Slope might, however, beg Mr. Harding to call upon him. Not disappointed with his achievement Mr. Slope went his way. He first posted the precious note which he had in his pocket, and then pursued other enterprises in which we must follow him in other chapters.

Mrs. Proudie, having received such satisfaction as was to be derived from slamming her husband's door, did not at once betake herself to Mrs. Quiverful. Indeed for the first few moments after her repulse she felt that she could not again see that lady. She would have to own that she had been beaten, to confess that the diadem had passed from her brow, and the sceptre from her hand! No, she would send a message to her with the promise of a letter on the next day or the day after. Thus resolving, she betook herself to her bed-room. But here she again changed her mind. The air of that sacred enclosure somewhat restored her courage, and gave her more heart. As Achilles warmed at the sight of his armour, as Don Quixote's heart grew strong when he grasped his lance, so did Mrs. Proudie look forward to fresh laurels, as her eye fell on her husband's pillow. She would not despair. Having so resolved, she descended with dignified mien and refreshed countenance to Mrs. Quiverful.

The scene in the bishop's study took longer in the acting than in the telling. We have not, perhaps, had the whole of the conversation. At any rate Mrs. Quiverful was beginning to be very impatient, and was thinking that farmer Subsoil would be tired of waiting for her, when Mrs. Proudie returned. Oh! who can tell the palpitations of that maternal heart, as the suppliant looked into the face of the great lady to see written there either a promise of house, income, comfort and future competence, or else the doom of continued and ever increasing poverty. Poor mother! poor wife! There was little there to comfort you!

"Mrs. Quiverful," thus spoke the lady with considerable austerity, and without sitting down herself, "I find that your husband has behaved in this matter in a very weak and foolish manner."

Mrs. Quiverful immediately rose upon her feet, thinking it disrespectful to remain sitting while the wife of the bishop stood. But she was desired to sit down again, and made to do so, so that Mrs. Proudie might stand and preach over her. It is generally considered an offensive thing for a gentleman to keep his seat while another is kept standing before him, and we presume the same law holds with regard to ladies. It often is so felt; but we are inclined to say that it never produces half the discomfort or half the feeling of implied inferiority that is shown by a great man who desires his visitor to be seated while he himself speaks from his legs. Such a solecism in good breeding, when construed into English, means this; "The accepted rules of courtesy in the world require that I should offer you a seat; if I did not do so, you would bring a charge against me in the world of being arrogant and ill-mannered; I will obey the world; but, nevertheless, I will not put myself on an equality with you. You may sit down, but I won't sit with you. Sit, therefore, at my bidding, and I '11 stand and talk at you!"

This was just what Mrs. Proudie meant to say; and Mrs. Quiverful, though she was too anxious and too flurried thus to translate the full meaning of the manoeuvre, did not fail to feel its effect. She was cowed and uncomfortable, and a second time essayed to rise from her chair.

"Pray be seated, Mrs. Quiverful; pray keep your seat. Your husband, I say, has been most weak and most foolish. It is im possible, Mrs. Quiverful, to help people who will not help themselves. I much fear that I can now do nothing for you in this matter."

"Oh! Mrs. Proudie,—don't say so," said the poor woman again jumping up.

"Pray be seated Mrs. Quiverful. I much fear that I can do nothing further for you in this matter. Your husband has, in a most unaccountable manner, taken upon himself to resign that which I was empowered to offer him. As a matter of course the bishop expects that his clergy shall know their own minds. What he may ultimately do,—what we may finally decide on doing,—I cannot now say. Knowing the extent of your family —"

"Fourteen children, Mrs. Proudie, fourteen of them! and barely bread,—barely bread! It's hard for the children of a clergyman, it's hard for one who has always done his duty respectably!" Not a word fell from her about herself; but the tears came streaming down her big coarse cheeks, on which the dust of the August road had left its traces.

Mrs. Proudie has not been portrayed in these pages as an agreeable or an amiable lady. There has been no intention to impress the reader much in her favour. It is ordained that all novels should have a male and a female angel, and a male and a female devil. If it be considered that this rule is obeyed in these pages, the latter / sharacter must be supposed to have fallen to the lot of Mrs. Proudie. But she was not all devil. There was a heart inside that stiff-ribbed bodice, though not, perhaps, of large dimensions, and certainly not easily accessible. Mrs. Quiverful, however, did gain access, and Mrs. Proudie proved herself a woman. Whether it was the fourteen children with their probable bare bread and their possible bare backs, or the respectability of the father's work, or the mingled dust and tears on the mother's face, we will not pretend to say. But Mrs. Proudie was touched.

She did not show it as other women might have done. She did not give Mrs. Quiverful eau-de-Cologne, or order her a glass of wine. She did not take her to her toilet table, and offer her the use 3f brushes and combs, towels and water. She did not say soft little speeches and coax her kindly back to equanimity. Mrs. Quiverful, despite her rough appearance, would have been as amenable to such little tender cares as any lady in the land. But none such were forthcoming. Instead of this, Mrs. Proudie Blapped one hand upon the other, and declared,—not with an oath; for as a lady and a Sabbatarian and a she-bishop, she could not not swear,—but with an adjuration, "that she wouldn't have it done."

The meaning of this was that she wouldn't have Mr. Quiverful's promised appointment cozened away by the treachery of Mr. Slope and the weakness of her husband. This meaning she very soon explained to Mrs. Quiverful.

"Why was your husband such a fool," said she, now dismounted from her high horse and sitting confidentially down close to her visitor, "as to take the bait which that man threw to him? If he had not been so utterly foolish nothing could have prevented your going to the hospital."

Poor Mrs. Quiverful was ready enough with her own tongue in accusing her husband to his face of being soft, and perhaps did not always speak of him to her children quite so respectfully as she might have done. But she did not at all like to hear him abused by others, and began to vindicate him, and to explain that of course he had taken Mr. Slope to be an emissary from Mrs. Proudie herself; that Mr. Slope was thought to be peculiarly her friend; and that, therefore, Mr. Quiverful would have been failing in respect to her had he assumed to doubt what Mr. Slope had said.

Thus mollified Mrs. Proudie again declared that "she would not have it done," and at last sent Mrs. Quiverful home with an assurance that to the furthest stretch of her power and influence in the palace, the appointment of Mr. Quiverful should be insisted on. As she repeated the word "insisted," she thought of the bishop in his night-cap, and with compressed lips slightly shook her head. Oh! my aspiring pastors, divines to whose ears nolo episcopari are the sweetest of words, which of you would be a bishop on such terms as these?

Mrs. Quiverful got home in the farmer's cart, not indeed with a light heart, but satisfied that she had done right in making her visit.

CHAPTER XXVII.

A LOVE SCENE.

Mr. Slope, as we have said, left the palace with a feeling of considerable triumph. Not that he thought that his dif-ficulties were all over; he did not so deceive himself; but he felt that he had played his first move well;—as well as the pieces on the board would allow; and that he had nothing with which to reproach himself. He first of all posted the letter to the archbishop, and having made that sure he proceeded to push the advantage which he had gained. Had Mrs. Bold been at home, he would have called on her; but he knew that she was at Plumstead, so he wrote the following note. It was the beginning of what, he trusted, might be a long and tender series of epistles.

"My dear Mrs. Bold,—You will understand perfectly that I cannot at present correspond with your father. I heartily wish that I could, and hope the day may be not long distant when mists shall have cleared away, and we may know each other. But I cannot preclude myself from the pleasure of sending you these few lines to say that Mr. Q. has to-day, in my presence, resigned any title that he ever had to the wardenship of the hospital, and that the bishop has assured me that it is his intention to offer it to your esteemed father.

"Will you, with my respectful compliments, ask him, who I believe is now a fellow-visitor with you, to call on the bishop either on Wednesday or Thursday, between ten and one. *This is by the 'bishop's desire.* If you will so far oblige me as to let me have a line naming either day, and the hour which will suit Mr. Harding,

Vol. n. H

I will take care that the servants shall have orders to show him in without delay. Perhaps I should say no more,—but still I wish you could make your father understand that no subject will be mooted between his lordship and him, which will refer at all to the method in which he may choose to perform his duty. I, for one, am persuaded that no clergyman could perform it more satisfactorily than he did, or than he will do again.

'' On a former occasion I was indiscreet and much too impatient, considering your father's age and my own. I hope he will not now refuse my apology. I still hope also that, with your aid and sweet pious labours, we may live to attach such a Sabbath school to the old endowment, as may, by God's grace and furtherance, be a blessing to the poor of this city.

'' You will see at once that this letter is confidential. The subject, of course, makes it so. But, equally of course, it is for your parent's eye as well as for your own, should you think proper to show it to him.

"I hope my darling little friend Johnny is as strong as ever,— dear little fellow. Does he still continue his rude assaults on those beautiful long silken tresses?

"I can assure you your friends miss you from Barchester sorely; but it would be cruel to begrudge you your sojourn among flowers and fields during this truly sultry weather.

"Pray believe me, my dear Mrs. Bold, "Yours most sincerely,
  "Obadiah Slope.
  "Barchester, Friday."

Now this letter, taken as a whole, and with the consideration that Mr. Slope wished to assume a great degree of intimacy with Eleanor, would not have been bad,—but for the allusion to the tresses. Gentlemen do not write to ladies about their tresses, uuless they are on very intimate terms indeed. But Mr. Slope could not be expected to be aware of this. He longed to put a little affection into his epistle, and yet he thought it injudicious, aa the letter would, he knew, be shown to Mr. Harding. He would have insisted that the letter should be strictly private and seen by no eyes but Eleanor's own, had he not felt that such an injunction would have been disobeyed. He therefore restrained his passion, did not sign himself "yours affectionately," and contented himself instead with the compliment to the tresses.

Having finished this letter, he took it to Mrs. Bold's house, and learning there, from the servant, that things were to be sent out to Plumstead that afternoon, left it, with many injunctions, in her hands.

We will now follow Mr. Slope so as to complete the day with him, and then return to his letter and its momentous fate in the next chapter.

There is an old song which gives us some very good advice about courting;—

"It's gude to be off with the auld luve Before ye he on wi' the new."

Of the wisdom of this maxim Mr. Slope was ignorant, and accordingly, having written his letter to Mrs. Bold, he proceeded to call upon the Signora Neroni. Indeed it was hard to say which was the old love and which the new, Mr. Slope having been smitten with both so nearly at the same time. Perhaps he thought it not amiss to have two strings to his bow. But two strings to Cupid's bow are always dangerous to him on whose behalf they are to be used. A man should remember that between two stools he may fall to the ground.

But in sooth Mr. Slope was pursuing Mrs. Bold in obedience to his better instincts, and the Signora in obedience to his worser. Had he won the widow and worn her no one could have blamed him. You, 0 reader, and I, and Eleanor's other friends would have received the story of such a winning with much disgust and disappointment; but we should have been angry with Eleanor, not with Mr. Slope. Bishop, male and female, dean and chapter and diocesan clergy in full congress, could have found nothing to disapprove of in such an alliance. Convocation itself, that mysterious and mighty synod, could in no wise have fallen foul of it. The possession of 1000Z. a year and a beautiful wife would not at all have hurt the voice of the pulpit charmer, or lessened the grace and piety of the exemplary clergyman.

But not of such a nature were likely to be his dealings with the Signora Neroni. In the first place he knew that her husband was living, and therefore he could not woo her honestly. Then again she had nothing to recommend her to his honest wooing had such been possible. She was not only portionless, but also from misfortune unfitted to be chosen as the wife of any man who wanted a useful mate. Mr. Slope was aware that she was a helpless, hopeless cripple.

But Mr. Slope could not help himself. He knew that he was wrong in devoting his time to the back drawing-room in Dr. Stanhope's house. He knew that what took place there would if divulged utterly ruin him with Mrs. Bold. He knew that scandal would soon come upon his heels and spread abroad among the black coats of Barchester some tidings, exaggerated tidings, of the sighs which he poured into the lady's ears. He knew that he was acting against the recognised principles of his life, against those laws of conduct by which he hoped to achieve much higher success. But as we have said, he could not help himself. Passion, for the first time in his life,—passion was too strong for him.

As for the Signora, no such plea can be put forward for her, for in truth she cared no more for Mr. Slope than she did for twenty others who had been at her feet before him. She willingly, nay greedily, aoccepted his homage. He was the finest fly that Barchester had hitherto afforded to her web; and the Signora was a powerful spider that made wondrous webs, and could in no way live without catching flies. Her taste in this respect was abominable, for she had no use for the victims when caught. She could not eat them matrimonially, as young lady-flies do whose webs are most frequently of their mothers' weaving. Nor could she devour them by any escapade of a less legitimate description? Her unfortunate affliction precluded her from all hope of levanting with a lover. It would be impossible to run away with a lady who required three servants to move her from a sofa.

The Signora was subdued by no passion. Her time for love was gone. She had lived out her heart, such heart as she had ever had, in her early years, at an age when Mr. Slope was thinking of the second book of Euclid and his unpaid bill at the buttery hatch. In age the lady was younger than the gentleman; but in feelings, in knowledge of the affairs of love, in intrigue, he was immeasurably her junior. It was necessary to her to have some man at her feet. It was the one customary excitement of her life. She delighted in the exercise of power which this gave her; it was now nearly the only food for her ambition; she would boast to her sister that she could make a fool of any man, and the sister, as little imbued with feminine delicacy as herself, good naturedly thought it but fair that such amusement should be afforded to a poor invalid who was debarred from the ordinary pleasures of life.

Mr. Slope was madly in love, but hardly knew it. The Signora spitted him, as a boy does a cockchafer on a cork, that she might enjoy the energetic agony of his gyrations. And she knew very well what she was doing.

Mr. Slope having added to his person all such adornments as are possible to a clergyman making a morning visit, such as a clean neck tie, clean handkerchief, new gloves, and a soupijon of not unnecessary scent, called about three o'clock at the doctor's door. At about this hour the Signora was almost always alone in the back drawing-room. The mother had not come down. The doctor was out or in his own room. Bertie was out, and Charlotte at any rate left the room if any one called whose object was specially with her sister. Such was her idea of being charitable and sisterly.

Mr. Slope, as was his custom, asked for Mrs. Stanhope, and was told, as was the servant's custom, that the Signora was in the drawing-room. Upstairs he accordingly went. He found her, as he always did, lying on her sofa with a French volume before her, and a beautiful little inlaid writing ease open on her table At the moment of his entrance she was in the act of writing. "Ah my friend," said she, putting out her left hand to him across her desk, "I did not expect you to-day, and was this very instant writing to you."

Mr. Slope, taking the soft fair delicate hand in his, and very soft and fair and delicate it was, bowed over it his huge red head and kissed it. It was a sight to see, a deed to record if the author could fitly do it, a picture to put on canvas. Mr. Slope was big, awkward, cumbrous, and having his heart in his pursuit was ill at ease. The lady was fair, as we have said, and delicate; every thing

about her was fine and refined; her hand in his looked like a rose lying among carrots, and when he kissed it he looked as a cow might do on finding such a flower among her food. She was graceful as a couchant goddess, and, moreover, as self-possessed as Venus must have been when courting Adonis. Oh, that such grace and such beauty should have condescended to waste itself on such a pursuit!

"I was in the act of writing to you," said she, "but now my scrawl may go into the basket;" and she raised the sheet of gilded note paper from off her desk as though to tear it.

"Indeed it shall not," said he, laying the embargo of half a stone weight of human flesh and blood upon the devoted paper. "Nothing that you write for my eyes, Signora, shall be so desecrated," and he took up the letter, put that also among the carrots and fed on it, and then proceeded to read it.

"Gracious me! Mr. Slope," said she, "I hope you don't mean to say that you keep all the trash I write to you. Half my time I don't know what I write, and when I do, I know it is only fit for the back of the fire. I hope you have not that ugly trick of keeping letters."

"At any rate, I don't throw them into a waste-paper basket. If destruction is their doomed lot, they perish worthily, and are burnt on a pyre, as Dido was of old."

"With a steel pen stuck through them, of course," said she, "to make the simile more complete. Of all the ladies of my acquaintance I think Lady Dido was the most absurd. Why did she not do as Cleopatra did? Why did she not take out her ships and insist on going with him? She could not bear to lose the land she had got by a swindle; and then she could not bear the loss of her lover. So she fell between two stools. Mr. Slope, whatever you do, never mingle love and business."

Mr. Slope blushed up to his eyes, and over his mottled forehead to the very roots of his hair. He felt sure that the Signora knew all about his intentions with reference to Mrs. Bold. His conscience told him that he was detected.

His doom was to be spoken; he was to be punished for his duplicity, and rejected by the beautiful creature before him. Poor man. He little dreamt that had all his intentions with reference to Mrs. Bold been known to the Signora, it would only have added zest to that lady's amusement. It was all very well to have Mr. Slope at her feet, to show her power by making an utter fool of a clergyman, to gratify her own infidelity by thus proving the little strength which religion had in controlling the passions even of a religious man; but it would be an increased gratification if she could be made to understand that she was at the same time alluring her victim away from another, whose love if secured would be in every way beneficent and salutary.

The Signora had indeed discovered with the keen instinct of such a woman, that Mr. Slope was bent on matrimony with Mrs. Bold, but in alluding to Dido she had not thought of it. She instantly perceived, however, from her lover's blushes, what was on his mind, and was not slow in taking advantage of it.

She looked him full in the face, not angrily, nor yet with a smile, but with an intense and overpowering gaze; and then holding up her forefinger, and slightly shaking her head she said;— "Whatever you do, my friend, do not mingle love and business. Either stick to your treasure and your city of wealth, or else follow your love like a true man. But never attempt both. If you do, you'll have to die with a broken heart as did poor Dido. Which is it to be with you, Mr. Slope, love or money?"

Mr. Slope was not so ready with a pathetic answer as he usually was with touching episodes in his extempore sermons. He felt that he ought to say something pretty, something also that should remove the impression on the mind of his lady love. But he was rather put about how to do it. "Love," said he; "true overpowering love, must be the strongest passion a man can feel; it must control every other wish, and put aside every other pursuit. But with me love will never act in that way unless it be returned." And he threw upon the Signora a look of tenderness which was intended to make up for all the deficiencies of his speech.

"Take my advice," said she. "Never mind love. After all, what is it? The dream of a few weeks. That is all its joy. The disappointment of a life is its Nemesis. Who was ever successful in true love? Success in love argues that the love is false. True love is always despondent or tragical. Juliet loved; Haidee loved; Dido loved, and what came of it? Troilus loved and ceased to be a man."

"Troilus loved and was fooled," said the more manly chaplain. "A man may love and yet not be a Troilus. All women are not Cressids."

"No; all women are not Cressids. The falsehood is not always on the woman's side. Imogen was true, but how was she rewarded? Her lord believed her to be the paramour of the first he who came near her in his absence. Desdemona was true and was smothered. Ophelia was true and was driven mad. There is no happiness in love, except at the end of an English novel. But in wealth, money, houses, lands, goods and chattels, in the good things of this world, yes, in them there is something tangible, something that can be retained and enjoyed."

"Oh, no," said Mr. Slope, feeling himself bound to enter some protest against so very unorthodox a doctrine; "this world's wealth will make no one happy."

'' And what will make you happy,—you,—you?" said she, raising herself up, and speaking to him with energy across the table. '' From what source do you look for happiness? Do not say that you look for none? I shall not believe you. It is a search in which every human being spends an existence."

"And the search is always in vain," said Mr. Slope. "We look for happiness on earth, while we ought to be content to hope for it in heaven." "Pshaw! You preach a doctrine which you know you don't believe. It is the way with you all. If you know that there is no earthly happiness, why do you long to be a bishop or a dean? Why do you want lands and income?"

"I have the natural ambition of a man," said he.

"Of course you have, and the natural passions;—and therefore I say that you don't believe the doctrine you preach. St. Paul was an enthusiast. He believed so that his ambition and passions did not war against his creed. So does the Eastern fanatic who passes half his life erect upon a pillar. As for me, I will believe in no belief that does not make itself manifest by outward signs. I will think no preaching sincere that is not recommended by the practice of the preacher."

Mr. Slope was startled and horrified, but he felt that he could not answer. How could he stand up and preach the lessons of his Master, being there as he was, on the devil's business? He was a true believer, otherwise this would have been nothing to him. He had audacity for most things, but he had not audacity to make a plaything of the Lord's word. All this the Signora understood and felt much interest as she saw her cockchafer whirl round upon her pin.

"Your wit delights in such arguments," said he, "but your heart and your reason do not go along with them. "

"My heart!" said she; "you quite mistake the principles of my composition if you imagine that there is such a thing about me." After all, there was very little that was false in anything that the Signora said. If Mr. Slope allowed himself to be deceived it was bis own fault. Nothing could have been more open than her declarations about herself.

The little writing table with her desk was still standing before her, a barrier, as it were, against the enemy. She was sitting as nearly upright as she ever did, and he had brought a chair close to the sofa, so that there was only the corner of the table between him and her. It so happened that as she spoke her hand lay upon the table, and as Mr. Slope answered her he put his hand upon hers. "No heart!" said he. "That is a heavy charge which you bring against yourself, and one of which I cannot find you guilty."

She withdrew her hand, not quickly and angrily as though insulted by his touch, but gently and slowly. "You are in no condition to give a verdict on the matter," said she, as you have not tried me. No; don't say that you intend doing so, for you know you have no intention of the kind. Nor indeed have I either. As for you, you will take your vows where they will result in something more substantial than the pursuit of such a ghost-like, ghastly love as mine"

"Your love should be sufficient to satisfy the dream of a monarch," said Mr. Slope, not quite clear as to the meaning of his words.

"Say an archbishop, Mr. Slope," said she. Poor fellow! she was very cruel to him. He went round again upon his cork on this allusion to his profession. He tried, however, to smile, and gently accused her of joking on a matter, which was, he said, to him of such vital moment.

"Why,—what gulls do you men make of us," she replied. "How you fool us to the top of our bent; and of all men you clergymen are the most fluent of your honeyed caressing words. Now look me in the face. Mr. Slope, boldly and openly."

Mr. Slope did look at ner with a languishing loving eye, and as he did so, he again put forth his hand to get hold of hers.

'' I told you to look at me boldly, Mr. Slope; but confine your boldness to your eyes.

"Oh, Madeline!" he sighed.

"Well, my name is Madeline," said she; "but none except my own family usually call me so. Now look me in the face, Mr. Slope. Am I to understand that you say you love me?"

Mr. Slope never had said so. If he had come there with anyformed plan at all, his intention was to make love to the lady without uttering any such declaration. It was, however, quite impossible that he should now deny his love. He had, therefore, nothing for it, but to go down on his knees distractedly against the sofa, and swear that he did love her with a love passing the love of man.

The Signora received the assurance with very little palpitation or appearance of surprise. "And now answer me another question," said she;."when are you to be married to my dear friend Eleanor Bold?"

Poor Mr. Slope went round and round in mortal agony. In such a condition as his it was really very hard for him to know what answer to give. And yet no answer would be his surest condemnation. He might as well at once plead guilty to the charge brought against him. "Why do you accuse me of such dissimulation?" said he.

"Dissimulation! I said nothing of dissimulation. I made no charge against you7 and make none. Pray don't defend yourself to me. You swear that you are devoted to my beauty, and yet you are on the eve of matrimony with another. I feel this to be rather a compliment. It is to Mrs. Bold that you must defend yourself. That you may find difficult;—unless, indeed, you can keep her in the dark. You clergymen are cleverer than other men."

"Signora, I have told you that I loved you, and now you rail at me?"

"Kail at you! God bless the man; what would he have? Come, answer me this at your leisure,—not without thinking now, but leisurely and with consideration;—Are you not going to be married to Mrs. Bold?"

"I am not," said he. And as he said it, he almost hated, with an exquisite hatred, the woman whom he could not help loving with an exquisite love.

"But surely you are a worshipper of hers?"

"I am not," said Mr. Slope, to whom the word worshipper was peculiarly distasteful. The Signora had conceived that it would be so.

"I wonder at that," said she. "Do you not admire her? To my eye she is the perfection of English beauty. And then she is rich too.' I should have thought she was just the person to attract you. Come, Mr. Slope, let me give you advice on this matter. Marry the charming widow. She will be a good mother to your children, and an excellent mistress of a clergyman's household."

"Oh, Signora, how can you be so cruel?"

"Cruel," said she, changing the voice of banter which she had been using for one which was expressively earnest in its tone; "is that cruelty?"

"How can I love another, while my heart is entirely your own?"

"If that were cruelty, Mr. Slope; what might you say of me if I were to declare that I returned your passion? What would you think if I bound you even by a lover's oath to do daily penance at this couch of mine? What can I give in return for a man's love? Ah, dear friend, you have not realised the conditions of my fate."

Mr. Slope was not on his knees all this time. After his declaration of love he had risen from them as quickly as he thought consistent with the new position which he now filled, and as he stood was leaning on the back of his chair. This outburst of tenderness on the Signora's part quite overcame him, and made him feel for the moment that he could sacrifice everything to be assured of the love of the beautiful creature before him, maimed, lame, and already married as she was.

"And can I not sympathise with your lot?" said he, now seating himself on her sofa, and pushing away the table with his foot.

"Sympathy is so near to pity!" said she. "If you pity me, cripple as I am, I shall spurn you from me."

"Oh, Madeline, I will only love you," and again he caught her hand and devoured it with kisses. Now she did not draw it from him, but sat there as he kissed it, looking at him with her great eyes, just as a great spider would look at a great fly that was quite securely caught.

"Suppose Signor Neroni were to come to Barchester," said she, "would you make his acquaintance?" "Signor Neroni!" said he.

'' Would you introduce him to the bishop, and Mrs. Proudie, and the young ladies?" said she, again having recourse to that horrid quizzing voice which Mr. Slope so particularly hated.

"Why do you ask such a question?" said he.

"Because it is necessary that you should know that there is a Signor Neroni. I think you had forgotten it."

"If I thought that you retained for that wretch one particle of the love of which he was never worthy, I would die before I would distract you by telling you what I feel. No! were your husband the master of your heart, I might perhaps love you;—but you should never know it."

"My heart again! how you talk. And you consider then, that if a husband be not master of his wife's heart, he has no right to her fealty. If a wife ceases to love, she may cease to be true. Is that your doctrine on this matter, as a minister of the Church of England?"

Mr. Slope tried hard within himself to cast off the pollution with which he felt that he was defiling his soul. He strove to tear himself away from the noxious siren that had bewitched him. But he could not do it. He could not be again heart free. He had looked for rapturous joy in loving this lovely creature, and he already found that he met with little but disappointment and selfrebuke. He had come across the fruit of the Dead Sea, so sweet and delicious to the eye, so bitter and nauseous to the taste. He had put the apple to his mouth, and it had turned to ashes between his teeth. Yet he could not tear himself away. He knew, he could not but know, that she jeered at him, ridiculed his love, and insulted the weakness of his religion. But she half permitted his adoration, and that half permission added such fuel to his fire that all the fountain of his piety could not quench it. He began to feel savage, irritated, and revengeful. He meditated some severity of speech, some taunt that should cut her, as her taunts cut him. He reflected as he stood there for a moment, silent before her, that if he desired to quell her proud spirit, he should do so by being prouder even than herself; that if he wished to have her at his feet suppliant for his love it behoved him to conquer her by indifference. All this passed through his mind. As far as dead knowledge went, he knew, or thought he knew, how a woman should be tamed. But when he essayed to bring his tactics to bear, he failed like a child. What chance has dead knowledge with experience in any of the transactions between man and man? What possible chance between man and woman? Mr. Slope loved furiously, insanely, and truly; but he had never played the game of love. The Signora did not love at all, but she was up to every move of the board. It was Philidor pitted against a school-boy.

And so she continued to insult him, and he continued to bear it.

"Sacrifice the world for love!" said she, in answer to some renewed vapid declaration of his passion; "how often has the same thing been said, and how invariably with the same falsehood!"

"Falsehood," said he. "Do you say that I am false to you? Do you say that my love is not real?"

"False? Of course it is false, false as the father of falsehood; —if indeed falsehoods need a sire and are not self-begotten since the world began. You are ready to sacrifice the world for love? Come, let us see what you will sacrifice. I care nothing for nuptial vows. The wretch,—I think you were kind enough to call him so, —whom I swore to love and obey, is so base that he can only be thought of with repulsive disgust. In the council chamber of my heart I have divorced him. To me that is as good as though aged lords had gloated for months over the details of his licentious life. I care nothing for what the world can say. Will you be as frank? Will you take me to your home as your wife? Will you call me Mrs. Slope before bishop, dean, and prebendaries?" The poor tortured wretch stood silent, not knowing what to say. "What! you won't do that. Tell me, then, what part of the world is it that you will sacrifice for my charms?"

"Were you free to marry, I would take you to my house tomorrow and wish no higher privilege."

"I am free," said she, almost starting up in her energy. For though there was no truth in her pretended regard for her clerical admirer, there was a mixture of real feeling in the scorn and satire with which she spoke of love and marriage generally. "I am free; free as the winds. Come; will you take me as I am? Have

your wish. Sacrifice the world, and prove yourself a true man."

Mr. Slope should have taken her at her word. She would have drawn back, and he would have had the full advantage of the offer. But he did not. Instead of doing so, he stood wrapt in astonishment, passing his fingers through his lank red hair, and thinking as he stared upon her animated countenance that her wondrous beauty grew more and more wonderful as he gazed on it. "Ha! ha! ha!" she laughed out loud. "Come, Mr. Slope; don't talk of sacrificing the world again. People beyond one-andtwenty should never dream of such a thing. You and I, if we have the dregs of any love left in us, if we have the remnants of a passion remaining in our hearts, should husband our resources better. We are not in our premiere jeunesse. The world is a very nice place. Your world, at any rate, is so. You have all manner of fat rectories to get, and possible bishoprics to enjoy. Come, confess! On second thoughts you would not sacrifice such things for the smiles of a lame lady?"

It was impossible for him to answer this. In order to be in any way dignified, he felt that he must be silent.

"Come," said she,—"don't boody with me; don't be angry because I speak out some home truths. Alas, the world, as I have found it, has taught me bitter truths. Come, tell me that I am forgiven. Are we not to be friends?" and she again put out her hand to him. He sat himself down in the chair beside her, and took her proffered hand and leant over her. "There," said she, with her sweetest softest smile,—a smile to withstand which a man should be cased in triple steel, "there; seal your forgiveness on it," and she raised it towards his face. He kissed it again and again, and stretched over her as though desirous of extending the charity of his pardon beyond the hand that was offered to him. She managed, however, to check his ardour. For one so easily allured as this poor chaplain, her hand was surely enough.

"Oh, Madeline!" said he, "tell me that you love me,—do you, —do you love

me?"

"Hush," said she. "There is my mother's step. Our tete-atete has been of monstrous length. Now you had better go. But we shall see you soon again, shall we not I"

Mr. Slope promised that he would call again on the following day.

"And, Mr. Slope," she continued, "pray answer my note. You have it in your hand, though I declare during these two hours you have not been gracious enough to read it. It is about the Sabbath school and the children. You know how anxious I am to have them here. I have been learning the catechism myself, on purpose. You must manage it for me next week. I will teach them, at any rate, to submit themselves to their spiritual pastors and masters."

Mr. Slope said but little on the subject of Sabbath schools, but he made his adieu, and betook himself home with a sad heart, troubled mind, and uneasy conscience.

CHAPTER XXVm. MRS. BOLD IS ENTERTAINED BY DE. AND MRS. GBANTLY AT ELUM8TEAD.

It will be remembered that Mr. Slope, when leaving his billet doux at the house of Mrs. Bold, had been informed that it would be sent out to her at Plumstead that afternoon. The archdeacon and Mr. Harding had in fact come into town together in the brougham, and it had been arranged that they should call for

Eleanor's parcels as they left on their way home. Accordingly they did so call, and the maid, as she handed to the coachman a small basket and large bundle carefully and neatly packed, gave in at the carriage window Mr. Slope's epistle. The archdeacon, who was sitting next to the window, took it, and immediately recognised the hand-writing of his enemy.

"Who left this?" said he.

"Mr. Slope called with it himself, your reverence," said the girl; "and was very anxious that missus should have it to-day."

So the brougham drove off, and the letter was left in the archdeacon's hand. He looked at it as though he held a basket of adders. He could not have thought worse of the document had he read it and discovered it to be licentious and atheistical. He did, moreover, what so many wise people are accustomed to do in similar circumstances; he immediately condemned the person to whom the letter was written, as though she were necessarily a particeps criminis.

Poor Mr. Harding, though by no means inclined to forward Mr. Slope's intimacy with his daughter, would have given anything VOL. II. i to have kept the letter from his son-in-law. But that was now impossible. There it was in his hand; and the archdeacon looked as thoroughly disgusted as though he were quite sure that it contained all the rhapsodies of a favoured lover.

"It's very hard on me," said he, after awhile, "that this should go on under my roof." Now here the archdeacon was certainly most unreasonable. Having invited his sister-in-law to his house, it was a natural consequence that she should receive her letters there. And if Mr. Slope chose to write to her, his letter would, as a matter of course, be sent after her. Moreover, the very fact of an invitation to one's house implies confidence on the part of the inviter. He had shown that he thought Mrs. Bold to be a fit person to stay with him by his asking her to do so, and it was most cruel to her that he should complain of her violating the sanctity of his roof-tree when the laches committed were none of her committing.

Mr. Harding felt this; and felt also that when the archdeacon talked thus about his roof, what he said was most offensive to himself as Eleanor's father. If Eleanor did receive a letter from Mr. Slope what was there in that to pollute the purity of Dr. Grantly's household? He was indignant that his daughter should be so judged and so spoken of; and he made up his mind that even as Mrs. Slope she must be dearer to him than any other creature on God's earth. He almost broke out and said as much;—but for the moment he restrained himself.

"Here," said the archdeacon, handing the offensive missile to his father-in-law; "I am not going to be the bearer of his love letters. You are her father, and may do as you think fit with it."

By doing as he thought fit with it, the archdeacon certainly meant that Mr. Harding would be justified in opening and reading the letter, and taking any steps which might in consequence be necessary. To tell the truth Dr. Grantly did feel rather a stronger curiosity than was justified by his outraged virtue to see the contents of the letter. Of course he could not open it himself, but he wished to make Mr. Harding understand that he, as Eleanor's father, would be fully justified in doing so. The idea of such a proceeding never occurred to Mr. Harding. His authority over Eleanor ceased when she became the wife of John Bold. He had not the slightest wish to pry into her correspondence. He consequently put the letter into his pocket, and only wished that he had been able to do so without the archdeacon's knowledge. They both sat silent during half the journey home, and then Dr. Grantly said, "Perhaps Susan had better give it to her. She can explain to her pister, better than either you or I can do how deep is the disgrace of such an acquaintance."

"I think you are very hard upon Eleanor," replied Mr. Harding. "I will not allow that she has disgraced herself, nor do I think it likely that she will do so. She has a right to correspond with whom she pleases, and I shall not take upon myself to blame her because she gets a letter from Slope."

"I suppose," said Dr. Grantly, "you don't wish her to marry the man! I suppose you'll admit that she would disgrace herself if she did do so!"

"I do not wish her to marry him," said the perplexed father. "I do not like him, and do not think he would make a good husband. But if Eleanor chooses to do so, I shall certainly not think that she disgraces herself."

"Good heavens!" exclaimed Dr. Grantly, and threw himself back into the corner of his brougham. Mr. Harding said nothing more, but commenced playing a dirge, with an imaginary fiddle bow upon an imaginary violoncello,

for which there did not appear to be quite room enough in the carriage; and he continued the tune, with sundry variations, till he arrived at the rectory door.

The archdeacon had been meditating sad things in his mind. Hitherto he had always looked on his father-in-law as a true partisan, though he knew him to be a man devoid of all the combative qualifications for that character. He had felt no fear that Mr. Harding would go over to the enemy, though he had never counted much on the ex-warden's prowess in breaking the hostile ranks. Now, however, it seemed that Eleanor, with her wiles, had completely trepanned and bewildered her father, cheated him out of his judgment, robbed him of the predilections and tastes of his life, and caused him to be tolerant of a man whose arrogance and vulgarity would, a few years since, have been unendurable to him. That the whole thing was as good as arranged between Eleanor and Mr. Slope there was no longer any room to doubt. That Mr. Harding knew that such was the case could hardly be doubted. It was too manifest that he at any rate suspected it, and was prepared to sanction it.

And, to tell the truth, such was the case. Mr. Harding disliked Mr. Slope as much as it was in his nature to dislike any man. Had his daughter wished to do her worst to displease him by a second marriage, she could hardly have succeeded better than by marrying Mr. Slope. But, as he said to himself now very often, what right had he to condemn her if she did nothing that was really wrong? If she liked Mr. Slope it was her affair. It was indeed miraculous to him that a woman with such a mind, so educated, so refined, so nice in her tastes, should like such a man. Then he asked himself whether it was possible that she did so?

Ah, thou weak man; most charitable, most Christian, but weakest of men! Why couldst thou not have asked herself? Was she not the daughter of thy loins, the child of thy heart, the best beloved to thee of all humanity? Had she not proved to thee, by years of closest affection, her truth and goodness and filial obedience? And yet, knowing and feeling all this, thou couldst endure to go groping in darkness, hearing her named in strains which wounded thy loving heart, and being unable to defend her as thou shouldst have done!

Mr. Harding had not believed, did not believe, that his daughter meant to marry this man; but he feared to commit himself to such an opinion. If she did do it there would be then no means of retreat. The wishes of his heart were;—First, that there should be no truth in the archdeacon's surmises; and in this wish he would have fain trusted entirely, had he dared so to do; Secondly, that the match might be prevented, if unfortunately, it had been contemplated by Eleanor; Thirdly, that should she be so infatuated as to marry this man, he might justify her conduct and declare that no cause existed for his separating himself from her.

He wanted to believe her incapable of such a marriage; he wanted to show that he so believed of her; but he wanted also to be able to say hereafter, that she had done nothing amiss if she should unfortunately prove herself to be different from what he thought her to be.

Nothing but affection could justify such fickleness; but affection did justify it. There was but little of the Roman about Mr. Harding. He could not sacrifice his Lucretia even though she should be polluted by the accepted addresses of the clerical Tarquin at the palace. If Tarquin could be prevented, well and good; but if not, the father would still open his heart to his daughter, and accept her as she presented herself, Tarquin and all.

Dr. Grantly's mind was of a stronger calibre, and he was by no means deficient in heart. He loved with an honest genuine love his wife and children and friends. He loved his father-in-law; and was quite prepared to love Eleanor too, if she would be one of his party, if she would be on his side, if she would regard the Slopes and the Proudies as the enemies of mankind, and acknowledge and feel the comfortable merits of the Gwynnes and Arabins. He wished to be what he called "safe" with all those whom he had admitted to the penetralia

of his house and heart. He could luxuriate in no society that was deficient in a certain feeling of faithful staunch high-churchism, which to him was tantamount to freemasonry. He was not strict in his lines of definition. He endured without impatience many different shades of Anglochurch conservatism; but with the Slopes and Proudies he could not go on all fours.

He was wanting in, moreover,—or perhaps it would be more correct to say, he was not troubled by—that womanly tenderness which was so peculiar to Mr. Harding. His feelings towards his friends were, that while they stuck to him he would stick to them; that he would work with them shoulder and shoulder; that he would lie faithful to the faithful. He knew nothing of that beautiful love which can be true to a false friend.

And thus these two men, each miserable enough in his own way, returned to Plumstead.

It was getting late when they arrived there, and the ladies had already gone up to dress. Nothing more was said as the two parted in the hall. As Mr. Harding passed to his own room he knocked at Eleanor's door and handed in the letter. The archdeacon hurried to his own territory, there to unburden his heart to his faithful partner.

What colloquy took place between the marital chamber and the adjoining dressing-room shall not be detailed. The reader, now intimate with the persons concerned, can well imagine it. The whole tenor of it also might be read in Mrs. Grantly's brow as she came down to dinner.

Eleanor, when she received the letter from her father's hand, had no idea from whom it came. She had never seen Mr. Slope's hand-writing, or if so had forgotten it; and did not think of him as she twisted the letter as people do twist letters when they do not immediately recognise their correspondents either by the writing or the seal. She was sitting at her glass brushing her hair, and rising every other minute to play with her boy who was sprawling on the bed, and who engaged pretty nearly the whole atten-

tion of the maid as well as of his mother.

At last, sitting before her toilet table, she broke the seal, and turning over the leaf saw Mr. Slope's name. She first felt surprised, and then annoyed, and then anxious. As she read it she became interested. She was so delighted to find that all obstacles to her father's return to the hospital were apparently removed that she did not observe the fulsome language in which the tidings were conveyed. She merely perceived that she was commissioned to tell her father that such was the case, and she did not realise the fact that such a communication should not have been made, in the first instance, to her by an unmarried young clergyman. She felt, on the whole, grateful to Mr. Slope, and anxious to get on her dress that she might run with the news to her father. Then she came to the allusion to her own pious labours, and she said in her heart that Mr. Slope was an affected ass. Then she went on again and was offended by her boy being called Mr. Slope's darling. He was nobody's darling but her own. Or at any rate not the darling of a disagreeable stranger like Mr. Slope. Lastly she arrived at the tresses and felt a qualm of disgust. She looked up in the glass, and there they were before her, long and silken, certainly, and very beautiful. I will not say but that she knew them to be so, but she felt angry with them and brushed them roughly and carelessly. She crumpled the letter up with angry violence, and resolved, almost without thinking of it, that she would not show it to her father. She would merely tell him the contents of it. She then comforted herself again with her boy, had her dress fastened, and went down to dinner.

As she tripped down the stairs she began to ascertain that there was some difficulty in her situation. She could not keep from her father the news about the hospital, nor could she comfortably confess the letter from Mr. Slope before the Grantlys. Her father had already gone down. She had heard his step upon the lobby. She resolved therefore to take him aside, and tell him her little bit of news. Poor girl! she had no idea how severely the unfortunate letter had already been discussed.

When she entered the drawing room the whole party were there, including Mr. Arabin, and the whole party looked glum and sour. The two girls sat silent and apart as though they were aware that something was wrong. Even Mr. Arabin was solemn and silent. Eleanor had not seen him since breakfast. He had been the whole day at St. Ewold's, and such having been the case it was natural that he should tell how matters were going on there. He did nothing of the kind, however, but remained solemn and silent. They were all solemn and silent. Eleanor knew in her heart that they had been talking about her, and her heart misgave her as she thought of Mr. Slope and his letter. At any rate she felt it to be quite impossible to speak to her father alone while matters were in this state.

Dinner was soon announced and Dr. Grantly, as was his wont, gave Eleanor his arm. But he did so as though the doing it were an outrage on his feelings rendered necessary by sternest necessity. With quick sympathy Eleanor felt this, and hardly put her fingers on his coat sleeve. It may be guessed in what way the dinner-hour was passed. Dr. Grantly said a few words to Mr. Arabin, Mr. Arabin said a few words to Mrs. Grantly, she said a few words to her father, and he tried to say a few words to Eleanor. She felt that she had been tried and found guilty of something, though she knew not what. She longed to say out to them all, "Well; what is it that I have done; out with it, and let me know my crime; for heaven's sake let me hear the worst of it;" but she could not. She could say nothing, but sat there silent, half feeling that she was guilty, and trying in vain to pretend even to eat her dinner.

At last the cloth was drawn, and the ladies were not long following it. When they were gone the gentlemen were somewhat more sociable but not much so. They could not of course talk over Eleanor's sins. The archdeacon had indeed so far betrayed his sister-in-law as to whisper into Mr. Arabin's ear in the study, as they met there before din-

ner, a hint of what he feared. He did so with the gravest and saddest of fears, and Mr. Arabin became grave and apparently sad enough as he heard it. He opened his eyes and his mouth and said in a sort of whisper "Mr. Slope!" in the same way as he might have said "The Cholera!" had his friend told him that that horrid disease was in his nursery. "I fear so, I fear so," said the archdeacon, and then together they left the room.

We will not accurately analyse Mr. Arabin's feelings on receipt of such astounding tidings. It will suffice to say that he was surprised, vexed, sorrowful, and ill at ease. He had not perhaps thought very much about Eleanor, but he had appreciated her influence, and had felt that close intimacy with her in a country house was pleasant to him, and also beneficial. He had spoken highly of her intelligence to the archdeacon, and had walked about the shrubberies with her, carrying her boy on his back. When Mr. Arabin had called Johnny his darling, Eleanor was not at all angry.

Thus the three men sat over their wine, all thinking of the same subject, but unable to speak of it to each other. So we will leave them, and follow the ladies into the drawing-room.

Mrs. Grantly had received a commission from her husband, and had undertaken it with some unwillingness. He had desired her to speak gravely to Eleanor, and to tell her that, if she persisted in her adherence to Mr. Slope, she could no longer look for the countenance of her present friends. Mrs. Grantly probably knew her sister better than the doctor did, and assured him that it would be in vain to talk to her. The only course likely to be of any service in her opinion was to keep Eleanor away from Barehester. Perhaps she might have added, for she had a very keen eye in such things, that there might also be ground for hope in keeping Eleanor near Mr. Arabin. Of this, however, she said nothing. But the archdeacon would not be talked over. He spoke much of his conscience, and declared that if Mrs. Grantly would not do it he would. So instigated, the lady undertook the task, stating, however, her full

conviction that her interference would be worse than useless. And so it proved.

As soon as they were in the drawing-room Mrs. Grantly found some excuse for sending her girls away, and then began her task. She knew well that she could exercise but very slight authority over her sister. Their various modes of life, and the distance between their residences, had prevented any very close confidence. They had hardly lived together since Eleanor was a child. Eleanor had moreover, especially in latter years, resented in a quiet sort of way the dictatorial authority which the archdeacon seemed to exercise over her father, and on this account had been unwilling to allow the archdeacon's wife to exercise authority over herself.

"You got a note just before dinner, I believe," began the eldest sister.

Eleanor acknowledged that she had done so, and felt that she turned red as she acknowledged it. She would have given anything to have kept her colour, but the more she tried to do so the more signally she failed.

"Was it not from Mr. Slope?"

Eleanor said that the letter was from Mr. Slope.

"Is he a regular correspondent of yours, Eleanor?"

"Not exactly," said she, already beginning to feel angry at the cross-examination. She determined,—and why it would be difficult to say,—that nothing should induce her to tell her sister Susan what was the subject of the letter. Mrs. Grantly, she knew, was instigated by the archdeacon, and she would not plead to any arraignment made against her by him.

"But, Eleanor dear, why do you get letters from Mr. Slope at all, knowing, as you do, he is a person so distasteful to papa, and to the archdeacon, and indeed to all your friends?"

"In the first place, Susan, I don't get letters from him; and in the next place, as Mr. Slope wrote the one letter which I have got, and as I only received it, which I could not very well help doing, as papa handed it to me, I think you had better ask Mr. Slope instead of me."

"What was his letter about, Eleanor?"

"I cannot tell you," said she, "because it was confidential. It was on business respecting a third person."

"It was in no way personal to yourself, then?"

"I won't exactly say that, Susan," said she, getting more and more angry at her sister's questions.

"Well, I must say it's rather singular," said Mrs. Grantly, affecting to laugh, "that a young lady in your position should receive a letter from an unmarried gentleman of which she will not tell the contents and which she is ashamed to show to her sister."

"I am not ashamed," said Eleanor blazing up; "I am not ashamed of anything in the matter; only I do not choose to be cross-examined as to my letters by any one."

"Well, dear," said the other, "I cannot but tell you that I do not think Mr. Slope a proper correspondent for you."

"If he be ever so improper how can I help his having written to me? But you are all prejudiced against him to such an extent, that that which would be kind and generous in another man is odious and impudent in him. I hate a religion that teaches one to be so onesided in one's charity."

'' I am sorry, Eleanor, that you hate the religion you find here; but surely you should remember that in such matters the archdeacon must know more of the world than you do. I don't ask you to respect or comply with me, although I am, unfortunately, so many years your senior; but surely, in such a matter as this, you might consent to be guided by the archdeacon. He is most anxious to be your friend if you will let him."

"In such a matter as what?" said Eleanor very testily. "Upon my word I don't know what this is all about."

"We all want you to drop Mr. Slope."

"You all want me to be as illiberal as yourselves. That I shall never be. I see no harm in Mr. Slope's acquaintance, and I shall not insult the man by telling him that I do. He has thought it necessary to write to me, and I do not want the archdeacon's advice about the letter. .If I did I would ask it."

"Then, Eleanor, it is my duty to tell you,"—and now she spoke with a tremendous gravity, '' that the archdeacon thinks that such a correspondence is disgraceful, and that he cannot allow it to go on in his house."

Eleanor's eyes flashed fire as she answered her sister, jumping up from her seat as she did so. "You may tell the archdeacon that wherever I am I shall receive what letters I please and from whom I please. And as for the word disgraceful, if Dr. Grantlj has used it of me he has been unmanly and inhospitable," and she walked off to the door. "When papa comes from the diningroom I will thank you to ask him to step up to my bed-room. I will show him Mr. Slope's letter, but I will show it to no one else." And so saying she retreated to her baby.

She had no conception, even yet, of the crime with which she was charged. The idea that she could be thought by her friends to regard Mr. Slope as a lover, had never flashed upon her. She conceived that they were all prejudiced and illiberal in their persecution of him, and therefore she would not join in the persecution, even though she greatly disliked the man.

Eleanor was very angry as she seated herself in a low chair by her open window at the foot of her child's bed. "To dare to say I have disgraced myself," she repeated to herself more than once. "How papa can put up with that man's arrogance! I will certainly not sit down to dinner in his house again unless he begs my pardon for that word." And then a thought struck her that Mr. Arabin might perchance hear of her " disgraceful" correspondence with Mr. Slope, and she turned crimson with pure vexation. Oh, if she had known the truth? If she could have conceived that Mr. Arabin had been informed as a fact that she was going to marry Mr. Slope!

She had not been long in her room before her father joined her. As he left the drawing-room Mrs. Grantly took her husband into the recess of the window, and told him how signally she had failed.

"I will speak to her myself before I go to bed," said the archdeacon.

"Pray do no such thing," said she;

"you can do no good and will only make an unseemly quarrel in the house. You have no idea how headstrong she can be."

The archdeacon declared that as to that he was quite indifferent. He knew his duty and would do it. Mr. Harding was weak in the extreme in such matters. He would not have it hereafter on his conscience that he had not done all that in him lay to prevent so disgraceful an alliance. It was in vain that Mrs. Grantly assured him that speaking to Eleanor angrily would only hasten such a crisis, and render it certain if at present there were any doubt. He was angry, self-willed, and sore. The fact that a lady of his household had received a letter from Mr. Slope had wounded his pride in the sorest place, and nothing could control him.

Mr. Harding looked worn and woebegone as he entered his daughter's room. These sorrows worried him sadly. He felt that if they were continued he must go to the wall in the manner so kindly prophesied to him by the chaplain. He knocked gently at his daughter's door, waited till he was distinctly bade to enter, and then appeared as though he and not she were the suspected criminal. Eleanor's arm was soon within his, and she had soon kissed his forehead and caressed him, not with joyous but with eager love. "Oh, papa," she said, "I do so want to speak to you. They have been talking about me down stairs to-night; don't you know they have, papa?"

Mr. Harding confessed with a sort of murmur that the archdeacon had been speaking of her.

"I shall hate Dr. Grantly soon."

"Oh my dear!"

'' Well; I shall. I cannot help it. He is so uncharitable, so unkind, so suspicious of every one that does not worship himself! And then He is so monstrously arrogant to other people who have a right to their opinions as well as he has to his own."

"He is an earnest eager man, my dear; but he never means to be unkind."

"He is unkind, papa, most unkind. There; I got that letter from Mr. Slope before dinner. It was you yourself who gave it to me. There; pray read it. It is all for you. It should have been addressed to you. You know how they have been talking about it down stairs. You know how they behaved to me at dinner. And since dinner Susan has been preaching to me till I could not remain in the room with her. Bead it, papa; and then say whether that is a letter that need make Dr. Grantly so outrageous."

Mr. Harding took his arm from his daughter's waist and slowly read the letter. She expected to see his countenance lit with joy as he learnt that his path back to the hospital was made so smooth; but she was doomed to disappointment, as had once been the case before on a somewhat similar occasion. His first feeling was one of unmitigated disgust that Mr. Slope should have chosen to interfere in his behalf. He had been anxious to get back to the hospital, but he would have infinitely sooner resigned all pretensions to the place, than have owed it in any manner to Mr. Slope's influence in his favour. Then he thoroughly disliked the tone of Mr. Slope's letter. It was unctuous, false, and unwholesome, like the man. He saw, which Eleanor had failed to see, that much more had been intended than was expressed. The appeal to Eleanor's pious labours as separate from his own grated sadly against his feelings as a father. And then when he came to the "darling boy" and the "silken tresses," he slowly closed and folded the letter in despair. It was impossible that Mr. Slope should so write unless he had been encouraged. It was impossible Eleanor should have received such a letter, and have received it without annoyance, unless she were willing to encourage him. So at least Mr. Harding argued to himself.

How hard it is to judge accurately of the feelings of others. Mr. Harding, as he came to the close of the letter, in his heart condemned his daughter for indelicacy, and it made him miserable to do so. She was not responsible for what Mr. Slope might write. True. But then she expressed no disgust at it. She had rather expressed approval of the letter as a whole. She had given it to him

to read, as a vindication for herself and also for him. The father's spirits sank within him as he felt that he could not acquit her.

And yet it was the true feminine delicacy of Eleanor's mind which brought her on this condemnation. Listen to me, ladies, and I beseech *you* to acquit her. She thought of this man, this Lover of whom she was so unconscious, exactly as her father did, exactly as the Grantlys did. At least she esteemed him personally as they did. But she believed him to be in the main an honest man, and one truly inclined to assist her father. She felt herself bound, after what had passed, to show this letter to Mr. Harding. She thought it necessary that he should know what Mr. Slope had to say. But she did not think it necessary to apologise for, or condemn, or even allude to the vulgarity of the man's tone,—which arose, as does all vulgarity, from ignorance. It was nauseous to her to have a man like Mr. Slope commenting on her personal attractions; and sue did not think it necessary to dilate with her father upon what was nauseous. She never supposed they could disagree on such a subject. It would have been painful for her to point it out, painful for her to speak strongly against a man of whom, on the whole, she was anxious to think and speak well. In encountering such a man she had encountered what was disagreeable, as she might do in walking the streets. But in such encounters she never thought it necessary to dwell on what disgusted her.

And he, foolish weak loving man, would not say one word, though one word would have cleared up everything. There would have been a deluge of tears, and in ten minutes every one in the house would have understood how matters really were. The father would have been delighted. The sister would have kissed her sister and begged a thousand pardons. The archdeacon would have apologised and wondered, and raised his eyebrows, and gone to bed a happy man. And Mr. Arabin,— Mr. Arabin would have dreamt of Eleanor, have awoke in the morning

with ideas of love, and retired to rest the next evening with schemes of marriage. But, alas! all this was not to be. »

Mr. Harding slowly folded the letter, handed it back to her, kissed her forehead and bade God bless her. He then crept slowly away to his own room.

As soon as he had left the passage another knock was given at Eleanor's door, and Mrs. Grantly's very demure own maid, entering on tiptoe, wanted to know would Mrs. Bold be so kind as to speak to the archdeacon for two minutes, in the archdeacon's study, if not disagreeable. The archdeacon's compliments, and he wouldn't detain her two minutes.

Eleanor thought it was very disagreeable; she was tired and fagged and sick at heart; her present feelings towards Dr. Grantly were anything but those of affection. She was, however, no coward, and therefore promised to be in the study in five minutes. So she arranged her hair, tied on her cap, and went down with a palpitating heart.

CHAPTER XXIX.

A SERIOTTS INTERVIEW.

There are people who delight in serious interviews, especially when to them appertains the part of offering advice or administering rebuke, and perhaps the archdeacon was one of these. Yet on this occasion he did not prepare himself for the coming conversation with much anticipation of pleasure. Whatever might be his faults he was not an inhospitable man, and he almost felt that he was sinning against hospitality in upbraiding Eleanor in his own house. Then, also he was not quite sure that he would get the best of it. His wife had told him that he decidedly would not, and he usually gave credit to what his wife said. He was, however, so convinced of what he considered to be the impropriety of Eleanor's conduct, and so assured also of his own duty in trying to check it, that his conscience would not allow him to take his wife's advice and go to bed quietly.

Eleanor's face as she entered the room was not such as to reassure him. As a rule she was always mild in manner and gentle in conduct; but there was that in her eye which made it not an easy task to scold her. In truth she had been little used to scolding. No one since her childhood had tried it but the archdeacon, and he had generally failed when he did try it. He had never done so since her marriage; and now, when he saw her quiet easy step, as she entered his room, he almost wished that he had taken his wife's advice.

He began by apologising for the trouble he was giving her. She begged him not to mention it, assured him that walking down stairs was no trouble to her at all, and then took a seat and waited patiently for him to begin his attack.

"My dear Eleanor," he said, "I hope you believe me when I assure you that you have no sincerer friend than I am." To this Eleanor answered nothing, and therefore he proceeded. "If you had a brother of your own I should not probably trouble you with what I am going to say. But as it is I cannot but think that it must be a comfort to you to know that you have near you one who is as anxious for your welfare as any brother of your own could be."

"I never had a brother," said she.

"I know you never had and it is therefore that I speak to you."

"I never had a brother," she repeated; "but I have hardly felt the want. Papa has been to me both father and brother."

"Your father is the fondest and most affectionate of men. But—"

"He is;—the fondest and most affectionate of men and the best of counsellors. While he lives I can never want advice."

This rather put the archdeacon out. He could not exactly contradict what his sister-in-law said about her father; and yet he did not at all agree with her. He wanted her to understand that he tendered his assistance because her father was a soft good-natured gentleman, not sufficiently knowing in the ways of the world; but he could not say this to her. So he had to rush into the subject matter of his proffered counsel without any acknowledgment on her part that she could need it, or would be grateful for it. '' Susan tells me that you received a letter this evening from Mr. Slope."

"Yes; papa brought it in the brougham. Did he not tell you?" "And Susan says that you objected to let her know what it was about."

"I don't think she asked me. But had she done so I should noi have told her. I don't think it nice to be asked about one's letters.. If one wishes to show them one does so without being asked."

"True. Quite so. "What you say is *qvite* true. But is not the

Vol. n. IE fact of your receiving letters from Mr. Slope, which you do not wish to show to your friends, a circumstance which must excite some,— some surprise,—some suspicion—"

"Suspicion!" said she, not speaking above her usual voice, speaking still in a soft womanly tone, but yet with indignation; "suspicion! Who suspects me, and of what?" And then there was a pause, for the archdeacon was not quite ready to explain the ground of his suspicion. "No, Dr. Grantly, I did not choose to show Mr. Slope's letter to Susan. I could not show it to any one till papa had seen it. If you have any wish to read it now, you can do so," and she handed the letter to him over the table.

This was an amount of compliance which he had not at all expected, and which rather upset him in his tactics. However, he took the letter, perused it carefully, and then refolding it, kept it on the table under his hand. To him it appeared to be in almost every respect the letter of a declared lover; it seemed to corroborate his worst suspicions; and the fact of Eleanor's showing it to him was all but tantamount to a declaration on her part that it was her pleasure to receive love-letters from Mr. Slope. He almost entirely overlooked the real subject-matter of the epistle; so intent was he on the forthcoming courtship and marriage.

"I'll thank you to give it me back, if you please, Dr. Grantly."

He took it in his hand and held it up, but made no immediate overture to return it. "And Mr. Harding has seen this?" said he.

"Of course he has," said she. It was written that he might see it. It refers solely to his business. Of course I

showed it to him."

"And, Eleanor, do you think that that is a proper letter for you— for a person in your condition—to receive from Mr. Slope?"

"Quite a proper letter," said she, speaking, perhaps, a little out of obstinacy;—perhaps forgetting at the moment the objectionable mention of her silken curls.

"Then, Eleanor, it is my duty to tell you that I wholly differ from you."

"So I suppose," said she, instigated now by sheer opposition and determination not to succumb. "You think Mr. Slope is a messenger direct from Satan. I think he is an industrious. well meaning clergyman. It's a pity that we differ as we do. But, as we do differ, we had probably better not talk about it."

Here Eleanor undoubtedly put herself in the wrong. She might probably have refused to talk to Dr. Grantly on the matter in dispute without any impropriety; but having consented to listen to him, she had no business to tell him that he regarded Mr. Slope as an emissary from the evil one; nor was she justified in praising Mr. Slope, seeing that in her heart of hearts she did not think well of him. She was, however, wounded in spirit, and angry and bitter. She had been subjected to contumely and cross-questioning and ill-usage through the whole evening. No one, not even Mr. Arabin, not even her father, had been kind to her. All this she attributed to the prejudice and conceit of the archdeacon, and therefore she resolved to set no bounds to her antagonism to him. She would neither give nor take quarter. He had greatly presumed in daring to question her about her correspondence, and she was determined to show that she thought so.

"Eleanor, you are forgetting yourself," said he, looking very sternly at her. "Otherwise you would never tell me that I conceive any man to be a messenger from Satan."

"But you do," said she. "Nothing is too bad for him. Give me that letter, if you please;" and she stretched out her hand and took it from him. "He has been doing his best to serve papa; doing more than any of papa's friends could do; and yet, because he is the chaplain of a bishop whom you don't like you speak of him as though he had no right to the usage of a gentleman."

"He has done nothing for your father."

' I believe that he has done a great deal; and, as far as I am concerned, I am grateful to him. Nothing that you can say can prevent my being so. I judge people by their acts, and his, as far as I can see them, are good." She then paused for a moment. "If you have nothing further to say, I shall be obliged by being permitted to say pood night. I am very tired."

Dr. Grantly had, as he thought, done his best to be gracious t his sister-in-law. He had endeavoured not to be harsh to her, and had striven to pluck the sting from his rebuke. But he did not intend that she should leave him without hearing him. "I have something to say, Eleanor; and I fear I must trouble you to hear it. You profess that it is quite proper that you should receive from Mr. Slope such letters as that you have in your hand. Susan and I think very differently. You are, of course, your own mistress, and much as we both must grieve should anything separate you from us, we have no power to prevent you froir taking steps which may lead to such a separation. If you are so wilful as to reject the counsel of your friends, you must be allowed to cater for yourself. But Eleanor, I may at any rate ask you this. Is it worth your while to break away from all those you have loved, — from all who love you,—for the sake of Mr. Slope?"

"I don't know what you mean, Dr. Grantly. I don't know what you're talking about. I don't want to break away from anybody."

"But you will do so if you connect yourself with Mr. Slope Eleanor, I must speak out to you. You must choose between your sister and myself and our friends, and Mr. Slope and his friends.. I say nothing of your father as you may probably understand his feelings better than I do."

"What do you mean, Dr. Grantly?

What am I to understand? I never heard such wicked prejudice in my life."

"It is no prejudice, Eleanor. I have known the world longer than you have done. Mr. Slope is altogether beneath you. You ought to know and feel that he is so. Pray,—pray think of this before it is too late."

"Too late!"

"Or if you will not believe me, ask Susan. You cannot think she is prejudiced against you. Or even consult your father; he is. not prejudiced against you. Ask Mr. Arabin"

"You haven't spoken to Mr. Arabin about this I" said she, jumping up and standing before him.

"Eleanor, all the world in and about Barchester will be speaking of it soon."

"But have you spoken to Mr. Arabin about me and Mr. Slope?" "Certainly I have, and he quite agrees with me." "Agrees with what?" said she. "I think you are trying to drive me mad."

"He agrees with me and Susan that it is quite impossible you should be received at Plumstead as Mrs. Slope."

Not being favourites with the tragic muse we do not dare to attempt any description of Eleanor's face when she first heard the name of Mrs. Slope pronounced as that which would or should or might at some time appertain to herself. The look, such as it was, Dr. Grantly did not soon forget. For a moment or two she could find no words to express her deep anger and deep disgust. And, indeed, at this conjuncture, words did not come to her very freely.

"How dare you be so impertinent?" at last she said; and then hurried out of the room, without giving the archdeacon the opportunity of uttering another word. It was with difficulty she contained herself till she reached her own room; and then locking the door, she threw herself on her bed and sobbed as though her heart would break.

But even yet she had no conception of the truth. She had no idea that her father and her sister had for days past conceived in sober earnest the idea that she was going to marry this man. She did not even then believe that the archdeacon thought that she would do so. By

some manoeuvre of her brain, she attributed the origin of the accusation to Mr. Arabin, and as she did so her anger against him was excessive, and the vexation of her spirit almost unendurable. She could not bring herself to think that the charge was made seriously. It appeared to her most probable that the archdeacon and Mr. Arabin had talked over her objectionable acquaintance with Mr. Slope; that Mr. Arabin, in his jeering, sarcastic way, had suggested the odious match as being the severest way of treating with contumely her acquaintance with his enemy; and that the archdeacon, taking the idea from him, thought proper to punish her by the allusion. The whole night she lay awake thinking of what had been said, and this appeared to be the most probable solution.

But the reflection that Mr. Arabin should have in any way mentioned her name in connection with that of Mr. Slope waa overpowering; and the spiteful ill-nature of the archdeacon, in repeating the charge to her, made her wish to leave his house almost before the day had broken. One thing was certain. Nothing should make her stay there beyond the following morning, and nothing should make her sit down to breakfast in company with Dr. Grantly. When she thought of the man whose name had been linked with her own, she cried from sheer disgust. It was only because she would be thus disgusted, thus pained and shocked and cut to the quick, that the archdeacon had spoken the horrid word. He wanted to make her quarrel with Mr. Slope, and therefore he had outraged her by his abominable vulgarity. She determined that at any rate he should know that she appreciated it.

Nor was the archdeacon a bit better satisfied with the result of his serious interview than was Eleanor. He gathered from it, as indeed he could hardly fail to do, that she was very angry with him; but he thought that she was thus angry, not because she was suspected of an intention to marry Mr. Slope, but because such an intention was imputed to her as a crime. Dr. Grantly regarded this supposed union with disgust; but it never occurred to him that Eleanor was outraged because she looked at it exactly in the same light.

He returned to his wife vexed and somewhat disconsolate, but, nevertheless, confirmed in his wrath against his sister-in-law. "Her whole behaviour," said he, "has been most objectionable. She handed me his love letter to read as though she were proud of it. And she is proud of it She is proud of having this slavering, greedy man at her feet. She will throw herself and John Bold's money into his lap. She will ruin her boy, disgrace her father and you, and be a wretched miserable woman."

His spouse who was sitting at her toilet table, continued her avocations, making no answer to all this. She had known that the archdeacon would gain nothing by interfering; but she was too charitable to provoke him by saying so while he was in such deep sorrow.

"This comes of a man making such a will as that of Bold's," he continued. "Eleanor is no more fitted to be trusted with such an amount of money in her own hands than is a charity-school girl. " Still Mrs. Grantly made no reply. "But I have done my duty. I can do nothing further. I have fold her plainly that she cannot be allowed to form a link of connection between me and that man. From henceforward it will not be in my power to make her welcome at Plumstead. I cannot have Mr. Slope's love letters coming here. Susan, I think you had better let her understand that as her mind on this subject seems to be irrevocably fixed, it will be better for all parties that she should return to Barchester." Now Mrs. Grantly was angry with Eleanor, nearly as angry as her husband; but she had no idea of turning her sister out of the house. She, therefore, at length spoke out, and explained to the archdeacon, in her own mild seducing way, that he was fuming and fussing and fretting himself very unnecessarily. She declared that things, if left alone, would arrange themselves much better than he lould arrange them; and at last succeeded in inducing him to go to bed in a somewhat less inhospitable state of mind.

On the following morning Eleanor's maid was commisioned to send word into the dining-room that her mistress was not well enough to attend prayers, and that she would breakfast in her own room, Here she was visited by her father and declared to him her intention of returning immediately to Barchester. He was hardly surprised by the announcement. All the household seemed to be aware that something had gone wrong. Every one walked about with subdued feet, and people's shoes seemed to creak more than usual. There was a look of conscious intelligence on the faces of the women; and the men attempted, but in vain, to converse as though nothing were the matter. All this had weighed heavily on the heart of Mr. Harding; and when Eleanor told him that her immediate return to Barchester was a necessity, he merely sighed piteously, and said that he would be ready to accompany her.

But here she objected strenuously. She had a great wish, she said, to go alone;—a great desire that it might be seen that her father was not implicated in her quarrel with Dr. Grantly. To this at last he gave way; but not a word passed between them about Mr. Slope, —not a word was said, not a question asked as to the serious interview on the preceding evening. There was, indeed, very little confidence between them, though neither of them knew why it should be so. Eleanor once asked him whether he would not call upon the bishop; but he answered rather tartly that he did not know; —he did not think he should, but he could not say just at present. And so they parted. Each was miserably anxious for some show of affection, for some return of confidence, for some sign of the feeling that usually bound them together. But none was given. The father could not bring himself to question his daughter about her supposed lover; and the daughter would not sully her mouth by repeating the odious word with which Dr. Grantly had roused her wrath. And so they parted.

There was some trouble in arranging the method of Eleanor's return. She begged her father to send for a postchaise; but when Mrs. Grantly heard of this, she objected strongly. If Eleanor would go away in dudgeon with the archdeacon why should she let all the servants and all the neighbourhood know that she had done so? So at last Eleanor consented to make use of the Plumstead carriage; and as the archdeacon had gone out immediately after breakfast and was not to return till dinner-time, she also consented to postpone her journey till after lunch, and to join the family at that time. As to the subject of the quarrel not a word was said by any one. The affair of the carriage was arranged by Mr. Harding, who acted as Mercury between the two ladies; they, when they met, kissed each other very lovingly, and then sat down each to her crochet work as though nothing was amiss in all the world.

CHAPTER XXX. ANOTHER IOYE SCENK.

But there was another visitor at the rectory whose feelings in this unfortunate matter must be somewhat strictly analysed. Mr. Arabin had heard from his friend of the probability of Eleanor's marriage with Mr. Slope with amazement, but not with incredulity. It has been said that he was not in love with Eleanor, and up to this period this certainly had been true. But as soon as he heard that she loved some one else he began to be very fond of her himself. He did not make up his mind that he wished to have her for his wife; he had never thought of her, and did not now think of her, in connection with himself; but he experienced an inward indefinable feeling of deep regret, a gnawing sorrow, an unconquerable depression of spirits, and also a species of self-abasement that he,— he, Mr. Arabin,—had not done something to prevent that other he, that vile he, whom he so thoroughly despised, from carrying off this sweet prize.

Whatever man may have reached the age of forty unmarried without knowing something of such feelings must have been very successful or else very cold-hearted.

Mr. Arabin had never thought of trimming the sails of his bark so that he might sail as convoy to this rich argosy. He had seen that Mrs. Bold was beautiful, but he had not dreamt of making her beauty his own. He knew that Mrs. Bold was rich, but he had had no more idea of appropriating her wealth than that of Dr. Grantly. He had discovered that Mrs. Bold was intelligent, warm-hearted, agreeable, sensible, all, in fact, that a man could wish his wife to be; but the higher were her attractions, the greater her claims to consideration, the less had he imagined that he might possibly become the possessor of them. Such had been his instinct rather than his thoughts,—so humble and so diffident. Now his diffidence was to be rewarded by his seeing this woman, whose beauty was to his eyes perfect, whose wealth was such as to have deterred him from thinking of her, whose widowhood would have silenced him had he not been so deterred, by his seeing her become the prey of Obadiah Slope!

On the morning of Mrs. Bold's departure he got on his horse to ride over to St. Ewold's. As he rode he kept muttering to himself a line from Van Artevelde,

"How little flattering is woman's love."

And then he strove to recall his mind and to think of other affairs, his parish, his college, his creed,—but his thoughts would revert to Mr. Slope and the Flemish chieftain.— "When we think upon it,

How little flattering is woman's love,
Given commonly to whosoe'er is nearest
And propped with most advantage."

Tt was not that Mrs. Bold should marry any one but him; he had not put himself forward as a suitor; but that she should marry Mr. Slope;—and so he repeated over again— "Outward grace
Nor inward light is needful;—day by day
Men wanting both are mated with the best
And loftiest of God's feminine creation,
Whose love takes no distinction but of gender,
And ridicules the very name of choice."

And so he went on, troubled much in his mind. He had but an uneasy ride of it that morning, and little good did he do at St. Ewold's.

The necessary alterations in his house were being fast completed, and he walked through the rooms, and went up and down the stairs, and rambled through the garden; but he could not wake himself to much interest about them. He stood still at every window to look out and think upon Mr. Slope. At almost every window he had before stood and chatted with Eleanor. She and Mrs. Grantly had been there continually, and while Mrs. Grantly had been giving orders, and seeing that orders had been complied with, he and Eleanor had conversed on all things appertaining to a clergyman's profession. He thought how often he had laid down the law to her, and how sweetly she had borne with his somewhat dictatorial decrees. He remembered her listening intelligence, her gentle but quick replies, her interest in all that concerned the church, in all that concerned him; and then he struck his riding whip against the window sill, and declared to himself that it was impossible that Eleanor Bold should marry Mr. Slope.

And yet he did not really believe, as he should have done, that it was impossible. He should have known her well enough to feel that it was truly impossible. He should have been aware that Eleanor had that within her which would surely protect her from such degradation. But he, like so many others, was deficient in confidence in woman. He said to himself over and over again that it was impossible that Eleanor Bold should become Mrs. Slope, and yet he believed that she would do so. And so he rambled about, and could do and think of nothing. He was thoroughly uncomfortable, thoroughly ill at ease, cross with himself, and every body else, and feeding in his heart on animosity towards Mr. Slope. This was not as it should be, as he knew and felt; but he could not help himself. In truth Mr. Arabin was now in love with Mrs. Bold, though ignorant of the fact himself. He was in love, and, though forty years old, was in love

without being aware of it. He fumed and fretted, and did not know what was the matter, as a youth might do at one-and-twenty. And so having done no good at St. Ewold's, he rode back much earlier than was usual with him, instigated by some inward unacknowledged hope that he might see Mrs. Bold before she left.

Eleanor had not passed a pleasant morning. She was irritated with every one, and not least with herself. She felt that she had been hardly used, but she felt also that she had not played her own lards well. She should have held herself so far above suspicion as o have received her sister's innuendoes and the archdeacon's lecture vith indifference. She had not done this, but had shown herself angry and sore, and was now ashamed of her own petulance, and yet unable to discontinue it.

The greater part of the morning she had spent alone; but after a while her father joined her. He had fully made up his mind that, come what come might, nothing should separate him from his younger daughter. It was a hard task for liim to reconcile himself to the idea of seeing her at the head of Mr. Slope's table; but he got through it. Mr. Slope, as he argued to himself, was a respectable man and a clergyman; and he, as Eleanor's father, had no right even to endeavour to prevent her from marrying such a one. He longed to tell her how he had determined to prefer her to all the world, how he was prepared to admit that she was not wrong, how thoroughly he differed from Dr. Grantly; but he could not bring himself to mention Mr. Slope's name. There was yet a chance that they were all wrong in their surmise! Being thus in doubt, he could not bring himself to speak openly to her on the subject.

He was sitting with her in the drawing-room, with his arm round her waist, saying every now and then some little soft words of affection, and working hard with his imaginary fiddle-bow, when Mr. Arabin entered the room. He immediately got up, and the two made some trite remarks to each other, neither thinking of what he was saying, while Eleanor kept her seat on the sofa mute and moody. Mr. Arabin was included in the list of those against whom her anger was excited. He, too, had dared to talk about '.ier acquaintance with Mr. Slope. He, too, had dared to blame her or not making an enemy of his enemy. She had not intended to iee him before her departure, and was now but little inclined to be gracious.

There was a feeling through the whole house that something was OTong. Mr. Arabin, when *ha* saw Eleanor, could not succeed in looking or in speaking as though he knew nothing of all thia He could not be cheerful and positive and contradictory with her, as was his wont. He had not been two minutes in the room before he felt that he had done wrong to return; and the moment he heard her voice, he thoroughly wished himself back at St. Ewold's. Why, indeed, should he have wished to have aught further to say to the future wife of Mr. Slope?

"I am sorry to hear that you are to leave us so soon," said he, striving in vain to use his ordinary voice. In answer to this she muttered something about the necessity of her being in Barchester, and betook herself most industriously to her crochet work.

Then there was a little more trite conversation between Mr. Arabin and Mr. Harding; trite, and hard, and vapid, and senseless. Neither of them had anything to say to the other, and yet neither at such a moment liked to remain silent. At last Mr. Harding, taking advantage of a pause, escaped out of the room, and Eleanor and Mr. Arabin were left together.

"Your going will be a great break-up to our party," said he. She again muttered something which was all but inaudible; but kept her eyes fixed upon her work. "We have had a very pleasant month here," said he; "at least I have; and I am sorry it should be so soon over. "

"I have already been from home longer than I intended," said she; "and it is time that I should return."

"Well; pleasant hours and pleasant days must come to an end. It is a pity that so few of them are pleasant; or per-

haps, rather"

"It is a pity, certainly, that men and women do so much to destroy the pleasantness of their days," said she, interrupting him. "It is a pity that there should be so little charity abroad."

"Charity should begin at home," said he; and he was proceeding to explain that he as a clergyman could not be what she would call charitable at the expense of those principles which he considered it his duty to teach, when he remembered that it would be worse than vain to argue on such a matter with the future wife of Mr. Slope. "But you are just leaving us," he continued, "and I will na weary your last hour with another lecture. As it is, I fear I hava given you too many."

"You should practise as well as preach, Mr. Arabin?"

"Undoubtedly I should. So should we all. All of us who presume to teach are bound to do our utmost towards fulfilling our own lessons. I thoroughly allow my deficiency in doing so. But I do not quite know now to what you allude. Have you any special reason for telling me now that I should practise as well as preach?"

Eleanor made no answer. She longed to let him know the cause of her anger, to upbraid him for speaking of her disrespectfully, and then at last to forgive him, and so part friends. She felt that she would be unhappy to leave him in her present frame of mind; but yet she could hardly bring herself to speak to him of Mr. Slope. And how could she allude to the innuendo thrown out by the archdeacon, and thrown out, as she believed, at the instigation of Mr. Arabin? She wanted to make him know that he was wrong, to make him aware that he had ill-treated her, in order that the sweetness of her forgiveness might be enhanced. She felt that she liked him too well to be contented to part with him in displeasure; and yet she could not get over her deep displeasure without some explanation, some acknowledgment on his part, some assurance that he would never again so sin against her.

"Why do you tell me that I should practise what I preach?" continued he.

"All men should do so."

"Certainly. That is as it were understood and acknowledged. But you do not say so to all men, or to all clergymen. The advice, good as it is, is not given except in allusion to some special deficiency. If you will tell me my special deficiency I will endeavour to profit by the advice."

She paused for a while, and then, looking full in his face, she said, "You are not bold enough, Mr. Arabin, to speak out to me openly and plainly, and yet you expect me, a woman, to speak openly to you. Why did you speak calumny of me to Dr. Grantly behind my back?"

"Calumny!" said he, and his whole face became suffused with blood; "what calumny? If I have spoken calumny of you, I will beg your pardon, and his to whom I spoke it, and God's pardon also. But what calumny have I spoken of you to Dr. Grantly?"

She also blushed deeply. She could not bring herself to ask him whether he had not spoken of her as another man's wife. "You know that best yourself," said she; "but I ask you as a man of honour, if you have not spoken of me as you would not have spoken of your own sister; or rather I will not ask you," she continued, rinding that he did not immediately answer her. '' I will not put you to the necessity of answering such a question. Dr. Grantly has told me what you said."

"Dr. Grantly certainly asked me for my advice, and I gave it. He asked me"

"I know he did, Mr Arabin. He asked you whether he would be doing right to receive me at Plumstead, if I continued my acquaintance with a gentleman who happens to be personally disagreeable to yourself and to him?"

"You are mistaken, Mrs. Bold. I have no personal knowledge of Mr. Slope. I never met him in my life."

"You are not the less individually hostile to him. It is not for me to question the propriety of your enmity; but I had a right to expect that my name should not have been mixed up in your hostilities. This has been done, and been done by you in a manner the most injurious and the most distressing to me as a woman. I must confess, Mr. Arabin, that from you I expected a different sort of usage."

As she spoke, she with difficulty restrained her tears; but she did restrain them. Had she given way and sobbed aloud, as in such cases a woman should do, he would have melted at once, implored her pardon, perhaps knelt at her feet and declared his love. Everything would have been explained, and Eleanor would have gone back to Barchester with a contented mind. How easily would she have forgiven and forgotten the archdeacon's suspicions had she but heard the whole truth from Mr. Arabin. She did not cry, and Mr. Arabin did not melt.

"You do me an injustice," said he. "My advice was asked by Dr. Grantly, and I was obliged to give it."

"Dr. Grantly has been most officious, most impertinent. I have as complete a right to form my acquaintance as he has to form his. What would you have said, had I consulted you as to the propriety of my banishing Dr. Grantly from my house because he knows Lord Tattenham Corner? I am sure Lord Tattenham is quite as objectionable an acquaintance for a clergyman as Mr. Slope is for a clergyman's daughter."

"I do not know Lord Tattenham Corner."

"No; but Dr. Grantly does. It is nothing to me if he knows all the young lords on every racecourse in England. I shall not interfere with him; nor shall he with me."

"I am sorry to differ with you, Mrs. Bold; but as you have spoken to me on this matter, and especially as you blame me for what little I said on the subject, I must tell you that I do differ from you. Dr. Grantly's position as a man in the world gives him a right to choose his own acquaintances, subject to certain influences. If he chooses them badly, those influences will be used. If he consorts with persons unsuitable to him his bishop will interfere. What the bishop is to Dr. Grantly, Dr. Grantly is to you."

"I deny it. I utterly deny it," said Eleanor, jumping from her seat, and literally flashing before Mr. Arabin, as she stood on the drawing-room floor. He had never seen her so excited, he had never seen her look half so beautiful. "I utterly deny it," said she. "Dr. Grantly has no sort of jurisdiction over me whatsoever. Do you and he forget that I am not altogether alone in the world? Do you forget that I have a father? Dr. Grantly, I believe, always has forgotten it."

"From you, Mr. Arabin," she continued, "I would have listened to advice, because I should have expected it to have been given as one friend may advise another; not as a schoolmaster gives an order to a pupil. I might have differed from you; on this matter I should have done so; but had you spoken to me in your usual manner and with your usual freedom I should not have been angry. But now, was it manly of you, Mr. Arabin, to speak of me in this way, so disrespectful,—so,?I cannot bring myself to repeat what you said. You must understand what I feel. Was it just of you to speak of me in such a way, and to advise my sister's husband to turn me out of my sister's house, because I chose to know a man of whose doctrine you disapprove?"

"I have no alternative left to me, Mrs. Bold," said he, standing with his back to the fire-place, looking down intently at the carpet pattern, and speaking with a slow measured voice, "but to tell you plainly what did take place between me and Dr. Grantly."

"Well," said she, finding that he paused for a moment.

"I am afraid that what I may say may pain you."

"It cannot well do so more than what you have already done," said she.

"Dr. Grantly asked me whether I thought it would be prudent for him to receive you in his house as the wife of Mr. Slope, and I told him that I thought it would be imprudent. Believing it to be utterly impossible that Mr. Slope and"

"Thank you, Mr. Arabin, that is sufficient. I do not want to know your reasons," said she, speaking with a terribly calm voice. '' I have shown to this gentleman the commonplace civility of a neighbour; and because I have done so, because I have not indulged against him in all the rancour and hatred which you and Dr. Grantly consider due to all clergymen who do not agree with yourselves, you conclude that I am to marry him;—or rather you do not conclude so;—no rational man could really come to such an outrageous conclusion without better ground;—you have not thought so;—but, as I am in a position in which such an accusation must be peculiarly painful, it is made in order that I may be terrified into hostility against this enemy of yours!"

As she finished speaking, she walked to the drawing-room VOL. II. L window and stepped out into the garden. Mr. Arabin was left in the room, still occupied in counting the pattern on the carpet. He had, however, distinctly heard and accurately marked every word that she had spoken. Was it not clear from what she had said, that the archdeacon had been wrong in imputing to her any attachment to Mr. Slope? Was it not clear that Eleanor was still free to make another choice? It may seem strange that he should for a moment have had a doubt; and yet he did doubt. She had not absolutely denied the charge. She had not expressly said that it was untrue. Mr. Arabin understood little of the nature pf a woman's feelings, or he would have known how improbable it was that she should make any clearer declaration than she had done. Few men do understand the nature of a woman's heart till years have robbed such understanding of its value. And it is well that it should be so, or men would triumph too easily.

Mr. Arabin stood counting the carpet, unhappy, wretchedly unhappy, at the hard words that had been spoken to him; and yet happy, exquisitely happy, as he thought that after all the woman whom he so regarded was not to become the wife of the man whom he so much disliked. As he stood there he began to be aware that he was himself in love. Forty years had passed over his head, and as yet woman's beauty had never given him an uneasy hour. His present hour was very uneasy.

Not that he remained there for half or a quarter of that time. In spite of what Eleanor had said, Mr. Arabin was, in truth, a manly man. Having ascertained that he loved this woman, and having now reason.to believe that she was free to receive his love, at least if she pleased to do so, he followed her into the garden to make such wooing as he could.

He was not long in finding her. She was walking to and fro beneath the avenue of elms that stood in the archdeacon's grounds, skirting the churchyard. What had passed between her and Mr. Arabin, had not, alas, tended to lessen the acerbity of her spirit. She was very angry; more angry with him than with any one. How could he have so misunderstood her? She had been so intimate with him, had allowed him such latitude iu what-he had chosen to say to her, had complied with his ideas, cherished his views, fostered his precepts, cared for his comforts, made much of him in every way in which a pretty woman can make much of an unmarried man without committing herself or her feelings! She had been doing this, and while she had been doing it he had regarded her as the affianced wife of another man. As she passed along the avenue, every now and then an unbidden tear would force itself on her cheek, and as she raised her hand to brush it away she stamped with her little foot upon the sward with very spite to think that she had been so treated.

Mr. Arabin was very near to her when she first saw him, and she turned short round and retraced her steps down the avenue, trying to rid her cheeks of all trace of the tell-tale tears. It was a needless endeavour, fpr Mr. Arabin was in a state of mind that hardly allowed him to observe such trifles. He followed her down the walk, and overtook her just as she reached the end of it.

He had not considered how he would address her. He had not thought what he would say. He had only felt that it was wretchedness to him to quarrel with her, and that it would be happiness to be allowed to love her. And yet he could not lower himself by asking her pardon.

He had done her no wrong. He had not calumniated her, not injured her, as she had accused him of doing. He could not confess sins of which he had not been guilty. He could only let the past be past,. and ask her as to her and his hopes for the future.

"I hope we are not to part as enemies?" said hev

"There shall be no enmity on my part," said Eleanor. "I endeavour to avoid all enmities. It would be a hollow pretence were I to say that there can bo true friendship between us after what has j ust passed. People cannot make their friends of those whom they despise."

"And am I despised?"

"I must have been so before you could have spoken of me as yu did. And I was deceived, cruelly deceived. I believed that you thought well of me. I believed that you esteemed me."

"Thought well of you and esteemed you!" said he. "In justifying myself before you, I must use stronger words than those." He paused for a moment, and Eleanor's heart beat with painful violence within her bosom as she waited for him to go on. "I have esteemed, do esteem you, as I never yet esteemed any woman. Think well of you! I never thought to think so well, so much of any human creature. Speak calumny of you! Insult you! Wilfully injure you! I wish it were my privilege to shield you from calumny, insult, and injury. Calumny! ah, me. 'Twere almost better that it were so. Better than to worship with a sinful worship; sinful and vain also." And then he walked along beside her, with his hands clasped behind his back, looking down on the grasj beneath his feet, and utterly at a loss how to express his meaning. And Eleanor walked beside him determined at least to give him no assistance.

"Ah, me!" he uttered at last, speaking rather to himself than to her. "Ah me! these Plumstead walks were pleasant enough, if one could have but heart's ease; but without that the dull dead stones of Oxford were far preferable. And St. Ewold's too! Mrs. Bold, I am beginning to think that I mistook myself when I came hither. A Eomish priest now would have escaped all this Oh, Father of heaven! how good for us would it be, if thou couldest vouchsafe to us a certain rule."

'' And have we not a certain rule, Mr. Arabin?"

"Yes; yes, surely; 'Lead us not into temptation but deliver us from evil.' But what is temptation? What is evil? Is this evil, —is this temptation?"

Poor Mr. Arabin! It would not come out of him, that deep true love of his. He could not bring himself to utter it in plain language that would require and demand an answer. He knew not how to say to the woman by his side, "Since the fact is that you do not love that other man, that you are not to be his wife, can you love me, will you be my wife?" These were the words whirl were in his heart, but with all his sighs he could not draw them to his lips. He would have given anything, everything for power to ask this simple question; but glib as was his tongue in pulpits and on platforms, now he could not find a word wherewith to express the plain wish of his heart.

And yet Eleanor understood him as thoroughly as though he had declared his passion with all the elegant fluency of a practised Lothario. With a woman's instinct she followed every bend of his mind, as he spoke of the pleasantness of Plumstead and the stones of Oxford, as he alluded to the safety of the Romish priest and the hidden perils of temptation. She knew that-it all meant love. She knew that this man at her side, this accomplished scholar, this practised orator, this great polemical combatant, was striving and striving in vain to tell her that his heart was no longer his own.

She knew this, and felt a joy in knowing it; and yet she would not come to his aid. He had offended her deeply, had treated her unworthily, the more unworthily seeing that he had learnt to love her, and Eleanor could not bring herself to abandon her revenge. She did not ask herself whether or no she would ultimately accept his love. She did not even acknowledge to herself that she now perceived it with pleasure. At the present moment it did not touch her heart. It merely appeased her pride and flattered her vanity. Mr. Arabin had dared to associate her name with that of Mr. Slope, and now her spirit was soothed by finding that he would fain associate it with his own. And so she walked on beside him inhaling incense, but giving out no sweetness in return.

"Answer me this," said Mr. Arabin, stopping suddenly in his walk, and stepping forward so that he faced his companion. 'Answer me this one question. You do not love Mr. Slope? You do not intend to be his wife?"

Mr. Arabin certainly did not go the right way to win such a voman as Eleanor Bold. Just as her wrath was evaporating, as fc was disappearing before the true warmth of his untold love, he: o-kindled it by a most useless repetition of his original sin. Had he known what he was about he should never have mentioned Mr. Slope's name before Eleanor Bold, till he had made her all his own. Then, and not till then, he might have talked of Mr. Slope with as much triumph as he chose.

"I shall answer no such question," said she; "and what is more, I must tell you that nothing can justify your asking it. Good morning!"'

And so saying she stepped proudly across the lawn, and passing through the drawing-room window joined her father and sister at lunch in the dining-room. Half an hour afterwards she was in the carriage, and so she left Plumstead without again seeing Mr. Arabin.

His walk was long and sad among the sombre trees that overshadowed the churchyard. He left the archdeacon's grounds that he might escape attention, and sauntered among the green hillocks under which lay at rest so many of the once loving swains and forgotten beauties of Plumstead. To his ears Eleanor's last words sounded like a knell never to be reversed. He could not comprehend that she might be angry with him, indignant with him, remorseless with him, and yet love him. He could not make up his mind whether or no Mr. Slope was in truth a favoured rival. If not, why should she not have answered his question?

Poor Mr. Arabin;—untaught, illiterate, boorish, ignorant man! That at forty years of age you should know so little of the workings of a woman's heart 1 CHAPTER XXXL THE BISHOP'S LIBRARY.

And thus the pleasant party at Plumstead was broken up. It had been a very pleasant party as long as they had all remained in good humour with one another. Mrs. Grantly had felt her house to be gayer and brighter than it had been for many a long day, and the archdeacon had been aware that the month had passed pleasantly without attributing the pleasure to any other special merits than those of his own hospitality. Within three or four days of Eleanor's departure Mr. Harding had also returned, and Mr. Arabin had gone to Oxford to spend one week there previous to his settling at the vicarage of St. Ewold's. He had gone laden with many messages to Dr. Gwynne touching the iniquity of the doings in Barchester palace, and the peril in which it was believed the hospital still stood in spite of the assurances contained in Mr. Slope's inauspicious letter.

During Eleanor's drive into Barchester she had not much opportunity of reflecting on Mr. Arabin. She had been constrained to divert her mind both from his sins and his love by the necessity of conversing with her sister and maintaining the appearance of parting with her on good terms. When the carriage reached her own door, and while she was in the act of giving her last kiss to her sister and nieces, Mary Bold ran out and exclaimed,

"Oh! Eleanor,—have you heard?—oh! Mrs. Grantly, have you heard what has happened? The poor dean!"

"Good heavens!" said Mrs. Cirantly; "what;—what has happened?" 'This morning at nine he had a fit of apoplexy, and he has not spoken since. I very much fear that by this time he is no more."

Mrs. Grantly had been very intimate with the dean, and was therefore much shocked.. Eleanor had not known him so well; nevertheless she was sufficiently acquainted with his person and manners to feel startled and grieved also at the tidings she now received. "I will go at once to the deanery," said Mrs. Grantly. "The archdeacon, I am sure, will be there. If there is any news to send you I will let Thomas call before he leaves town." And so the carriage drove off, leaving Eleanor and her baby with Mary Bold.

Mrs. Grantly had been quite right. The archdeacon was at the deanery. He had come into Barchester that morning by himself, not caring to intrude himself upon Eleanor, and he also immediately on his arrival had heard of the dean's fit. There was, as we have before said, a library or reading room connecting the cathedral with the dean's house. This was generally called the bishop's library, because a certain bishop of Barchester was supposed to have added it to the cathedral. It was built immediately over a portion of the cloisters, and a flight of stairs descended from it into the room in which the cathedral clergymen put their surplices on and off. As it also opened directly into the dean's house, it was the passage through which that dignitary usually went to his public devotions. Who had or had not the right of entry into it, it might be difficult to say; but the people of Barchester believed that it belonged to the dean, and the clergymen of Barchester believed that it belonged to the chapter.

On the morning in question most of the resident clergymen who constituted the chapter, and some few others, were here assembled, and among them as usual the archdeacon towered with high authority. He had heard of the dean's fit before he was over the bridge which led into the town, and had at once come to the well known clerical trysting place. He had been there by eleven o'clock, and had remained ever since. From time to time the medical men who had been called in came through from the deanery into the library, uttered little bulletins, and then returned. There was it appears very little hope of the old man's rallying, indeed no hope of any thing like a final recovery. The only question was whether he must die at once speechles3, unconscious, stricken to death by his first heavy fit; or whether by due aid of medical skill he might not be so far brought back to this world as to become conscious of his state, and enabled to address one prayer to his Maker before he-was called to meet Him face to face at the judgment seat.

Sir Omicron Pie had been sent for from London. That great man had shown himself a wonderful adept at keeping life still moving within an old man's heart in the case of good old Bishop Grantly, and it might be reasonably expected that he would be equally successful with a dean. In the mean time Dr. Fillgrave and Mr. Eereehild were doing their best; and poor Miss Trefoil sat at the head of her father's bed, longing, as in such cases daughters do long, to be allowed to do something to show her love; if it were only to chafe his feet with her hands, or wait in menial offices on those autocratic doctors; anything so that now in the time of need she might be of use.

The archdeacon alone of the attendant clergy had been admitted for a moment into the sick man's chamber. He had crept in with creaking shoes, had said with smothered voice a word of consolation to the sorrowing daughter, had looked on the distorted face of his old friend with solemn but yet eager scrutinising eye, as though he said in his heart " and so some day it will probably be with me;" and then, having whispered an unmeaning word or two to the doctors, had creaked his way back again into the library.

"He'll never speak again, I fear," said the archdeacon as he noiselessly closed the door, as though the unconscious dying man, from whom all sense had fled, would have heard in his distant chamber the spring of the lock which was now so carefully handled.

"Indeed! indeed! is he so bad?" said the meagre little prebendary, turning over in his own mind all the probable candidates for the deanery, and wondering whether the archdeacon would think it worth his while to accept it. "The fit must have been very violent." "When a man over seventy has a stroke of apoplexy it seldom comes very lightly," said the burly chancellor.

"He was an excellent, sweet-tempered man," said one of the vicars choral. "Heaven knows how we shall repair his loss."

"He was indeed, said a minor canon; "and a great blessing to all those privileged to take a share of the services of our cathedral. I suppose the government will appoint, Mr. Archdeacon. I trust we may have no stranger."

"We will not talk about his successor," said the archdeacon, "while there is yet hope."

"Oh no, of course not," said the minor canon. "It would be exceedingly indecorous! but"

"I know of no man," said the meagre little prebendary, "who has better interest with the present government than Mr. Slope."

"Mr. Slope!" said two or three at once almost sotto voice. "Mr. Slope dean of Barchester!"

"Pooh!" exclaimed the burly chancellor.

"The bishop would do anything for him," said the little prebendary.

"And so would Mrs. Proudie," said the vicar choral.

"Pooh!" said the chancellor.

The archdeacon had almost turned pale at the idea. What if Mr. Slope should become dean of Barchester? To be sure there was no adequate ground, indeed no ground at all, for presuming that such a desecration could even be contemplated. But nevertheless it was on the cards. Dr. Proudie had interest with the government, and the man carried as it were Dr. Proudie in his pocket. How should they all conduct themselves if Mr. Slope were to become dean of Barchester? The bare idea for a moment struck even Dr. Grantly dumb.

"It would certainly not be very pleasant for us to have Mr. Slope at the deanery," said the little prebendary, chuckling inwardly at the evident consternation which his surmise had created.

'' About as pleasant and as probable as having you in the palace," said the chancellor.

"I should think such an appointment highly improbable," said the minor canon, "and, moreover, extremely inju-dicious. Should not you, Mr. Archdeacon?"

"I should presume such a thing to be quite out of the question," said the archdeacon; "but at the present moment I am thinking rather of our poor friend who is lying so near us than of Mr. Slope."

"Of course, of course," said the vicar choral with a very solemn air; "of course you are. So are we all. Poor Dr. Trefoil; the best of men, but"

"It's the most comfortable dean's residence in England," said a second prebendary. "Fifteen acres in the grounds. It is better than many of the bishops' palaces."

"And full two thousand a year," said the meagre doctor.

"It is cut down to 1,200?." said the chancellor.

"No," said the second prebendary. "It is to be fifteen. A special case was made."

"No such thing," said the chancellor.

"You '11 find I'm right," said the prebendary.

'/1'm sure I read it in the report," said the minor canon.

"Nonsense," said the chancellor. "They couldn't do it. There were to be no exceptions but London and Durham. "

"And Canterbury and York," said the vicar choral, modestly.

"What do you say, Grantly?" said the meagre little doctor.

"Say about what?" said the archdeacon, who had been looking as though he were thinking about his friend the dean, but who had in reality been thinking about Mr. Slope.

"What is the next dean to have, twelve or fifteen?"

"Twelve," said the archdeacon authoritatively, thereby putting an end at once to all doubt and dispute among his subordinates as far as that subject was concerned.

"Well, I certainly thought it was fifteen," said the minor canon.

"Pooh!" said the burly chancellor. At this moment the door opened, and in came Dr. Fillgrave.

"How is he?" "Is he conscious?" "Can

he speak?" "I hope not dead?" "No worse news, doctor, I trust?" "I hope, I trust, something better, doctor?" said half a dozen voices all at once, each in a tone of extremest anxiety. It was pleasant to see how popular the good old dean was among his clergy.

"No change, gentlemen; not the slightest change;—but a telegraphic message has arrived;—Sir Omicron Pie will be here by the 9.15 P.m. train. If any man can do anything Sir Omicron Pie will do it. But all that skill can do has been done."

"We are sure of that, Dr. Fillgrave," said the archdeacon; "we are quite sure of that. But yet you know"

"Oh! quite right," said the doctor, "quite right. I should have done just the same. I advised it at once. I said to Rerechild at once that with such a life and such a man, Sir Omicron should be summoned;—of course I knew expense was nothing;—so distinguished, you know, and so popular. Nevertheless, all that human skill can do has been done."

Just at this period Mrs. Grantly's carriage drove into the close, and the archdeacon went down to confirm the news which she had heard before.

By the 9.15 P.m. train Sir Omicron Pie did arrive. And in the course of the night a sort of consciousness returned to the poor old dean. Whether this was due to Sir Omicron Pie is a question on which it may be well not to offer an opinion. Dr. Fillgrave was very clear in his own mind, but Sir Omicron himself is thought to have differed from that learned doctor. At any rate Sir Omicron expressed an opinion that the dean had yet some days to live.

For the eight or ten next days, accordingly, the poor dean remained in the same state, half conscious and half comatose, and the attendant clergy began to think that no new appointment would be necessary for some few months to come.

CHAPTER XXXII.

A NEW CANDIDATE FOR ECCLESIASTICAL HONOURS.

The dean's illness occasioned much mental turmoil in other placos besides the deanery and adjoining library; and the idea which occurred to the meagre little prebendary about Mr. Slope did not occur to him alone.

The bishop was sitting listlessly in his study when the news reached him of the dean's illness. It was brought to him by Mr. Slope, who of course was not the last person in Barchester to hear it. It was also not slow in finding its way to Mrs. Proudie's ears. It may be presumed that there was not just then much friendly intercourse between these two rival claimants for his lordship's obedience. Indeed, though living in the same house, they had not met since the stormy interview between them in the bishop's study on the preceding day.

On that occasion Mrs. Proudie had been defeated. That the prestige of continual victory should have been torn from her standards was a subject of great sorrow to that militant lady; but though defeated, she was not overcome. She felt that she might yet recover her lost ground, that she might yet hurl Mr. Slope down to the dust from which she had picked him, and force her sinning lord to sue for pardon in sackcloth and ashes.

On that memorable day, memorable for his mutiny and rebellion against her high behests, he had carried his way with a high hand, and had really begun to think it possible that the days of his slavery were counted. He had begun to hope that he was now about to enter into a free land, a land delicious with milk which he himself might quaff, and honey which would not tantalise him by being only honey to the eye. When Mrs. Proudie banged the door, as she left his room, he felt himself every inch a bishop. To be sure his spirit had been a little cowed by his chaplain's subsequent lecture; but on the whole he was highly pleased with himself, and flattered himself that the worst was over. "Ce n'est que le premier pas qui coute," he reflected; and now that the first step had been so magnanimously taken all the rest would follow easily.

He met his wife as a matter of course at dinner where little or nothing was said that could ruffle the bishop's happiness. His daughters and the servants were present and protected him.

He made one or two trifling remarks on the subject of his projected visit to the archbishop, in order to show to all concerned that he intended to have his own way; and the very servants perceiving the change transferred a little of their reverence from their mistress to their master. All which the master perceived; and so also did the mistress. But Mrs. Proudie bided her time.

After dinner he returned to his study where Mr. Slope soon found him, and there they had tea together and planned many things. For some few minutes the bishop was really happy; but as the clock on the chimney piece warned him that the stilly hours of night were drawing on, as he looked at his chamber candlestick and knew that he must use it, his heart sank within him again. He was as a ghost all whose power of wandering free through these upper regions ceases at cock-crow; or rather he was the opposite of the ghost, for till cock-crow he must again be a serf. And would that be all? Could he trust himself to come down to breakfast a free man in the morning?

He was nearly an hour later than usual, when he betook himself to his rest. Eest! what rest? However, he took a couple of glasses of sherry, and mounted the stairs. Par be it from us to follow him thither. There are some things which no novelist, no historian, should attempt;—some few scenes in life's drama which even no poet should dare to paint. Let that which passed between Dr. Proudie and his wife on this night be understood to be among them.

Ha came down the following morning a sad and thoughtful man. He was attenuated in appearance;—one might almost say emaciated. I doubt whether his now grizzled locks had not palpably become more grey than on the preceding evening. At any rate he had aged materially. Years do not make a man old gradually and at an even pace. Look through the world and see if this is not so always, except in those rare cases in which the human being lives and dies without joys and without sorrows, like a vegetable. A man shall be possessed of florid youthful blooming health till, it matters not what age; thirty,—forty,—fifty. Then comes some nipping frost, some period of agony, that robs the fibres of the body of their succulence, and the hale and hearty man is counted among the old.

He came down and breakfasted alone. Mrs. Proudie being indisposed took her coffee in her bed-room, and her daughters waited upon her there. He ate his breakfast alone, and then, hardly knowing what he did, he betook himself to his usual seat in his study. He tried to solace himself with his coming visit to the archbishop. That effort of his own free will at any rate remained to him as an enduring triumph. But somehow, now that he had achieved it, he did not seem to care so much about it. It was his ambition that had prompted him to take his place at the archiepiscopal table, and his ambition was now quite dead within him.

He was thus seated when Mr. Slope made his appearance, with breathless impatience.

"My lord, the dean is dead."

"Good heavens!" exclaimed the bishop, startled out of his apathy by an announcement so sad and so sudden.

"He is either dead or now dying. He has had an apoplectic fit, and I am told that there is not the slightest hope. Indeed, I do not doubt that by this time he is no more."

Bells were rung, and servants were immediately sent to inquire. In the sourse of the morning, the bishop, leaning on his chaplain's arm, himself called at the deanery door. Mrs. Proudie sent to Miss Trefoil all manner of offers of assistance. The Miss Proudies sent also, and there was immense sympathy between the palace and the deanery. The answer to all inquiries was unvaried. The dean was just the same; and Sir Omicron Pie was expected down by the 9.15 P.m. train.

And then Mr. Slope began to meditate, as others also had done, as to who might possibly be the new dean; and it occurred to him as it had also occurred to others, that it might be pos-

sible that he should be the new dean himself. And then the question as to the twelve hundred, or fifteen hundred, or two thousand, ran in his mind, *ep* it had run through those of the other clergymen in the cathedral library.

Whether it might be two thousand, or fifteen, or twelve hundred, it would in any case undoubtedly be a great thing for him, if he could get it. The gratification to his ambition would be greater even than that of his covetousness. How glorious to out-top the archdeacon in his own cathedral city; to sit above prebendaries and canons, and have the cathedral pulpit and all the cathedral services altogether at his own disposal!

But it might be easier to wish for this than to obtain it. Mr. Slope, however, was not without some means of forwarding his views, and he at any rate did not let the grass grow under his feet. In the first place he thought,—and not vainly,—that he could count upon what assistance the bishop could give him. He immediately changed his views with regard to his patron; he made up his mind that if he became dean, he would hand his lordship back again to his wife's vassalage; and he thought it possible that his lordship might not be sorry to rid himself of one of his mentors. Mr. Slope had also taken some steps towards making his name known to other men in power. There was a certain chief-commissioner of national schools who at the present moment was presumed to stand especially high in the good graces of the government big wigs, and with him Mr. Slope had contrived to establish a sort of epistolary intimacy. He thought that he might safely apply to Sir Nicholas Fitzwhiggin; and he felt sure that if Sir Nicholas chose to exert himself, the promise of such a piece of preferment would be had for the asking for.

Then he also had the press at his bidding, or flattered himself that he had so. The daily Jupiter had taken his part in a verythorough manner in those polemical contests of his with Mr. Arabin. He had on more than one occasion absolutely had an interview with a gentleman on the staff of that paper, who, if

not the editor, was as good as the editor; and had long been in the habit of writing telling letters on all maimer of ecclesiastical abuses, which he signed with his initials, and sent to his editorial friend with private notes signed in his own name. Indeed, he and Mr. Towers,—such was the name of the powerful gentleman of the press with whom he was connected,—were generally very amiable with each other. Mr. Slope's little productions were always printed and occasionally commented upon; and thus, in a small sort of way, he had become a literary celebrity. This public life had great charms for him, though it certainly also had its drawbacks. On one occasion, when speaking in the presence of reporters, he had failed to uphold and praise and swear by that special line of conduct which had been upheld and praised and sworn by in the Jupiter, and then he had been much surprised and at the moment not a little irritated to find himself lacerated most unmercifully by his old ally. He was quizzed and bespattered and made a fool of, just as though, or rather worse than if, he had been a constant enemy instead of a constant friend. He had hitherto not learnt that a man who aspires to be on the staff of the Jupiter must surrender all individuality. But ultimately this little castigation had broken no bones between him and his friend Mr. Towers. Mr. Slope was one of those who understood the world too well to show himself angry with such a potentate as the Jupiter. He had kissed the rod that scourged him, and now thought that he might fairly look for his reward. He determined that he would at once let Mr. Towers know that he was a candidate for the place which was about to become vacant. More than voi. n. M one piece of preferment had lately been given away much in accordance with advice tendered to the government in the columns of the Jupiter.

But it was incumbent on Mr. Slope first to secure the bishop. Tie specially felt that it behoved him to do this before the visit to the archbishop was made. It was really quite providential that the dean should have fallen ill just at the very nick of time. If Dr. Proudie could be instigated to take the matter up warmly, he might manage a good deal while staying at the archbishop's palace. Feeling this very strongly Mr. Slope determined to sound the bishop that very afternoon He was to start on the following morning to London, and therefore not a moment could be lost with safety.

He went into the bishop's study about five o'clock and found him still sitting alone. It might have been supposed that he had hardly moved since the little excitement occasioned by his walk to the dean's door. He still wore on his face that dull dead look of half unconscious suffering. He was doing nothing, reading nothing, thinking of nothing, but simply gazing on vacancy when Mr. Slope for the second time that day entered his room.

"Well, Slope," said he, somewhat impatiently; for, to tell the truth, he was not anxious just at present to have much conversation with Mr. Slope.

"Your lordship will be sorry to hear that as yet the poor dean has shown no sign of amendment."

"Oh,—ah,—hasn't he? Poor man! I'm sure I'm very sorry. I suppose Sir Omicron has not arrived yet?"

"No; not till the 9.15 P.m. train."

"I wonder they didn't have a special. They say Dr. Trefoil is very rich."

"Very rich, I believe," said Mr. Slope. "But the truth is all the doctors in London can do no good;—no other good than to show that every possible care has been taken. Poor Dr. Trefoil is not long for this world, my lord."

"I suppose not;—I suppose not."

"Oh no; indeed, his best friends could not wish that he should outlive such a shock, for his intellects cannot possibly survive it." "Poor man! poor man!" said the bishop.

"It will naturally be a matter of much moment to your lordship who is to succeed him," said Mr. Slope. "It would be a great thing if you could secure the appointment for some person of your own way of thinking on important points. The party hostile to us are very strong here in Barchester;—much too strong."

"Yes, yes. If poor Dr. Trefoil is to go, it will be a great thing to get a good man in his place."

"It will be everything to your lordship to get a man on whose co-operation you can reckon. Only think what trouble we might have if Dr. Grantly, or Dr. Hyandry, or any of that way of thinking, were to get it."

"It is not very probable that Lord will give it to any of that school. Why should he?"

"No. Not probable; certainly not; but it's possible. Great interest will probably be made. If I might venture to advise your lordship, I would suggest that you should discuss the matter with his grace next week. I have no doubt that your wishes, if made known and backed by his grace, would be paramount with Lord."

"Well, I don't know that; Lord has always been very kind to me, very kind. But I am unwilling to interfere in such matters unless asked. And indeed, if asked, I don't know whom, at this moment, I should recommend."

Mr. Slope, even Mr. Slope, felt at the present rather abashed. He hardly knew how to frame his little request in language sufficiently modest. He had recognised and acknowledged to himself the necessity of shocking the bishop in the first instance by the temerity of his application, and his difficulty was how best to remedy that by his adroitness and eloquence. "I doubted myself," said he, "whether your lordship would have any one immediately in your eye, and it is on this account that I venture to submit to you an idea that I have been turning over in my own mind If poor Dr. Trefoil must go, I really do not see why, with your lordship's assistance, I should not hold the preferment myself."

"You!" exclaimed the bishop, in a manner that Mr. Slope could hardly have considered complimentary.

The ice was now broken, and Mr. Slope became fluent enough. "I have been thinking of looking for it. If your lordship will press the matter on the archbishop, I do not doubt but I shall succeed. You see I shall be the first to move, which is a great matter. Then I

can count upon assistance from the public press. My name is known, I may say, somewhat favourably known to that portion of the press which is now most influential with the government, and I have friends also in the government. But, nevertheless, it is to you, my lord, that I look for assistance. It is from your hands that I would most willingly receive the benefit. And, which should ever be the chief consideration in such matters, you must know better than any other person whatsoever what qualifications I possess."

The bishop sat for a while dumbfounded. Mr. Slope dean of Barchester! The idea of such a transformation of character would never have occurred to his own unaided intellect. At first he went on thinking why, for what reasons, on what account, Mr. Slope should be dean of Barchester. But by degrees the direction of his thoughts changod, and he began to think why, for what reasons, on what account, Mr. Slope should not be dean of Barchester As far as he himself, the bishop, was concerned, he could well spare the services of his chaplain. That little idea of using Mr. Slope as a counterpoise to his wife had well nigh evaporated. He had all but acknowledged the futility of the scheme. If indeed he could have slept in his chaplain's bed-room instead of his wife's, there might have been something in it. But. And thus as

Mr. Slope was speaking, the bishop began to recognise the idea that that gentleman might become dean of Barchester without impropriety;—not moved, indeed, by Mr. Slope's eloquence, for he did not follow the tenor of his speech; but led thereto by his own cogitations.

"I need not say," continued Mr. Slope, "that it would be my chief desire to act in all matters connected with the cathedral as far as possible in accordance with your views. I know your lordship so well,—and I hope you know me well enough to have the same feelings,—that I am satisfied that my being in that position would add materially to your own comfort and enable you to extend the sphere of your useful influence. As I said before, it is most desirable that there should be but one opinion among the dignitaries of the same diocese. I doubt much whether I would accept such an appointment in any diocese in which I should be constrained to differ much from the bishop. In this case there would be a delightful uniformity of opinion."

Mr. Slope perfectly well perceived that the bishop did not follow a word that he said, but nevertheless he went on talking. He knew it was necessary that Dr. Proudie should recover from his surprise, and he knew also that he must give him the opportunity of appearing to have been persuaded by argument. So he went on, and produced a multitude of fitting reasons all tending to show that no one on earth could make so good a dean of Barchester as himself, that the government and the public would assuredly coincide in desiring that he, Mr. Slope, should be dean of Barchester; but that for high considerations of ecclesiastical polity it would be especially desirable that this piece of preferment should be so bestowed through the instrumentality of the bishop of the diocese.

"But I really don't know what I could do in the matter," said the bishop.

'' If you would mention it to the archbishop; if you could tell his grace that you consider such an appointment very desirable; that you have it much at heart with a view to putting an end to schism in the diocese; if you did this with your usual energy, you would probably find no difficulty in inducing his grace to promise that he would mention it to Lord. Of course you would let the archbishop know that I am not looking for the preferment solely through his intervention; that you do not exactly require him to ask it as a favour; that you expect that I shall get it through other sources,—as is indeed the case; but that you are very anxious that his grace should express his approval of such an arrangement to Lord."

It ended in the bishop promising to do as he was bid. Not that he so promised without a stipulation. "About that hospital," he said, in the middle of the con-

ference. "I was never so troubled in my life;" which was about the truth. "You haven't spoken to Mr. Harding since I saw you?"

Mr. Slope assured his patron that he had not.

"Ah well, then;—I think upon the whole it will be better to let Quiverful have it. It has been half promised to him, and he has a large family and is very poor. I think on the whole it will be better to make out the nomination for Mr. Quiverful."

"But, my lord," said Mr. Slope, still thinking that he was bound to make a fight for his own view on this matter, and remembering that it still behoved him to maintain his lately acquired supremacy over Mrs. Proudie, lest he should fail in his views regarding the deanery,—" but, my lord, I am really much afraid"

"Remember, Mr. Slope," said the bishop, "lean hold out no sort of hope to you in this matter of succeeding poor Dr. Trefoil. I will certainly speak to the archbishop, as you wish it, but I cannot think."

"Well, my lord," said Mr. Slope, fully understanding the bishop, and in his turn interrupting him, "perhaps your lordship is right about Mr. Quiverful. I have no doubt I can easily arrange matters with Mr. Harding, and I will make out the nomination for your signature as you direct."

'"Yes, Slope, I think that will be best; and you may be sure that any little I can do to forward your views shall be done. " And so they parted.

Mr. Slope had now much business on his hands. He had to make his daily visit to the Signora. This common prudence should have now induced him to omit, but he was infatuated; and could not bring himself to be commonly prudent. He determined therefore that he would drink tea at the Stanhopes'; and he determined also, or thought that he determined, that having done so he would go thither no more. He had also to arrange his matters with Mrs. Bold. He was of opinion that Eleanor would grace the deanery as perfectly as she would the chaplain's cottage; and he thought'

moreover, that Eleanor's fortune would excellently repair any dilapidations, and also curtailments in the dean's stipend which might have been made by that ruthless ecclesiastical commission.

Touching Mrs. Bold his hopes now soared high. Mr. Slope was one of that numerous multitude of swains who think that all is fair in love, and he had accordingly not refrained from using the services of Mrs. Bold's own maid. From her he had learnt much of what had taken place at Plumstead; not exactly with truth, for "the own maid" had not been able to divine the exact truth, but with some sort of similitude to it. He had been told that the archdeacon and Mrs. Grantly and Mr. Harding and Mr. Arabin had all quarrelled with "missus" for having received a letter from Mr. Slope; that "missus" had positively refused to give the letter up; that she had received from the archdeacon the option of giving up either Mr. Slope and his letter, or else the society of Plumstead rectory; and that "missus" had declared with much indignation, that "she didn't care a straw for the society of Plumstead rectory," and that she wouldn't give up Mr. Slope for any of them.

Considering the source from whence this came it was not quite so untrue as might have been expected. It showed pretty plainly what had been the nature of the conversation in the servants' hall; and coupled as it was with the certainty of Eleanor's sudden return, it appeared to Mr. Slope to be so far worthy of credit as to justify him in thinking that the fair widow would in all human probability accept bis offer.

All this work was therefore to be done. It was desirable he thought that he should make his offer before it was known that Mr. Quiverful was finally appointed to the hospital. In his letter to Eleanor he had plainly declared that Mr. Harding was to have the appointment. It would be very difficult to explain this away; and were he to write another letter to Eleanor, telling the truth and throwing the blame on the bishop, it would naturally injure him in her estimation. He determined therefore to let that matter disclose itself as it would, and to lose no time in throwing himself at her feet.

Then he had to solicit the assistance of Sir Nicholas Fitzwhiggin and Mr. Towers, and he went directly from the bishop's presence to compose his letters to those gentlemen. As Mr. Slope was esteemed an adopt at letter writing, they shall be given in full.

"(Private.) "Palace, Barchester, Sept. 185—.

"My dear Sir Nicholas,—I hope that the intercourse which has been between us will preclude you from regarding my present application as an intrusion. You cannot I imagine have yet heard that poor dear old Dr. Trefoil has been seized with apoplexy. It is a subject of profound grief to every one in Barchester, for he has always been an excellent man;—excellent as a man and as a clergyman. He is, however, full of years, and his life could not under any circumstances iave been much longer spared. You may probably have known him.

"There is, it appears, no probable chance of his recovery. Sir Omicron Pie is, I believe, at present with him. At any rate the medical men here have declared that one or two days more must limit the tether of his mortal coil. I sincerely trust that his soul may wing its flight to that haven where it may for ever be at rest and for ever be happy.

"The bishop has been speaking to me about the preferment, and he is anxious that it should be conferred on me. I confess that I can hardly venture, at my age, to look for such advancement; but I am so far encouraged by his lordship, that I believe I shall be induced to do so. His lordship goes to to-morrow, and is intent on mentioning the subject to the archbishop.

"I know well how deservedly great is your weight with the present government. In any matter touching church preferment you would of course be listened to. Now that the matter has been put into my head, I am of course anxious to be successful. If you can assist me by your good word, you will confer on me one additional favour.

"I had better add, that Lord cannot as yet know of this piece of preferment

having fallen in, or rather of its certainty of falling; for poor dear Dr. Trefoil is past hope. Should Lord first hear it from you, that might probably be thought to give you a fair claim to express your opinion.

"Of course our grand object is that we should all be of one opinion in church matters. This is most desirable at Barchester; it is this that makes our good bishop so anxious about it. You may probably think it expedient to point this out to Lord if it shall be in your powerto oblige me by mentioning the subject to his lordship.

"Believe me, my dear Sir Nicholas,
"Your most faithful servant,
"obadiah Slope."

His letter to Mr. Towers was written in quite a different strain. Mr. Slope conceived that he completely understood the difference in character and position of the two men whom he addressed. He knew that for such a man as Sir Nicholas Fitzwhiggin a little flummery was necessary, and that it might be of the easy everyday description. Accordingly his letter to Sir Nicholas was written currente calamo, with very little trouble. But to such a man as Mr. Towers it was not so easy to write a letter that should be effective and yet not offensive, that should carry its point without undue interference. It was not difficult to flatter Dr. Proudie or Sir Nicholas Fitzwhiggin, but very difficult to flatter Mr. Towers without letting the flattery declare itself. This, however, had to be done. Moreover, this letter must, in appearance at least, be written without effort, and be fluent, unconstrained, and demonstrative of no doubt or fear on the part of the writer. Therefore the epistle to Mr. Towers was studied, and recopied, and elaborated at the cost of so many minutes, that Mr. Slope had hardly time to dress himself and reach Dr. Stanhope's that evening. When despatched it ran as follows j—

"Private. "Barchester. Sept. 185—."

He purposely omitted any allusion to the "palace," thinking that Mr. Towers might not like it. A great man, he remembered, had been once much condemned for dating a letter from Windsor

Castle.

"My dear Sir,—We were all a good deal shocked here this morning by hearing that poor old Dean Trefoil had been stricken with apoplexy. The fit took him about 9 A.m. I am writing now to save the post, and he is still alive, but past all hope, or possibility I believe, of living. Sir Omicron Pie is here, or will be very shortly; but all that even Sir Omicron can do, is to ratify the sentence of his less distinguished brethren that nothing can be done. Poor Dr. Trefoil's race on this side the grave is run. I do not know whether you knew him. He was a good, quiet, charitable man of the old school of course,—as any clergyman over seventy years of age must necessarily be.

"But I do not write merely with the object of sending you such news as this; doubtless some one of your Mercuries will have seen and heard and reported so much; I write, as you usually do yourself, rather with a view to the future than to the past.

"Rumour is already rife here as to Dr. Trefoil's successor, and among those named as possible future deans your humble servant is, I believe, not the least frequently spoken of. In short I am looking for the preferment. You may probably know that since Bishop Proudie came to this diocese I have exerted myself here a good deal; and I may certainly say not without some success. He and I are nearly always of the same opinion on points of doctrine as well as church discipline, and therefore I have had, as his confidential chaplain, very much in my own hands; but I confess to you that I have a higher ambition than to remain the chaplain of any bishop.

"There are no positions in which more energy is now needed than those of our deans. The whole of our enormous cathedral establishments have been allowed to go to sleep,—nay, they are all but dead, and ready for the sepulchre! And yet of what prodigious moment they might be made, if, as was intended, they were so managed as to lead the way and show an example for all our parochial clergy!

"The bishop here is most anxious for

my success. Indeed, he goes to-morrow to press the matter on the archbishop. I believe also I may count on the support of at least one most effective member of the government. But I confess that the support of the Jupiter, if I be thought worthy of it, would be more gratifying to me than any other; more gratifying if by it I should be successful; —and more gratifying also, if, although so support-ed, I should be unsuccessful.

"The time has, in fact, come in which no government can venture to fill up the high places of the Church in defian-ce of the public press. The age of ho-nourable bishops and noble deans has gone by; and any clergyman, however humbly born, can now hope for success, if his industry, talent, and character be Sufficient to call forth the manifest opinion of the public in his favour.

"At the present moment we all feel that any counsel given in such matters by the Jupiter has the greatest weight;— is, indeed, generally followed; and we feel also,—I am speaking of clergymen of my own age and standing,—that it should be so. There can be no patron less interested than the Jupiter, and none that more thoroughly understands the wants of the people.

"I am sure you will not suspect me of asking from you any support which the paper with which you are connected cannot conscientiously give me. My ob-ject in writing is to let you know that I am a candidate for the appointment. It is for you to judge whether or no you can assist my views. I should not, of course, have written to you on such a matter had I not believed,—and I have had good reason so to believe,—that the Jupiter approves of my views on ecclesiastical polity.

"The bishop expresses a fear that I may be considered too young for such a sta-tion, my age being thirty-six. I cannot think that at the present day any hesita-tion need be felt on such a point. The public has lost its love for antiquated servants. If a man will ever be fit to do good work he will be fit at thirty-six years of age.

"Believe me very faithfully yours,

"Obadiah Slope.

"T. Towers, Esq..
"Court,
"Middle Temple."

Having thus exerted himself, Mr. Slope posted his letters, and passed the remainder of the evening at the feet of his mistress.

Mr. Slope will be accused of deceit in his mode of canvassing. It will be said that he lied in the application he made to each of his three patrons. I believe it must be owned that he did so. He could not hesitate on account of his youth, and yet be quite assured that he was not too young. He could not count chiefly on the bishop's support, and chiefly also on that of the newspaper. He did not think that the bishop was going to to press the matter on the archbishop. It must be owned that in his canvassing Mr. Slope was as false as he well could be.

Let it, however, be asked of those who are conversant with such matters, whether he was more false than men usually are on such occasions. We Eng-lish gentlemen hate the name of a lie; but how often do we find public men who believe each other's words?

CHAPTER XXXIII. MRS. PROUDIE VIC-TRIX.

The next week passed over at Barches-ter with much apparent tranquillity. The hearts, however, of some of the inhabi-tants were not so tranquil as the streets of the city. The poor old dean still con-tinued to live, just as Sir Omicron Pie had prophesied that he would do, much to the amazement, and some thought disgust, of Dr. Fillgrave. The bishop still remained away. He had stayed a day or two in town, and had also re-mained longer at the archbishop's than he had intended. Mr. Slope had as yet received no line in answer to either of his letters; but he had learnt the cause of this. Sir Nicholas was stalking a deer, or attending the Queen, in the Highlands; and even the indefatigable Mr. Towers had stolen an autumn holiday and had made one of the yearly tribe who now ascend Mont Blanc. Mr. Slope learnt that he was not expected back till the last day of September.

Mrs. Bold was thrown much with the Stanhopes of whom she became fonder

and fonder. If asked, she would have said that Charlotte Stanhope was her es-pecial friend, and so she would have thought. But, to tell the truth, she liked Bertie nearly as well. She had no more idea of regarding him as a lover than she would have had of looking at a big tame dog in such a light. Bertie had become very intimate with her, and made little speeches to her, and said little things of a sort very different from the speeches and sayings of other men. But then this was almost always done before his sis-ters; and he, with his long silken beard, his light blue eyes and strange dress, was so unlike other men! She adtnitted him to a kind of familiarity which she had never known with any one else, and of which she by no means understood the danger. She blushed once at finding that she had called him Bertie, and on the same day only barely remembered her position in time to check herself from playing upon him some personal practical joke to which she was instigat-ed by Charlotte.

In all this Eleanor was perfectly ir no-cent, and Bertie Stanhope could hard-ly be called guilty. But every familiarity into which Eleanor was entrapped was deliberately planned by his sister. She knew well how to play her game, and played it without mercy; she knew, none so well, what was her brother's character, and she would have handed over to him the young widow, and the young widow's money, and the money of the widow's child, without remorse. With her pretended friendship and warm cordiality, she strove to connect Eleanor so closely with her brother as to make it impossible that she should go back even if she wished it. But Char-lotte Stanhope knew really nothing of Eleanor's character; did not even under-stand that there were such characters. She did not comprehend that a young and pretty woman could be playful and familiar with a man such as Bertie Stan-hope, and yet have no idea in her head, no feeling in her heart, that she would have been ashamed to own to all the world. Charlotte Stanhope did not in the least conceive that her new friend was a woman whom nothing could entrap into an inconsiderate marriage, whose mind would have revolted from the slightest impropriety had she been aware that any impropriety existed.

Miss Stanhope, however, had tact enough to make herself and her father's house very agreeable to Mrs. Bold. There was with them all an absence of stiffness and formality which was peculiarly agreeable to Eleanor after the great dose of clerical arrogance which she had lately been constrained to take. She played chess with them, walked with them, and drank tea with them; studied or pretended to study astronomy; assisted them in writing stories in rhyme, in turning prose tragedy into comic verse, or comic stories into would-be tragic poetry. She had no idea before that she had any such talents. She had not conceived the possibility of her doing such things as she now did. She found with the Stanhopes new amusements and employments, new pursuits, which in themselves could not be wrong, and which were exceedingly alluring.

Is it not a pity that people who are bright and clever should so often be exceedingly improper? and that those who are never improper should so often be dull and heavy? Now Charlotte Stanhope was always bright, and never heavy;—but then her propriety was doubtful.

But during all this time Eleanor by no means forgot Mr. Arabin, nor did she forget Mr. Slope. She had parted from Mr Arabin in her anger. She was still angry at what she regarded as his impertinent interference; but nevertheless she looked forward to meeting him again, and also looked forward to forgiving him. The words that Mr. Arabin had uttered still sounded in her ears. She knew that if not intended for a declaration of love, they did signify that he loved her; and she felt also that if he ever did make such a declaration it might be that she should not receive it unkindly. She was still angry with him, very angry with him; so angry that she would bite her lip and stamp her foot as she thought of what he had said and done. But nevertheless she yearned to

let him know that he was forgiven. All that she required was that he should own that he had sinned.

She was to meet him at Ullathorne on the last day of the present month. Miss Thorne had invited all the country round to a breakfast on the lawn. There were to be tents, and archery, and dancing for the ladies on the lawn, and for the swains and girls in the paddock. There were to be fiddlers and fifers, races for the boys, poles to be climbed, ditches full of water to be jumped over, horse-collars to be grinned through,—this latter amusement was an addition of the stewards, and not arranged by Miss Thorne in the original programme,— and every game to be played which, in a long course of reading, Miss Thorne could ascertain to have been played in the good days of Queen Elizabeth. Everything of more modern growth was to be tabooed, if possible. On one subject Miss Thorne was very unhappy. She had been turning in her mind the matter of a bull-ring, but could not succeed in making anything of it. She would not for the world have done, or allowed to be done, anything that was cruel. As to the promoting the torture of a bull for the amusement of her young neighbours, it need hardly be said that Miss Thorne would be the last to think of it. And yet there was something so charming in the name. A bullring, however, without a bull would only be a memento of the decadence of the times, and she felt herself constrained to abandon the idea. Quintains, however, she was determined to have, and had poles and swivels and bags of flour prepared accordingly. She would no doubt have been anxious for something small in the way of a tournament; but, as she said to her brother, that had been tried, and the age had proved itself too decidedly inferior to its fore-runners to admit of such a pastime. Mr. Thorne did not seem to participate much in her regret, feeling perhaps that a full suit of chain-armour would have added but little to his own personal comfort.

This party at Ullathorne had been planned in the first place as a sort of welcoming to Mr. Arabin on his en-

trance into St. Ewold's parsonage. An intended harvest-home gala for the labourers and their wives and children had subsequently been amalgamated with it, and thus it had grown to its present dimensions. All the Plumstead party had of course been asked, and at the time of the invitation Eleanor had intended to have gone with her sister. Now her plans were altered, and she was going with the Stanhopes. The Proudies were also to be there; and as Mr. Slope had not been included in the invitation to the palace, the Signora, whose impudence never deserted her, asked pemiission of Miss Thorne to bring him.

This permission Miss Thorne gave, having no other alternative; but she did so with a trembling heart, fearing Mr. Arabin would be offended. Immediately on his return she apologised, almost with tears;—so dire an enmity was presumed to range between the twc gentlemen. But Mr. Arabin comforted her by an assurance that he should meet Mr. Slope with the greatest pleasure imaginable, and made her promise that she would introduce them to each other.

But this triumph of Mr. Slope's was not so agreeable to Eleanor, who since her return to Barchester had done her best to avoid him. She would not give way to the Plumstead folk when they so ungenerously accused her of being in love with this odious man; but, nevertheless, knowing that she was so accused, she was fully alive to the expediency of keeping out of his way and dropping him by degrees. She had seen very little of him since her return. Her servent had been instructed to say to all visitors that she was out. She could not bring herself to specify Mr. Slope particularly, and in order to avoid him she had thus debarred herself from all her friends. She had excepted Charlotte Stanhope, and by degrees a few others also. Once she had met him at the Stanhopes'; but, as a rule, Mr. Slope's visits there were made in the morning, and hers in the evening. On that one occasion Charlotte had managed to preserve her from any annoyance. This was very good-natured on the part of Charlotte, as Eleanor thought, and also very sharp-witted, as Eleanor had told her friend nothing of her reasons for wishing to avoid that gentleman. The fact, however, was, that Charlotte had learnt from her sister that Mr. Slope would probably put himself forward as a suitor for the widow's hand, and she was consequently sufficiently alive to the expediency of guarding Bertie's future wife from any danger in that quarter.

Nevertheless the Stanhopes were pledged to take Mr. Slope with them to Ullathorne. An arrangement was therefore necessarily made, which was very disagreeable to Eleanor. Dr. Stanhope, with herself, Charlotte, and Mr. Slope, were to go together, and Bertie was to follow with his sister Madeline. It was clearly visible by Eleanor's face that this assortment was very disagreeable to her; and Charlotte, who was much encouraged thereby in her own little plan, made a thousand apologies.

"I see you don't like it, my dear," said she, "but we could not manage otherwise. Bertie would give his eyes to go with you, VOL. II. N but Madeline cannot possibly go without him. Nor could we possibly put Mr. Slope and Madeline in the same carriage without any one else. They'd both be ruined for ever, you know, and not admitted inside Ullathorne gates, I should imagine, after such an impropriety."

"Of course that wouldn't do," said Eleanor; "but couldn't I go in the carriage with the Signora and your brother?"

"Impossible!" said Charlotte. "When she is there, there is only room for two. " The Signora, in truth, did not care to do her travelling in the presence of strangers.

"Well, then," said Eleanor, "you are all so kind, Charlotte, and so good to me, that I am sure you won't be offended; but I think I 'll not go at all."

"Not go at all!—What nonsense!—indeed you shall." It had been absolutely determined in family council that Bertie should propose on that very occasion.

"Or I can take a fly," said Eleanor. "You know I am not embarrassed by so many difficulties as you young ladies. I can go alone."

"Nonsense! my dear. Don't think of such a thing; after all it is only for an hour or so; and, to tell the truth, I don't know what it is you dislike so. I thought you and Mr. Slope were great friends. What is it you dislike?"

"Oh! nothing particular," said Eleanor; "only I thought it would be a family party."

"Of course it would be much nicer, much more snug, if Bertie could go with us. It is he that is badly treated. I can assure you he is much more afraid of Mr. Slope than you are. But you see Madeline cannot go out without him,—and she, poor creature, goes out so seldom! I am sure you don't begrudge her this, though her vagary does knock about our own party a little."

Of course Eleanor made a thousand protestations, and uttered a thousand hopes that Madeline would enjoy herself. And of course she had to give way, and undertake to go in the carriage with Mr. Slope. In fact, she was driven either to do this, or to explain why she would not do so. Now she could not bring herself to explain to Charlotte Stanhope all that had passed at Plumstead.

But it was to her a sore necessity. She thought of a thousand little schemes for avoiding it; she would plead illness, and not go at all; she would persuade Mary Bold to go although not asked, and then make a necessity of having a carriage of her own to take her sister-in-law; anything, in fact, she could do, rather than be seen by Mr. Arabin getting out of the same carriage with Mr. Slope. However, when the momentous morning came she had no scheme matured, and then Mr. Slope handed her into Dr. Stanhope's carriage, and following her steps, sat opposite to her.

The bishop returned on the eve of the Ullathorne party, and was received at home with radiant smiles by the partner of all his cares. On his arrival he crept up to his dressing-room with somewhat of a palpitating heart. He had overstayed his allotted time by three days, and was not without much fear of penalties. Nothing, however, could be more affectionately cordial than the greeting he received. The girls came out and kissed him in a manner that was quite soothing to his spirit; and Mrs. Proudie, "albeit unused to the melting mood," squeezed him in her arms, and almost in words called him her dear, darling, good, pet, little bishop. All this was a very pleasant surprise.

Mrs. Proudie had somewhat changed her tactics;—not that she had seen any cause to disapprove of her former line of conduct, but she had now brought matters to such a point that she calculated that she might safely do so. She had got the better of Mr. Slope, and she now thought well to show her husband that when allowed to get the better of everybody, when obeyed by him and permitted to rule over others, she would take care that he should have his reward. Mr. Slope had not a chance against her. Not only could she stun the poor bishop by her midnight anger, but she could assuage and soothe him, if she so willed, by daily indulgences. She could furnish his room for him, turn him out as smart a bishop as any on the bench, give him good dinners, warm fires, and an easy life. All this she would do if he would but be quietly obedient. But if not,!To speak sooth, however, his suftermgs on tftai dreadful night had been so poignant, as to leave him little spirit for further rebellion.

As soon as he had dressed himself he returned to his room.

"I hope you enjoyed yourself at," said she, seating herself on one side of the fire while he remained in his arm-chair on the other, stroking the calves of his legs. It was the first time he had had a fire in his room since the summer, and it pleased him; for the good bishop loved to be warm and cozy. Yes, he said, he had enjoyed himself very much. Nothing could be more polite than the archbishop; and Mrs. Archbishop had been equally charming.

Mrs. Proudie was delighted to hear it. Nothing, she declared, pleased her so much as to think

"Her bairn respectit like the lave."

She did not put it precisely in these words, but what she said came to the same thing; and then having petted and fondled her little man sufficiently, she proceeded to business. "The poor dean is still alive," said she.

"So I hear; so I hear," said the bishop. "I'll go to the deanery directly after breakfast to-morrow."

"We are going to this party at Ullathorne to morrow morning, my dear; we must be there early, you know,—by twelve o'clock I suppose."

"Oh,—ah!" said the bishop; "then I'll certainly call the next day."

"Was much said about it at?" asked Mrs. Proudie.

"About what?" said the bishop.

"Pilling up the dean's place," said Mrs. Proudie. As she spoke a spark of the wonted fire returned to her eye, and the bishop felt himself to be a little less comfortable than before.

"Pilling up the dean's place,—that is, if the dean dies? Very little, my dear. It was mentioned, just mentioned."

"And what did you say about it, bishop?" "Why, I said that I thought that if, that is, should,—should the dean die, that is, I said I thought "As he went on stammering and floundering, he saw that his wife's eye was fixed sternly on him. Why should he encounter such evil for a man whom he loved so slightly as Mr. Slope? Why should he give up his enjoyments and his ease, and such dignity as might be allowed to him, to fight a losing battle for a chaplain? The chaplain after all, if successful, would be as great a tyrant as his wife. Why fight at all? why contend? why be uneasy? From that moment he determined to fling Mr. Slope to the winds, and take the goods the gods provided.

"I am told," said Mrs. Proudie, speaking very slowly, "that Mr. Slope is looking to be the new dean."

"Yes,—certainly, I believe he is," said the bishop.

"And what does the archbishop say about that?" asked Mrs. Proudie.

"Well, my dear, to tell the truth, I promised Mr. Slope to speak to the archbishop. Mr. Slope spoke to me about it. It is very arrogant of him, I must say,—but that is nothing to me."

"Arrogant!" said Mrs. Proudie. "It is

the most impudent piece of pretension I ever heard of in my life. Mr. Slope Dean of Barchester, indeed!" And what did you do in the matter, bishop?"

"Why, my dear, I did speak to the archbishop."

"You don't mean to tell me," said Mrs. Proudie, "that you are going to make yourself ridiculous by lending your name to such a preposterous attempt as this? Mr. Slope Dean of Barchester, indeed!" And she tossed her head, and put her arms a-kimbo, with an air of confident defiance that made her husband quite sure that Mr. Slope never would be Dean of Barchester. In truth, Mrs. Proudie was all but invincible. Had she married Petruchio, it may be doubted whether that arch wife-tamer would have been able to keep her legs out of those garments which are presumed by men to be peculiarly unfitted for feminine use.

"It is preposterous, my dear." "Then why have you endeavoured to assist him?"

"Why,—my dear, I haven't assisted him—much."

"But why have you done it at all? Why have you mixed your name up in anything so ridiculous? What was it you did say to the archbishop?"

"Why, I just did mention it. I just did say that,—that in the event of the poor dean's death, Mr. Slope would,—would"

"Would what?"

"I forget how I put it,—would take it if he could get it; something of that sort. I did'nt say much more than that."

" You shouldn't have said anything at all. And what did the archbishop say?"

"He did'nt say anything; he just bowed and rubbed his hands. Somebody else came up at that moment, and as we were discussing the new parochial universal school committee, the matter of the new dean dropped. After that I didn't think it wise to renew it."

"Eenew it! I am very sorry you ever mentioned it. What will the archbishop think of you?"

"You may be sure, my dear, the archbishop thought very little about it."

'' But why did you think about it, bishop? How could you think of making such a creature as that Dean of Barchester?—Dean of Barchester! I suppose he'll be looking for a bishopric some of these days,—a man that hardly knows who his own father was; a man that I found without bread to his mouth, or a coat to his back! Dean of Barchester, indeed! I'll dean him."

Mrs. Proudie considered herself to be in politics a pure Whig. All her family belonged to the Whig party. Now, among all ranks of Englishmen and Englishwomen—Mrs. Proudie should, I think, be ranked among the former, on the score of her great strength of mind,—no one is so hostile to lowly born pretenders to high station as the pure Whig.

The bishop thought it necessary to exculpate himself. "Why, my dear," said he, "it appeared to me that you and Mr. Slope did not get on quite so well as you used to do."

"Get on!" said Mrs. Proudie, moving her foot uneasily on the hearth-rug, and compressing her lips in a manner that betokened much danger to the subject of their discourse.

"I began to find that he was objectionable to you,"—Mrs. Proudie's foot worked on the hearth-rug with great rapidity,— "and that you would be more comfortable if he was out of the palace,"—Mrs. Proudie smiled, as a hyena may probably smile before he begins his laugh,—" and therefore I thought that if he got this place, and so ceased to be my chaplain, you might be pleased at such an arrangement."

And then the hyena laughed out. Pleased at such an arrangement! pleased at having her enemy converted into a dean with twelve hundred a year! Medea, when she describes the customs of her native country,—I am quoting from Eobson's edition,— assures her astonished auditor that in her land captives, when taken, are eaten. "You pardon them?" says Medea. "We do indeed," says the mild Grecian. "We eat them!" says she of Colchis, with terrific energy. Mrs. Proudie was the Medea of Barchester. She had no idea of not eating Mr. Slope. Pardon him! merely get rid of him! make a dean of him! It was not so they did with their captives in her country, among people of her sort! Mr. Slope had no such mercy to expect. She would pick him to the very last bone.

"Oh, yes, my dear, of course he'll cease to be your chaplain," said she. "After what has passed, that must be a matter of course. I couldn't for a moment think of living in the same house with such a man. Besides, he has shown himself quite unfit for such a situation;—making broils and quarrels among the clergy, getting you, my dear, into scrapes, and taking upon himself as though he were as good as bishop himself. Of course he'll go. But because he leaves the palace, that is no reason why he should get into the deanery."

"Oh, of course not!" said the bishop; "but to save appearances you know, my dear"

"I don't want to save appearances. I want Mr. Slope to appear just what he is,—a false, designing, mean, intriguing man. *J.* have my eye on him; he little knows what I see. He is misconducting himself in the most disgraceful way with that lame Italian woman. That family is a disgrace to Barchester, and Mr. Slope is a disgrace to Barchester! If he doesn't look well to it, he'll have his gown stripped off his back instead of having a dean's hat on his head. Dean, indeed! The man has gone mad with arrogance."

The bishop said nothing further to excuse either himself or his chaplain, and having shown himself passive and docile, was again taken into favour. They soon went to dinner, and he spent the pleasantest evening he had had in his own house for a long time. His daughter played and sang to him as he sipped his coffee and read his newspaper, and Mrs. Proudie asked good-natured little questions about the archbishop; and then he went happily to bed, and slept as quietly as though Mrs. Proudie had been Griselda herself. While shaving himself in the morning and preparing for the festivities of Ullathorne he fully resolved to run no more tilts against a warrior so fully armed at all

points as was Mrs. Proudie.

CHAPTER XXXIV. OXFORD—THE MASTER AND TUTOR OF LAZARUS.

Mr. Arabin, as we have said, had but a sad walk of it under the trees of Plumstead churchyard. He did not appear to any of the family till dinner time, and then he seemed, as far as their judgment went, to be quite himself. He had, as was his wont, asked himself a great many questions, and given himself a great many answers; and the upshot of this was that he had set himself down for an ass. He had determined that he was much too old and much too rusty to commence the manoeuvres of love-making; that he had let the time slip through his hands which should have been used for such purposes; and that now he must He on his bed as he had made it. Then he asked himself whether in truth he did love this woman; and he answered himself, not without a long struggle, but at last honestly, that he certainly did love her. He then asked himself whether he did not also love her money; and he again answered himself that he did so. But here he did not answer honestly. It was and ever had been his weakness to look for impure motives for his own conduct. No doubt, circumstanced as he was, with a small living and a fellowship, accustomed as he had been to collegiate luxuries and expensive comforts, he might have hesitated to marry a penniless woman had he felt ever so strong a predilection for the woman herself; no doubt Eleanor's fortune put all such difficulties out of the question; but it was equally without doubt that his love for her had crept upon him without the slightest idea on his part that he could ever benefit his own condition by sharing her wealth.

When he had stood on the hearth-rug, counting the pattern, and counting also the future chances of his own life, the remembrances of Mrs. Bold's comfortable income had not certainly damped his first assured feeling of love for her. And why should it have done so? Need it have done so with the purest of men? Be that as it may, Mr. Arabin decided against himself. He decided that it had done so in his case, and that he was not

the purest of men.

He also decided, which was more to his purpose, that Eleanor did not care a straw for him, and that very probably she did care a straw for his rival. Then he made up his mind not to think of her any more, and went on thinking of her till he was almost in a state to drown himself in the little brook which ran at the bottom of the archdeacon's grounds.

And ever and again his mind would revert to the Signora Neroni, and he would make comparisons between her and Eleanor Bold, not always in favour of the latter. The Signora had listened to him, and flattered him, and believed in him; at least she had told him so. Mrs. Bold had also listened to him, but had never flattered him; had not always believed in him; and now had broken from him in violent rage. The Signora, too, was the more lovely woman of the two, and had also the additional attraction of her affliction; —for to him it was an attraction.

But he never could have loved the Signora Neroni as he felt that he now loved Eleanor! Then he flung stones into the brook, instead of flinging in himself, and sat down on its margin as sad a gentleman as you shall meet in a summer's day.

He had heard the dinner-bell ring as he sat in the churchyard, and he knew that it was time to recover his self-possession. He felt that he was disgracing himself in his own eyes, that he had been idling his time and neglecting the high duties which he had taken upon himself to perform. He should have spent this afternoon among the poor at St. Ewold's, instead of wandering about at Plumstead, an ancient love-lorn swain, dejected and sighing, full of imaginary sorrows and Wertherian grief. He was thoroughly ashamed of himself, and determined to lose no time in retrieving *m* his character, so damaged in his own eyes. Thus when he appeared at dinner he was as animated as ever, and was the author of most of the conversation which graced the archdeacon's board on that evening. Mr. Harding was ill at ease and sick at heart, and did not care to appear more comfortable than he really was. "What little he did say was said to his daughter. He thought that the archdeacon and Mr. Arabia had leagued together against Eleanor's comfort; and his wish now was to break away from the pair, and undergo in his Barchester lodgings whatever Fate had in store for him. He hated the name of the hospital. His attempt to regain his lost inheritance there had brought upon him so much suffering. As far as he was concerned Mr. Quiverful was now welcome to the place.

And the archdeacon was not very lively. The poor dean's illness was of course discussed in the first place. Dr. Grantly did not mention Mr. Slope's name in connexion with the expected event of Dr. Trefoil's death; he did not wish to say anything about Mr. Slope just at present, nor did he wish to make known his sad surmises; but the idea that his enemy might possibly become Dean of Barchester made him very gloomy. Should such an event take place, such a dire catastrophe come about, there would be an end to his life as far as his life was connected with the city of Barchester. He must give up all his old haunts, all his old habits, and live quietly as a retired rector at Plumstead. It had been a severe trial for him to have Dr. Proudie in the palace;—but with Mr. Slope also in the deanery, he felt that he should be unable to draw his breath in Barchester close.

Thus it came to pass that in spite of the sorrow at his heart Mr. Arabin was apparently the gayest of the party. Both Mr. Harding and Mrs. Grantly were in a slight degree angry with him on account of his want of gloom. To the one it appeared as though he were triumphing at Eleanor's banishment, and to the other that he was not affected as he should have been by all the sad circumstances of the day, Eleanor's obstinacy, Mr. Slope's success, and the poor dean's apoplexy. And so they were all at cross purposes.

Mr. Harding left the room almost together with the ladies, and then the archdeacon opened his heart to Mr. Arabin. He still harped upon the hospital. "What did that fellow mean," said he,

"by saying in his letter to Mrs. Bold, that if Mr. Harding would call on the bishop it would be all right? Of course I would not be guided by anything he might say; but still it may be well that Mr. Harding should see the bishop. It would be foolish to let the thing slip through our fingers because Mrs. Bold is determined to make a fool of herself. "

Mr. Arabin hinted that he was not quite so sure that Mrs. Bold would make a fool of herself. He said that he was not convinced that she did regard Mr. Slope so warmly as she was supposed to do. The archdeacon questioned and cross-questioned him about this, but elicited nothing; and at last remained firm in his own conviction that he was destined, malgris lui, to be the brother-inlaw of Mr. Slope. Mr. Arabin strongly advised that Mr. Harding should take no step regarding the hospital in connexion with, or in consequence of, Mr. Slope's letter. "If the bishop really means to confer the appointment on Mr. Harding," argued Mr. Arabin, "he will take care to let him have some other intimation than a message conveyed through a letter to a lady. Were Mr. Harding to present himself at the palace he might merely be playing Mr. Slope's game;" and thus it was settled that nothing should be done till the great Dr. Grwynne's arrival, or at any rate without that potentate's sanction.

It was droll to observe how these men talked of Mr. Harding as though he were a puppet, and planned their intrigues and small ecclesiastical manoeuvres in reference to Mr. Harding's future position, without dreaming of taking him into their confidence. There was a comfortable house and income in question, and it was very desirable, and certainly very just, that Mr. Harding should have them; but that, at present, was not the main point. It was expedient to beat the bishop, and if possible to smash Mr. Slope. Mr. Slope had set up, or was supposed to have set up, a rival candidate. Of all things the most desirable would have been to have had Mr. Quiverful's appointment published to the public, and then annulled by the

clamour of an indignant world, loud in the defence of Mr. Harding's rights. But of such an event the chance was small; a slight fraction only of the world would be indignant, and that fraction would be one not accustomed to loud speaking. And then the preferment had in a sort of way been offered to Mr. Harding, and had in a sort of way been refused by him.

Mr. Slope's wicked, cunning hand had been peculiarly conspicuous in the way in which this had been Drought to pass, and it was the success of Mr. Slope's cunning which was so painfully grating to the feelings of the archdeacon. That which of all things he most dreaded was that he should be out-generaled by Mr. Slope; and just at present it appeared probable that Mr. Slope would turn his flank, steal a march on him, cut off his provisions, carry his strong. town by a coup de main, and at last beat him thoroughly in a regular pitched battle. The archdeacon felt that his flank had been turned when desired to wait on Mr. Slope instead of the bishop, that a march had been stolen when Mr. Harding was induced to refuse the bishop's offer, that his provisions would be cut off when Mr. Quiverful got the hospital, that Eleanor was the strong town doomed to be taken, and that Mr. Slope, as Dean of Barchester, would be regarded by all the world as the conqueror in the final conflict.

Dr. Gwynne was the Deus ex machina who was to come down upon the Barchester stage, and bring about deliverance from these terrible evils. But how can melodramatic denouements be properly brought about, how can vice and Mr. Slope be punished, and virtue and the archdeacon be rewarded, while the avenging god is laid up with the gout? In the mean time evil may be triumphant, and poor innocence, transfixed to the earth by an arrow from Dr. Proudie's quiver, may lie dead upon the ground, not to be resuscitated even by Dr. Gwynne.

Two or three days after Eleanor's departure Mr. Arabin went to Oxford, and soon found himself closeted with the august head of his college. It was quite clear that Dr. Gwynne was not very sanguine as to the effects of his journey to Barchester, and not over anxious to interfere with the bishop. He had had tne gout but was very nearly convalescent, and Mr. Arabin at once saw that had the mission been one of which the master thoroughly approved, he would before this have been at Plumstead.

As it was Dr. Gwynne was resolved on visiting his friend, and willingly promised to return to Barchester with Mr. Arabin. He could not bring himself to believe that there was any probability that Mr. Slope would be made Dean of Barchester. Rumour, he said, had reached, even his ears, not at all favourable to that gentleman's character, and he expressed himself strongly of opinion that any such appointment was quite out of the question. At this stage of the proceedings, the master's right-hand man, Tom Staple, was called in to assist at the conference. Tom Staple was the Tutor of Lazarus, and moreover a great man at Oxford. Though universally known by a species of nomenclature so very undignified Tom Staple was one who maintained a high dignity in the University. He was, as it were, the leader of the Oxford tutors, a body of men who consider themselves collectively as being by very little, if at all, second in importance to the heads themselves. It is not always the case that the master, or warden, or provost, or principal can hit it off exactly with his tutor. A tutor is by no means indisposed to have a will of hie own. But at Lazarus they were great friends and firm allies at the time of which we are writing.

Tom Staple was a hale strong man of about forty-five; short in stature, swarthy in face, with strong sturdy black hair, and crisp black beard, of which very little was allowed to show itself in shape of whiskers. He always wore a white neckcloth, clean indeed, but not tied with that scrupulous care which now distinguishes some of our younger clergy. He was, of course, always clothed in a seemly suit of solemn black. Mr. Staple was a decent cleanly liver, not over addicted to any sensuality; but nevertheless a somewhat warmish hue was beginning to adorn his nose, the peculiar effect, as his friends averred, of a certain pipe of port, introduced into the cellars of Lazarus the very same year in which the tutor entered it as a freshman. There was also, perhaps, a little redolence of port wine, as it were the slightest possible twang, in Mr. Staple's voice.

In these latter days Tom Staple was not a happy man. University reform had long been his bugbear, and now was his bane. It was not with him as with most others, an affair of politics, respecting which, when the need existed, he could, for parties' sake or on behalf of principle, maintain a certain amount of necessary zeal. It was not with him a subject for dilettante warfare, and courteous common-place opposition. To him it was life and death. The statu quo of the University was his only idea of life, and any reformation was as bad to him as death. He would willingly have been a martyr in the cause, had the cause admitted of martyrdom.

At the present day, unfortunately, public affairs will allow of no martyrs, and therefore it is that there is such a deficiency of zeal. Could gentlemen of 10,000?. a year have died on their own doorsteps in defence of protection, no doubt some half-a-dozen glorious old baronets would have so fallen, and the school of protection would at this day have been crowded with scholars. Who can fight strenuously in any combat in which there is no danger? Tom Staple would have willingly been impaled before a committee of the House, could he by such self-sacrifice have infused his own spirit into the component members of the hebdomadal board.

Tom Staple was one of those who in his heart approved of the credit system which had of old been in vogue between the students and tradesmen of the University. He knew and acknowledged to himself that it was useless in these degenerate days publicly to contend with the Jupiter on such a subject. The Jupiter had undertaken to rule the University, and Tom Staple was well aware that the Jupiter was too powerful for him. But in secret, and among his safe companions, he would argue that the system of credit was an ordeal good for young men to undergo.

The bad men, said he, the weak and worthless, blunder into danger and burn their feet; but the good men, they who have any character, they who have that within them which can reflect credit on their Alina Mater, they come through scatheless. What merit will there be to a young man to get through safely, if he he guarded and protected and restrained like a school-boy? By so doing, the period of the ordeal is only postponed, and the manhood of the man will be deferred from the age of twenty to that of twenty-four. If you bind him with leading-strings at college, he will break loose while eating for the bar in London; bind him there, and he will break loose afterwards, when he is a married man. The wild oats must be sown somewhere. 'Twas thus that Tom Staple would argue of young men; not, indeed, with much consistency, but still with some practical knowledge of the subject gathered from long experience.

And now Tom Staple proffered such wisdom as he had for the assistance of Dr. Gwynne and Mr. Arabin. "Quite out of the question," said he, arguing that Mr. Slope could not possibly be made the new Dean of Barchester.

"So I think," said the master. "He has no standing, and, if all I hear be true, very little character."

"As to character," said Tom Staple, "I don't think much of that. They rather like loose parsons for deans; a little fast living, or a dash of infidelity, is no bad recommendation to a cathedral close. But they couldn't make Mr. Slope. The last two deans have been Cambridge men; you'll not show me an instance of their making three men running from the same University. We don't get our share, and never shall, I suppose; but we must at least have one out of three."

"Those sort of rules are all gone by now," said Mr. Arabin.

"Everything has gone by, I believe," said Tom Staple. "The cigar has been smoked out, and we are the ashes."

"Speak for yourself, Staple," said the master.

"I speak for all," said the tutor, stoutly. "It is coming to that, that there will be no life left anywhere in the country. No one is any longer fit to rule himself, or those belonging to him. The Government is to find us all in everything, and the press is to find the Government. Nevertheless, Mr. Slope won't be Dean of Barchester."

"And who will be warden of the hospital?" said Mr. Arabin.

"I hear that Mr. Quiverful is already appointed," said Tom Staple.

"I think not," said the master. "And I think, moreover, that Dr. Proudie will not be so short-sighted as to run against such a rock. Mr. Slope should himself have sense enough to prevent it."

"But perhaps Mr. Slope may have no objection to see his patron on a rock," said the suspicious tutor.

"What could he get by that?" asked Mr. Arabin.

"It is impossible to see the doubles of such a man," said Mr. Staple. "It seems quite clear that Bishop Proudie is altogether in his hands, and it is equally clear that he has been moving heaven and earth to get this Mr. Quiverful into the hospital although he must know that such an appointment would be most damaging to the bishop. It is impossible to understand such a man, and dreadful to think," added Tom Staple, sighing deeply, " that the welfare and fortunes of good men may depend on his intrigues."

Dr. Gwynne or Mr. Staple were not in the least aware, nor even was Mr. Arabin, that this Mr. Slope, of whom they were talking, had been using his utmost efforts to put their own candidate into the hospital; and that in lieu of being permanent in the palace, his own expulsion therefrom had been already decided on by the high powers of the diocese.

"I'll tell you what," said the tutor, "if this Quiverful is thrust into the hospital and Dr. Trefoil does die, I should not wonder if the Government were to make Mr. Harding Dean of Barchester. They would feel bound to do something for him after all that wan said when he resigned. Dr. Gwynne at that moment made no reply to this suggestion; but

it did not the less impress itself on his mind. If Mr. Harding could not be warden of the hospital, why should he not be Dean of Barchester?

And so the conference ended without any very fixed resolution, and Dr. Gwynne and Mr. Arabin prepared for their journey ta Plumstead on the morrow.

Vol. 11. o CHAPTER XXXV.

Miss Thorne's Fete Champetre.

The day of the Ullathorne party arrived and all the world were there;—or at least so much of the world as had been included in Miss Thorne's invitation. As we have said, the bishop returned home on the previous evening, and on the same evening, and by the same train, came Dr. Gwynne and Mr. Arabin from Oxford. The archdeacon with his brougham was in waiting for the Master of Lazarus, so that there was a goodly show of church dignitaries on the platform of the railway.

The Stanhope party was finally arranged in the odious manner already described, and Eleanor got into the doctor's carriage full of apprehension and presentiment of further misfortune,—whereas Mr. Slope entered the vehicle elate with triumph.

He had received that morning a very civil note from Sir Nicholas Fitzwhiggin; not promising much indeed; but then Mr. Slope knew, or fancied that he knew, that it was not etiquette for government officers to make promises. Though Sir Nicholas promised nothing he implied a good deal;—declared his conviction that Mr. Slope would make an excellent dean, and wished him every kind of success. To be sure he added that, not being in the cabinet, he was never consulted on such matters, and that even if he spoke on the subject his voice would go for nothing. But all this Mr. Slope took for the prudent reserve of official life. To complete his anticipated triumphs, another letter was brought to him just as he was about to start to Ullathorne.

Mr. Slope also enjoyed the idea of handing Mrs. Bold out of Dr. Stanhope's carriage before the multitude at Ullathorne gate as much as Eleanor

dreaded the same ceremony. He had fully made up his mind to throw himself and his fortune at the widow's feet, and had almost determined to seleet the present propitious morning for doing so. The Signora had of late been less than civil to him. She had indeed admitted his visits, and listened, at any rate without anger, to his love; but she had tortured him and reviled him, jeered at him and ridiculed him, while she allowed him to call her the most beautiful of living women, to kiss her hand, and to proclaim himself with reiterated oaths her adorer, her slave, and worshipper.

Miss Thome was in great perturbation, yet in great glory, on the morning of the gala day. Mr. Thome also, though the party was none of his giving, had much heavy work on his hands. But perhaps the most overtasked, the most anxious, and the most effective of all the Ullathorne household was Mr. Plomacy, the steward. This last personage had, in the time of Mr. Thome's father, when the Directory held dominiom in France, gone over to Paris with letters in his boot-heel for some of the royal party; and such had been his good luck that he had returned safe. He had then been very young and was now very old, but the exploit gave him a character for political enterprise and secret discretion which still availed him as thoroughly as it had done in its freshest gloss. Mr. Plomacy had been steward of Ullathorne for more than fifty years, and a very easy life he had of it. Who could require much absolute work from a man who had carried safely at his heel that which if discovered would have cost him his head? Consequently Mr. Plomacy never worked hard, and of latter years had never worked at all. He had a taste for timber, and therefore he marked the trees that were to be cut down; he had a taste for gardening, and would therefore allow no shrub to be planted or bed to be made without his express sanction. In these matters he was sometimes driven to run counter to his mistress, but he rarely allowed his mistress to carry the point against him.

But on occasions such as the present Mr. Plomacy came out strong. He had the honour of the family at heart; he thoroughly appreciated the duties of hospitality; and therefore, when gala doings were going on, always took the management into his own hands and reigned supreme over master and mistress.

To give Mr. Plomacy his due, old as he was, he thoroughly understood such work as he had in hand, and did it well.

The order of the day was to be as follows. The quality, as the upper classes in rural districts are designated by the lower with so much true discrimination, were to eat a breakfast, and the non-quality were to eat a dinner. Two marquees had been erected for these two banquets, that for the quality on the esoteric or garden side of a certain deep ha-ha; and that for the non-quality on the exoteric or paddock side of the same. Both were of huge dimensions; that on the outer side was, one may say, on an egregious scale; but Mr. Plomacy declared that neither would be sufficient. To remedy this, an auxiliary banquet was prepared in the diningroom, and a subsidiary board was to be spread *sub dio* for the accommodation of the lower class of yokels on the Ullathorne property.

No one who has not had a hand in the preparation of such an affair can understand the manifold difficulties which Miss Thorne encountered in her project. Had she not been made throughout of the very finest whalebone, riveted with the best Yorkshire steel, she must have sunk under them. Had not Mr. Plomacy felt how much was justly expected from a man who at one time carried the destinies of Europe in his boot, he would have given way; and his mistress, so deserted, must have perished among her poles and canvas.

In the first place there was a dreadful line to be drawn. Who were to dispose themselves within the ha-ha, and who without? To this the unthinking will give an off-hand answer, as they will to every ponderous question. Oh;—the bishop and such like within the ha-ha; and Farmer Greenacre and such like without. True, my unthinking friend; but who shall define these such-likes? It

is in such definitions that the whole difficulty of society consists. To seat the bishop on an arm chair on the lawn and place Farmer Greenacre at the end of a long table in the paddock is easy enough; but where will you put Mrs. Lookaloft, whose husband, though a tenant on the estate, hunts in a red coat, whose daughters go to a fashionable seminary in Barchester, who calls her farm house Rose bank, and who has a pianoforte in her drawing-room? The Misses Lookaloft, as they call themselves, won't sit contented among the bumpkins. Mrs. Lookaloft won't squeeze her fine clothes on a bench and talk familiarly about cream and ducklings to good Mrs. Greenacre. And yet Mrs. Lookaloft is no fit companion and never has been the associate of the Thornes and the Grantlys. And if Mrs. Lookaloft be admitted within the sanctum of fashionable life, if she be allowed with her three daughters to leap the ha-ha, why not the wives and daughters of other families also? Mrs. Greenacre is at present well contented with the paddock, but she might cease to be so if she saw Mrs. Lookaloft on the lawn. And thus poor Miss Thorne had a hard time of it.

And how was she to divide her guests between the marquee and the parlour? She had a countess coming, an Honourable John and an Honourable George, and a whole bevy of Ladies Amelia, Bosina, Margaretta, &c.; she had a leash of baronets with their baronnettes; and, as we all know, she had a bishop. If she put them on the lawn, no one would go into the parlour; if she put them into the parlour, no one would go into the tent. She thought of keeping the old people in the house, and leaving the lawn to the lovers. She might as well have seated herself at once in a hornet's nest. Mr. Plomacy knew better than this. "Bless your soul, Ma'am," said he, "there won't be no old ladies;—not one, barring yourself and old Mrs. Clantantram."

Personally Miss Thorne accepted this distinction in her favour as a compliment to her good sense; but nevertheless she had no desire to be closeted on the

coming occasion with Mrs. Clantantram. She gave up all idea of any arbitrary division of her guests, and determined if possible to put the bishop on the lawn and the countess in the house, to sprinkle the baronets, and thus divide the attractions. What to do with the Lookalofts even Mr. Plomacy could not decide. They must take their chance. They had been specially told in the invitation that all the tenants had been invited; and they might probably have the good sense to stay away if they objected to mix with the rest of the tenantry.

Then Mr. Plomacy declared his apprehension that the Honourable Johns and Honourable Georges would come in a sort of amphibious costume, half morning half evening, satin neckhandkerchiefs, frock coats, primrose gloves, and polished boots; and that, being so dressed, they would decline riding at the quintain, or taking part in any of the athletic games which Miss Thorne had prepared with so much fond care. If the Lord Johns and Lord Georges didn't ride at the quintain, Miss Thorne might be sure that nobody else would.

"But," said she, in dolorous voice, all but overcome by her cares; "it was specially signified that there were to be sports."

"And so there will be, of course," said Mr. Plomacy. "They'll all be sporting with the young ladies in the laurel walks. Them's the sports they care most about now-a-days. *Ji* you gets the young men at the quintain you'll have all the young women in the pouts."

"Can't they look on, as their great grandmothers did before them?" said Miss Thorne.

"It seems to me that the ladies ain't contented with looking now-a-days. Whatever the men do they'll do. If you'll have side saddles on the nags, and let them go at the quintain too, it'll answer capital, no doubt."

Miss Thorne made no reply. She felt that she had no good ground on which to defend her sex of the present generation from the sarcasm of Mr. Plomacy. She had once declared, in one of her warmer moments, "that now-a-days the gentlemen were all women, and the ladies all men." She could not alter the debased character of the age. But, such being the case, why should she take on herself to cater for the amusement of people of such degraded tastes? This question she asked herself more than once, and she could only answer herself with a sigh. There was her own brother Wilfred, on whose shoulders rested all the ancient honours of Ullathorne house; it was very doubtful whether even he would consent to "go at the quintain," as Mr. Plomacy not injudiciously expressed it.

And now the morning arrived. The Ullathorne household was early on the move. Cooks were cooking in the kitchen long before daylight, and men were dragging out tables and hammering red baize on to benches at the earliest dawn. With what dread eagerness did Miss Thorne look out at the weather as soon as the parting veil of night permitted her to look at all! In this respect at any rate there was nothing to grieve her. The glass had been rising for the last three days, and the morning broke with that dull chill steady grey haze which in autumn generally presages a clear and dry day. By seven she was dressed and down. Miss Thorne knew nothing of the modern luxury of deshabilles. She would as soon have thought of appearing before her brother without her stockings as without her stays;— and Miss Thorne's stays were no trifle.

And yet there was nothing for her to do when down. She fidgeted out to the lawn, and then back into the kitchen. She put on her high-heeled clogs, and fidgeted out into the paddock. Then she went into the small home park where the quintain was erected. The pole and cross bar and the swivel, and the target and the bag of flour were all complete. She got up on a carpenter's bench and touched the target with her hand; it went round with beautiful ease; the swivel had been oiled to perfection. She almost wished to take old Plomacy at his word, to get on a side saddle and have a tilt at it herself. What must a young man be, thought she, who could prefer maundering among laurel trees with a wishy washy school girl to such fun as this?"

Well," said she aloud to herself, "one man can take a horse to water, but a thousand can't make him drink. There it is. If they haven't the spirit to enjoy it, the fault shan't be mine;" and so she returned to the house.

At a little after eight her brother came down, and they had a sort of scrap breakfast in his study. The tea was made without the customary urn, and they dispensed with the usual rolls and toast. Eggs also were missing, for every egg in the parish had been whipped into custards, baked into pies, or boiled into lobster salad. The allowance of fresh butter was short, and Mr. Thorne was obliged to eat the leg of a fowl without having it devilled in the manner he loved.

"I have been looking at the quintain, Wilfred," said she, "and it appears to be quite right."

"Oh;—ah; yes;" said he. "It seemed to be so yesterday when I saw it." Mr. Thorne was beginning to be rather bored by his sister's love of sports, and had especially no affection for this quintain post.

"I wish you'd just try it after breakfast," said she. "You could have the saddle put on Mark Antony, and the pole is there all handy. You can take the flour bag off, you know, if you think Mark Antony won't be quick enough," added Miss Thorne, seeing that her brother's countenance was not indicative of complete accordance with her little proposition.

Now Mark Antony was a valuable old hunter, excellently suited to Mr. Thorne's usual requirements, steady indeed at his fences, but extremely sure, very good in deep ground, and safe on the roads. But he had never yet been ridden at a quintain, and Mr. Thorne was not inclined to put him to the trial, either with or without the bag of flour. He hummed and hawed, and finally declared that he was afraid Mark Antony would shy.

"Then try the cob," said the indefatigable Miss Thorne.

"He's in physic," said Wilfred.

"There's the Beelzebub colt," said his sister. "I know he's in the stable, because I saw Peter exercising him just

now."

"My dear Monica, he's so wild, that it's as much as I can do to manage him at all. He'd destroy himself and me too, if I attempted to ride him at such a rattletrap as that."

A rattletrap! The quintain that she had put up with so much anxious care; the game that she had prepared for the amusement of the stalwart yeomen of the country; the sport that had been honoured by the affection of so many of their ancestors! It cut her to the heart to hear it so denominated by her own brother. There were but the two of them left together in the world; and it had ever been one of the rules by which Miss Thorne had regulated her conduct through life, to say nothing that could provoke her brother. She had often had to suffer from his indifference to time-honoured British customs; but she had always suffered in silence. It was part of her creed that the head of the family should never be upbraided in his own house; and Miss Thorne had lived up to her creed. Now, however, she was greatly tried. The colour mounted to her ancient cheek, and the fire blazed in her still bright eye; but yet she said nothing. She resolved that, at any rate, to him nothing more should be said about the quintain that day.

She sipped her tea in silent sorrow, and thought with painful regret of the glorious days when her great ancestor Ealfried had successfully held Ullathorne against a Norman invader. There was no such spirit now left in her family except that small useless spark which burnt in her own bosom. And she herself,—was not she at this moment intent on entertaining a descendant of those very Normans, a vain proud countess with a frenchified name, who would only think that she graced Ullathorne too highly by entering its portals? Was it likely that an honourable John, the son of an Earl De Courcy, should ride at a quintain in company with Saxon yeomen? And why should she expect her brother to do that which her brother's guests would decline to do?

Some dim faint idea of the impracticability of her own views flitted across her brain. Perhaps it was necessary that races doomed to live on tho same soil should give way to each other, and adopt each other's pursuits. Perhaps it was impossible that after more than five centuries of close intercourse, Normans should remain Normans, and Saxons Saxons. Perhaps after all her neighbours were wiser than herself. Such ideas did occasionally present themselves to Miss Thorne's mind, and make her sad enough. But it never occurred to her that her favourite quintain was but a modern copy of a Norman knight's amusement,—an adaptation of the noble tourney to the tastes and habits of the Saxon yeomen. Of this she was ignorant, and it would have been cruelty to instruct her.

When Mr. Thorne saw the tear in her eye he repented himself of his contemptuous expression. By him also it was recognised as a binding law that every whim of his sister was to be respected. He was not perhaps so firm in his observances to her, as she was in hers to him. But his intentions were equally good, and whenever he found that he had forgotten them it was matter of grief to him. "My dear Monica," said he, "I beg your pardon. I don't in the least mean to speak ill of the game. When I called it a rattletrap, I merely meant that it was so for a man of my age. You know you always forget that I an't a young man."

"I am quite sure you are not an old man, Wilfred," said she, accepting the apology in her heart, and smiling at him with the tear still on her cheek.

"If I was five-and-twenty, or thirty," continued he, "I should like nothing better than riding at the quintain all day."

"But you are not too old to hunt or to shoot," said she. "If you can jump over a ditch and hedge I am sure you could turn the quintain round."

"But when I ride over the hedges, my dear,—and it isn't very often I do that,—but when I do ride over the hedges there isn't any bag of flour coming after me. Think how I'd look taking the countess out to breakfast with the back of my head all covered with meal."

Miss Thorne said nothing further. She didn't like the allusion to the count-

ess. She couldn't be satisfied with the reflection that the sports of Ullathorne should be interfered with by the personal attentions necessary for a Lady De Courcy. But she saw that it was useless for her to push the matter further. It was conceded that Mr. Thorne was to be spared the quintain; and Miss Thorne determined to trust wholly to a youthful knight of hers, an immense favourite, who, as she often declared, was a pattern to the young men of the age, and an excellent sample of an English yeoman.

This was Farmer Greenacre's eldest son; who, to tell the truth, had from his earliest years taken the exact measure of Miss Thome's foot. In his boyhood he had never failed to obtain from her apples, pocket money, and forgiveness for his numerous trespasses; and now in his early manhood he got privileges and immunities which were equally valuable. He was allowed a day or two's shooting in September; he schooled the squire's horses; got slips of trees out of the orchard, and roots of flowers out of the garden; and had the fishing of the little river altogether in his own hands. He had undertaken to come mounted on a nag of his father's, and show the way at the quintain post. Whatever young Greenacre did the others would do after him. The juvenile Lookalofts might stand aloof, but the rest of the youth of Ullathorne would be sure to venture if Harry Greenacre showed the way. And so Miss Thome made up her mind to dispense with the noble Johns and Georges, and trust, as her ancestors had done before her, to the thews and sinews of native Ullathorne growth.

At about nine the lower orders began to congregate in the paddock and park, under the surveillance of Mr. Plomacy and the head gardener and head groom, who were sworn in as his deputies, and were to assist him in keeping the peace and promoting the sports. Many of the younger inhabitants of the neighbourhood, thinking that they could not have too much of a good thing, had come at a very early hour, and the road between the house and the church had been thronged for some time before the gates were thrown open.

And then another difficulty of huge dimensions arose, a difficulty which Mr. Plomacy had indeed foreseen and for which he was in some sort provided. Some of those who wished to share Miss Thome's hospitality were not so particular as they should have been as to the preliminary ceremony of an invitation. They doubtless conceived that they had been overlooked by accident; and instead of taking this in dudgeon, as their betters would have done, they good-naturedly put up with the slight, and showed that they did so by presenting themselves at the gate in their Sunday best.

Mr. Plomacy, however, well knew who were welcome and who wore not. To some, even though uninvited, he allowed ingress. "Don't be too particular, Plomacy," his mistress had said; '' especially with the children. If they live anywhere near, let them in."

Acting on this hint Mr. Plomacy did let in many an eager urchin, and a few tidily dressed girls with their swains, who in no way belonged to the property. But to the denizens of the city he was inexorable. Many a Barchester apprentice made his appearance there that day, and urged with piteous supplication that he had been working all the week in making saddles and boots for the use of Ullathorne, in compounding doses for the horses, or cutting up carcases for the kitchen. No such claim was allowed. Mr. Plomacy knew nothing about the city apprentices; he was to admit the tenants and labourers on the estate; Miss Thome wasn't going to take in the whole city of Barchester; and so on.

Nevertheless, before the day was half over, all this was found to be useless. Almost anybody who chose to come made his way into the park, and the care of the guardians was transferred to the tables on which the banquet was spread. Even here there was many an unauthorised claimant for a place, of whom it was impossible to get quit without more commotion than the place and food were worth.

CHAPTER XXXVI. TTLLATHORNE SPORTS.—ACT I.

The trouble in civilised life of entertaining company, as it is called too generally without much regard to strict veracity, is so great that it cannot but be matter of wonder that people are so fond of attempting it. It is dim cult to ascertain what is the quid pro quo. If they who give such laborious parties, and who endure such toil and turmoil in the vain hope of giving them successfully, really enjoyed the parties given by others, the matter could be understood. A sense of justice would induce men and women to undergo, in behalf of others, those miseries which others had undergone in their behalf. But they all profess that going out is as great a bore as receiving; and to look at them when they are out, one cannot but believe them.

Entertain! Who shall have sufficient self-assurance, who shall feel sufficient confidence in his own powers to dare to boast that he can entertain his company? A clown can sometimes do so, and sometimes a dancer in short petticoats and stuffed pink legs; —occasionally, perhaps, a singer. But beyond these, success in this art of entertaining is not often achieved. Young men and girls linking themselves kind with kind, pairing like birds in spring because nature wills it,—they, after a simple fashion, do entertain each other. Few others even try.

Ladies, when they open their houses, modestly confessing, it may be presumed, their own incapacity, mainly trust to wax candles and upholstery. Gentlemen seem to rely on their white waistcoats. To these are added, for the delight of the.more sensual, champagne and such good things of the table as fashion allows to be still considered as comestible. Even in this respect the world is deteriorating. All the good soups are now tabooed; and at the houses of one's accustomed friends, small barristers, doctors, government clerks, and such like, (for we cannot all of us always live as grandees, surrounded by an elysium of livery servants), one gets a cold potato handed to one as a sort of finale to one's slice of mutton. Alas! for those happy days when one could say to one's neighbourhood, "Jones, shall I give you some mashed turnip?—may I

trouble you for a little cabbage?" And then the pleasure of drinking wine with Mrs. Jones and Miss Smith; —with all the Joneses and all the Smiths! These latter-day habits are certainly more economical.

Miss Thorne, however, boldly attempted to leave the modern beaten track, and made a positive effort to entertain her guests. Alas! she did so with but moderate success. They had all their own way of going, and would not go her way. She piped to them, but they would not dance. She offered to them good honest household cake, made of currants and flour and eggs and sweetmeat; but they would feed themselves on trashy wafers from the shop of the Barchester pastry-cook, on chalk and gum and adulterated sugar. Poor Miss Thorne! yours is not the first honest soul that has vainly striven to recall the glories of happy days gone by! If fashion suggests to a Lady De Courcy that when invited to a dejeuner at twelve she ought to come at three, no eloquence of thine will teach her the advantage of a nearer approach to punctuality.

She had fondly thought that when she called on her friends to come at twelve, and specially begged them to believe that she meant it, she would be able to see them comfortably seated in their tents at two. Vain woman,—or rather ignorant woman,— ignorant of the advances of that civilisation which the world had witnessed while she was growing old. At twelve she found herself alone, dressed in all the glory of the newest of her many suits of raiment; with strong shoes, however, and a serviceable bonnet on her head, and a warm rich shawl on her shoulders. Thus clad she peered out into the tent, went to the ha-ha, and satisfied herself that at any rate the youngsters were amusing themselves, spoke a word to Mrs. Greenacre over the ditch, and took one look at the quintain. Three or four young farmers were turning the machine round and round, and poking at the bag of flour in a manner not at all intended by the inventor of the game; but no mounted sportsmen were there. Miss Thome looked at her watch. It was

only fifteen minutes past twelve, and it was understood that Harry Greenacre was not to begin till the half hour.

Miss Thorne returned to her drawing-room rather quicker than was her wont, fearing that the countess might come and find none to welcome her. She need not have hurried, for no one was there. At half-past twelve she peeped into the kitchen; at a quarter to one she was joined by her brother; and just then the first fashionable arrival took place. Mrs. Clantantram was announced.

No announcement was necessary, indeed; for the good lady's voice was heard as she walked across the courtyard to the house scolding the unfortunate postilion who had driven her from Barchester. At the moment Miss Thorne could not but be thankful that the other guests were more fashionable, and were thus spared the fury of Mrs. Clantantram's indignation.

"Oh Miss Thorne, look here!" said she, as soon as she found herself in the drawing-room; "do look at my roquelaure! It's clean spoilt, and for ever. I wouldn't but wear it because I knew you wished us all to be grand to-day; and yet I had my misgivings. Oh dear, oh dear! It was five-and-twenty shillings a yard." The Barchester post horses had misbehaved in some unfortunate manner just as Mrs. Clantantram was getting out of the chaise, and had nearly thrown her under the wheel.

Mrs. Clantantram belonged to other days, and therefore, though she had but little else to recommend her, Miss Thorne was to a certain extent fond of her. She sent the roquelaure away to be cleaned, and lent her one of her best shawls out of her own wardrobe.

The next comer was Mr. Arabin, who was immediately informed of Mrs. Clantantram's misfortune, and of her determination to pay neither master nor post-boy; although, as she remarked, she intended to get her lift home before she made known her mind upon that matter. Then a good deal of rustling was heard in the sort of lobby that was used for the ladies' outside cloaks; and the door having been thrown wide open, the servant announced, not in the most confident of voices, Mrs. Lookaloft, and the Miss Lookalofts, and Mr. Augustus Lookaloft.

Poor man!—we mean the footman. He knew, none better, that Mrs. Lookaloft had no business there, that she was not wanted there, and would not be welcome. But he had not the courage to tell a stout lady with a low dress, short sleeves, and satin at eight shillings a yard, that she had come to the wrong tent He had not dared to hint to young ladies with white dancing shoes and long gloves, that there was a place ready for them in the paddock. And thus Mrs. Lookaloft carried her point, broke through the guards, and made her way into the citadel. That she would have to pass an uncomfortable time there, she had surmised before. But nothing now could rob her of the power of boasting that she had consorted on the lawn with the squire and Miss Thorne, with a countess, a bishop, and the county grandees, while Mrs. Greenacre and such like were walking about with the ploughboys in the park. It was a great point gained by Mrs. Lookaloft, and it might be fairly expected that from this time forward the tradesmen of Barchester would, with undoubting pens, address her husband as T. Lookaloft, Esquire.

Mrs. Lookaloft's pluck carried her through everything, and she walked triumphant into the Ullathorne drawing-room; but her children did feel a little abashed at the sort of reception they met with. It was not in Miss Thorne's heart to insult her own guests; but neither was it in her disposition to overlook such effrontery. "Oh, Mrs. Lookaloft, is this you," said she; "and your daughters and son? Well, we're very glad to see you; but I'm sorry you've come in such low dresses, as we are all going out of doors. Could we lend you anything?"

"Oh dear no! thank ye, Miss Thorne," said the mother: "the girls and myself are quite used to low dresses, when we're out."

"Are you, indeed?" said Miss Thorne shuddering; but the shudder was lost on Mrs. Lookaloft,

"And where's Lookaloft?" said the master of the house, coming up to welcome his tenant's wife. Let the faults of the family be what they would, he could not but remember that their rent was well paid. He was therefore not willing to give them a cold shoulder.

"Such a headache, Mr. Thorne!" said Mrs. Lookaloft. "In fact he couldn't stir, or you may be certain on such a day he would not have absented hisself."

"Dear me," said Miss Thorne. "If he is so ill, I'm sure you'd wish to be with him."

"Not at all!" said Mrs. Lookaloft. "Not at all, Miss Thorne. It is only bilious you know, and when he's that way he can bear nobody nigh him." The fact however was that Mr. Lookaloft, having either more sense or less courage than his wife, had not chosen to intrude on Miss Thorne's drawing-room; and as he could not very well have gone among the plebeians while his wife was with the patricians, he thought it most expedient to remain at Rosebank.

Mrs. Lookaloft soon found herself on a sofa, and the Miss Lookalofts on two chairs, while Mr. Augustus stood near the door; and here they remained till in due time they were seated all four together at the bottom of the dining-room table.

Then the Grantlys came; the archdeacon and Mrs. Grantly and the two girls, and Dr. Gwynne and Mr. Harding; and as ill luck would have it, they were closely followed by Dr. Stanhope's carriage. As Eleanor looked out of the carriage window, she saw her brother-in-law helping the ladies out, and threw herself back into her seat, dreading to be discovered. She had had an odious journey. Mr. Slope's civility had been more than ordinarily greasy; and now, though he had not in fact said anything which she could notice, she had for the first time entertained a suspicion VOL. II. P that he was intending to make love to her. Was it after all true that she had been conducting herself in a way that justified the world in thinking that she liked the man? After all, could it be possible that the archdeacon and Mr. Arabin were right, and that she was wrong? Charlotte Stanhope had also been

watching Mr. Slope, and had come to the conclusion that it behoved her brother to lose no further time, if he meant to gain the widow. She almost regretted that it had not been contrived that Bertie should be at Ullathorne before them.

Dr. Grantly did not see his sister-in-law in company with Mr. Slope, but Mr. Arabin did. Mr. Arabin came out with Mr. Thorne to the front door to welcome Mrs. Grantly, and he remained in the courtyard till all their party had passed on. Eleanor hung back in the carriage as long as she well could, but she was nearest to the door, and when Mr. Slope, having alighted, offered her his hand, she had no alternative but to take it. Mr. Arabin, standing at the open door while Mrs. Grantly was shaking hands with some one within, saw a clergyman alight from the carriage whom he at once knew to be Mr. Slope, and then he saw this clergyman hand out Mrs. Bold. Having seen so much, Mr. Arabin, rather sick at heart, followed Mrs. Grantly into the house.

Eleanor was, however, spared any further immediate degradation, for Dr. Stanhope gave her his arm across the courtyard, and Mr. Slope was fain to throw away his attention upon Charlotte.

They had hardly passed into the house, and from the house to the lawn, when, with a loud rattle and such noise as great men and great women are entitled to make in their passage through the world, the Proudies drove up. It was soon apparent that no everyday comer was at the door. One servant whispered to another that it was the bishop, and the word soon ran through all the hanger-son and strange grooms and coachmen about the place. There was quite a little cortege to see the bishop and his "lady" walk across the courtyard, and the good man was pleased to see that the church was held in such respect in the parish of St. Ewold's.

And now the guests came fast and thick, and the lawn began to be crowded, and the room to be full. Voices buzzed, silk rustled against silk, and muslin crumpled against muslin. Miss Thorne became more happy than she had been, and again bethought her of her sports. There were targets and bows and arrows prepared at the further end of the lawn. Here the gardens of the place encroached with a somewhat wide sweep upon the paddock, and gave ample room for the doings of the toxophilites. Miss Thorne got together such daughters of Diana as could bend a bow, and marshalled them to the targets. There were the Grantly girls and the Proudie girls and the Chadwick girls, and the two daughters of the burly chancellor, and Miss Knowle; and with them went Frederick and Augustus Chadwick, and young Knowle of Knowle park, and Frank Foster of the Elms, and Mr. Vellem Deeds the dashing attorney of the High Street, and the Rev. Mr. Green, and the Kev. Mr. Brown, and the Kev. Mr. White, all of whom, as in duty bound, attended the steps of the three Miss Proudies.

"Did you ever ride at the quintain, Mr. Foster?" said Miss Thome, as she walked with her party, across the lawn.

"The quintain?" said young Foster, who considered himself a dab at horsemanship. "Is it a sort of gate, Mjsb Thome?" Miss Thome had to explain the noble game she spoke of, and Frank Foster had to own that he never had ridden at the quintain.

"Would you like tocomeand see?" said Miss Thome. "There'll be plenty here without you, if you like it."

"Well, I don't mind," said Frank; "I suppose the ladies can come too."

"Oh yes," said Miss Thome; "those who like it; I have no doubt they'll go to see your prowess, if you'll ride, Mr. Foster."

Mr. Foster looked down at a most unexceptionable pair of pantaloons, which had arrived from London only the day before. They were the very things,—at least he thought so,—for a picnic or fete champetre; but he was not prepared to ride in them. Nor was he more encouraged than had been Mr. Thome, by the idea of being attacked from behind by the bag of flour which Miss Thorne had graphically described to him.

"Well, I don't know about riding, Miss Thorne," said he; "I fear I'm not

quite prepared."

Miss Thorne sighed, but said nothing further. She left the toxophilites to their bows and arrows and returned towards the house. But as she passed by the entrance to the small park, she thought that she might at any rate encourage the yeomen by her presence, as she could not induce her more fashionable guests to mix with them in their manly amusements. Accordingly she once more betook herself to the quintain post.

Here to her great delight she found Harry Greenacre ready mounted, with his pole in his hand, and a lot of comrades standing round him, encouraging him to the assault. She stood at a little distance and nodded to him in token of her good pleasure.

"Shall I begin, ma'am?" said Harry, fingering his long staff in a rather awkward way, while his horse moved uneasily beneath him, not accustomed to a rider armed with such a weapon.

"Yes; yes," said Miss Thorne, standing triumphant as the queen of beauty, on an inverted tub which some chance had brought thither from the farm-yard.

"Here goes then," said Harry, as he wheeled his horse round to get the necessary momentum of a sharp gallop. The quintain post stood right before him, and the square board at which he was to tilt was fairly in his way. If he hit that duly in the middle, and maintained his pace as he did so, it was calculated that he would be carried out of reach of the flour bag, which, suspended at the other end of the cross-bar on the post, would swing round when the board was struck. It was also calculated that if the rider did not maintain his pace, he would get a blow from the flour bag just at the back of his head, and bear about him the signs of his awkwardness to the great amusement of the lookers-on.

Harry Greenacre did not object to being powdered with flour in the service of his mistress, and therefore gallantly touched his steed with his spur, having laid his lance in rest to the best of his ability. But his ability in this respect was not great, and his appurtenances probably not very good; consequently, he struck his horse with his pole unin-

tentionally on the side of the head as he started. The animal swerved and shied, and galloped off wide of the quintain. Harry well accustomed to manage a horse, but not to do so with a twelve-foot rod on his arm, lowered his right hand to the bridle and thus the end of the lance came to the ground, and got between the legs of the steed. Down came rider and steed and staff. Young Greenacre was thrown some six feet over the horse's head, and poor Miss Thome almost fell off her tub in a swoon.

"Oh gracious, he's killed," shrieked a woman who was near him when he fell.

"The Lord be good to him! his poor mother, his poor mother!" said another.

"Well, drat them dangerous plays all the world over," said an old crone.

"He has broke his neck sure enough, if ever man did," said a fourth.

Poor Miss Thorne! She heard all this and yet did not quite swoon. She made her way through the crowd as best she could, sick herself almost to death. Oh, his mother—his poor mother! How could she ever forgive herself. The agony of that moment was terrific. She could hardly get to the place where the poor lad was lying, as three or four men in front were about the horse which had risen with some difficulty; but at last she found herself close to the young farmer.

"Has he marked himself? for heaven's sake tell me that; has he marked his knees?" said Harry, slowly rising and rubbing his left shoulder with his right hand, and thinking only of his horse's legs. Miss Thorne soon found that he had not broken his neck, nor any of his bones, nor been injured in any essential way. But from that time forth she never instigated any one to ride at a quintain.

Eleanor left Dr. Stanhope as soon as she could do so civilly, and went in quest of her father whom she found on the lawn in oompany with Mr. Arabin. She was not sorry to find them together. She was anxious to disabuse at any rate her father's mind as to this report which had got abroad respecting her, and would have been well pleased to have been able to do the same with regard to

Mr. Arabin. She put her own through her father's arm, coming up behind his back, and then tendered her hand also to the vicar of St. Ewold's.

"And how did you come?" said Mr. Harding, when the first greeting was over.

"The Stanhopes brought me," said she; "their carriage was obliged to come twice, and has now gone back for the Signora." As she spoke she caught Mr. Arabin's eye, and saw that he was looking pointedly at her with a severe expression. She understood at once the accusation contained in his glance. It said as plainly as an eye can speak, "Yes, you came with the Stanhopes; but you did so in order that you might be in company with Mr. Slope."

"Our party," said she, still addressing her father, "consisted of the doctor and Charlotte Stanhope, myself, and Mr. Slope." As she mentioned the last name she felt her father's arm quiver slightly beneath her touch. At the same moment Mr. Arabin turned away from them, and joining his hands behind hia back strolled slowly away by one of the paths.

"Papa," said she, "it was impossible to help coming in the same carriage with Mr. Slope; it was quite impossible. I had promised to come with them before I dreamt of his coming, and afterwards I could not get out of it without explaining and giving rise to talk. You weren't at home, you know; I couldn't possibly help it." She said all this so quickly that by the time her apology was spoken she was quite out of breath.

"I don't know why you should have wished to help it, my dear," said her father.

'' Yes, papa, you do; you must know; you do know all the things they said at Plumstead. I am sure you do. You know all the archdeacon said. How unjust he was; and Mr. Arabin too. He's a horrid man, a horrid odious man, but"

"Who is an odious man, my dear? Mr. Arabin?"

"No; but Mr. Slope. You know I mean Mr. Slope. He's the most odious man I ever met in my life, and it was most unfortunate my having to come

here in the same carriage with him. But how could I help it?"

A great weight began to move itself off Mr. Harding's mind. So, after all, the archdeacon with all his wisdom, and Mrs. Grantly with all her tact, and Mr. Arabin with all his talent, were in the wrong. His own child, his Eleanor, the daughter of whom he was so proud was not to become the wife of a Mr. Slope. He had been about to give his sanction to the marriage, so certified had he been of the fact; and now he learnt that this imputed lover of Eleanor's was at any rate as much disliked by her as by any one of the family. Mr. Harding, however, was by no means sufficiently a man of the world to conceal the blunder he had made. He could not pretend that he had entertained no suspicion. He could not make believe that he had never joined the archdeacon in his surmises. He was greatly surprised, and gratified beyond measure, and he could not help showing that such was the case.

"My darling girl," said he, "I am so delighted, so overjoyed. My own child; you have taken such a weight off my mind."

"But surely, papa, *you* didn't think."

"I didn't know what to think, my dear. The archdeacon told me that"

"The archdeacon!" said Eleanor, her face lighting up with passion. "A man like the archdeacon might, one would think, be better employed than in traducing his sister-in-law, and creating bitterness between a father and his daughter!"

"He didn't mean to do that, Eleanor."

""What did he mean then? Why did he interfere with me, and fill your mind with such falsehood?"

"Never mind it now, my child; never mind it now. We shall all know you better now."

'' Oh, papa, that you should have thought it!—that you should have suspected me!"

"I don't know what you mean by suspicion, Eleanor. There would be nothing disgracef ui, you know; nothing wrong in such a marriage. Nothing that could have justified my interfering as your father." And Mr. Harding would

have proceeded in his own defence to make out that Mr. Slope after all was a very good sort of man, and a very fitting second husband for a young widow, had he not been interrupted by Eleanor's greater energy.

"It would be disgraceful," said she. "It would be wrong. It would be abominable. Could I do such a horrid thing, I should expect no one to speak to me. Ugh "and she shuddered as she thought of the matrimonial torch which her friends had been so ready to light on her behalf. "I don't wonder at Dr. Grantly; I don't wonder at Susan; but, oh papa, I do wonder at you. How could you, how could you believe it?" Poor Eleanor, as she thought of her father's defalcation, could resist her tears no longer, and was forced to cover her face with her handkerchief.

The place was not very opportune for her grief. They were walking through the shrubberies, and there were many people near them. Poor Mr. Harding stammered out his excuse as best he could, and Eleanor with an effort controlled her tears, and returned her handkerchief to her pocket. She did not find it difficult to forgive her father, nor could she altogether refuse to join him in the returning gaiety of spirit to which her present avowal gave rise. It was such a load off his heart to think that he should not be called on to welcome Mr. Slope as his son-in-law! It was such a relief to him to find that his daughter's feelings and his own were now, as they ever had been, in unison. He had been so unhappy for the last six weeks about this wretched Mr. Slope! He was so indifferent as to the loss of the hospital, so thankful for the recovery of his daughter, that, strong as was the ground for Eleanor's anger, she could not find it in her heart to be long angry with him. "Dear papa," she said, hanging closely to his arm, "never suspect me again. Promise me that you never will. Whatever I do, you may be sure I shall tell you first; you may be sure I shall consult you."

And Mr. Harding did promise, and owned his sin, and promised again. And so, while he promised amendment and she uttered forgiveness, they returned together to the drawing-room windows.

And what had Eleanor meant when she declared that whatever she did, she would tell her father first? What was she thinking of doing?

80 ended the first act of the melodrama which Eleanor was called on to perform this day at Ullathorne. THE SIGNORA NERONI, THE COUNTESS DE COURCY, AND MRS.

PROUDIE MEET EACH OTHER AT UL-LATHORNE.

And now there were new arrivals. Just as Eleanor reached the drawing-room the Signora was being wheeled into it. She had been brought out of the carriage into the dining-room and there placed on a sofa, and was now in the act of entering the other room, by the joint aid of her brother and sister, Mr. Arabin, and two servants in livery. She was all in her glory, and looked so pathetically happy, so full of affliction and grace, was so beautiful, so pitiable, and so charming, that it was almost impossible not to be glad she was there.

Miss Thorne was unaffectedly glad to welcome her. In fact, the Signora was a sort of lion; and though there was no drop of the Leohunter blood in Miss Thorne's veins, she nevertheless did like to see attractive people at her house. The Signora was attractive, and on her first settlement in the dining-room she had whispered two or three soft feminine words into Miss Thorne's ear, which, at the moment, had quite touched that lady's heart.

"Oh, Miss Thorne; where is Miss Thorne?" she said, as soon as her attendants had placed her in her position just before one of the windows, from whence she could see all that was going on upon the lawn; "How am I to thank you for permitting a creature like me to be here? But if you knew the pleasure you give me, I am sure you would excuse the trouble I bring with me." And as she spoke she squeezed the spinster's little hand between her own.

"We are delighted to see you here," said Miss Thorne; "you give us no trouble at all, and we think it a great favour conferred by you to come and see us;

don't we Wilfred?"

"A very great favour indeed," said Mr. Thorne, with a gallant bow, but of a somewhat less cordial welcome than that conceded by his sister. Mr. Thorne had heard perhaps more of the antecedents of his guest than his sister had done, and had not as yet undergone the power of the Signora's charms.

But while the mother of the last of the Neros was thus in her full splendour, with crowds of people gazing at her and the elite of the company standing round her couch, her glory was paled by the arrival of the Countess De Courcy. Miss Thorne had now been waiting three hours for the countess, and could not therefore but show very evident gratification when the arrival at last took place. She and her brother of course went off to welcome the titled grandees, and with them, alas, went many of the Signora's admirers.

"Oh, Mr. Thorne," said the countess, while in the act of being disrobed of her fur cloaks, and re-robed in her gauze shawls, "what dreadful roads you have; perfectly frightful." It happened that Mr. Thorne was way-warden for the district, and not liking the attack, began to excuse his roads. "Oh yes, indeed they are," said the countess, not minding him in the least, "perfectly dreadful; are they not, Margaretta? Why, my dear Miss Thorne, we left Courcy Castle just at eleven; it was only just past eleven, was it not, John? and"

"Just past one, I think you mean," said the Honourable John, turning from the group and eyeing the Signora through his glass. The Signora gave him back his own, as the saying is, and more with it; so that the young nobleman was forced to avert his glance, and drop his glass.

"I say, Thorne," whispered he, "who the deuce is that on the sofa?"

"Dr. Stanhope's daughter," whispered back Mr. Thorne. "Signora Neroni, she calls herself." "Whew-ew-ew!" whistled the Honourable John. "The devil she is! I have heard no end of stories about that filly. You must positively introduce me, Thorne; you positively must."

Mr. Thorne, who was respectability itself, did not quite like having a guest about whom the Honourable John De Courcy had heard no end of stories; but he couldn't help himself. He merely resolved that before he went to bed he would let his sister know somewhat of the history of the lady she was so willing to welcome. The innocence of Miss Thorne, at her time of life, was perfectly charming; but even innocence may be dangerous.

"John may say what he likes," continued the countess, urging her excuses to Miss Thorne; "I am sure we were past the castle gate before twelve, weren't we, Margaretta?"

"Upon my word I don't know," said the Lady Margaretta, "for I was half asleep. But I do know that I was called sometime in the middle of the night, and was dressing myself before daylight."

Wise people, when they are in the wrong, always put themselves right by finding fault with the people against whom they have sinned. Lady De Courcy was a wise woman; and therefore, having treated Miss Thorne very badly by staying away till three o'clock, she assumed the offensive and attacked Mr. Thorne's roads. Her daughter, not less wise, attacked Miss Thorne's early hours. The art of doing this is among the most precious of those usually cultivated by persons who know how to live. There is no withstanding it. Who can go systematically to work, and having done battle with the primary accusation and settled that, then bring forward a counter-charge and support that also? Life is not long enough for such labours. A man in the right relies easily on his rectitude, and therefore goes about unarmed. His very strength is his weakness. A man in the wrong knows that he must look to his weapons. Hia very weakness is his strength. The one is never prepared for combat, the other is always ready. Therefore it is that in this world the man that is in the wrong almost invariably conquers the man that is in the right,—and invariably despises him. A man must be an idiot or else an angel who after the age of forty shall attempt to be just to his neighbours. Many like the Lady Margaretta have learnt their lesson at a much earlier age. But this of course depends on the school in which they have been taught.

Poor Miss Thorne was altogether overcome. She knew very well that she had been ill treated, and yet she found herself making apologies to Lady De Courcy. To do her ladyship justice, she received them very graciously, and allowed herself with her train of daughters to be led towards the lawn.

There were two windows in the drawing-room wide open for the countess to pass through; but she saw that there was a woman on a sofa, at the third window, and that that woman had, as it were, a following attached to her. Her ladyship therefore determined to investigate the woman. The De Courcys were hereditarily short sighted, and had been so for thirty centuries at least. So Lady De Courcy, who when she entered the family had adopted the family habits, did as her son had done before her, and taking her glass to investigate the Signora Neroni, pressed in among the gentlemen who surrounded the couch, and bowed slightly to those whom she chose to honour by her acquaintance.

In order to get to the window she had to pass close to the front of the couch, and as she did so she stared hard at the occupant. The occupant in return stared hard at the countess. The countess who since her countess-ship commenced had been accustomed to see all eyes, not royal, ducal or marquesal, fall before her own, paused as she went on, raised her eyebrows, and stared even harder than before. But she had now to do with one who cared little for countesses. It was, one may say, impossible for mortal man or woman to abash Madeline Neroni. She opened her large bright lustrous eyes wider and wider, till she seemed to be all eyes. She gazed up into the lady's face, not as though she did it with an effort, but as if she delighted in doing it. She used no glass to assist her effrontery, and needed none. The faintest possible smile of derision played round her mouth, and her nostrils were slightly dilated, as if in sure anticipation of her triumph. And it was

sure. The Countess De Courcy, in spite of her thirty centuries and De Courcy castle, and the fact that Lord De Courcy was grand master of the ponies to the Prince of Wales, had not a chance with her. At first the little circlet of gold wavered in the countess's hand, then the hand shook, then the circlet fell, the countess's head tossed itself into the air, and the countess's feet shambled out to the lawn. She did not however go so fast but what she heard the Signora's voice, asking; "Who on earth is that woman, Mr. Slope?" "That is Lady De Courcy."

"Oh, ah. I might have supposed so. Ha, ha, ha. Well, that's as good as a play." It was as good as a play to any there who had eyes to observe it, and wit to comment on what they observed.

But the Lady De Courcy soon found a congenial spirit on the lawn. There she encountered Mrs. Proudie, and as Mrs. Proudie was not only the wife of a bishop, but was also the cousin of an earl, Lady De Courcy considered her to be the fittest companion she was likely to meet in that assemblage. They were accordingly delighted to see each other. Mrs. Proudie by no means despised a countess, and as this countess lived in the county and within a sort of extensive visiting distance of Barchester, she was glad to have this opportunity of ingratiating herself.

"My dear Lady De Courcy, I am so delighted," said she, looking as little grim as it was in her nature to do. "I hardly expected to see you here. It is such a distance, and then you know, such a crowd."

"And such roads, Mrs. Proudie! I really wonder how the people ever get about. But I don't suppose they ever do. "

"Well, I really don't know; but I suppose not. The Thornes donlt, I know," said Mrs. Proudie. "Very nice person, Miss Thorne, isn't she?"

"Oh, delightful, and so queer. I've known her these twenty years. A great pet of mine is dear Miss Thorne. She is so very strange, you know. She always makes me think of the Esquimaux and the Indians. Isn't her dress quite delightful?"

'.'Delightful," said Mrs. Proudie. "I wonder now whether she paints. Did you ever see such colour?"

"Oh, of ceurse." said Lady De Courcy; "that is, I have no doubt she does. But, Mrs. Proudie, who is that woman on the sofa by the window? just step this way and you'll see her, there;

"and the countess led her to a spot where she could plainly see the Signora's well-remembered face and figure.

She did not however do so without being equally well seen by the Signora. "Look, look," said that lady to Mr. Slope, who was still standing near to her; "see the high spiritualities and temporalities of the land in league together, and all against poor me. I'll wager my bracelet, Mr. Slope, against your next sermon, that they've taken up their position there on purpose to pull me to pieces. Well; I can't rush to the combat, but I know how to protect myself if the enemy come near me."

But the enemy knew better. They could gain nothing by contact with the Signora Neroni, and they could abuse her as they pleased at a distance from her on the lawn. "She's that horrid Italian woman, Lady De Courcy; you must have heard of her."

"What Italian woman?" said her ladyship, quite alive to the coming story. "I don't think I've heard of any Italian woman coming into the country. She doesn't look Italian either."

"Oh, you must have heard of her," said Mrs. Proudie. "No, she's not absolutely Italian. She is Dr. Stanhope's daughter,— Dr. Stanhope the prebendary; and she calls herself the Signora Neroni."

"Oh-h-h-h!" exclaimed the countess.

"I was sure you had heard of her," continued Mrs. Proudie. "I don't know anything about her husband. They do say that some man named Neroni is still alive. I believe she did marry such a man abroad, but I do not at all know who or what he was."

"Ah-h-h-h!" said the countess, shaking her head with much intelligence, as every additional "h" fell from her lips. "I know all about it now. I have heard George mention her. George knows all about her. George heard about her in Rome."

"She's an abominable woman, at any rate," said Mrs. Proudie.

"Insufferable," said the countess.

"She made her way into the palace once before I knew anything about her; and I cannot tell you how dreadfully indecent her conduct was."

"Was it?" said the delighted countess.

"Insufferable," said the prelatess.

"But why does she lie on a sofa?" asked Lady De Courcy.

"She has only one leg," replied Mrs. Proudie.

"Only one leg!" said Lady De Courcy, who felt to a certain degree dissatisfied that the Signora was thus incapacitated. "Was she born so?"

"Oh, no," said Mrs. Proudie,—and her ladyship felt somewhat recomforted by the assurance,—" she had two. But that Signor Neroni beat her, I believe, till she was obliged to have one amputated. At any rate, she entirely lost the use of it."

"Unfortunate creature!" said the countess, who herself knew something of matrimonial trials.

"Yes," said Mrs. Proudie; "one would pity her, in spite of her past bad conduct, if she now knew how to behave herself. But she does not. She is the most insolent creature I ever put my eyes on."

"Indeed she is," said Lady De Courcy.

"And her conduct with men is so abominable, that she is not fit to be admitted into any lady's drawing-room."

"Dear me!" said the countess, becoming again excited, happy, and merciless.

"You saw that man standing near her,—the clergyman with the red hair?"

"Yes, yes."

"She has absolutely ruined that man. The bishop, or I should rather take the blame on myself, for it was I,—I brought him down from London to Barchester. He is a tolerable preacher, an active young man, and I therefore introduced him to the bishop. That woman, Lady De Courcy, has got hold of him, and has so disgraced him, that I am forced to require that he shall leave

the palace; and I doubt very much whether he won't lose his gown!"

"Why what an idiot the man must be!" said the countess. "You don't know the intriguing villany of that woman," said Mrs. Proudie, remembering her torn flounces. "But you say she has only got one leg!"

"She is as full of mischief as tho' she had ten. Look at her eyes, Lady De Courcy. Did you ever see such eyes in a decent woman's head?"

"Indeed I never did, Mrs. Proudie."

" And her effrontery, and her voice; I quite pity her poor father, who is really a good sort of man." "Dr. Stanhope, isn't he?"

"Yes, Dr. Stanhope. He is one of our prebendaries,—a good quiet sort of man himself. But I am surprised that he should let his daughter conduct herself as she does."

"I suppose he can't help it," said the countess.

"But a clergyman, you know, Lady De Courcy! He should at any rate prevent her from exhibiting in public, if he cannot induce her to behave at home. But he is to be pitied. I believe he has a desperate life of it with the lot of them. That apish-looking man there, with the long beard and the loose trousers,—he is the woman's brother. He is nearly as bad as she is. They are both of them infidels."

"Infidels!" said Lady De Courcy, "and their father a prebendary!"

"Yes, and likely to be the new dean too," said Mrs. Proudie.

"Oh, yes, poor dear Dr. Trefoil!" said the countess, who had once in her life spoken to that gentleman; "I was so distressed to hear it, Mrs. Proudie. And so Dr. Stanhope is to be the new dean! He comes of an excellent family, and I wish him success in spite of his daughter. Perhaps, Mrs. Proudie, when he is dean they'll be better able to see the error of their ways."

To this Mrs. Proudie said nothing. Her dislike of the Signora Neroni was too deep to admit of her even hoping that that lady should see the error of her ways. Mrs. Proudie looked on the Signora as one of the lost,—one of those

beyond the reach of

Vol. Ii. a

Christian charity, and was therefore able to enjoy the luxury of hating her, without the drawback of wishing her eventually well out of her sins.

Any further conversation between these congenial souls was prevented by the advent of Mr. Thorne, who came to lead the countess to the tent. Indeed, he had been desired to do so some ten minutes since; but he had been delayed in the drawing-room by the Signora. She had contrived to detain him, to get him near to her sofa, and at last to make him seat himself on a chair close to her beautiful arm. The fish took the bait, was hooked, and caught, and landed. Within that ten minutes he had heard the whole of the Signora's history in such strains as she chose to use in telling it. He learnt from the lady's own bps the whole of that mysterious tale to which the Honourable George had merely alluded. He discovered that the beautiful creature lying before him had been more sinned against than sinning. She had owned to him that she had been weak, confiding and indifferent to the world's opinion, and that she had therefore been ill-used, deceived and evil spoken of. She had spoken to him of her mutilated limb, her youth destroyed in its fullest bloom, her beauty robbed of its every charm, her life blighted, her hopes withered; and as she did so, a tear dropped from her eye to her cheek. She had told him of these things, and asked for his sympathy.

What could a good-natured genial Anglo-Saxon Squire Thorne do but promise to sympathise with her? Mr. Thorne did promise to sympathise; promised also to come and see the last of the Neros, to hear more of those fearful Roman days, of those light and innocent but dangerous hours which flitted by so fast on the shores of Como, and to make himself the confidant of the Signora's sorrows.

We need hardly say that he dropped all idea of warning his sister against the dangerous lady. He had been mistaken;—never so much mistaken in his life. He had always regarded that Honourable George as a coarse brutal-minded young man; now he was more convinced than ever that he was so. It was by such men as the Honourable George that the reputations of such women as Madeline Neroni were imperilled and damaged. He would go and see the lady in her own house. He was fully sure in his own mind of the soundness of his own judgment. If he found her, as he believed he should do, an injured well-disposed warm-hearted woman, he would get his sister Monica to invite her out to Ullathorne.

"No," said she, as at her instance he got up to leave her, and declared that he himself would attend upon her wants; " no, no, my friend; I positively put a veto upon your doing so. What, in your own house, with an assemblage round you such as there is here! Do you wish to make every woman hate me and every man stare at me? I lay a positive order on you not to come near me again to-day. Come and see me at home. It is only at home that I can talk. It is only at home that I really can live and enjoy myself. My days of going out, days such as these, are rare indeed. Come and see me at home, Mr. Thorne, and then I will not bid you to leave me."

It is, we believe, common with young men of five and twenty to look on their seniors,—on men of, say, double their own age,—as so many stocks and stones,—stocks and stones, that is, in regard to feminine beauty. There never was a greater mistake. Women, indeed, generally know better; but on this subject men of one age are thoroughly ignorant of what is the very nature of mankind of other ages. No experience of what goes on in the world, no reading of history, no observation of life, has any effect in teaching the truth. Men of fifty don't dance mazurkas, being generally too fat and wheezy; nor do they sit for the hour together on river banks at their mistresses' feet, being somewhat afraid of rheumatism. But for real true love, love at first sight, love to devotion, love that robs a man of his sleep, love that " will gaze an eagle blind," love that "will hear the lowest sound when the suspicious tread of theft is stopped," love that is "like a Hercules, still climbing trees in the Hesperides,"—we believe the best age is from forty-five to seventy. Up to that men are generally given to mere flirting.

At the present moment Mr. Thorne, setat. fifty, was over head and ears in love at first sight with the Signora Madeline Vesey Neroni, nata Stanhope.

Nevertheless he was sufficiently master of himself to offer his arm with all propriety to Lady De Courcy, and the countess graciously permitted herself to be led to the tent. Such had been Miss Thorne's orders, as she had succeeded in inducing the bishop to lead old Lady Knowle to the top of the dining-room. One of the baronets was sent off in quest of Mrs. Proudie and found that lady on the lawn not in the best of humours. Mr. Thorne and the countess had left her too abruptly; she had in vain looked about for an attendant chaplain, or even a stray curate; they were all drawing long bows with the young ladies at the bottom of the lawn, or finding places for their graceful cotoxophilites in some snug corner of the tent. In such position Mrs. Proudie had been wont in earlier days to fall back upon Mr. Slope; but now she could never fall back upon him again. She gave her head one shake as she thought of her lone position, and that shake was as good as a week deducted from Mr. Slope's longer sojourn in Barchester. Sir Harkaway Gorse, however, relieved her present misery, though his doing so by no means mitigated the sinning chaplain's doom.

And now the eating and drinking began in earnest. Dr. Grantly, to his great horror, found himself leagued to Mrs. Clantantram. Mrs. Clantantram had a great regard for the archdeacon, which was not cordially returned; and when she, coming up to him, whispered in his ear, "Come, archdeacon, I'm sure you won't begrudge an old friend the favour of your arm," and then proceeded to tell him the whole history of her roquelaure, he resolved that he would shake her off before he was fifteen minutes older. But latterly the archdeacon had not been successful in his resolutions; and on the present occasion Mrs. Clantantram stuck to him till the banquet was over.

Dr. Gwynne got a baronet's wife, and Mrs. Grantly fell to the lot of a baronet. Charlotte Stanhope attached herself to Mr. Harding in order to make room for Bertie, who succeeded in Bitting down in the dining-room next to Mrs. Bold. To speak sooth, now that he had love in earnest to make, his heart almost failed him.

Eleanor had been right glad to avail herself of his arm, seeing that Mr. Slope was hovering nigh her. In striving to avoid that terrible Charybdis of a Slope she was in great danger of falling into an unseen Scylla on the other hand, that Scylla being Bertie Stanhope. Nothing could be more gracious than she was to Bertie. She almost jumped at his proffered arm. Charlotte perceived this from a distance, and triumphed in her heart; Bertie felt it, and was encouraged; Mr. Slope saw it, and glowered with jealousy. Eleanor and Bertie sat down to table in the diningroom; and as she took her seat at his right hand, she found that Mr. Slope was already in possession of the chair at her own.

As these things were going on in the dining-room Mr. Arabia was hanging enraptured and alone over the Signora's sofa; and Eleanor from her seat could look through the open door and soe that he was doing so.

CHAPTER XXXVm. THE BISHOP BREAKFASTS, AND THE DEAN DIES.

The bishop of Barchester said grace over the well-spread board in the Ullathorne dining-room; and while he did so the last breath was flying from the dean of Barchester as he lay in his sick room in the deanery. "When the bishop of Barchester raised his first glass of champagne to his lips the deanship of Barchester was a good thing in the gift of the prime minister. Before the bishop of Barchester had left the table, the minister of the day was made aware of the fact at his country seat in Hampshire, and had already turned over in his mind the names of five very respectable aspirants for the preferment. It is at present only necessary to say that Mr. Slope's name was not among the five.

'' 'Twas merry in the hall when the beards wagged all;" and the clerical beards wagged merrily in the hall of Ullathorne that day. It was not till after the last cork had been drawn, the last speech made, the last nut cracked, that tidings reached and were whispered about that the poor dean was no more. It was well for the happiness of the clerical beards that this little delay took place, as otherwise decency would have forbidden them to wag at all.

But there was one sad man among them that day. Mr. Arabin's beard did not wag as it should have done. He had come there hoping the best, striving to think the best, about Eleanor; turning over in his mind all the words he remembered to have fallen from her about Mr. Slope, and trying to gather from them a conviction unfavourable to his rival. He had not exactly resolved to come that day to some decisive proof as to the widow's intention; but' he c had meant, if possible, to re-cultivate his friendship with Eleanor; and in his present frame of mind any such re-cultivation must have ended in a declaration of love.

He had passed the previous night alone at his new parsonage, and it was the first night that he had so passed. It had been dull and sombre enough. Mrs. Grantly had been right in saying that a priestess would be wanting at St. Ewold's. He had sat there alone with his glass before him, and then with his teapot, thinking about Eleanor Bold. As is usual in such meditations he did little but blame her; blame her for liking Mr. Slope, and blame her for not liking him; blame her for her cordiality to himself, and blame her for her want of cordiality; blame her for being stubborn, headstrong, and passionate; and yet the more he thought of her the higher she rose in his affection. If only it should turn out, if only it could be made to turn out, that she had defended Mr. Slope, not from love, but on principle, all would be right. Such principle in itself would be admirable, loveable, womanly. He felt that he could be pleased to allow Mr. Slope just so much favour as that. But

if And then Mr. Arabin poked his fire most unneces sarily, spoke crossly to his new parlour-maid who came in for the tea-things, and threw himself back in his chair determined to go to sleep. Why had she been so stiffnecked when asked a plain question? She could not but have known in what light he regarded her. Why had she not answered a plain question, and so put an end to his misery? Then, instead of going to sleep in his arm-chair, Mr. Arabin walked about the room as though he had been possessed.

On the following morning when he attended Miss Thorne's behests he was still in a somewhat confused state. His first duty had been to converse with Mrs. Clantantram, and that lady had found it impossible to elicit the slightest sympathy from him on the subject of her roquelaure. Miss Thorne had asked him whether Mrs. Bold was coming with the Grantlys; and tho two names of Bold and Grantly together had nearly made him jump from his seat.

He was in this state of confused uncertainty, hope, and doubt, when he saw Mr. Slope, with his most polished smile, handing Eleanor out of her carriage. He thought of nothing more. He never considered whether the carriage belonged to her or to Mr. Slope, or to any one else to whom they might both be mutually obliged without any concert between themselves. This sight in his present state of mind was quite enough to upset him and his resolves. It was clear as noonday. Had he seen her handed into a carriage by Mr. Slope at a church door with a white veil over her head, the truth could not be more manifest. He went into the house, and, as we have seen, soon found himself walking with Mr. Harding. Shortly afterwards Eleanor came up; and then he had to leave his companion, and either go about alone br find another. "While in this state he was encountered by the archdeacon.

"I wonder," said Dr. Grantly, "if it be true that Mr. Slope and Mrs. Bold came here together. Susan says she is almost sure she saw their faces in the same carriage as she got out of her own.

" Mr. Arabin had nothing for it but to bear his testimony to the correctness of Mrs. Grantly's eyesight. "It is perfectly shameful," said the archdeacon; "or I should rather say, shameless. She was asked here as my guest; and if she be determined to disgrace herself, she should have feeling enough not to do so before my immediate friends. I wonder how that man got himself invited. I wonder whether she had the face to bring him."

To this Mr. Arabin could answer nothing, nor did he wish to answer anything. Though he abused Eleanor to himself, he did not choose to abuse her to any one else, nor was he well pleased to hear any one else speak ill of her. Dr. Grantly, however, was very angry, and did not spare his sister-in-law. Mr. Arabin therefore left him as soon as he could, and wandered back into the house. He had not been there long, when the Signora was brought in. For some time he kept himself out of temptation, and merely hovered round her at a distance; but as soon as Mr. Thome had left her, he yielded himself up to the basilisk, and allowed himself to be made prey of.

It is impossible to say how the knowledge had been acquired, but the Signora had a sort of instinctive knowledge that Mr. Arabin was an admirer of Mrs. Bold. Men hunt fores by the aid of dogs, and are aware that they do so by the strong organ of smell with which the dog is endowed. They do not, however, in the least comprehend how such a sense can work with such acuteness. The organ by which women instinctively, as it were, know and feel how other women are regarded by men, and how also men are regarded by other women, is equally strong, and equally incomprehensible. A glance, a word, a motion, suffices. By some such acute exercise of her feminine senses the Signora was aware that Mr. Arabin loved Eleanor Bold; and therefore, by a further exercise of her peculiar feminine propensities, it was quite natural for her to entrap Mr. Arabin into her net.

The work was half done before she came to Ullathorne, and when could she have a better opportunity of completing it? She had had almost enough of Mr. Slope, though she could not quite resist the fun of driving a very sanctimonious clergyman to madness by a desperate and ruinous passion. Mr. Thorne had fallen too easily to give much pleasure in the chase. His position as a man of wealth might make his alliance of value, but as a lover he was very second-rate. We may say that she regarded him somewhat as a sportsman does a pheasant. The bird is so easily shot, that he would not be worth the shooting were it not for the very respectable appearance that he makes in a larder. The Signora would not waste much time in shooting Mr. Thorne, but still he was worth bagging for family uses.

But Mr. Arabin was game of another sort. The Signora was herself possessed of quite sufficient intelligence to know that Mr. Arabin was a man more than usually intellectual. She knew also, that as a clergyman he was of a much higher stamp than Mr. Slope, and that as a gentleman he was better educated than Mr. Thorne. She would never have attempted to drive Mr. Arabin into ridiculous misery as she did Mr. Slope, nor would she think it possible to dispose of him in ten minutes as she had done with Mr. Thorne.

Such were her reflections about Mr. Arabin. As to Mr. Arabin, it cannot be said that he reflected at all about the Signora. He knew that she was beautiful, and he felt that she was able to charm him. He required charming in his present misery, and therefore he went and stood at the head of her couch. She knew all about it. Such were her peculiar gifts. It was her nature to see that he required charming, and it was her province to charm him. As the Eastern idler swallows his dose of opium, as the London reprobate swallows his dose of gin, so with similar desires and for similar reasons did Mr. Arabin prepare to swallow the charms of the Signora Neroni.

"Why an't you shooting with bows and arrows, Mr. Arabin?" said she, when they were nearly alone together in the drawingroom; "or talking with young ladies in shady bowers, or turning your talents to account in some way? What was a bachelor like you asked here for? Don't you mean to earn your cold chicken and champagne? Were I you I should be ashamed to be so idle."

Mr. Arabin murmured some sort of answer. Though he wished to be charmed, he was hardly yet in a mood to be playful in return.

"Why, what ails you, Mr. Arabin?" said she. "Here you are in your own parish; Miss Thorne tells me that her party is given expressly in your honour; and yet you are the only dull man at it. Your friend Mr. Slope was with me a few minutes since, full of life and spirits. Why don't you rival him?"

It was not difficult for so acute an observer as Madeline Neroni to see that she had hit the nail on the head and driven the bolt home. Mr. Arabin winced visibly before her attack, and she knew at once that he was jealous of Mr. Slope.

"But I look on you and Mr. Slope as the very antipodes of men," said she. "There is nothing in which you are not each the reverse of the other, except in belonging to the same profession: and even in that you are so unlike as perfectly to maintain the rule. He is gregarious; you are given to solitude. He is active, you are passive. He works, you think. He likes women, you despise them. He is fond of position and power,—and so are you, but for directly different reasons. He loves to be praised. You very foolishly abhor it. He will gain his rewards, which will be an insipid useful wife, a' comfortable income, and a reputation for sanctimony. You will also gain yours."

"Well, and what will they be?" said Mr. Arabin, who knew that he was being flattered, and yet suffered himself to put up with it. "What will be my rewards?"

"The heart of some woman whom you will be too austere to own that you love, and the respect of some few friends which you will be too proud to own that you value."

"Eich rewards," said he; "but of little worth if they are to be so treated."

"Oh; you are not to look for such success as awaits Mr. Slope. He is born to be a successful man. He suggests to himself an object, and then starts for it with eager intention. Nothing will deter him from his pursuit. He will have no scruples, no fears, no hesitation. His desire is to be a bishop with a rising family. The wife will come first, and in due time the apron. You will see all this, and then"

"Well, and what then?"

"Then you will begin to wish that you had done the same."

Mr. Arabin looked placidly out at the lawn, and resting his shoulder on the head of the sofa, rubbed his chin with his hand. It was a trick he had when he was thinking deeply; and what the Signora said made him think. Was it not all true? Would he not hereafter look back, if not at Mr. Slope, at some others, perhaps not equally gifted with himself, who had risen in the world while: he had lagged behind, and then wish that he had done the same?. "Is not such the doom of all speculative men of talent?" said she. "Do they not all sit rapt as you now are, cutting imaginary silken cords with their fine edges, while those not so highly tempered sever the every-day Gordian knots of the world's struggle, and win wealth and renown? Steel too highly polished, edges too sharp. do not do for this world's work, Mr. Arabin."

Who was this woman that thus read the secrets of his heart, and re-uttered to Mm the unwelcome bodings of his own soul? He looked full into her face when she had done speaking, and said, "Am I one of those foolish blades, too sharp and too fine to do a useful day's work?"

"Why do you let the Slopes of the world out-distance you?'' said she. '' Is not the blood in your veins as warm as his? Does not your pulse beat as fast? Has not God made you a man, and intended you to do a man's work here; ay, and to take a man's wages also?"

Mr. Arabin sat ruminating and rubbing his face, and wondering why these things were said to him; but he replied nothing. The Signora went on. "The greatest mistake any man ever made is to suppose that the good things of the world are not worth the winning. And it is a mistake so opposed to the religion which you preach! Why does God permit his bishops one after another to have their five thousands and ten thousands a year if such wealth be bad and not worth having? Why are beautiful things given to us, and luxuries and pleasant enjoyments, if they be not intended to be used? They must be meant for some one, and what is good for a layman cannot surely be bad for a clerk. You try to despise these good things, but you only try; you don't succeed."

"Don't I," said Mr. Arabin, still musing, and not knowing what he said.

"I ask you the question; do you succeed?"

Mr. Arabin looked at her piteously. It seemed to him as though he were being interrogated by some inner spirit of his own, to whom he could not refuse an answer, and to whom he did not dare to give a false reply.

"Come, Mr. Arabin, confess; do you succeed? Is money so contemptible? Is worldly power so worthless? Is feminine beauty a trifle to be so slightly regarded by a wise man?"

"Feminine beauty!" said he, gazing into her face, as though all the feminine beauty in the world were concentrated there. "Why do you say I do not regard it?"

"Ii you look at me like that, Mr. Arabin, I shall alter my opinion;—or should do so, were I not of course aware that I have no beauty of my own worth regarding."

The gentleman blushed crimson, but the lady did not blush at all. A slightly increased colour animated her face, just so much so as to give her an air of special interest. She expected a compliment from her admirer, but she was rather grateful than otherwise by finding that he did not pay it to her. Messrs. Slope and Thome, Messrs. Brown, Jones and Robinson, they all paid her compliments. She was rather in hopes that she would ultimately succeed in inducing Mr. Arabin to abuse her.

"But your gaze," said she, " is one of wonder, and not of admiration. You wonder at my audacity in asking you such questions about yourself.

"Well, I do rather," said he.

'' Nevertheless I expect an answer, Mr. Arabin. "Why were women made beautiful if men are not to regard them?" "But men do regard them," he replied. "And why not you?"

"You are begging the question, Madame Neroni."

"I am sure I shall beg nothing, Mr. Arabin, which you will not grant, and I do beg for an answer. Do you not as a rule think women below your notice as companions? Let us see. There is the widow Bold looking round at you from her chair this minute. What would you say to her as a companion for life?"

Mr. Arabin, rising from his position, leaned over the sofa and looked through the drawing-room door to the place where Eleanor was seated between Bertie Stanhope and Mr. Slope. She at once caught his glance, and averted her own. She was not pleasantly placed in her present position. Mr. Slope was doing his best to attract her attention; and she was striving to prevent his doing so by talking to Mr. Stanhope, while her mind was intently fixed on Mr. Arabin and Madame Neroni. Bertie Stanhope endeavoured to take advantage of her favours, but he was thinking more of the manner in which he would by-and-by throw himself at her feet, than of amusing her at the present moment.

"There," said the Signora. "She was stretching her beautiful neck to look at you, aud now you have disturbed her. Well I declare, I believe I am wrong about you. I believe that you do think Mrs. Bold a charming woman. Your looks seem to say so; and by her looks I should say that she is jealous of me. Come, Mr. Arabin, confide in me, and if it is so, I'll do all in my power to make up the match."

It is needless to say that the Signora was not very sincere in her offer. She was never sincere on such subjects. She never expected others to be so, nor did she expect others to think her so. Such matters were her playthings, her billiard table, her hounds and hunters, her waltzes and polkas, her picnics and summer-day excursions. She had little else to amuse her, and therefore played at love-making in all its forms. She was now playing at it with Mr. Arabin, and did not at all expect the earnestness and truth of his answer. "All in your power would be nothing," said he; "for Mrs. Bold is, I imagine, already engaged to another."

"Then you own the impeachment yourself."

"You cross-question me rather unfairly," he replied, "and I do not know why I answer you at all. Mrs. Bold is a very beautiful woman, and as intelligent as beautiful. It is impossible to know her without admiring her."

"So you think the widow a very beautiful woman?"

"Indeed I do."

"And one that would grace the parsonage of St. Ewold's."

"One that would well grace any man's house."

"And you really have the effrontery to tell me this," said she; —"to tell me, who, as you very well know, set up to be a beauty myself, and who am at this very moment taking such an interest in your affairs, you really have the effrontery to tell me that Mrs. Bold is the most beautiful woman you know!"

"I did not say so," said Mr. Arabin; "you are more beautiful."

"Ah, come now; that is something like. I thought you could not be so unfeeling."

"You are more beautiful; perhaps more clever."

"Thank you, thank you, Mr. Arabin. I knew that you and I should be friends." "But"

"Not a word further. I will not hear a word further. If you talk till midnight, you cannot improve what you have said. " "But Madame Neroni, Mrs. Bold"

"I will not hear a word about Mrs. Bold. Dread thoughts of strychnine did pass across my brain, but she is welcome to the second place."

"Her place"

"I won't hear anything about her or her place. I am satisfied, and that is enough. But, Mr. Arabin, I am dying with hunger. Beautiful and clever as I am, you know I cannot go to my food, and yet you do not bring it to me."

This at any rate was so true as to make it necessary that Mr. Arabin should act upon it, and he accordingly went into the diningroom and supplied the Signora's wants.

'' And yourself?" said she.

"Oh," said he, "I am not hungry; I never eat at this hour."

"Come, come, Mr. Arabin, don't let love interfere with your appetite. It never does with mine. Give me half a glass more champagne, and then go to the table. Mrs. Bold will do me an injury if you stay talking to me any longer."

Mr. Arabin did as he was bid. He took her plate and glass from her, and going into the dining-room, helped himself to a sandwich from the crowded table and began munching it in a corner. As he was doing so, Miss Thorne, who had hardly sat down for a moment, came into the room, and seeing him standing, was greatly distressed. "Oh, my dear Mr. Arabin," said she, "have you never sat down yet? I am so distressed. You of all men too."

Mr. Arabin assured her that he had only just come into the room. "That is the very reason why you should lose no more time. Come, I'll make room for you. Thank 'ee, my dear," she said, seeing that Mrs. Bold was making an attempt to move from her chair, "but I would not for worlds see you stir, for all the ladies 'would think it necessary to follow. But, perhaps, if Mr. Stanhope has done,—just for a minute, Mr. Stanhope,—till I can get Another chair."

And so Bertie had to rise to male way for his rival. This he did, as he did everything, with an air of good-humoured pleasantry which made it impossible for Mr. Arabin to refuse the proffered seat.

"His bishopric let another take," said Bertie;—the quotation being certainly not appropriate, either for the occasion or the person spoken to. "I have eaten and am satisfied. Mr.. Arabin, pray take my chair. I wish for your sake that it really was a bishop's seat."

Mr. Arabin did sit down, and as he did so, Mrs. Bold got up as though to follow her neighbour.

"Pray, pray don't move," said Miss Thome, almost forcing Eleanor back into her chair. "Mr. Stanhope is not going to leave us. He will stand behind you like a true knight as he is. And now I think of it, Mr. Arabin, let me introduce you to Mr. Slope. Mr. Slope, Mr. Arabin." And the two gentlemen bowed stiffly to each other across the lady whom they both intended to marry, while the other gentleman who also intended to marry her stood behind, watching them.

The two had never met each other before, and the present was certainly not a good opportunity for much cordial conversation even if cordial conversation between them had been possible. As it was, the whole four who formed the party seemed as though their tongues were tied. Mr. Slope, who was wide awake to what he hoped was his coming opportunity, was not much concerned in the interest of the moment. His wish was to see Eleanor move, that he might pursue her. Bertie was not exactly in the same frame of mind; the evil day was near enough; there was no reason why he should precipitate it. He had made up his mind to marry Eleanor Bold if he could, and was resolved to-day to take the first preliminary step towards doing so. But there was time enough before him. He was not going to make an offer of marriage over the table-cloth. Having thus good-naturedly made way for Mr. Arabin, he was willing also to let him talk to the future Mrs. Stanhope as long as they remained in their present position.

Mr. Arabin, having bowed to Mr. Slope, began eating his food without saying a word further. He was full of thought, and though he ate he did so unconsciously.

But poor Eleanor was the most to be pitied. The only friend on whom she thought she could rely, was Bertie Stanhope, and he, it seemed, was determined to desert her. Mr. Arabin did not attempt to address her. She said a few words in reply to some remarks from Mr. Slope, and then feeling the situation too much for her, started from her chair in spite of Miss Thorne, and hurried from the

room. Mr. Slope followed her, and young Stanhope lost the occasion.

Madeline Neroni, when she was left alone, could not help pondering much on the singular interview she had had with this singular man. Not a word that she had spoken to him had been intended by her to be received as true, and yet he had answered her in the very spirit of truth. He had done so, and she had been aware that he had so done. She had wormed from him his secret; and he, debarred as it would seem from man's usual privilege of lying, had innocently laid bare his whole soul to her. He loved Eleanor Bold, but Eleanor was not in his eye so beautiful as herself. He would fain have Eleanor for his wife, but yet he had acknowledged that she was the less gifted of the two. The man had literally been unable to falsify his thoughts when questioned, and had been compelled to be true malgre lui, even when truth must have been so disagreeable to hin.

This teacher of men, this Oxford pundit, this double-distilled quintessence of university perfection, this writer of religious treatises, this speaker of ecclesiastical speeches, had been like a little child in her hands. She had turned him inside out, and read his very heart as she might have done that of a young girl. She could not but despise him for his facile openness, and yet she liked him for it too. It was a novelty to her, a new trait in a man's VOL. II H character. She felt also that she could never so completely make a fool of him as she did of the Slopes and Thornes. She felt that she never could induce Mr. Arabin to make protestations to her that were not true, or to listen to nonsense that was mere nonsense.

It was quite clear that Mr. Arabin was heartily in love with Mrs. Bold, and the Signora, with very unwonted good nature, began to turn it over in her mind whether she could not do him a good turn. Of course Bertie was to have the first chance. It was an understood family arrangement that her brother was, if possible, to marry the widow Bold. Madeline knew too well his necessities and what was due to her sister to interfere with so excellent a plan, as long as it might be feasible. But she had strong suspicion that it was not feasible. She did not think it likely that Mrs. Bold would accept a man in her brother's position, and she had frequently said so to Charlotte. She was inclined to believe that Mr. Slope had more chance of success; and with her it would be a labour of love to rob Mr. Slope of his wife.

And so the Signora resolved, should Bertie fail, to do a goodnatured act for once in her life, and give up Mr. Arabia to the woman whom he loved.

CHAPTER XXXIX. THE LOOKALOFTS AND THE GREENACRES.

On the whole, Miss Thorne's provision for the amusement and feeding of the outer classes in the exoteric paddock was not unsuccessful. Two little drawbacks to the general happiness did take place, but they were of a temporary nature, and apparent rather than real. The first was the downfall of young Harry Greenacre, and the other the uprise of Mrs. Lookaloft and her family.

As to the quintain, it became more popular among the boys on foot, than it would ever have been among the men on horseback, even had young Greenacre been more successful. It was twirled round and round till it was nearly twirled out of the ground; and the bag of flour was used with great gusto in powdering the backs and heads of all who could be coaxed within its vicinity.

Of course it was reported all through the assemblage that Harry was dead, and there was a pathetic scene between him and his mother when it was found that he had escaped scatheless from the fall. A good deal of beer was drunk on the occasion, and the quintain was "dratted" and "bothered," and very generally anathematised by all the mothers who had young sons likely to be placed in similar jeopardy. But the affair of Mrs. Lookaloft was of a more serious nature. "I do tell 'ee plainly,—face to face,— she be there in madam's drawing-room; herself and Gussy, and them two walloping gals, dressed up to their very eyeses." This was said by a very positive, very indignant, and very fat farmer's wife, who was sitting on the

end of a bench leaning on the handle ot a huge cotton umbrella.

"But you didn't zee her, Dame Guffern?" said Mrs. Greenacre, whom this information, joined to the recent peril undergone by her son, almost overpowered. Mr. Greenacre held just as much land as Mr. Lookaloft, paid his rent quite as punctually, and his opinion in the vestry-room was reckoned to be every whit as good. Mrs. Lookaloft's rise in the world had been wormwood to Mrs. Greenacre. She had no taste herself for the sort of finery which had converted Barleystubb farm into Eosebank, and which had occasionally graced Mr. Lookaloft's letters with thedignity of esquirehood. She had no wish to convert her own homestead into Violet Villa, or to see her gudeman go about with a new-fangled handle to his name. But it was a mortal injury to her that Mrs. Lookaloft should be successful in her hunt after such honours. She had abused and ridiculed Mrs. Lookaloft to the extent of her little power. She had pushed against her going out of church, and had excused herself with all the easiness of equality. "Ah, dame, I axes pardon; but you be grown so mortal stout these times." She had inquired with apparent cordiality of Mr. Lookaloft, after "the woman that owned him," and had, as she thought, been on the whole able to hold her own pretty well against her aspiring neighbour. Now, however, she found herself distinctly put into a separate and inferior class. Mrs. Lookaloft was asked into the Ullathorne drawing-room merely because she called her house Eosebank, and had talked over her husband into buying pianos and silk dresses instead of putting his money by to stock farms for his sons.

Mrs. Greenacre, much as she reverenced Miss Thorne and highly as she respected her husband's landlord, could not but look on this as an act of injustice done to her and hers. Hitherto the Lookalofts had never been recognised as being of a different class from the Greenacres. Their pretensions were all self-pretensions, their finery was all paid for by themselves and not granted to them by others. The local sovereigns

of the vicinity, the district fountains of honour, had hitherto conferred on them the stamp of no rank. Hitherto their crinoline petticoats, late hours, and mincing gait had been a fair subject of Mrs. Greenacre's raillery, and this raillery had been a safety valve for her envy. Now, however, and from henceforward, the case would be very different. Now the Lookalofts would boast that their aspirations had been sanctioned by the gentry of the country. Now they would declare with some show of truth that their claims to peculiar consideration had been recognised. They had sat as equal guests in the presence of bishops and baronets; they had been curtseyed to by Miss Thorne on her own drawing-room carpet; they were about to sit down to table in company with a live countess! Bab Lookaloft, as she had always been called by the young Greenacres in the days of their juvenile equality, might possibly sit next to the Honourable George, and that wretched Gussy might be permitted to hand a custard to the Lady Margaretta De Courcy.

The fruition of those honours, or such of them as fell to the lot of the envied family, was not such as should have caused much envy. The attention paid to the Lookalofts by the De Courcys was very limited, and the amount of entertainment which they received from the bishop's society was hardly in itself a recompense for the dull monotony of their day. But of what they endured Mrs. Greenacre took no account. She thought only of what she considered they must enjoy, and of the dreadfully exalted tone of living which would be manifested by the Rosebank family, as the consequence of their present distinction.

"But did 'ee zee 'em there, dame; did 'ee zee 'em there with your own eyes?" asked poor Mrs. Greenacre; still hoping that there might be some ground for doubt.

"And how could I do that unless so be I was there myself?" asked Mrs. Guffern. "I didn't zet eyes on none of them this blessed morning, but I zee'd them as did. You know our John; well, he

will be for keeping company with Betsey Busk, madame's own maid, you know. And Betsey isn't none of your common kitchen wenches. So Betsey, she come out to our John, you know, and she's always vastly polite to me. So before she took so much as one turn with John, she told me every ha'porth that was going on up in the house." "Did she now?" said Mrs. Greenacre.
"Indeed she did,"'said Mrs. Guffern.

"And she told you them people was up there in the drawingroom?"

"She told me she zee'd them come in,—that they was dressed finer by half nor any of the family, with all their neokses and buzoms stark naked as a born babby."

"The minxes!" exclaimed Mrs. Greenacre, who felt herself more put about by this than any other mark of aristocratic distinction which her enemies had assumed.

"Yes, indeed," continued Mrs. Guffern, "as naked as you please, while all the quality was dressed just as you and I be, Mrs. Greenacre."

"Drat their impudence," said Mrs. Greenacre, from whose wellcovered bosom all milk of human kindness was receding, as far as the family of the Lookalofts were concerned.

"So says I," said Mrs. Guffern; "and so says my goodman, Thomas Guffern, when he hear'd it. 'Molly,' says he to me, 'if ever you takes to going about o' mornings with yourself all naked in them ways, I begs you won't come back no more to the old _ house.' So says I, 'Thomas, no more I wull.' 'But,' says he, 'drat it, how the deuce does she manage with her rheumatiz, and she not a rag on her:'" and Mrs. Guffern laughed loudly as she thought of Mrs. Lookaloft's probable sufferings from rheumatic attacks.

"But to liken herself that way to folk that ha' blood in their veins," said Mrs. Greenacre.

"Well, but that warn't all neither that Betsey told. There they all swelled into madam's drawing-room, like so many turkey cocks, as much as to say, 'and who dare say no to us?' and Gregory was thinking of telling of 'em to come down here, only his heart failed him 'oause of the grand way they was dressed So in they went; but madam looked at them as glum as death."

"Well now," said Mrs. Greenacre, greatly relieved. "So they wasn't axed different from us at all then?"

"Betsey says that Gregory says that madam wasn't a bit toe well pleased to see them where they was, and that, to his behoving, they was expected to come here just like the rest of us."

There was consolation in this. Not that Mrs. Greenacre was altogether satisfied. She felt that justice to herself demanded that Mrs. Lookaloft should not only not be encouraged, but that she should also be absolutely punished. What had been done at that scriptural banquet, of which Mrs. Greenacre so often read the account to her family? Why had not Miss Thorne boldly gone to the intruder and said, "Friend, thou hast come up hither to high places not fitted to thee. Go down lower, and thou wilt find thy mates." Let the Lookalofts be treated at the present moment with ever so cold a shoulder, they would still be enabled to boast hereafter of their position, their aspirations, and their honour.

"Well, with all her grandeur, I do wonder that she be so mean," continued Mrs. Greenacre, unable to dismiss the subject. "Did you hear, goodman?" she went on, about to repeat the whole story to her husband who then came up. "There's dame Lookaloft and Bab and Gussy and the lot of 'em all sitting as grand as fivepence in madam's drawing-room, and they not axed no more nor you nor me. Did you ever hear tell the like o' that?"

"Well, and what for should'nt they?" said Farmer Greenacre.

"Likening theyselves to the quality, as though they was estated folk, or the like o' that!" said Mrs. Guffern.

"Well, if they likes it and madam likes it, they's welcome for me," said the farmer. "Now I likes this place better, cause I be more at home like, and don't have to pay for them fine clothes for the missus. Every one to his taste, Mrs. Guffern, and if neighbour Lookaloft thinks that he has the best of it, he's welcome."

Mrs. Greenacre sat down by her husband's side to begin the heavy work of the banquet, and she did so in some measure with restored tranquillity, but nevertheless she shook her head at her gossip to show that in this instance she did not quite approve of her husband's doctrine.

"And I'll tell 'ee what, dames," continued he; "if so be that we cannot enjoy the dinner that madam gives us because Mother Lookaloft is sitting up there on a grand sofa, I think we ought all to go home. If we greet at that, what'll we do when true sorrow comes across us? How would you be now, dame, if the boy there had broke his neck when he got the tumble?" Mrs. Greenacre was humbled and said nothing further on the matter. But let prudent men, such as Mr. Greenacre, preach as they will, the family of the Lookalofts certainly does occasion a good deal of heart-burning in the world at large.

It was pleasant to see Mr. Plomacy, as leaning on his stout stick he went about among the rural guests, acting as a sort of head constable as well as master of the revels. "Now, young 'un, if you can't manage to get along without that screeching, you'd better go to the other side of the twelve-acre field, and take your dinner with you. Come, girls, what do you stand there for, twirling of your thumbs? come out, and let the lads see you; you've no need to be so ashamed of your faces. Hollo! there, who are you? how did you make your way in here?" This last disagreeable question was put to a young man of about twenty-four, who did not, in Mr. Plomacy's eye, bear sufficient vestiges of a rural education and residence.

"If you please, your worship, Master Barrell the coachman let me in at the church wicket, 'cause I do be working mostly al'ays for the family."

"Then Master Barrell the coachman may let you out again," said Mr. Plomacy, not even conciliated by the magisterial dignity which had been conceded to him. "What's your name? and what trade are you, and who do you work for?"

"I'm Stubbs, your worship, Bob Stubbs; and,—and,—and."

"And what's your trade, Stubbs?"

"Plaisterer, please your worship."

"I'll plaister you, and Barrell too; you'll just walk out of this 'ere field as quick as you walked in. We don't want no plaisterers; when we do, we'll send for 'em. Come, my buck, walk."

Stubbs the plasterer was much downcast at this dreadful edict. He was a sprightly fellow, and had contrived since his egress into the Ullathorne elysium to attract to himself a forest nymph, to whom he was whispering a plasterer's usual soft nothings, when he was encountered by the great Mr. Plomacy. It was dreadful to be thus dissevered from his dryad, and sent howling back to a Barchester pandemonium just as the nectar and ambrosia were about to descend on the fields of asphodel. He began to try what prayers would do, but city prayers were vain against the great rural potentate. Not only did Mr. Plomacy order his exit, but raising his stick to show the way which led to the gate that had been left in the custody of that false Cerberus Barrell, proceeded himself to see the edict of banishment carried out.

The goddess Mercy, however, the sweetest goddess that ever sat upon a cloud, and the dearest to poor frail erring man, appeared on the field in the person of Mr. Greenacre. Never was interceding goddess more welcome.

"Come, man," said Mr. Greenacre, "never stick at trifles such a day as this. I know the lad well. Let him bide at my axing. Madam won't miss what he can eat and drink, I know."

Now Mr. Plomacy and Mr. Greenacre were sworn friends. Mr. Plomacy had at his own disposal as comfortable a room as there was in Ullathorne House; but he was a bachelor, and alone there; and, moreover, smoking 'in the house was not allowed even to Mr. Plomacy. His moments of truest happiness were spent in a hugo arm-chair in the warmest corner of Mrs. Greenacre's beautifully clean front kitchen. 'Twas there that the inner man dissolved itself, and poured itself out in streams of

pleasant chat; 'twas there that he was respected and yet at his ease; 'twas there, and perhaps there only, that he could unburden himself from the ceremonies of life without offending the dignity of those above him, or incurring the familiarity of those below. 'Twas there that his long pipe was always to be found on the accustomed chimney board, not only permitted but encouraged.

Such being the state of the case, it was not to be supposed that Mr. Plomacy could refuse such a favour to Mr. Greenacre; but nevertheless he did not grant it without some further show of austere authority. "Eat and drink, Mr. Greenacre! No. It's not what he eats and drinks; but the example such a chap shows, coming in where he's not invited;—a chap of his age too. He too that never did a day's work about Ullathorne since he was born. Plaisterer! I'll plaister him!"

"He worked long enough for me, then, Mr. Plomacy. And a good hand he is at setting tiles as any in Barchester," said the other, not sticking quite to veracity, as indeed mercy never should. "Come, come, let him alone to-day, and quarrel with him tomorrow. You wouldn't shame him before his lass there?"

"It goes against the grain with me, then," said Mr. Plomacy. "And take care, you Stubbs, and behave yourself. If I hear a row I shall know where it comes from. I'm up to you Barchester journeymen. I know what stuff you're made of."

And so Stubbs wont off happy, pulling at the forelock of his shock head of hair in honour of the steward's clemency, and giving another double pull at it in honour of the farmer's kindness. And as he went he swore within his grateful heart that if ever Farmer Greenacre wanted a day's work done for nothing, he was the lad to do it for him. Which promise it was not probable that he would ever be called on to perform.

But Mr. Plomacy was not quite happy in his mind, for he thought of the unjust steward, and began to reflect whether he had not made for himself friends of

the mammon of unrighteousness. This, however, did not interfere with the manner in which he performed his duties at the bottom of the long board; nor did Mr. Greenacre perform his the worse at the top on account of the good wishes of Stubbs the plasterer. Moreover, the guests did not think it anything amiss when Mr. Plomacy, rising to say grace, pvayed that God would make them all truly thankful for the good things which Madame Thome in her great liberality had set before them!

All this time the quality in the tent on the lawn were getting on swimmingly; that is, if champagne without restriction can enable quality folk to swim. Sir Harkaway Gorse proposed the health of Miss Thorne, and likened her to a blood race-horse, always in condition, and not to be tired down by any amount of work. Mr. Thorne returned thanks, saying he hoped his sister would always be found able to run when called upon, and then gave the health and prosperity of the De Courcy family. His sister was very much honoured by seeing so many of them at her poor board. They were all aware that important avocations made the absence of the earl necessary. As his duty to his prince had called him from his family hearth, he, Mr. Thorne, could not venture to regret that he did not see him at Ullathorne; but nevertheless he would venture to say,—that was to express a wish,—an opinion he meant to say. And so Mr. Thorne became somewhat gravelled, as country gentlemen in similar circumstances usually do; but he ultimately sat down, declaring that he had much satisfaction in drinking the noble earl's health, together with that of the countess, and all the family of De Courcy castle.

And then the Honourable George returned thanks. We will not follow him through the different periods of his somewhat irregular eloquence. Those immediately in his neighbourhood found it at first rather difficult to get him on his legs, but much greater difficulty was soon experienced in inducing him to resume his seat. One of two arrangements should certainly be made in these days; either let all speech-making on festive occasions be utterly tabooed and made as it were impossible; or else let those who are to exercise the privilege be first subjected to a competing examination before the civil service examining commissioners. As it is now, the Honourable Georges do but little honour to our exertions in favour of British education.

In the dining-room the bishop went through the honours of the day with much more neatness and propriety. He also drank Miss Thorne's health, and did it in a manner becoming the bench which he adorned. The party there, was perhaps a little more dull, a shade less lively than that in the tent. But what was lost in mirth, was fully made up in decorum.

And so the banquets passed off at the various tables with great eclat and universal delight.

CHAPTER XL. UXLATHORNE SPORTS. ACT II.

"That which has made them drunk, has made me bold." 'Twas thus that Mr. Slope encouraged himself as he left the dining-room in pursuit of Eleanor. He had not indeed seen in that room any person really intoxicated; but there had been a good deal of wine drunk, and Mr. Slope had not hesitated to take his share, in order to screw himself up to the undertaking which he had in hand. He is not the first man who has thought it expedient to call in the assistance of Bacchus on such an occasion.

Eleanor was out though the window and on the grass before she perceived that she was followed. Just at that moment the guests were nearly all occupied at the tables. Here and there were to be seen a constant couple or two who preferred their own sweet discourse to the jingle of glasses or the charms of rhetoric which fell from the mouths of the Honourable George and the bishop of Barchester; but the grounds were as nearly vacant as Mr. Slope could wish them to be.

Eleanor saw that she was pursued, and as a deer, when escape is no longer possible, will turn to bay and attack the hounds, so did she turn upon Mr. Slope. "Pray don't let me take you from the room." said she, speaking with all the stiffness which she knew how to use. "I have come out to look for a friend. I must beg of you, Mr. Slope, to go back. "

But Mr. Slope would not be thus entreated. He had observed all day that Mrs. Bold was not cordial to him, and this had to a certain extent oppressed him. But he did not deduce from this any assurance that his aspirations were in vain. He saw that she was angry with him. Might she not be so because he had so long tampered with her feelings;— might it not arise from his having, as he knew was the case, caused her name to be bruited about in conjunction with his own, without having given her the opportunity of confessing to the world that henceforth their names were to be one and the same? Poor lady! He had within him a certain Christian conscience-stricken feeling of remorse on this head. It might be that he had wronged her by his tardiness. He had, however, at the present moment imbibed too much of Mr. Thorne's champagne to have any inward misgivings. He was right in repeating the boast of Lady Macbeth; he was not drunk; but he was bold enough for anything. It was a pity that in such a state he could not have encountered Mrs. Proudie.

"You must permit me to attend you," said he; "I could not think of allowing you to go alone."

"Indeed you must, Mr. Slope," said Eleanor still very stiffly; "for it is my special wish to be alone."

The time for letting the great secret escape him had already come. Mr. Slope saw that it must be now or never, and he was determined that it should be now. This was not his first attempt at winning a fair lady. He had been on his knees, looked unutterable things with his eyes, and whispered honeyed words before this. Indeed he was somewhat an expert at these things, and had only to adapt to the perhaps different taste of Mrs. Bold the well-remembered rhapsodies which had once so much gratified Olivia Proudie.

"Do not ask me to leave you, Mrs Bold," said he with an impassioned look, impassioned and sanctified as well, with that sort of look which is not uncommon with gentlemen of Mr. Slope's school, and which may perhaps be called the tender-pious. "Do not ask me to leave you, till I have spoken a few words with which my heart is full;—which I have come hither purposely to say."

Eleanor saw how it was now. She knew directly what it was she was about to go through, and very miserable the knowledge made her. Of course she could refuse Mr. Slope, and there would be an end of that, one might say. But there would not be an end of it as far as Eleanor was concerned. The very fact of Mr. Slope's making an offer to her would be a triumph to the archdeacon, and in a great measure a vindication of Mr. Arabin's conduct. The widow could not bring herself to endure with patience the idea that she had been in the wrong. She had defended Mr. Slope, she had declared herself quite justified in admitting him among her acquaintance, had ridiculed the idea of his considering himself as more than an acquaintance, and had resented the archdeacon's caution in her behalf. Now it was about to be proved to her in a manner sufficiently disagreeable that the archdeacon had been right, and she herself had been entirely wrong.

"I don't know what you can have to say to me, Mr. Slope, that you could not have said when we were sitting at table just now;" and she closed her lips, and steadied her eyeballs, and looked at him in a manner that ought to have frozen him.

But gentlemen are not easily frozen when they are full of champagne, and it would not at any time have been easy to freeze Mr. Slope. "There are things, Mrs. Bold, which a man cannot well say before a crowd; which perhaps he cannot well say at any time; which indeed he may most fervently desire to get spoken, and which he may yet find it almost impossible to utter. It is such things as these, that I now wish to say to you." Then the tender-pious look was repeated, with a little more emphasis even than before.

Eleanor had not found it practicable to stand stock still before the dining-room window, and there receive his offer in full view of Miss Thorne's guests. She had therefore in self-defence walked on, and thus Mr. Slope had gained his object of walking with her. He now offered her his arm.

"Thank you, Mr. Slope, I am much obliged to you; but for the very short time that I shall remain with you I shall prefer walking alone."

"And must it be so short?" said he; "must it be—"

"Yes," said Eleanor, interrupting him; "as short a spossible, if you please, sir."

"I had hoped, Mrs. Bold,—I had hoped—."

'' Pray hope nothing, Mr. Slope, as far as I am concerned; praj do not; I do not know, and need not know what hope you mean Our acquaintance is very slight, and will probably remain so. Pray let that be enough. There is at any rate no necessity for us to quarrel."

Mrs. Bold was certainly treating Mr. Slope rather cavalierly, and he felt it so. She was rejecting him before he had offered himself, and informed him at the same time that he was taking a great deal too much on himself to be so familiar. She did not even make an attempt

"From such a sharp and waspish word as 'no'
To pluck the sting."

He was still determined to be very tender and very pious, seeing that in spite of all Mrs. Bold had said to him, he not yet abandoned hope; but he was inclined also to be somewhat angry. The widow was bearing herself, as he thought, with too high a hand, —was speaking of herself in much too imperious a tone. She had clearly no idea that an honour was being conferred on her. Mr. Slope would be tender as long as he could, but he began to think, if that failed, it would not be amiss if he also mounted himself for a while on his high horse. Mr. Slope could undoubtedly be very tender, but he could be very savage also, and he knew his own abilities.

"That is cruel," said he, "and unchristian too. The worst of us are all still

bidden to hope. What have I done that you should pass on me so severe a sentence?" Then he paused a moment, during which the widow walked steadily on with measured step, saying nothing further.

"Beautiful woman," at last he burst forth; "beautiful woman, you cannot pretend to be ignorant that I adore you. Yes, Eleanor, yes, I love you. I love you with the truest affection which man can bear to woman. Next to my hopes of heaven are my hopes of possessing you. " Mr. Slope's memory here played him false, or he would not have omitted the deanery. "How sweet to walk to heaven with you by my side, with you for my guide, mutual guides. Say, Eleanor, dearest Eleanor, shall we walk that sweet path together?" Eleanor had no intention of ever walking together with Mr. Slope on any other path than that special one of Miss Thome's which they now occupied; but as she had been unable to prevent the expression of Mr. Slope's wishes and aspirations, she resolved to hear him out to the end, before she answered him. "Ah! Eleanor," he continued, and it seemed to be his idea that as he had once found courage to pronounce her Christian name, he could not utter it often enough. "Ah! Eleanor, will it not be sweet, with the Lord's assistance, to travel hand in hand through this mortal valley which his mercies will make pleasant to us, till hereafter we shall dwell together at the foot of his throne?" And then a more tenderly pious glance than ever beamed from the lover's eyes. "Ah! Eleanor—"

"My name, Mr. Slope, is Mrs. Bold," said Eleanor, who, though determined to hear out the tale of his love, was too much disgusted by his blasphemy to be able to bear much more of it.

"Sweetest angel, be not so cold," said he, and as he said it the champagne broke forth, and he contrived to pass his arm round her waist. Hte did this with considerable cleverness, for up to this point Eleanor had contrived with tolerable success to keep her distance from him. They had got into a walk nearly enveloped by shrubs, and Mr. Slope therefore no doubt considered that as they

were now alone it was fitting that he should give her some outward demonstration of that affection of which he talked so much. It may perhaps be presumed that the same stamp of measures had been found to succeed with Olivia Proudie. Be this as it may, it was not successful with Eleanor Bold.

She sprang from him as she would have jumped from an adder, but she did not spring far; not, indeed, beyond arm's length; and then, quick as thought, she raised her little hai.d and dealt him a

Vol. Ii. a box on the ear with such right good will, that it sounded among the trees like a miniature thunder-clap.

And now it is to be feared that every well-bred reader of these pages will lay down the book with disgust, feeling that, after all, the heroine is unworthy of sympathy. She is a hoyden, one will say. At any rate she is not a lady, another will exclaim. I have suspected her all through, a third will declare. She has no idea of the dignity of a matron, or of the peculiar propriety which her position demands. At one moment she is romping with young Stanhope; then she is making eyes at Mr. Arabin! anon she comes to fisty-cuffs with a third lover; and all before she is yet a widow of two years' standing.

She cannot altogether be defended; and yet it may be averred that she is not a hoyden, not given to romping, nor prone to boxing. It were to be wished devoutly that she had not struck Mr. Slope in the face. In doing so she derogated from her dignity and committed herself. Had she been educated in Belgravia, had she been brought up by any sterner mentor than that fond father, had she lived longer under the rule of a husband, she might, perhaps, have saved herself from this great fault. As it was, the provocation was too much for her, the temptation to instant resentment. of the insult too strong. She was too keen in the feeling of independence, a feeling dangerous for a young woman, but one in which her position peculiarly tempted her to indulge. And then Mr. Slope's face, tinted with a deeper dye than usual by the wine he had drunk, simpering and puckering itself with pseudo piety and tender grimaces, seemed specially to call for such punishment. She had, too, a true instinct as to the man. He was capable of rebuke in this way and in no other. To him the blow from her little hand was as much an insult as a blow from a man would have been to another. It went direct to his pride. He conceived himself lowered in his dignity, and personally outraged. He could almost have struck at her again in his rage. Even the pain was a great annoyance to him, and the feeling that his clerical character had been wholly disregarded, sorely vexed him.

There are such men; men who can endure no taint on their personal self-respect, even fiom a woman;—men whose bodies are to themselves such sacred temples, that a joke against them is desecration, and a rough touch downright sacrilege. Mr. Slojie was such a man; and therefore the slap on the face that he got from Eleanor was, as far as he was concerned, the fittest rebuke which could have been administered to him.

But, nevertheless, she should not have raised her hand against the man. Ladies' hands, so soft, so sweet, so delicious to the touch, so graceful to the eye, so gracious in their gentle doings, were not made to belabour men's faces. The moment the deed was done Eleanor felt that she had sinned against all propriety, and would have given little worlds to recall the blow. Ia her first agony of sorrow she all but begged the man's pardon. Her next impulse, however, and the one which she obeyed, was to run away.

"I never, never will speak another word to you," she said, gasping with emotion and the loss of breath which her exertion and violent feelings occasioned her, and so saying she put foot to the ground and ran quickly back along the path to the house.

But how shall I sing the divine wrath of Mr. Slope, or how invoke the tragic muse to describe the rage which swelled the celestial bosom of the bishop's chaplain? Such an undertaking by no means befits the low-heeled buskin of modern fiction. The painter put a veil over Agamemnon's face when called on to depict the father's grief at the early doom of his devoted daughter. The god, when he resolved to punish the rebellious winds, abstained from mouthing empty threats. We will not attempt to tell with what mighty surgings of the inner heart Mr. Slope swore to revenge himself on the woman who had disgraced him, nor will we vainly strive to depict his deep agony of soul.

There he is, however, alone in the garden walk, and we must contrive to bring him out of it. He was not willing to come forth quite at once. His cheek was stinging with the weight of Eleanor's fingers, and he fancied that every one who looked at him would bo able to see on his face the traces of what he had endured. He. stood awhile, becoming redder and redder with rage. He stood motionless, undecided, glaring with his eyes, thinking of the pains and penalties of Hades, and meditating how he might best devote his enemy to the infernal gods with all the passion of his accustomed eloquence. He longed in his heart to be preaching at her. 'Twas thus that he was ordinarily avenged of sinning mortal men and women. Could he at once have ascended his Sunday rostrum and fulminated at her such denunciations as his spirit delighted in, his bosom would have been greatly eased.

But how preach to Mr. Thome's laurels, or how preach indeed at all in such a vanity fair as this now going on at Ullathorne? And then he began to feel a righteous disgust at the wickedness of the doings around him. He had been justly chastised for lending, by his presence, a sanction to such worldly lures. The gaiety of society, the mirth of banquets, the laughter of the young, and the eating and drinking of the elders were, for awhile, without excuse in his sight. What had he now brought down upon himself by sojourning thus in the tents of the heathen? He had consorted with idolaters round the altars of Baal; and therefore a sore punishment had come upon him. He then thought of the Signora Neroni, and his soul within him was full of sorrow. He had an inkling,— a true inkling,—that he was a wicked, sinful man; but it led him in no right direction; he could admit no charity in his heart. He felt debasement coming on him, and he longed to shake it off, to rise up in his stirrup, to mount to high places and great power,—that he might get up into a mighty pulpit and preach to the world a loud sermon against Mrs. Bold.

There he stood fixed to the gravel for about ten minutes. Fortune favoured him so far that no prying eyes came to look upon him in his misery. Then a shudder passed over his whole frame; he collected himself, and slowly wound his way round to the lawn, advancing along the path and not returning in the direction which Eleanor had taken. When he reached the tent he found the bishop standing there in conversation with the master of Lazarus. His lordship had come out to air himself after the exertion of his speech. A

"This is very pleasant,—very pleasant, my lord, is it not?" said Mr. Slope with his most gracious smile, and pointing to the tent; "very pleasant. It is delightful to see so many persons enjoying themselves so thoroughly."

Mr. Slope thought he might force the bishop to introduce him to Dr. Gwynne. A very great example had declared and practised the wisdom of being everything to everybody, and Mr. Slope was desirous of following it. His maxim was never to lose a chance. The bishop, however, at the present moment was not very anxious to increase Mr. Slope's circle of acquaintance among his clerical brethren. He had his own reasons for dropping any marked allusion to his domestic chaplain, and he therefore made his shoulder rather cold for the occasion.

"Very, very," said he without turning round, or even deigning to look at Mr. Slope. "And therefore, Dr. Gwynne, I really think that you will find that the hebdomadal board will exercise as wide and as general an authority as at the present moment. I, for one, Dr. Gwynne"

"Dr. Gwynne," said Mr. Slope, raising his hat, and resolving not to be outwitted by such an insignificant little goose as the bishop of Barchester. The master of Lazarus also raised his hat and bowed very politely to Mr. Slope. There is not a more courteous gentleman in the queen's dominions than the master of Lazarus. "My lord, said Mr. Slope, "pray do me the honour of introducing me to Dr. Gwynne. The opportunity is too much in my favour to be lost."

The bishop had no help for it. "My chaplain, Dr. Gwynne," said he; "my present chaplain, Mr. Slope." He certainly made the introduction as unsatisfactory to the chaplain as possible, and by the use of the word present, seemed to indicate that Mr. Slope might probably not long enjoy the honour which he now held. But Mr. Slope cared nothing for this. He understood the innuendo, and disregarded it. It might probably come to pass that he would be in a situation to resign his chaplaincy before the bishop was in a situation to dismiss him from it. What need the future dean of Barchester care for the bishop, or for the bishop's wife? Had not Mr. Slope, just as he was entering Dr. Stanhope's carriage, received an all-important note from Tom Towers of the Jupiter? Had he not that note this moment in his pocket?

So disregarding the bishop, he began to open out a conversation with the master of Lazarus.

But suddenly an interruption came, not altogether unwelcome to Mr. Slope. One of the bishop's servants came up to his master's shoulder with a long, grave face, and whispered into the bishop's oar.

"What is it, John?" said the bishop "The dean, my lord; he is dead.''

Mr. Slope had no further desire to converse with the master of Lazarus, and was very soon on hie oad back to Barchester.

Eleanor, as we have said, having declared her intention of never holding further communication with Mr. Slope, ran hurriedly back towards the house. The thought, however, of what she had done grieved her greatly, and she could not abstain from bursting into tears. 'Tvras thus she played the second act in that day's melodrama.

CHAPTER XLI. MIIS. BOLD CONFIDES HER SORROW TO HER FRIEND MISS STANHOPE.

When Mrs. Bold came to the end of the walk and faced the lawn, she began to bethink herself what she should do. Was she to wait there till Mr. Slope caught her, or was she to go in among the crowd with tears in her eyes and passion in her face? She might in truth have stood there long enough without any reasonable fear of further immediate persecution from Mr. Slope; but we are all inclined to magnify the bugbears which frighten us. In her present state of dread she did not know of what atrocity he might venture to be guilty. Had any one told her a week ago that he would have put his arm round her waist at this party of Miss Thorne's she would have been utterly incredulous. Had she been informed that he would be seen on the following Sunday walking down the High-street in a scarlet coat and top-boots, she would not have thought such a phenomenon more improbable.

But this improbable iniquity he had committed; and now there was nothing she could not believe of him. In the first place it was quite manifest that he was tipsy; in the next place, it was to be taken as proved that all his religion was sheer hypocrisy; and finally the man was utterly shameless. She therefore stood watching for the sound of his footfall, not without some fear that he might creep out at her suddenly from among the bushes.

As she thus stood, she saw Charlotte Stanhope at a little distance from her walking quickly across the grass. Eleanor's handkerchief was in her hand, and putting it to her face so as to conceal her tears. she ran across the lawn and joined her friend. "Oh, Charlotte," she said, almost too much out of breath to speak very plainly; "I am so glad I have found you."

"Glad you have found me!" said Charlotte, laughing: "that's a good joke. Why Bertie and I have been looking for you everywhere. He swears that you have gone off with Mr. Slope, and is now on the point of hanging himself."

"Oh, Charlotte, don't," said Mrs. Bold.

"Why, my child, what on earth is the matter with you!" said Miss Stanhope, perceiving that Eleanor's hand trembled on her own arm, and finding also that her companion was still half choked by tears. "Goodness heaven! something has distressed you. What is it. What can I do for you?"

Eleanor answered her only by a sort of spasmodic gurgle in her throat. She was a good deal upset, as people say, and could not at the moment collect herself.

'' Come here, this way, Mrs. Bold; come this way, and we shall not be seen. What has happened to vex you so? What can I do for you? Can Bertie do anything?"

"Oh, no, no, no, no, no," said Eleanor. "There is nothing to be done. Only that horrid man"

"What horrid man?" asked Charlotte.

There are some moments in life in which both men and women feel themselves imperatively called on to make a confidence;—in which not to do so requires a disagreeable resolution and also a disagreeable suspicion. There are people of both sexes who never make confidences; who are never tempted by momentary circumstances to disclose their secrets; but such are generally dull, close, unimpassioned spirits, "gloomy gnomes, who live in cold dark mines." There was nothing of the gnome about Eleanor; and she therefore resolved to tell Charlotte Stanhope the whole story about Mr Slope. "That horrid man; that Mr. Slope," said she. "Did you not see that he followed me out of the dinin-groom?"

"Of course I did, and was sorry enough; but I could not help it. I knew you would be annoyed. But you and Bertie managed it badly between you."

"It was not his fault nor mine either. You know how I disliked the idea of coming in the carriage with that man."

"I am sure I am very sorry if that has led to it."

"I don't know what has led to it," said Eleanor, ahnost crying again. "But it has not been my fault."

"But what has he done, my dear?"

"He's an abominable, horrid, hypocritical man, and it would serve him right to tell the bishop all about it."

"Believe me, if you want to do him an injury, you had far better tell Mrs. Proudie. But what did he do, Mrs. Bold?"

"Ugh!" exclaimed Eleanor.

"Well, I must confess he's not very nice," said Charlotte Stanhope.

"Nice!" said Eleanor. "He is the most fulsome, fawning, abominable man I ever saw. What business had he to come to me?—I that never gave him the slightest tittle of encouragement; —I that always hated him though I did take his part when others ran him down."

"That's just where it is, my dear. He has heard that, and therefore fancied that of course you were in love with him."

This was wormwood to Eleanor. It was in fact the very thing which all her friends had been saying for the last month past; and which experience now proved to be true. Eleanor resolved within herself that she would never again take any man's part. The world with all its villany, and all its ill-nature, might wag as it liked; she would not again attempt to set crooked things straight. "But what did he do, my dear?" said Charlotte, who was really rather interested in the subject.

"He,—he—he—."

"Well,—come, it can't have been anything so very horrid, for the man was not tipsy."

"Oh, I am sure he was," said Eleanor. "I am sure he must have been tipsy."

"Well, I declare I didn't observe it. But what was it, my love?"

'' Why, I believe I can hardly tell you. He talked such horrid stuff that you never heard the like; about religion, and heaven, and love.—Oh, dear,—he is such a nasty man."

"I can easily imagine the sort of stuff he would talk. Well,— and then?"

"And then.—he took hold of me."

"Took hold of you?"

"Yes,—he somehow got close to me, and took hold of me."

"By the waist?"

"Yes," said Eleanor shuddering.

"And then?"

"Then I jumped away from him, and gave him a slap on tbo face;—and ran away along the path till I saw you."

"Ha, ha, ha!" Charlotte Stanhope laughed heartily at the finale to the tragedy. It was delightful to her to think that Mr. Slope had had his ears boxed. She did not quite appreciate the feeling which made her friend so unhappy at the result of the interview. To her thinking the matter had ended happily enough as regarded the widow, who indeed was entitled to some sort of triumph among her friends. Whereas to Mr. Slope would be due all those jibes and jeers which would naturally follow such an affair. His friends would ask him whether his ears tingled whenever he saw a widow; and he would be cautioned that beautiful things were made to be Looked at, and not to be touched.

Such were Charlotte Stanhope's views on such matters; but she did not at the present moment clearly explain them to Mrs. Bold. Her object was to endear herself to her friend; and therefore, having had her laugh, she was ready enough to offer sympathy. Could Bertie do anything? Should Bertie speak to the man, and warn him that in future he must behave with more decorum? Bertie, indeed, she declared, would be more angry than any one else when he heard to what insult Mrs. Bold had been subjected.

"But you won't tell him?" said Mrs. Bold with a look of horror.

"Not if you don't like it," said Charlotte; "but considering everything, I would strongly advise it. If you had a brother, you know, it would be unnecessary. But it is very right that Mr. Slope should know that you have somebody by you that will, and can protect you."

"But my father is here."

'' Yes, but it is so disagreeable for clergymen to have to quarrel with each other; and circumstanced as your father is just at this moment, it would be very inexpedient that there should be anything unpleasant between him and Mr. Slope. Surely you and Bertie are intimate enough for you to permit him to take your part."

Charlotte Stanhope was very anxious that her brother should at once on that very day settle matters with his future wife. Things had now come to that point between him and his father, and between him and his creditors, that he must either do so, or leave Barchester; either do that, or go back to his unwashed associates, dirty lodgings, and poor living at Carrara. Unless he could provide himself with an income, he must go to Carrara, or to.

His father the prebendary had not said this in so many words, but had he done so, he could not have signified it more plainly.

Such being the state of the case, it was very necessary that no more time should be lost. Charlotte had seen her brother's apathy, when he neglected to follow Mrs. Bold out of the room, with anger which she could hardly suppress. It was grievous to think that Mr. Slope should have so distanced him. Charlotte felt that she had played her part with sufficient skill. She had brought them together and induced such a degree of intimacy, that her brother was really relieved from all trouble and labour in the matter. And moreover, it was quite plain that Mrs. Bold was very fond of Bertie. A.nd now it was plain enough also that he had nothing to fear from his rival Mr. Slope.

There was certainly an awkwardness in subjecting Mrs. Bold to a second offer on the same day. It would have been well perhaps to have put the matter off for a week, could a week have been spared. But circumstances are frequently too peremptory to be arranged as we would wish to arrange them; and such was the case now. This being so, could not this affair of Mr. Slope's be turned to advantage? Could it not be made the excuse for bringing Bertie and Mrs. Bjld into still closer connection; into such close connection that they could not fail to throw themselves into each other's arms? Such was the game which Miss Stanhope now at a moment's notice resolved to play.

And very well she played it. In the first place, it. was arranged that Mr. Slope should not return in the Stanhopes' carriage to Barchester. It so happened that Mr. Slope was already gone, but of that of course they knew nothing. The Signora should be induced to go first, with only the servants and her sister, and Bertie should take Mr. Slope's place in the second journey. Bertie was to be told in confidence of the whole affair, and when the carriage was gone off with its first load, Eleanor was to be left under Bertie's special protection, so as to insure her from any further aggression from Mr. Slope. While the carriage was getting ready, Bertie was to seek out that gentleman and make him understand that he must provide himself with another conveyance back to Barchester. Their immediate object should be to walk about together in search of Bertie. Bertie, in short, was to be the Pegasus on whose wings they were to ride out of their present dilemma.

There was a warmth of friendship and cordial kindliness in all this, that was very soothing to the widow; but yet, though she gave way to it, she was hardly reconciled to doing so. It never occurred to her, that now that she had killed one dragon, another.vas about to spring up in her path: she had no remote idea that ihe would have to encounter another suitor in her proposed projector; but she hardly liked the thought of putting herself so much into the hands of young Stanhope. She felt that if she wanted protection, she should go to her father. She felt that she should ask him to provide a carriage for her back to Barchester. Mrs. Clantantram she knew would give her a seat. She knew that she should not throw herself entirely upon friends whose friendship dated as it were but from yesterday. But yet she could not say "no," to one who was so sisterly in her kindness, so eager in her good nature, so comfortably sympathetic as Charlotte Stanhope. And thus she gave way to all the propositions made to her.

They first went into the dining-room, looking for their champion, and from thence to the drawing-room. Here they found Mr. Arabin, still hanging over the Signora's sofa; or, rather, they found him sitting near her head, as a physician might have sat, had the lady been his patient. There was no other person in the room. The guests were some in the tent, some few still in the dining-room, some at the bows and arrows, but most of them walking with Miss Thorne through the park, and looking at the games that were going on.

All that had passed, and was passing between Mr. Arabin and the lady, it is unnecessary to give in detail. She was doing with him as she did with all others. It was her mission to make fools of men, and she was pursuing her mission with Mr. Arabin. She had almost got him to own his love for Mrs. Bold, and had subsequently almost induced him to acknowledge a passion for herself. He, poor man, was hardly aware what he was doing or saying, hardly conscious whether he was in heaven or in hell. So little had he known of female attractions of that peculiar class which the Signora owned, that he became affected with a kind of temporary delirium, when first subjected to its power. He lost his head rather than his heart, and toppled about mentally, reeling in his ideas as a drunken man does on his legs. She had whispered to him words that really meant nothing, but which coming from such beautiful lips, and accompanied by such lustrous glances, seemed to have a mysterious significance, which he felt though he could not understand.

In being thus be-sirened Mr. Arabin behaved himself very differently from Mr. Slope. The Signora had said truly, that the two men were the contrasts of each other; that the one was all for action, the other all for thought. Mr. Slope, when this lady laid upon his senses the overpowering breath of her charms, immediately attempted to obtain some fruition, to achieve some mighty triumph. He began by catching at her hand, and progressed by kissing it. He made vows of love, and asked for vows in return. He promised everlasting devotion, knelt before her, and swore that had she been on Mount Ida, Juno would have had cause to hate her rather than Venus. But Mr. Arabin uttered no oaths, kept his hand mostly in his trousers pocket, and had no more

thought of kissing Madam Neroni, than of kissing the Countess De Courcy.

As soon as Mr. Arabin saw Mrs. Bold enter the room he blushed and rose from his chair; then he sat down again, and then again got up. The Signora saw the blush at once, and smiled at the poor victim, but Eleanor was too much confused to see anything.

"Oh, Madeline," said Charlotte, "I want to speak to you particularly; we must arrange about the carriage, you know;" and she stooped down to whisper to her sister. Mr. Arabin immediately withdrew to a little distance, and as Charlotte had in fact much to explain before she could make the new carriage arrangements intelligible, he had nothing to do but to talk to Mrs. Bold.

"We have had a very pleasant party," said he, using the tone he would have used had he declared that the sun was shining very brightly, or the rain falling very fast.

"Very," said Eleanor, who never in her life had passed a more unpleasant day.

"I hope Mr. Harding has enjoyed himself."

"Oh, yes, very much," said Eleanor, who had not seen her father since she parted from him soon after her arrival.

"He returns to Barchester to-night, I suppose."

"Yes, I believe so; that is, I think he is staying at Plumstead."

"Oh, staying at Plumstead," said Mr. Arabin. "He came from there this morning. I believe he is going back; he didn't exactly say, however."

"I hope Mrs. Grantly is quite well."

"She seemed to be quite well. She is here; that is, unless she has gone away."

"Oh, yes, to be sure. I was talking to her. Looking very welj indeed." Then there was a considerable pause; for Charlotte could not at once make Madeline understand why she was to be sent home in a hurry without her brother.

"Are you returning to Plumstead, Mrs. Bold?" Mr. Arabin merely asked this by way of making conversation, but he immediately perceived that he was approaching dangerous ground.

"No," said Mrs. Bold very quietly; "I

am going home to Barchester."

"Oh, ah, yes. I had forgotten that you had returned." And then Mr. Arabin, finding it impossible to say anything further, stood silent till Charlotte had completed her plans, and Mrs. Bold stood equally silent, intently occupied as it appeared in the arrangement of her rings.

And yet these two people were thoroughly in love with each other; and though one was a midille-aged clergyman, and the other a lady at any rate past the wishy-washy bread-and-butter period of life, they were as unable to tell their own minds to each other as any Damon and Phillis, whose united ages would not make up that to which Mr. Arabin had already attained.

Madeline Neroni consented to her sister's proposal, and then the two ladies again went off in quest of Bertie Stanhope.

CHAPTER XLII. TJLLATIIORNE SPORTS. ACT in.

And now Miss Thome's guests were beginning to take their departure, and the amusement of those who remained was becoming slack. It was getting dark, and ladies in morning costumes were thinking that if they were to appear by candle-light they ought to readjust themselves. Some young gentlemen had been heard to talk so loud that prudent mammas determined to retire judiciously, and the more discreet of the male sex, whose libations had been moderate, felt that there was not much more left for them to do.

Morning parties, as a rule, are failures. People never know how to get away from them gracefully. A picnic on an island or a mountain or in a wood may perhaps be permitted. There is no master of the mountain bound by courtesy to bid you stay while in his heart he is longing for your departure. But in a private house or in private grounds a morning party is a bore. One is called on to eat and drink at unnatural hours. One is obliged to give up the day which is useful, and is then left without resource for the evening which is useless. One gets home fagged and desceuvre, and yet at an hour too early for bed. There is

no comfortable resource left.

All this began now to be felt. Some young people had come with some amount of hope that they might get up a dance in the evening, and were unwilling to leave till all such hope was at an end. Others, fearful of staying longer than was expected, had ordered their carriages early, and were doing their best to go. solicitous for their servants and horses. The countess and her noble brood were among the first to leave, and as regarded the Hon. George, it was certainly time that he did so. Her ladyship was in a great fret and fume. Those horrid roads would, she was sure, be the death of her if unhappily she were caught in them by the dark night. The lamps she was assured were good, but no lamp could withstand the jolting of the roads of East Barsetshire. The De Courcy property lay in the western division of the county.

Mrs. Proudie could not stay when the countess was gone. So the bishop was searched for by the Revs. Messrs. Grey and Green, and found in one corner of the tent enjoying himself thoroughly in a disquisition on the hebdomadal board. He obeyed, however, the behests of his lady without finishing the sentence in which he was promising to Dr. Gwynne that his authority at Oxford should remain unimpaired, and the episcopal horses turned their noses towards the palatial stables. Then the Grantlys went. Before they did so, Mr. Harding managed to whisper a word into his daughter's ear. Of course, he said he would undeceive the Grantlys as to that foolish rumour about Mr. Slope.

"No, no, no," said Eleanor; "pray do not;—pray wait till I see you. You will be home in a day or two, and then I will explain to you everything."

"I shall be home to-morrow," said he.

"I am so glad," said Eleanor. "You will come and dine with me, and then we shall be so comfortable."

Mr. Harding promised. He did not exactly know what there was to be explained, or why Dr. Grantly's mind should not be disabused of the mistake into which he had fallen; but nevertheless he promised. He owed some repara-

tion to his daughter, and he thought that he might best make it by obedience.

And thus the people were thinning off by degrees as Charlotte and Eleanor walked about in quest of Bertie. Their search might have been long had they not happened to hear his voice. He was comfortably ensconced in the ha-ha, with his back to the sloping side, smoking a cigar, and eagerly engaged in conversation with some youngster from the further side of the county, whom he had

Vol. n. x never met before, who was also smoking under Bertie's pupilage, and listening with open ears to an account given by his companion of some of the pastimes of Eastern clime.

"Bertie, I am seeking you everywhere," said Charlotte. "Come up here at once."

Bertie looked up out of the ha-ha, and saw the two ladies before him. As there was nothing for him but to obey, he got up and threw away his cigar. From the first moment of his acquaintance with her he had liked Eleanor Bold. Had he been left to his own devices, had she been penniless, and had it then been quite out of the question that he should marry her, he would most probably have fallen violently in love with her. But now he could not help regarding her somewhat as he did the marble workshops at Carrara, as he had done his easel and palette, as he had done the lawyer's chambers in London; in fact, as he had invariably regarded everything by which it had been proposed to him to obtain the means of living. Eleanor Bold appeared before him, no longer as a beautiful woman, but as a new profession called matrimony. It was a profession indeed requiring but little labour, and one in which an income was insured to him. But nevertheless he had been as it were goaded on to it. His sister had talked to him of Eleanor, just as she had talked of busts and portraits. Bertie did not dislike money, but he hated the very thought of earning it. He was now called away from his pleasant cigar to earn it, by offering himself as a husband to Mrs. Bold. The work indeed was made easy enough; for in lieu of his having to seek the widow, the widow had apparently come to seek him.

He made some sudden absurd excuse to his auditor, and then throwing away his cigar, climbed up the wall of the ha-ha and joined the ladies on the lawn. "Come and give Mrs. Bold an arm," said Charlotte, "while I set you on a piece of duty which, as. a preux chevalier, you must immediately perform. Your personal danger will, I fear, be insignificant, as your antagonist is a clergyman."

Bertie immediately gave his arm to Eleanor, walking between her and his sister. He had lived too long abroad to fall into the Englishman's habit of offering each an arm to two ladies at the eamo time;—a habit, by the bye, which foreigners regard as an approach to bigamy, or a sort of incipient Mormonism.

The little history of Mr. Slope's misconduct was then told to Bertie by his sister, Eleanor's ears tingling the while. And well they might tingle. If it were necessary to speak of the outrage at all, why should it be spoken of to such a person as Mr. Stanhope, and why in her own hearing? She knew she was wrong and was unhappy and dispirited, and yet she could think of no way to extricate herself, no way to set herself right. Charlotte spared her as much as she possibly could, spoke of the whole thing as though Mr. Slope had taken a glass of wine too much, said that of course there would be nothing more about it, but that steps must be taken to exclude Mr. Slope from the carriage. "Mrs. Bold need be under no alarm about that," said Bertie, "for Mr. Slope has gone this hour past. He told me that business made it necessary that he should start at once for Barchester."

"He is not so tipsy, at any rate, but what he knows his fault," said Charlotte. "Well, my dear, that is one difficulty over. Now I'll leave you with your true knight, and get Madeline oil as quickly as I can. The carriage is here, I suppose, Bertie?"

"It has been here for the last hour."

"That's well. Good bye, my dear. Of course you'll come in to tea. I shall trust to you to bring her, Bertie; even by force il necessary." And so saying, Charlotte ran off across the lawn, leaving her brother alone with the widow.

As Miss Stanhope went off, Eleanor bethought herself tfcat as Mr. Slope had taken his departure there no longer existed any necessity for separating Mr. Stanhope from his sister Madeline, who so much needed his aid. It had been arranged that he should remain so as to preoccupy Mr. Slope's place in the carriage, and act as a social policeman to effect the exclusion of that disagreeable gentleman. But Mr. Slope had effected his own exclusion, and there was no possible reason now why Bertie should not go with his sister. At least Eleanor saw none, and she said as much.

"Oh, let Charlotte have her own way," said he. "She has arranged it, and there will be no end of confusion if we make another change. Charlotte always arranges everything in our house; and rules us like a despot."

"But the Signora?" said Eleanor.

"Oh, the Signora can do very well without me. Indeed, she will have to do without me," he added, thinking rather of his studies in Carrara, than of his Barchester hymeneals.

"Why, you are not going to leave us?" asked Eleanor.

It has been said that Bertie Stanhope was a man without principle. He certainly was so. He had no power of using active mental exertion to keep himself from doing evil. Evil had no ugliness in his eyes; virtue no beauty. He was void of any of these feelings which actuate men to do good. But he was perhaps equally void of those which actuate men to do evil. He got into debt with utter recklessness, thinking nothing as to whether the tradesmen would ever be paid or not. But he did not invent active schemes of deceit for the sake of extracting the goods of others. If a man gave him credit, that was the man's look-out. Bertie Stanhope troubled himself nothing further. In borrowing money he did the same; he gave people references to "his governor;" told them that the "old chap" had a good income; and agreed to pay sixty per cent, for the ac-commodation. All this he did without a scruple of conscience; but then he never contrived active villany.

In this affair of his marriage, it had been represented to him as a matter of duty that he ought to put himself in possession of Mrs. Bold's hand and fortune; and at first he had so regarded it. About her he had thought but little. It was the customary thing for men situated as he was to marry for money, and there was no reason why he should not do what others around him did. And so he consented. But now he began to see the matter in another light. He was setting himself down to catch this woman, as a cat Bits to catch a mouse. He was to catch her, and swallow her up. her and her child, and her houses and land, in order that he might live on her instead of on his father. There was a cold, calculating. cautious cunning about this quite at variance with Bertie's character. The prudence of the measure was quite as antagonistic to. his feelings as the iniquity.

And then, should he be successful, what would be the reward? Having satisfied his creditors with half of the widow's fortune, he would be allowed to sit down quietly at Barchester, keeping economical house with the remainder. His duty would be to rock the cradle of the late Mr. Bold's child, and his highest excitement a demure party at Plumstead rectory, should it ultimately turn out that the archdeacon would be sufficiently reconciled to receive him.

There was very little in the programme to allure such a man as Bertie Stanhope. Would not the Carrara workshop, or whatever worldly career fortune might have in store for him,—would not almost anything be better than this? The lady herself was undoubtedly all that was desirable; but the most desirable lady becomes nauseous when she has to be taken as a pill. He was pledged to his sister, however, and let him quarrel with whom he would, it behoved him not to quarrel with her. If she were lost to him all would be lost that he could ever hope to derive henceforward from the paternal roof-tree. His mother was apparently indifferent to his weal or woe, to his wants or his welfare. His father's brow got blacker and blacker from day to day, as the old man looked at his hopeless son. And as for Madeline,—poor Madeline, whom of all of them he liked the best,—she had enough to do to shift for herself. No; come what might, he must cling to his sister and obey her behests, let them be ever so stern;—or at the very least seem to obey them. Could not some happy deceit bring him through in this matter, so that he might save appearances with his sister, and yet not betray the widow to her ruin? What if he made a confederate of Eleanor? 'Twas in this spirit that Bertie Sfmbope set about his wooing.

"But you are not going to leave Barchester? " asked Eleanor.

"I do not know," he replied; "I hardly know yet what I am going to do. But it is at any rate certain that I must do something."

"You mean about your profession?" said she.

"Yes, about my profession, if you can call it one."

"And is it not one?" said Eleanor. "Were I a man, I know none I should prefer to it, except painting. And I believe the one is as much in your power as the other."

"Yes, just about equally so," said Bertie, with a little touch of inward satire directed at himself. He knew in his heart that he would never make a penny by either.

"I have often wondered, Mr. Stanhope, why you do not exert yourself more," said Eleanor, who felt a friendly fondness for the man with whom she was walking. "But I know it is very impertinent in me to say so."

"Impertinent!" said he. "Not so, but much too kind. It is much too kind in you to take any interest in so idle a scamp."

"But you are not a scamp, though you are perhaps idle; and I do take an interest in you; a very great interest," she added, in a voice which almost made him resolve to change his mind. "And when I call you idle, I know you are only so for the present moment. "Why can't you settle steadily to work here in Barchester?"

"And make busts of the bishop, dean, and chapter? or perhaps, if I achieve a great success, obtain a commission to put up an elaborate tombstone over a prebendary's widow, a dead lady with a Grecian nose, a bandeau, and an intricate lace veil; lying of course on a marble sofa, from among the legs of which Death will be creeping out and poking at his victim with a small toasting-fork. "

Eleanor laughed; but yet she thought that if the surviving prebendary paid the bill, the object of the artist as a professional man would, in a great measure, be obtained.

"I don't know about the dean and chapter and the prebendary's widow," said Eleanor. "Of course you must take them as they come. But the fact of your having a great cathedral in which such ornaments are required, could not but be in your favour."

"No real artist could descend to the ornamentation of a cathedral," said Bertie, who had his ideas of the high ecstatic ambition of art, as indeed all artists have who are not in receipt of a good income. "Buildings should be fitted to grace the sculpture, not the sculpture to grace the building."

"Yes, when the work of art is good enough to merit it. Do you, Mr. Stanhope, do something sufficiently excellent, and we ladies of Barchester will erect for it a fitting receptacle. Come, what shall the subject be?"

"I'll put you in your pony chair, Mrs. Bold, as Dannecker put Ariadne on her lion. Only you must promise to sit for me."

"My ponies are too tame, I fear, and my broad-brimmed straw hat will not look so well in marble as the lace veil of the prebendary's wife."

"If you will not consent to that, Mrs. Bold, I will consent to try no other subject in Barchester."

"You are determined, then, to push your fortune in other lands?"

"I am determined," said Bertie, slowly and significantly, as he tried to bring up his mind to a great resolve;—" I am determined in this matter to be guided wholly by you."

"Wholly by me!" said Eleanor, astonished at, and not quite liking, his altered manner.

"Wholly by you," said Bertie, dropping his companion's arm, and standing before her on the path. In their walk they had come exactly to the spot in which Eleanor had been provoked into slapping Mr. Slope's face. Could it be possible that this place was peculiarly unpropitious to her comfort? Could it be possible that she should here have to encounter yet another amorous swain?

"If you will be guided by me, Mr. Stanhope, you will set yourself down to steady and persevering work, and you will be be ruled by your father as to the place in which it will be most advisable for you to do so."

"Nothing could be more prudent, if only it were practicable. But now, if you will let me, I will tell you how it is that I will be guided by you, and why. Will you let me tell you?"

"I really do not know what you can have to tell."

"No;—you cannot know. It is impossible that you should. But we have been very good friends, Mrs. Bold, have we not?"

"Yes, I think we have," said she, observing in his demeanour an earnestness very unusual with him.

"You were kind enough to say just now that you took an interest in me, and I was perhaps vain enough to believe you."

"There is no vanity in that; I do so as your sister's brother;— and as my own friend also."

"Well, I don't deserve that you should feel so kindly towards me," said Bertie; "but upon my word I am very grateful for it," and he paused awhile, hardly knowing how to introduce the subject that he had in hand.

And it was no wonder that he found it difficult to introduce the subject. He had to make known to his companion the scheme that had been prepared to rob her of her wealth; he had to tell her that he had intended to marry her without loving her, or else that he loved her without intending to marry her; and he had also to bespeak from her not only his own pardon, but also that of his sister, and induce Mrs. Bold to protest in her future communion with Charlotte that an offer had been duly made to her and duly rejected. Bertie Stanhope was not prone to be very diffident of his own conversational powers, but it did seem to him that he was about to tax them almost too far. He hardly knew where to begin, and he hardly knew where he should end.

By this time Eleanor was again walking on slowly by his side, not taking his arm as she had heretofore done, but listening very intently for whatever Bertie might have to say to her.

"I wish to be guided by you," said he; "and, indeed, in this matter, there is no one else who can set me right."

"Oh, that must be nonsense," said she.

"Well, listen to me now, Mrs. Bold; and if you can help it, pray don't be angry with me." *"Angry,"* said she.

"You will have cause to be so. You. know how very much attached to you my sister Charlotte is." Eleanor acknowledged that she did.

"Indeed she is; I never knew her to love any one so warmly on so short an acquaintance. You know also how well she loves me?"

Eleanor now made no answer, but she felt the blood tingle in her cheek as she gathered from what he said the probable result of this double-barrelled love on the part of Miss Stanhope.

"I am her only brother, Mrs. Bold, and it is not to be wondered at that she should love me. But you do not yet know Charlotte;— you do not know how entirely the well-being of our family hangs on her. Without her to manage for us I do not know how we should get on from day to day. You cannot yet have observed all this."

Eleanor had indeed observed a good deal of this. She did not however now say so, but allowed him to proceed with his story.

"You cannot therefore be surprised that Charlotte should be most anxious to do the best for us all."

Eleanor said that she was not at all surprised.

"And she has had a very difficult game to play, Mrs. Bold,—a very difficult game. Poor Madeline's unfortunate marriage and terrible accident, my mother's ill health, my father's absence fivm England, and last, and worst, perhaps, my own roving, idle spirit have almost been too much for her. You cannot wonder if among all her cares one of the foremost is to see me settled in the world."

Eleanor on this occasion expressed no acquiescence. She certainly supposed that a formal offer was to be made, and could not but think that so singular an exordium was never before made by a gentleman in a similar position. Mr. Slope had annoyed her by the excess of his ardour. It was quite clear that no such danger was to be feared from Mr. Stanhope. Prudential motives alone actuated him. Not only was he about to make love because his sister told him, but he also took the precaution of explaining all this before he began. 'Twas thus, we may presume, that the matter presented itself to Mrs. Bold.

When he had got so far, Bertie began poking the gravel with a little cane which he carried. He still kept moving on, but very slowly, and his companion moved slowly by his side, not inclined to assist him in the task the performance of which appeared to be difficult to him. "Knowing how fond she is of yourself, Mrs. Bold, cannot you imagine what scheme should have occurred to her?"

"I can imagine no better scheme, Mr. Stanhope, than the one I proposed to you just now."

"No," said he, somewhat lack-a-daisically; "I suppose that would be the best; but Charlotte thinks another plan might be joined with it.—She wants me to marry you."

A thousand remembrances flashed across Eleanor's mind all in a moment,—how Charlotte had talked about and praised her brother, how she had continually contrived to throw the two of them together, how she had encouraged all manner of little intimacies, how she had with singular cordiality persisted in treating Eleanor as one of the family. All this had been done to secure her comfortable income for the benefit of one of the family!

Such a feeling as this is very bitter when it first impresses itself on a young mind. To the old such plots and plans, such matured schemes for obtaining the goods of this world without the trouble of earning them, such long-headed attempts to convert "tuum" into "meum," are the ways of life to which they are accustomed. 'Tis thus that many live, and it therefore behoves all those who are well to do in the world to be on their guard against those who are not. With them it is the success that disgusts, not the attempt. But Eleanor had not yet learnt to look on her money as a source of danger. She had not begun to regard herself as fair game to be hunted down by hungry gentlemen. She had enjoyed the society of the Stanhopes, she had greatly liked the cordiality of Charlotte, and had been happy in her new friends. Now she saw the cause of all this kindness, and her mind was opened to a new phase of human life.

"Miss Stanhope," said she, haughtily, "has been contriving for me a great deal of honour, but she might have saved herself the trouble. I am not sufficiently ambitious."

"Pray don't be angry with her, Mrs. Bold," said he,—" or with me either."

"Certainly not with you, Mr. Stanhope," said she, with considerable sarcasm in her tone. "Certainly not with you." "No,—nor with her," said he, imploringly.

"And why, may I ask you, Mr. Stanhope, have you told me this singular story? For I may presume I may judge by your manner of telling it, that,—that,—that you and your sister are not exactly of one mind on the subject."

"No; we are not."

"And if so," said Mrs. Bold, who was now really angry with the unnecessary insult which she thought had been offered to her, "and if so, why has it been worth your while to tell me all this?"

"I did once think, Mrs. Bold,—that you,—that you." The widow now again became entirely impassive, and would not lend the slightest assistance to her companion. "I did once think thai you perhaps might,—might have been taught to regard me as more than a friend."

"Never!" said Mrs. Bold, "never. If I have ever allowed myself to do anything to encourage such an idea, I have been very much to blame,—very much to blame indeed."

"You never have," said Bertie, who really had a good-natured anxiety to make what he said as little unpleasant as possible. "You never have, and I have seen for some time that I had no chance; but my sister's hopes ran higher. I have not mistaken you, Mrs. Bold, though perhaps she has."

"Then why have you said all this to me?"

"Because I must not anger her."

"And will not this anger her? Upon my word, Mr. Stanhope, I do not understand the policy of your family. Oh, how I wish I was at home!" And as she expressed the wish, she could restrain herself no longer, but burst out into a flood of tears.

Poor Bertie was greatly moved. "You shall have the carriage to yourself going home," said he; "at least you and my father. As for me I can walk, or for the matter of that it does not much signify what I do." He perfectly understood that part of Eleanor's grief arose from the apparent necessity of her going back to Barchester in the carriage with her second suitor.

This somewhat mollified her. "Oh, Mr. Stanhope," said she, "why should you have made me so miserable? What will you have gained by telling me all this?"

He had not even yet explained to her the most difficult part of his proposition. He had not told her that she was to be a party to the little deception which he intended to play off upon his sister. This suggestion had still to be made, and, as it was absolutely necessary, he proceeded to make it.

We need not follow him through the whole of his statement. At last, and not without considerable difficulty, he gave Eleanor to understand why he had let her into his confidence, seeing that he no longer intended her the honour of a formal offer. At last he made her comprehend the part which she was destined to play in this little family comedy.

But when she did understand it, she was only more angry with him than ever;—more angry, not only with him, but with Charlotte also. Her fair name was to be bandied about between them in different senses, and each sense false. She was to be played off by the sister against the father; and then by the brother against the sister. Her dear friend Charlotte, with all her agreeable sympathy and affection, was striving to sacrifice her for the Stanhope family welfare; and Bertie, who, as he now proclaimed himself, was over head and ears in debt, completed the compliment of owning that he did not care to have his debts paid at so great a sacrifice of himself. Then she was asked to conspire together with this unwilling suitor, for the sake of making the family believe that he had in obedience to their commands done his best to throw himself thus away!

She lifted up her face when he had finished, and looking at him with much dignity, even through her tears, she said;—"I regret to say it, Mr. Stanhope; but after what has passed, I believe that all intercourse between your family and myself had better cease."

"Well, perhaps it had," said Bertie naively; "perhaps that will be better, at any rate for a time; and then Charlotte will think you are offended at what I have done."

"And now I will go back to the house, if you please," said Eleanor. "I can find my way by myself, M. Stanhope. After what has passed," she added, "I would rather go alone."

"But I must find the carriage for you, Mrs. Bold, and I must tell my father that you will return with him alone, and I must make some excuse to him for not going with you; and I must bid the servant put you down at your own house, for I suppose you will not now choose to see them again in the close."

There was a truth about this, and a perspicuity in making arrangements for lessening her immediate embarrassment, which had some effect in soft-ening Eleanor's anger. So she suffered herself to walk by his side over the now deserted lawn till they came to the drawing-room window. There was something about Bertie Stanhope, which gave him, in the estimation of every one, a different standing from that which any other man would occupy under similar circumstances. Angry as Eleanor was, and great as was her cause for anger, she was not half as angry with him as she would have been with any one else. He was apparently so simple, so good-natured, so unaffected and easy to talk to, that she had already half-forgiven him before he was at the drawing-room window. When they arrived there Dr. Stanhope was sitting nearly alone with Mr. and Miss Thorne; one or two other unfortunates were there, who from one cause or another were still delayed in getting away; but they were every moment getting fewer in number.

As soon as he had handed Eleanor over to his father, Bertie started off to the front gate, in search of the carriage, and there waited leaning patiently against the front wall, and comfortably smoking a cigar till it came up. When he returned to the room Dr. Stanhope and Eleanor were alone with their hosts.

"At last, Miss Thorne," said he cheerily, "I have come to relieve you. Mrs. Bold and my father are the last roses of the very delightful summer you have given us, and desirable as Mrs. Bold's society always is, now at least you must be glad to see the last flowers plucked from the tree."

Miss Thorne declared that she was delighted to have Mrs. Bold and Dr. Stanhope still with her; and Mr. Thorne would have said the same, had he not been checked by a yawn, which he could not suppress.

"Father, will you give your arm to Mrs. Bold?" said Bertie: and so the last adieux were made, and the prebendary led out Mrs. Bold, followed by his son.

"I shall be home soon after you," said he, as the two got into the carriage.

"Are you not coming in the carriage?" said the father.

"No, no; I have some one to see on the road, and shall walk. John, mind you drive to Mrs. Bold's house first."

Eleanor looking out of the window, saw him with his hat in his hand, bowing to her with his usual gay smile, as though nothing had happened to mar the tranquillity of the day. It was many a long year before she saw him again. Dr. Stanhope hardly spoke to her on her way home; and she was safely deposited by John at her own hall-door before the carriage drove into the close.

And thus our heroine played the last act of tnat day's melodrama.

MH. AND MRS. QUIVERFUL ARE MADE HAPPY. MR. SLOPE IS

ENCOURAGED BY THE PRESS

Before she started for Ullathorne, Mrs. Proudie, careful souJ, caused two letters to be written, one by herself and one by her lord, to the inhabitants of Puddingdale vicarage, which made happy the hearth of those within it.

As soon as the departure of the horses left the bishop's stableroom free for other services, that humble denizen of the diocese started on the bishop's own pony with the two despatches. We have had so many letters lately that we will spare ourselves these. That from the bishop was simply a request that Mr. Quiverful would wait upon his lordship the next morning at 11 A.m.; and that from the lady was as simply a request that Mrs. Quiverful would do the same by her, though it was couched in somewhat longer and more grandiloquent phraseology.

It had become a point of conscience with Mrs. Proudie to urge the settlement of this great hospital question. She was resolved that Mr. Quiverful should have it. She was resolved that there should be no more doubt or delay, no more refusals and resignations, no more secret negotiations carried on by Mr. Slope on his own account in opposition to her behests.

"Bishop," she said, immediately after breakfast, on the morning of that eventful day, "have you signed the appointment yet?"

"No, my dear, not yet; it is not exactly signed as yet."

"Then do it," said the lady.

The bishop did it; and a very pleasant day indeed he spent at Ullathorne. And when he got home he had a glass of hot negus in his wife's sitting-room, and read the last number of the "Little Dorrit" of the day with great inward satisfaction. Oh, husbands, oh, my marital friends, what great comfort is there to be derived from a wife well obeyed!

Much perturbation and flutter, high expectation and renewed hopes, were occasioned at Puddingdale, by the receipt of these episcopal despatches. Mrs. Quiverful, whose careful ear caught the sound of the pony's feet as he trotted up to the vicarage kitchen door, brought them in hurriedly to her husband. She was at the moment concocting the Irish stew destined to satisfy the noonday wants of fourteen young birds, let alone the parent couple. She had taken the letters from the man's hands between the folds of her capacious apron, so as to save them from the contamination of the stew, and in this guise she brought them to her husband's desk.

They at once divided the spoil, each taking that addressed to the other. "Quiverful," said she with impressive voice, "you are to be at the palace at eleven to-morrow."

"And so are you, my dear," said he, almost gasping with the importance of the tidings: and then they exchanged letters.

"She'd never have sent for me again," said the lady, "if it wasn't all right."

"Oh! my dear, don't be too certain," said the gentleman. "Only think if it should be wrong."

"She'd never have sent for me, Q., if it wasn't all right," again argued the lady. "She's stiff and hard and proud as piecrust, but I think she's right at bottom." Such was Mrs. Quiverful's verdict about Mrs. Proudie, to which in after times she always adhered. People when they get their income doubled usually think that those through whose instrumentality this little ceremony is performed are right at bottom.

"Oh Letty!" said Mr. Quiverful, rising from his well-worn seat.

"Oh Q.!" said Mrs. Quiverful. Then the two, unmindful of the kitchen apron, the greasy fingers, and the adherent Irish stew, threw themselves warmly into each other's arms. "For heaven's sake don't let any one cajole you out of it again," said the wife.

"Let me alone for that," said the husband, with a look of almost fierce determination, pressing his fist as he spoke rigidly on his desk, as though he had Mr. Slope's head below his knuckles, and meant to keep it there.

"I wonder how soon it will be," said she.

"I wonder whether it will be at all," said he, still doubtful.

"Well, I won't say too much," said the lady. "The cup has slipped twice before, and it may fall altogether this time; but I'll not believe it. He'll give you the appointment to-morrow. You'll find he will."

"Heaven send he may," said Mr. Quiverful, solemnly. And who that considers the weight of the burden on this man's back, will say that the prayer was an improper one? There were fourteen of them,—fourteen of them living,—as Mrs. Quiverful had so powerfully urged in the presence of the bishop's wife. As long as promotion cometh from any human source, whether north or south, east or west, will not such a claim as this hold good, in spite of all our examination tests, detur digniori's and optimist tendencies? It is fervently to be hoped that it may. Till we can become divine we must be content to be human, lest in our hurry for a change we sink to something lower.

And then the pair sitting down lovingly together, talked over all their difficulties, as they so often did, and all their hopes, as they so seldom were enabled to do.

"You had better call on that man, Q. , as you come away from the palace," said Mrs. Quiverful, pointing to an angry call for money from the Barchester draper, which the postman had left at the vicarage that morning. Cormorant that he was, unjust, hungry cormorant! When rumour first got abroad that the Quiverfuls were to go to the hospital, this fellow with fawning eagerness had pressed his goods upon the wants of the poor clergyman. He had done so, feeling that he should be paid from tho hospital funds, and flattering himself that a man with fourteen

Vol. 11. u children, and money wherewithal to clothe them, could not but bn an excellent customer. As soon as the second rumour reached him. he applied for his money angrily.

And the "fourteen"—or such of them as were old enough to hope and discuss their hopes, talked over their golden future. The tall-grown girls whispered to each other of possible Barchester parties, of possible allowances for dress, of a possible piano,—the one they had in the vicarage was so weather-beaten with the storms of years and children as to be no longer worthy of the name,—of the pretty garden, and the pretty house. 'Twas of such things it most behoved them to whisper.

And the younger fry, they did not content themselves with whispers, but shouted to each other of their new playground beneath our dear ex-warden's well-loved elms, of their future own gardens, of marbles to be procured in the wished-for city, and of the rumour which had reached them of a Barchester school.

'Twas in vain that their cautious mother tried to instil into their breasts the very feeling she had striven to banish from that of their father; 'twas in vain that she repeated to the girls that "there's many a slip 'twixt the cup and the lip;" 'twas in vain she attempted to make the children believe that they were to live at Puddingdale all their lives. Hopes mounted high and would not have themselves quelled. The neighbouring farmers heard the news, and came in to congratulate them. 'Twas Mrs. Quiverful herself who had kindled the fire, and in the first outbreak of her renewed expectations she did it so thoroughly, that it was quite past her power to put it out again.

Poor matron! good honest matron! doing thy duty in the state to which thou hast been called, heartily if not contentedly; let the fire burn on;—on this occasion the flames will not scorch; they shall warm thee and thine. 'Tis ordained that that husband of thine, that Q. of thy bosom, shall reign supreme for years to come over the bedesmen of Hiram's hospital.

And the last in all Barchester to mar their hopes, had he heard and seen all that passed at Puddingdale that day, would have been Mr. Harding. What wants had he to set in opposition to those of such a regiment of young ravens? There are fourteen of them living! With him at any rate, let us say, that that argument would have been sufficient for the appointment of Mr. Quiverful.

In the morning, Q. and his wife kept their appointments with that punctuality which bespeaks an expectant mind. The friendly farmer's gig was borrowed, and in that they went, discussing many things by the way. They had instructed the household to expect them back by one, and injunctions were given to the eldest pledge to have ready by that accustomed hour the remainder of the huge stew which the provident mother had prepared on the previous day. The hands of the kitchen clock came round to two, three, four, before the farmer's gig-wheels were again heard at the vicarage gate. With what palpitating hearts were the returning wanderers greeted!

"I suppose, children, you all thought we were never coming back any more?" said the mother, as she slowly let down her solid foot till it rested on the step of the gig. Well, such a day as we've had!" Then leaning heavily on a big boy's shoulder, she stepped once more on terra firma.

There was no need for more than the tone of her voice to tell them that all was right. The Irish stew might burn itself to cinders now.

Then there was such kissing and hugging, such crying and laughing. Mr. Quiverful could not sit still at all, but kept walking from room to room, then out into the garden, then down the avenue into the road, then back again to his wife. She, however, lost no time so idly. "We must go to work at once, girls, and that in earnest. Mrs. Proudie expects us to be in the hospital house 04 the 15th of October."

Had Mrs. Proudie expressed a wish that they should all be there on the next morning, the girls would have had nothing to say against it.

"And when will the pay begin?" asked the eldest boy. "To-day, my dear," said the gratified mother.

"Oh,—that is jolly," said the boy.

"Mrs. Proudie insisted on our going down to the house," continued the mother; "and when there I thought I might save a journey by measuring some of the rooms and windows; so I got a knot of tape from Bobbins. Bobbins is as civil as you please, now."

"I wouldn't thank him," said Letty the younger.

"Oh, it's the way of the world, my dear. They all do just the same. You might just as well be angry with the turkey cock for gobbling at you. It's the bird's nature." And as she enunciated to her bairns the upshot of her practical experience, she pulled from her pocket the portions of tape which showed the length and breadth of the various rooms at the hospital house.

And so we will leave her happy in her toils.

The Quiverfuls had hardly left the palace, and Mrs. Proudie was still holding forth on the matter to her husband, when another visitor was announced in the person of Dr. Gwynne. The master of Lazarus had asked for the bishop, and not for Mrs. Proudie, and therefore, when he was shown into the study, he was surprised rather than rejoiced to find the lady there.

Going home in the carriage that evening from Ullathorne Dr. Gwynne had not without difficulty brought round his friend the archdeacon to a line of tactics much less bellicose than that which his own taste would have preferred. "It will be unseemly in us to show ourselves in a bad humour; and moreover we have no power in this matter, and it will therefore be bad policy to act as though we had." 'Twas thus the master of Lazarus argued. "If," he continued, "the bishop be determined to appoint another to the hospital, threats will not prevent him, and threats should not be lightly used by an archdeacon to his bishop. If he will place a stranger in the hospital we can only leave him to the indignation of others. It is probable that such a step may not eventually injure your father-in-law. I will see the bishop, if you will allow me,— alone." At this the archdeacon winced visibly "yes, alone; for so I shall be calmer: and then I shall at any rate learn what he does mean to do in the matter."

The archdeacon puffed and blew, put up the carriage window and then put it down again, argued the matter up to his own gate, and at last gave way. Everybody was against him, his own wife, Mr. Harding, and Dr. Gwynne. "Pray keep him out of hot water, Dr. Gwynne," Mrs. Grantly had said to her guest. "My dearest madam, I'll do my best," the courteous master had replied. 'Twas thus he did it; and earned for himself the gratitude of Mrs. Grantly.

And now we may return to the bishop's study.

Dr. Gwynne had certainly not foreseen the difficulty which here presented itself. He,—together with all the clerical world of England,—had heard it rumoured that Mrs. Proudie did not confine herself to her wardrobes, still-rooms, and laundries; but yet it had never occurred to him that if he called on a bishop at one o'clock in the day, he could by any possibility find him closeted with his wife; or that if he did so, the wife would remain longer than necessary to make her curtsey. It appeared, however, as though in the present case Mrs. Proudie had no idea of retreating.

The bishop had been very much pleased with Dr. Gwynne on the preceding day, and of course thought that Dr. Gwynne had been as much pleased with him. He attributed the visit solely to compliment, and thought it an extremely gracious and proper thing for the master of Lazarus to drive over from Plumstead specially to call at the palace so soon after his arrival in the country. The fact that they were not on the same side either in politics or doctrines made the compliment the greater. The bishop, therefore, was all smiles. And Mrs. Proudie, who liked people with good handles to their names was also very well disposed to welcome the master of Lazarus.

"We had a charming party at Ullathorne, Master, had we not?" said she. "I hope Mrs. Grantly got home without fatigue."

Dr. Gwynne said that they had all been a little tired, but were none the worse this morning.

"An excellent person, Miss Thorne," suggested the bishop.

"And an exemplary Christian, I am told," said Mrs. Proudie.

Dr. Gwynne declared that he was very glad to hear it.

"I have not seen her Sabbath-day schools yet," continued the lady, "but I shall make a point of doing so before long."

Dr. Gwynne merely bowed at this intimation. He had heard something of Mrs. Proudie and her Sunday schools, both from Dr. Grantly and Mr. Harding.

"By the bye, Master," continued the lady, "I wonder whether Mrs. Grantly would like me to drive over and inspect her Sabbathday school. I hear that it is most excellently kept."

Dr. Gwynne really could not say. He had no doubt Mrs. Grantly would be most happy to see Mrs. Proudie any day Mrs. Proudie would do her the honour of calling; that was, of course, if Mrs. Grantly should happen to be at home.

A slight cloud darkened the lady's brow. She saw that her offer was not taken in good part. This generation of unregenerated vipers was still perverse, stiffnecked, and hardened in their iniquity. "The archdeacon, I know," said she, "sets his face against these institutions."

At this Dr. Gwynne laughed slightly. It was but a smile. Had he given his cap for it he could not have helped it.

Mrs. Proudie frowned again. "'Suffer little children, and forbid them not,'" said she. "Are we not to remember that, Dr. Gwynne?' Take heed that ye despise not one of these little ones.' Are we not to remember that, Dr. Gwynne?" And at each of these questions she raised at him her menacing forefinger.

"Certainly, madam, certainly," said the master; "and so does the archdea-

con, I am sure, on week days as well as on Sundays."

"On week days you can't take heed not to despise them," said Mrs. Proudie, "because then they are out in the fields. On week days they belong to their parents, but on Sundays they ought to belong to the clergyman." And the finger was again raised.

The master began to understand and to share the intense disgust which the archdeacon always expressed when Mrs. Proudie's name was mentioned. What was he to do with such a woman as this? To take his hat and go would have been his natural resource; but then he did not wish to be foiled in his object.

"My lord," said he, "I wanted to ask you a question on business, if you could spare me one moment's leisure. I know I must apologise for so disturbing you; but in truth I will not detain you five minutes."

"Certainly, Master, certainly," said the bishop; "my time is quite yours. Pray make no apology, pray make no apology."

"You have a great deal to do just at the present moment, bishop. Do not forget how extremely busy you are at present," said Mrs. Proudie, whose spirit was now up; for she was angry with her visitor.

"I will not delay his lordship much above a minute," said the master of Lazarus, rising from his chair, and expecting that Mrs. Proudie would now go or else that the bishop would lead the way into another room. But neither event seemed likely to occur, and Dr. Gwynne stood for a moment silent in the middle of the room.

"Perhaps it's about Hiram's hospital?" suggested Mrs. Proudie.

Dr. Gwynne, lost in astonishment, and not knowing what else on earth to do, confessed that his business with the bishop was connected with Hiram's hospital.

"His lordship has finally conferred the appointment on Mr. Quiverful this morning," said the lady.

Dr. Gwynne made a simple reference to the bishop, and finding that the lady's statement was formally confirmed, he took his leave. "That comes of the re-form bill," he said to himself as he walked down the bishop's avenue. "Well, at any rate the Greekplay bishops were not so bad as that."

It has been said that Mr. Slope, as he started for Ullathorne, received a despatch from his friend, Mr. Towers, which had the effect of putting him in that high good-humour which subsequent events somewhat untowardly damped. It ran as follows. lis shortness will be its sufficient apology.

"My dear Sir,—I wish you every success. I don't know that I can help you, but if I can, I will.

"Yours ever,

"T T

"30/9/185—"

There was more in this than in all Sir Nicholas Fitzwhiggin's flummery; more than in all the bishop's promises, even had they been ever so sincere; more than in any archbishop's good word, even had it been possible to obtain it. Tom Towers would do for him what he could.

Mr. Slope had from his youth upwards been a firm believer in the public press. He had dabbled in it himself ever since he had taken his degree, and regarded it as the great arranger and distributor of all future British terrestrial affairs whatever. He had not yet arrived at the age, an age which sooner or later comes to most of us, which dissipates the golden dreams of youth. He delighted in the idea of wresting power from the hands of his country's magnates, and placing it in a custody which was at any rate nearer to his own reach. Sixty thousand broad sheets dispersing themselves daily among his reading fellow-citizens, formed in his eyes a better depot for supremacy than a throne at Windsor, a cabinet in Downing Street, or even an assembly at Westminster. And on this subject we must not quarrel with Mr. Slope, for the feeling is too general to be met with disrespect.

Tom Towers was as good, if not better than his promise. On the following morning the Jupiter, spouting forth public opinion with sixty thousand loud clarions, did proclaim to the world that Mr. Slope was the fitting man for the vacant post. It was pleasant for Mr. Slope to read the following lines in the Barchester news-room which he did within thirty minutes after the morning train from London had reached the city.

"It is just now five years since we called the attention of our readers to the quiet city of Barchester. From that day to this, we have in no way meddled with the affairs of that happy ecclesiastical community. Since then, an old bishop has died there, and a young bishop has been installed; but we believe we did not do more than give some customary record of the interesting event. Nor are we now about to meddle very deeply in the affairs of tlie diocese. If any of the chapter feel a qualm of conscience on reading thus far, let it be quieted. Above all, let the mind of the new bishop be at rest. We are now not armed for war, but approach the reverend towers of the old cathedral with an olive-branch in our hands.

"It will be remembered that at the time alluded to, now five years past, we had occasion to remark on the state of a charity in Barchester called Hiram's hospital. We thought that it was maladministered, and that the very estimable and reverend gentleman who held the office of warden was somewhat too highly paid for duties which were somewhat too easily performed. This gentleman,—and we say it in all sincerity and with no touch of sarcasm,—had never looked on the matter in this light before. We do not wish to take praise to ourselves whether praise be due to us or not. But the consequence of our remark was, that the warden did look into the matter, and finding on so doing that he himself could come to no other opinion than that expressed by us, he very creditably threw up the appointment. The then bishop as creditably declined to fill the vacancy till the affair was put on a better footing. Parliament then took it up; and we have now the satisfaction of informing our readers that Hiram's hospital will be immediately re-opened under new auspices. 'Heretofore, provision was made for the maintenance of twelve old men. This will now be ex-tended to the fair sex, and twelve elderly women, if any such can be found in Barchester, will be added to the establishment. There will be a matron; there will, it is hoped, be schools attached for the poorest of the children of the poor, and there will be a steward. The warden, for there will still be a warden, will receive an income more in keeping with the extent of the charity than that heretofore paid. The stipend we believe will be 45 0l. We may add that the excellent house which the former warden inhabited will still be attached to the situation.

"Barchester hospital cannot perhaps boast a world-wide reputation; but as we adverted to its state of decadence, we think it right also to advert to its renaissance. May it go on and prosper. Whether the salutary reform which has been introduced within its walls has been carried as far as could have been desired, may be doubtful. The important question of the school appears to be somewhat left to the discretion of the new warden. This might have been made the most important part of the establishment, and the new warden, whom we trust we shall not offend by the freedom of our remarks, might have been selected with some view to his fitness as schoolmaster. But we will not now look a gift horse in the mouth. May the hospital go on and prosper! The situation of warden has of course been offered to the gentleman who so honourably vacated it five years since; but we are given to understand that he has declined it. "Whether the ladies who have been introduced be in his estimation too much for his powers of control, whether it be that the diminished income does not offer to him sufficient temptation to resume his old place, or that he has in the meantime assumed other clerical duties, we do not know. We are, however, informed that he has refused the offer, and that the situation has been accepted by Mr. Quiverful, the vicar of Puddingdale.

"So much we think is due to Hiram redivivus. But while we are on the subject of Barchester, we will venture with all respectful humility to express our opinion on another matter, connected with the ecclesiastical polity of that ancient city. Dr. Trefoil, the dean, died yesterday. A short record of his death, giving his age, and the various pieces of preferment which he has at different times held, will be found in another column of this paper. The only fault we knew in him was his age, and as that is a crime of which we all hope to be guilty, we will not bear heavily on it. May he rest in peace! But though the great age of an expiring dean cannot be made matter of reproach, we are not inclined to look on such a fault as at all pardonable in a dean just brought to the birth. We do hope that the days of sexagenarian appointmerits are past. If we want deans, we must want them for some purpose. That purpose will necessarily be botter fulfilled by a man of forty than by a man of sixty. If we are to pay deans at all we are to pay them for some sort of work. That work, be it what it may, will be best performed by a workman in the prime of life. Dr. Trefoil, we see, was eighty when he died. As we have as yet completed no plan for pensioning superannuated clergymen, we do not wish to get rid of any existing deans of that age. But we prefer having as few such as possible. If a man of seventy be now appointed, we beg to point out to Lord that he will be past all use in a year or two, if indeed he be not so at the present moment. His lordship will allow us to remind him that all men are not evergreens like himself.

""We hear that Mr. Slope's name has been mentioned for this preferment. Mr. Slope is at present chaplain to the bishop. A better man could hardly be selected. He is a man of talent, young, active, and conversant with the affairs of the cathedral. He is moreover, we conscientiously believe, a truly pious clergyman. We know that his services in the city of Barchester have been highly appreciated. He is an eloquent preacher and a ripe scholar. Such a selection as this would go far to raise the confidence of the public in the present administration of church patronage, and would teach men to believe that from henceforth the establishment of our church will not af-

ford easy couches to worn-out clerical voluptuaries."

Standing at a reading-desk in the Barchester news-room Mr. Slope digested this article with considerable satisfaction. What was therein said as to the hospital was now comparatively matter of indifference to him. He was certainly glad that he had not succeeded in restoring to the place the father of that virago who had so audaciously outraged all decency in his person;—and was so far satisfied. But Mrs. Proudie's nominee was appointed, and he was so far dissatisfied. His mind, however, was now soaring above Mrs. Bold or Mrs. Proudie. He was sufficiently conversant with the tactics of the Jupiter to know that the pith of the article would lie in the last paragraph. The place of nonour was given to him, and it was indeed as honourable as even he could have wished. He was very grateful to his friend Mr. Towers, and with full heart looked forward to the day when he might entertain him in princely style at his own full-spread board in the deanery dining-room.

It had been well for Mr. Slope that Dr. Trefoil had died in the autumn. Those caterers for our morning repast, the staff of the Jupiter, had been sorely put to it for the last month to find a sufficiency of proper pabulum. Just then there was no talk of a new American president. No wonderful tragedies had occurred on railway trains in Georgia, or elsewhere. There was a dearth of broken banks, and a dead dean with the necessity for a live one was a godsend. Had Dr. Trefoil died in June, Mr. Towers would probably not have known so much about the piety of Mr. Slope.

And here we will leave Mr. Slope for a while in his triumph,— explaining, however, that his feelings were not altogether of a triumphant nature. His rejection by the widow, or rather the method of his rejection, galled him terribly. For days to come he positively felt the sting upon his cheek, whenever he thought of what had been done to him. He could not refrain from calling her by harsh names, speaking to himself as he walked through the streets of Barches-

ter. When he said his prayers, he could not bring himself to forgive her. When he strove to do so, his mind recoiled from the attempt, and in lieu of forgiving ran off in a double spirit of vindictiveness, dwelling on the extent of the injury he had received. And so his prayers dropped senseless from his lips.

And then the Signora! What would he not have given to be able to hate her also? As it was. he worshipped the very sofa on which she was ever lying. And thus it was not all rose colour with Mr. Slope, although his hopes ran high.

MES. BOLD AT HOME.

Poor Mrs. Bold, when she got home from Ullathorne on the evening of Miss Thorne's party, was very unhappy, and moreover, very tired. Nothing fatigues the body so much as weariness of spirit, and Eleanor's spirit was indeed weary.

Dr. Stanhope had civilly but not very cordially asked her in to tea, and her manner of refusal convinced the worthy doctor that he need not repeat the invitation. He had not exactly made himself a party to the intrigue which was to convert the late Mr. Bold's patrimony into an income for his hopeful son, but he had been well aware what was going on. And he was well aware also, when he perceived that Bertie declined accompanying them home in the carriage, that the affair had gone off.

Eleanor was very much afraid that Charlotte would have darted out upon her, as the prebendary got out at his own door, but Bertie had thoughtfully saved her from this, by causing the carriage to go round by her own house. This also Dr. Stanhope understood, and allowed to pass by without remark.

When she got home, she found Mary Bold in the drawing-room with the child in her lap. She rushed forward, and, throwing herself on her knees, kissed the little fellow till she almost frightened him. "Oh, Mary, I am so glad you did not go. It was an odious party."

Now the question of Mary's going had been one greatly mooted between them. Mrs. Bold, when invited, had been the guest of the Grantlys, and Miss Thorne, who had chiefly known Eleanor at the hospital or at Plumstead rectory, had forgotten all about Mary Bold. Her sister-in-law had implored her to go under her wing, and had offered to write to Miss Thorne, or to call on her. But Miss Bold had declined. In fact, Mr. Bold had not been verypopular with such people as the Thornes, and his sister would not go among them unless she were specially asked to do so.

"Well then," said Mary, cheerfully, "I have the less to regret."

"You have nothing to regret; but oh! Mary, I have,—so much, — so much." Then she began kissing her boy, whom her caresses had roused from his slumbers. When she raised her head, Mary saw that the tears were running down her cheeks.

"Good heavens, Eleanor, what is the matter? what has happened to you? Eleanor,—dearest Eleanor,—what is the matter?" and Mary got up with the boy still in her arms.

"Give him to me,—give him to me," said the young mother. "Give him to me, Mary," and she almost tore the child out of her sister's arms. The poor little fellow murmured somewhat at the disturbance, but nevertheless nestled himself close into his mother's bosom.

"Here, Mary, take the cloak from me. My own, own darling, darling, darling jewel. You are not false to me. Everybody else is false; everybody else is cruel. Mamma will care for nobody, nobody, nobody, but her own, own, own little man." Again she kissed and pressed the baby, and cried till the tears ran down over the child's face.

"Who has been cruel to you, Eleanor?" said Mary. I hope I have not. "

Now, in this matter, Eleanor had great cause for mental uneasiness. She could not certainly accuse her loving sister-in-law of cruelty; but she had to do that which was more galling; she had to accuse herself of imprudence against which her sister-in-law had warned her. Miss Bold had never encouraged Eleanor's acquaintance with Mr. Slope, and she had positively discouraged the friendship of the Stanhopes as far as her usual gentle mode of speaking had permitted. Eleanor had only laughed at her,

however, when she said that she disapproved of married women who lived apart from their husbands. and suggested that Charlotte

Stanhope never went to church. Now, however, Eleanor must either hold her tongue, which was quite impossible, or confess herself to have been utterly wrong, which was nearly equally so. So she staved off the evil day by more tears, and consoled herself by inducing little Johnny to rouse himself sufficiently to return her caresses.

"He is a darling;—as true as gold. What would mamma do without him? Mamma would lie down and die if she had not her own Johnny Bold to give her comfort." This and much more she said of the same kind, and for a time made no other answer to Mary's inquiries.

This kind of consolation from the world's deceit is very common. Mothers obtain it from their children, and men from their dogs. Some men even do so from their walking-sticks, which is just as rational. How is it that we can take joy to ourselves in that we are not deceived by those who have not attained the art to deceive us? In a true man, if such can be found, or a true woman, much consolation may indeed be taken.

In the caresses of her child, however, Eleanor did receive consolation; and may ill befall the man who would begrudge it to her. The evil day, however, was only postponed. She had to tell her disagreeable tale to Mary, and she had also to tell it to her father. Must it not, indeed, be told to the whole circle of her acquaintances before she could be made to stand all right with them? At the present moment there was no one to whom she could turn for comfort. She hated Mr. Slope. That was a matter of course; in that feeling she revelled. She hated and despised the Stanhopes; but that feeling distressed her greatly. She had, as it were, separated herself from her old friends to throw herself into the arms of this family; and then how had they intended to use her? She coidd hardly reconcile herself to her own father, who had believed ill of her. Mary

Bold had turned Mentor. That she could have forgiven had the Mentor turned out to be in the wrong; but Mentors in the right are not to be pardoned. She could not but hate the archdeacon; and now she hated him worse than ever, for she must in some sort humble herself before him. She hated her sister, for she was part and parcel of the archdeacon. And she would have hated Mr. Arabin if she could. He had pretended to regard her, and yet before her face he had hung over that Italian woman as though there had been no beauty in the world but hers,—no other woman worth a moment's attention. And Mr. Arabin would have to learn all this about Mr. Slope! She told herself that she hated him, and she knew that she was lying to herself as she did so. She had no consolation but her baby, and of that she made the most. Mary, though she could not surmise what it was that had so violently affected her sisterin-law, saw at once that her grief was too great to be kept under control, and waited patiently till the child should be in his cradle. "You'll have some tea, Eleanor," she said.

"Oh, I don't care," said she; though in fact she must have been very hungry, for she had eaten nothing at Ullathorne.

Mary quietly made the tea, and buttered the bread, laid aside the cloak, and made things look comfortable.

"He's fast asleep," said she; "you're very tired; let me take him up to bed."

But Eleanor would not let her sister touch him. She looked wistfully at her baby's eyes, saw that they were lost in the deepest slumber, and then made a sort of couch for him on the sofa. She was determined that nothing should prevail upon her to let him out of her sight that night.

"Come, Nelly," said Mary, "don't be cross with me. I at least have done nothing to offend you."

"I an't cross," said Eleanor.

"Are you angry then? Surely you can't be mgry with me."

"No, I an't angry;—at least not with you."

"If you are not, drink the tea I have made for you. I am sure you must want it."

Eleanor did drink it, and allowed herself to be persuaded. She ate and drank, and as the inner woman was recruited she felt a little more charitable towards the world at large. At last she found words to begin her story, and before she went to bed, she had made a clean breast of it and told everything;—everything, that is, as to the lovers she had rejected. Of Mr. Arabin she said not a word.

"I know I was wrong," said she, speaking of the blow she had given to Mr. Slope; "but I didn't know what he might do, and I had to protect myself."

"He richly deserved it," said Mary.

"Deserved it!" said Eleanor, whose mind as regarded Mr. Slope was almost bloodthirsty. "Had I stabbed him with a dagger, he would have deserved it. But what will they say about it at Plumstead?"

"I don't think I should tell them," said Mary. Eleanor began to think that she would not.

There could have been no kinder comforter than Mary Bold. There was not the slightest dash of triumph about her when she heard of the Stanhope scheme, nor did she allude to her former opinion when Eleanor called her late friend Charlotte a base, designing woman. She re-echoed all the abuse that was heaped on Mr. Slope's head, and never hinted that she had said as much before. "I told you so, I told you so!" is the croak of a true Job's comforter. But Mary, when she found her friend lying in her sorrow and scraping herself with potsherds, forbore to argue and to exult. Eleanor acknowledged the merit of the forbearance, and at length allowed herself to be tranquillised.

On the next day she did not go out of the house. Barchester she thought would be crowded with Stanhopes and Slopes; perhaps also with Arabins and Grantlys.-Indeed there was hardly any one among her friends whom she could have met without some cause of uneasiness.

In the course of the afternoon she heard that the dean was dead; and she also heard that Mr. Quiverful had been finally appointed to the hospital. In the evening her father came to her, and then the story, or as much of it as she could bring herself to tell him, had to be repeated. He was not in truth much surprised at Mr.

Vol. n. x

Slope's effrontery; but he was obliged to act as though he had been, to save his daughter's feelings. He was, however, anything but skilful in his deceit, and she saw through it.

"I see," said she, "that you think it only in the common course of things that Mr. Slope should hav" treated me in this way." She had said nothing to him about the embrace, nor yet of the way in which it had been met.

"I do not think it at all strange," said he, "that any one should admire my Eleanor."

"It is strange to me," said she, "that any man should have so mucn audacity, without ever having received the slightest encouragement."

To this Mr. Harding answered nothing. With the archdeacon it would have been the text for a rejoinder which would not have disgraced Bildad the Shuhite.

"But you'll tell the archdeacon?" asked Mr. Harding.

"Tell him what?" said she sharply.

"Or Susan?" continued Mr. Harding. "You'll tell Susan. You'll let them know that they wronged you in supposing that this man's addresses would be agreeable to you."

"They may find that out their own way," said she; "I shall not ever willingly mention Mr. Slope's name to either of them."

"But I may."

" I have no right to hinder you from doing anything that may be necessary to your own comfort, but pray do not do it for my sake. Dr. Grantly never thought well of me, and never will. I don't know now that I am even anxious that he should do so."

And then they went to the affair of the hospital. "But is it true, papa?"

"What, my dear?" said he. "About the dean? Yes, I fear quite true. Indeed I know there is no doubt about it."

"Poor Miss Trefoil. I am so sorry for her. But I did not mean mat," said Eleanor. "But about the hospital, papa?"

"Yes, my dear. I believe it is true that Mr. Quiverful is to have it."

"Oh, what a shame!"

"No, my dear, not at all; not at all a shame. I am sure I hope it will suit him. "

"But, papa, you know it is a shame. After all your hopes, all your expectations to get back to your old house, to see it given away in this way to a perfect stranger!"

"My dear, the bishop had a right to give it to whom he pleased."

"I deny that, papa. He had no such right. It is not as though you were a candidate for a new piece of preferment. If the bishop has a grain of justice —"

"The bishop offered it to me on his terms, and as I did not like the terms, I refused it. After that, I cannot complain. "

"Terms! he had no right to make terms."

"I don't know about that; but it seems he had the power. But to tell you the truth, Nelly, I am as well satisfied as it is. When the affair became the subject of angry discussion, I thoroughly wished to be rid of it altogether."

"But you did want to go back to the old house, papa. You told me so yourself."

"Yes, my dear, I did. For a short time I did wish it. And I was foolish in doing so. I am getting old now; and my chief worldly wish is for peace and rest. Had I gone back to the hospital I should have had endless contentions with the bishop, contentions with his chaplain, and contentions with the archdeacon. I am not up to this now; I am not able to meet such troubles; and therefore I am not ill-pleased to find myself left to the little church of St. Cuthbert's. I shall never starve," added he, laughing, "as long as you are here."

"But will you come and live with me, papa?" she said earnestly, taking him by both his hands. "If you will do that, if you will promise that, I will own that you are right."

"I will dine with you to-day at any rate."

"No; but live here altogether. Give up

that close, odious little room in High Street."

"My dear, it's a very nice little room; and you are really quite uncivil."

"Oh, papa, don't joke. It's not a nice place for you. You say you are growing old,—though I am sure you are not." '' Am not I, my dear?"

"No, papa, not old,—not to say old. But you are quite old enough to feel the want of a decent room to sit in. You know how lonely Mary and I are here. You know nobody ever sleeps in the big front bed-room. It is really unkind of you to remain up there alone, when you are so much wanted here."

"Thank you, Nelly,—thank you. But, my dear—."

"If you had been living here, papa, with us, as I really think you ought to have done, considering how lonely we are, there would have been none of all this dreadful affair about Mr. Slope."

Mr. Harding, however, did not allow himself to be talked over into giving up hi3 own and only little pied a terre in the High Street. He promised to come and dine with his daughter, and stay with her, and visit her, and do everything but absolutely live with her. It did not suit the peculiar feelings of the man to tell his daughter that though she had rejected Mr. Slope, and been ready to reject Mr. Stanhope, some other more favoured suitor would probably soon appear; and that on the appearance of such a suitor the big front bed-room might perhaps be more frequently in requisition than at present. But doubtless such an idea crossed his mind, and added its weight to the other reasons which made him decide on still keeping the close, odious little room in High Street.

The evening passed over quietly and in comfort. Eleanor was always happier with her father than with any one else. He had not, perhaps, any natural taste for baby-worship, but he was always ready to sacrifice himself, and therefore made an excellent third in a trio with his daughter and Mary Bold in singing the praises of the wonderful child.

They were standing together over their music in the evening, the baby having again been put to bed upon the sofa, when the servant brought in a very small note in a beautiful pink envelope. It quite filled the room with perfume as it lay upon the small salver. Mary Bold and Mrs. Bold were both at the piano, and Mr. Harding was sitting close to them, with the violoncello between his legs; so that the elegancy of the epistle was visible to them all.

"Please, ma'am, Dr. Stanhope's coachman says he is to wait for an answer," said the servant.

Eleanor got very red in the face as she took the note in her hand. She had never seen the writing before. Charlotte's epistles, to which she was well accustomed, were of a very different style and kind. She generally wrote on large note-paper; she twisted up her letters into the shape and sometimes into the size of cocked hats; she addressed them in a sprawling manly hand, and not unusually added a blot or a smudge, as though such were her own peculiar sign-manual. The address of this note was written in a beautiful female hand, and the gummed wafer bore on it an impress of a gilt coronet. Though Eleanor had never seen such a one before, she guessed that it came from the Signora. Such epistles were very numerously sent out from any house in which the Signora might happen to be dwelling, but they were rarely addressed to ladies. When the coachman was told by the lady's maid to take the letter to Mrs. Bold, he openly expressed his opinion that there was some mistake about it. Whereupon the lady's maid boxed the coachman's ears. Had Mr. Slope seen in how meek a spirit the coachman took the rebuke, he might have learnt a useful lesson, both in philosophy and religion.

The note was as follows.

"My dear Mrs. Bold,—May I ask you, as a great favour, to call on me to-morrow? You can say what hour will best suit you; but quite early, if you can. I need hardly say that if I could call upon you I should not take this liberty with you.

"I partly know what occurred the other day, and I promise you that you shall meet with no annoyance if you will

come to me, My brother leaves us for London to-day; from thence he goes tc Italy.

"It will probably occur to you that I should not thus intrude on you, unless I had that to say to you which may be of considerable moment. Pray therefore excuse me, even if you do not grant my request, and believe me,

"Very sincerely yours,

"M. Veset Neboxi.

"Thursday Evening."

The three of them sat in consultation on this epistle for some ten or fifteen minutes, and then decided that Eleanor should write a line saying that she would see the Signora the next morning, at twelve o'clock.

CHAPTER XLV. TIIE STANHOPES AT HOME

We must now return to the Stanhopes, and see how they behaved themselves on their return from Ullathorne.

Charlotte, who came back in the first homeward journey with her sister, waited in palpitating expectation till the carriage drove up to the door a second time. She did not run down or stand at the window, or show in any outward manner that she looked for anything wonderful to occur; but, when she heard the carriagewheels, she stood up with erect ears, listening for Eleanor's footfall on the pavement or the cheery sound of Bertie's voice welcoming her in. Had she heard either, she would have felt that all was right; but neither sound was there for her to hear. She heard only her father's slow step, as he ponderously let himself down from the carriage, and slowly walked along the hall, till he got into his own private room on the ground floor. "Send Miss Stanhope to me," he said to the servant.

"There's something wrong now," said Madeline, who was lying on her sofa in the back drawing-room.

"It's all up with Bertie," replied Charlotte. "I know; I know;" she said to the servant, as he brought up the message. "Tell my father I will be with Lim immediately."

"Bertie's wooing has gone astray," said Madeline; "I knew it would."

"It has been his own fault then. She

was ready enough, I am quito sure," said Charlotte, with that sort of ill-nature which is not uncommon when one woman speaks of another.

"What will you say to him now?" By "him," the Signora meant their father.

"That will be as I find him. He was ready to pay two hundred pounds for Bertie, to stave off the worst of his creditors, if this marriage had gone on. Bertie must now have the money instead, and go and take his chance."

"Where is he now?"

"Heaven knows;—smoking in the bottom of Mr. Thome's ha-ha, or philandering with some of those Miss Chadwicks. Nothing will ever make an impression on him. But he'll be furious if I don't go down."

"Don't be long, Charlotte, for I want my tea," said the Signora.

So Charlotte went down to her father. There was a very black cloud on the old man's brow; blacker than his daughter could ever yet remember to have seen there. He was sitting in hie own armchair, not comfortably over the fire, but in the middle of the room, waiting till she should come and listen to him.

"What has become of your brother?" he said, as soon as the door was shut.

"I should rather ask you," said Charlotte. "I left you both at TJllathorne when I came away. What have you done with Mrs. Bold?"

"Mrs. Bold! nonsense. The woman has gone home as she ought to do. And heartily glad I am that she should not be sacrificed to so heartless a reprobate."

"Oh, papa!"

"A heartless reprobate! Tell me now where he is, and what he is going to do. I have allowed myself to be fooled between you. Marriage, indeed! Who on earth that has money, or credit, or respect in the world to lose, would marry him?"

"It is no use your scolding me, papa. I have done the best I could for him and you."

"And Madeline is nearly as bad," said the prebendary, who was in truth very, very angry.

"Oh I suppose we are all bad," replied Charlotte.

The old man emitted a huge leonine sigh. If they were all bad, who had made them so? If they were unprincipled, selfish, and disreputable, who was to be blamed for the education which had had so injurious an effect?

"I know you'll ruin me among you," said he.

"Why, papa, what nonsense that is. You are living within your income this minute, and if there are any new debts I don't know of them. I am sure there ought to be none, for we are dull enough here."

"Are those bills of Madeline's paid?"

"No, they are not. Who was to pay them?"

"Her husband may pay them."

"Her husband! Would you wish me to tell her you say so? Do you wish to turn her out of your house?"

"I wish she would know how to behave herself." "Why, what on earth has she done now? Poor Madeline' To-day is only the second time she has gone out since we came to this vile town." He then sat silent for a time, thinking in what shape he would declare his resolve. "Well, papa," said Charlotte, "shall I stay here, or may I go up-stairs and give mamma her tea?"

"You are in your brother's confidence. Tell me what he is going to do?"

"Nothing, that I am aware of."

"Nothing;—nothing! nothing but eat and drink, and spend every shilling of my money he can lay his hands upon. I have made up my mind, Charlotte. He shall eat and drink no more in this house."

"Very well. Then I suppose he must go back to Italy." "He may go where he pleases."

"That's easily said, papa; but what does it mean? You can't let him."

"It means this," said the doctor, speaking more loudly than was his wont, and with wrath flashing from his eyes; "that as sure as God rules in heaven I will not maintain him any longer in idleness." "Oh, ruling in heaven!" said Charlotte. "It is no use talking about that. You must rule him here on earth; and the question is, how you can do it. You can't turn him out of the house

penniless, to beg about the street."

"He may beg where he likes."

"He must go back to Carrara. That is the cheapest place he can live at, and nobody there will give him credit for above two or three hundred pauls. But you must let him have the means of going."

"As sure as"

"Oh, papa, don't swear. You know you must do it. You were ready to pay two hundred pounds for him if this marriage came off. Half that will start him to Carrara."

"What? Give him a hundred pounds!"

"You know we are all in the dark, papa," said she, thinking it expedient to change the conversation. "For anything we know, he may be at this moment engaged to Mrs. Bold."

"Fiddlestick," said the father, who had seen the way in which Mrs. Bold had got into the carriage, while his son stood apart without even offering her his hand.

"Well, then, he must go to Carrara," said Charlotte

Just at this moment the lock of the front door was heard, and Charlotte's quick ears detected her brother's cat-like step in the hall. She said nothing, feeling that for the present Bertie had better keep out of her father's way. But Dr. Stanhope also heard the sound of the lock.

"Who's that?" he demanded. Charlotte made no reply, and he asked again, "Who is that that has just come in? Open the door. Who is it?"

"I suppose it is Bertie."

"Bid him come here," said the father. But Bertie, who was close to the door and heard the call, required no further bidding, but walked in with a perfectly unconcerned and cheerful air. It was this peculiar insouciance which angered Dr. Stanhope, even more than his son's extravagance.

"Well, sir?" said the doctor.

"And how did you get home, sir, with your fair companion?" said Bertie. "I suppose she is not up-stairs, Charlotte?"

"Bertie," said Charlotte, "papa is in no humour for joking. He is very angry with you."

"Angry!" said Bertie, raising his eye-brows, as though he had never yet given his parent cause for a single moment's uneasiness.

' Sit down, if you please, sir," said Dr. Stanhope very sternly, but not now very loudly. "And I'll trouble you to sit down too, Charlotte. Your mother can wait for her tea a few minutes."

Charlotte sat down on the chair nearest to the door, in somewhat of a perverse sort of manner; as much as though she would say;—Well, here I am; you shan't say I don't do what I am bid; but I'll be whipped if I give way to you. And she was determined not to give way. She too was angry with Bertie; but she was not the less ready on that account to defend him from his father. Bertie also sat down. He drew his chair close to the library-table, upon which he put his elbow, and then resting his face comfortably on one hand, he began drawing little pictures on a sheet of paper with the other. Before the scene was over he had completed admirable figures of Miss Thorne, Mrs. Proudie, and Lady De Courcy, and begun a family piece to comprise the whole set of the Lookalofts.

"Would it suit you, sir," said the father, "to give me some idea as to what your present intentions are;—what way of living you propose to yourself?"

"I'll do anything you can suggest, sir," replied Bertie.

"No; I shall suggest nothing further. My time for suggesting has gone by. I have only one order to give, and that is, that you leave my house."

"To-night?" said Bertie; and the simple tone of the question left the doctor without any adequately dignified method of reply.

"Papa does not quite mean to-night," said Charlotte; "at least I suppose not."

"To-morrow, perhaps," suggested Bertie.

"Yes, sir, to-morrow," said the doctor. "You shall leave this to-morrow."

"Very well, sir. Will the 4.30 P.m. train be soon enough?" and Bertie, as he asked, put the finishing touch to Miss Thorne's high-heeled boots.

"You may go how and when and where you please, so that you leave my house to-morrow. You have disgraced me, sir; you have disgraced yourself, and me, and your sisters."

"I am glad at least, sir, that I have not disgraced my mother," said Bertie.

Charlotte could hardly keep her countenance; but the doctor's brow grew still blacker than ever. Bertie was executing his chef d'oeuvre in the delineation of Mrs. Proudie's nose and mouth.

"You are a heartless reprobate, sir; a heartless, thankless, good-for-nothing reprobate. I have done with you. You are my son;—that I cannot help; but you shall have no more part or parcel in me as my child; nor I in you as your father. "

"Oh, papa, papa! you must not, shall not say so," said Charlotte.

"I will say so, and do say so," said the father, rising from his chair. "And now leave the room, sir."

"Stop, stop," said Charlotte; "why don't you speak, Bertie? Why don't you look up and speak? It is your manner that makes papa so angry."

"He is perfectly indifferent to all decency, to all propriety," said the doctor; and then he shouted out, "Leave the room, sir! Do you hear what I say?"

"Papa, papa, I will not let you part so. I know you will be sorry for it." And then she added, getting up and whispering into his ear, "Is he only to blame? Think of that. We have made our own bed, and, such as it is, we must lie on it. It is no use for us to quarrel among ourselves," and as she finished her whisper Bertie finished off the countess's bustle, which was so well done that it absolutely seemed to be swaying to and fro on the paper with its usual lateral motion. 1

"My father is angry at the present time," said Bertie, looking up for a moment from his sketches, "because I am not going to marry Mrs. Bold. What can I say on the matter? It is true thai I am not going to marry her. In the first place"

"That is not true, sir," said Dr. Stanhope; "but I will not argue with you."

"You were angry just this moment because I would not speak," said Bertie,

going on with a young Lookaloft.

"Give over drawing," said Charlotte, going up to him and taking the paper from under his hand. The caricatures, however, she preserved, and showed them afterwards to the friends of the Thornes, the Proudies, and De Courcys. Bertie, deprived of his occupation, threw himself back in his chair and waited further orders.

"I think it will certainly be for the best that Bertie should leave this at once,—perhaps to-morrow," said Charlotte; "but pray, papa, let us arrange some scheme together."

"If he will leave this to-morrow, I will give him 10?., and he shall be paid *51.* a month by the banker at Carrara as long as he stays permanently in that place."

"Well, sir! it won't be long," said Bertie; for I shall be starved to death in about three months."

"He must have marble to work with," said Charlotte.

"I have plenty there in the studio to last me three months," said Bertie. "It will be no use attempting anything large in so limited a time;—unless I do my own tombstone."

Terms, however, were ultimately come to, somewhat more liberal than those proposed, and the doctor was induced to shake hands with his son, and bid him good night. Dr. Stanhope would not go up to tea, but had it brought to him in his study by his daughter.

But Bertie went up-stairs and spent a pleasant evening. He finished the Lookalofts, greatly to the delight of his sisters, though the manner of portraying their decollete dresses was not the most refined. Finding how matters were going, he by degrees allowed it to escape from him that he had not pressed his suit upon the widow in a very urgent way.

"I suppose, in point of fact, you never proposed at all?" said Charlotte.

"Oh, she understood that she might have me if she wished," said he.

"And she didn't wish," said the Signora.

"You have thrown me over in the most shameful manner," said Charlotte. "I suppose you told her all about my little plan?"

"Well, it came out somehow; at least the most of it."

"There's an end of that alliance," said Charlotte; "but it doesn't matter much. I suppose we shall all be back at Como soon."

"I am sure I hope so," said the Signora; I'm sick of the sight of black coats. If that Mr. Slope comes here any more, he'll be the death of me."

"You've been the ruin of him, I think," said Charlotte.

"And as for a second black-coated lover of mine, I am going to make a present of him to another lady with most singular disinterestedness."

The next day, true to his promise, Bertie packed up and went off by the 4. 30 P.M. train, with *20l.* in his pocket, bound for the marble quarries of Carrara. And so he disappears from our scene.

At twelve o'clock on the day following that on which Bertie went, Mrs. Bold, true also to her word, knocked at Dr. Stanhope's door with a timid hand and palpitating heart. She was at once shown up to the back drawing-room, the folding doors of which were closed, so that in visiting the Signora Eleanor was not necessarily thrown into any communion with those in the front room. As she went up the stairs, she saw none of the family, and was so far saved much of the annoyance which she had dreaded.

"This is very kind of you, Mrs. Bold;—very kind, after what has happened," said the lady on the sofa with her sweetest smile. "You wrote in such a strain that I could not but come to you. " "I did, I did; I wanted to force you to see me." "Well, Signora; I am here."

"How cold you are to me. But I suppose I must put up with that. I know you think you have reason to be displeased with us all. Poor Bertie! if you knew all, you would not be angry with him."

"I am not angry with your brother;— not in the least. But I hope you did not send for me here to talk about him."

"If you are angry with Charlotte, that is worse; for you have no warmer friend in all Barchester. But I did *not* send for

you to talk about this. Pray bring your chair nearer, Mrs. Bold, so that I may look at you. It is so unnatural to see you keeping so far off from me." Eleanor did as she was bid, and brought her chair close to the sofa. "And now, Mrs. Bold, I am going to tell you something which you may perhaps think indelicate; but yet I know that I am right in doing so."

Hereupon Mrs. Bold said nothing, but felt inclined to shake in her chair. The Signora, she knew, was not very particular, and that which to her appeared to be indelicate might to Mrs. Bold appear to be extremely indecent.

"I believe you know Mr. Arabin?"

Mrs. Bold would have given the world not to blush, but her blood was not at her own command. She did blush up to her forehead, and the Signora, who had made her sit in a special light in order that she might watch her, saw that she did so.

"Yes,—I am acquainted with him. That is, slightly. He is an intimate friend of Dr. Grantly, and Dr. Grantly is my brother-inlaw."

"Well; if you know Mr. Arabin, I am sure you must like him I know and like him much. Everybody that knows him must like him."

Mrs. Bold felt it quite impossible to say anything in reply to this. Her blood was rushing about her body she knew not how or why. She felt as though she were swinging in her chair; and she knew that she was not only red in the face, but also almost suffocated with heat. However she sat still and said nothing.

"How stiff you are with me, Mrs. Bold," said the Signora; '' and I the while am doing for you all that one woman can do to serve another."

A kind of thought came over the widow's mind that perhaps the Signora's friendship was real, and that at any rate it could not hurt her; and another kind of thought, a glimmering of a thought, came to her also,—that Mr. Arabin was too precious to be lost. She despised the Signora; but might she not stoop to conquer? It should be but the smallest fraction of a stoop! "I don't want to be stiff;

" she said, "but your questions are so very singular."

"Well, then, I will ask you one more singular still," said Madeline Neroni, raising herself on her elbow and turning her own face full upon her companion's. "Do you love him, love him with all your heart and soul, with all the love your bosom can feel? For I can tell you that he loves you, adores you, worships you, thinks of you and nothing else, is now thinking of you as he attempts to write his sermon for next Sunday's preaching. What would I not give to be loved in such a way by such a man,— that is, if I were an object fit for any man to love!"

Mrs. Bold got up from her seat and stood speechless before the woman who was now addressing her in this impassioned way. When the Signora thus alluded to herself, the widow's heart was softened, and she put her own hand, as though caressingly, on that of her companion which was resting on the table. The Signora grasped it and went on speaking.

"What I tell you is God's own truth; and it is for you to use it as may be best for your own happiness. But you must not betray me. He knows nothing of this. He knows nothing of my knowing his inmost heart. He is simple as a child in these matters. He told me his secret in a thousand ways because he could not dissemble; but he does not dream that he has told it. You know it now, and I advise you to use it."

Eleanor returned the pressure of the other's hand with an infinitesimal soupqon of a squeeze.

"And remember," continued the Signora, "he is not like other men. You must not expect him to come to you with vows and oaths and pretty presents, to kneel at your feet, and kiss your shoestrings. If you want that, there are plenty to do it; but he won't be one of them." Eleanor's bosom nearly burst with a sigh; but Madeline, not heeding her, went on. "With him, yea will stand for yea, and nay for nay. Though his heart should break for it, the woman who shall reject him once, will have rejected him once and for all. Remember that. And now, Mrs. Bold, I will not keep you, for you are fluttered. I partly guess what use you will make of what I have said to you. If ever you are a happy wife in that man's house, we shall be far away; but I shall expect you to write me one line to say that you have forgiven the sins of the family."

Eleanor half whispered that she would, and then, without uttering another word, crept out of the room, and down the stairs, opened the front door for herself without hearing or seeing any one, and found herself in the close.

It would be difficult to analyse Eleanor's feelings as she walked home. She was nearly stupefied by the things that had been said to her. She felt sore that her heart should have been so searched and riddled by a comparative stranger, by a woman whom she had never liked and never could like. She was mortified that the man whom she owned to herself that she loved should have concealed his love from her and shown it to another. There was much to vex her proud spirit. But there was, nevertheless, an under-stratum of joy in all this which buoyed her up wondrously. She tried if she could disbelieve what Madame Neroni had said to her; but she found that she could not. It was true; it must be true. She could not, would not, did not doubt it.

On one point she fully resolved to follow the advice given her. If it should ever please Mr. Arabia to put such a question to her as that suggested, her "yea " should be "yea." Would not all her miseries be at an end. if she could talk of them to him openly, with her head resting on his shoulder P ME. SLOPE'S PARTING INTERVIEW WITH THE SIGNORA.

On the following day the Signora was in her pride. She was dressed in her brightest of morning dresses, and had quite a levee round her couch. It was a beautifully bright October afternoon. All the gentlemen of the neighbourhood were in Barchester, and those who had the entry of Dr. Stanhope's house were in the Signora's back drawing-room. Charlotte and Mrs. Stanhope were in the front room, and such of the lady's squires as could not for the moment get near the centre of attraction had to waste their fragrance on the mother and sister.

The first who came and the last to leave was Mr. Arabin. This was the second visit he had paid to Madame Neroni since he had met her at Ullathorne. He came he knew not why, to talk about he knew not what. But, in truth, the feelings which now troubled him were new to him, and he could not analyse them. It may seem strange that he should thus come dangling about Madame Neroni because he was in love with Mrs. Bold; but it was nevertheless the fact; and though he could not understand why he did so, Madame Neroni understood it well enough.

She had been gentle and kind to him, and had encouraged his staying. Therefore he stayed on. She pressed his hand when he first greeted her; she made him remain near her; and whispered to him little nothings. And then her eye, brilliant and bright, was now mirthful, now melancholy, and invincible in either way! "What man with warm feelings, blood unchilled, and a heart not guarded by a triple steel of experience could have withstood those eyes! The lady, it is true, intended to do him no mortal injury, she merely chose to inhale a slight breath of incense before she handed the casket over to another. Whether Mrs. Bold would willingly have spared even so much is another question.

And then came Mr. Slope. All the world now knew that Mr. Slope was a candidate for the deanery, and that he was generally considered to be the favourite. Mr. Slope, therefore, walked rather largely upon the earth. He gave to himself a portly air, such as might become a dean, spoke but little to other clergymen, and shunned the bishop as much as possible. How the meagre little prebendary, and the burly chancellor, and all the minor canons and vicars choral, ay, and all the choristers too, cowered and shook and walked about with long faces when they read or heard of that article in the Jupiter. Now were coming the days when nothing would avail to keep the impure spirit from the cathedral pulpit. That pulpit would indeed be his own. Precentors, vicars, and choristers might hang up their harps on the willows. Ichabod! Ichabod! the glory of their house was departing from them.

Mr. Slope, great as he was with embryo grandeur, still came to see the Signora. Indeed, he could not keep himself away. He dreamed of that soft hand which he had kissed so often, and of that imperial brow which his lips had once pressed, and he then dreamed also of further favours.

And Mr. Thorne was there also. It was the first visit he had ever paid to the Signora, and he made it not without due preparation. Mr. Thorne was a gentleman usually precise in his dress, and prone to make the most of himself in an unpretending way. The grey hairs in his whiskers were eliminated perhaps once a month; those on. his head were softened by a mixture which we will not call a dye; it was only a wash. His tailor lived in St. James's Street, and his bootmaker at the corner of that street and Piccadilly. He was particular in the article of gloves, and the getting up of his shirts was a matter not lightly thought of in the Ullathorne laundry. On the occasion of the present visit he had rather overdone his usual efforts, and caused some little uneasiness to his sister, who had not hitherto received very cordially the proposition for a lengthened visit from the Signora at Ullathorne.

There were others also there,—young men about the city who had not much to do, and who were induced by the lady's charms to neglect that little; but all gave way to Mr. Thorne, who was somewhat of a grand signior, as a country gentleman always is in a provincial city.

"Oh, Mr. Thorne, this is so kind of you!" said the Signora. "You promised to come; but I really did not expect it. I thought you country gentlemen never kept your pledges."

"Oh, yes, sometimes," said Mr. Thorne, looking rather sheepish, and making his salutations a little too much in the style of the last century.

"You deceive none but your consti—stit—stit; what do you call the people that carry you about in chairs and pelt you with eggs and apples when they make you a member of Parliament?"

"One another also, sometimes, Signora," said Mr. Slope, with a deanish sort of smirk on his face. "Country gentlemen do deceive one another, sometimes, don't they, Mr. Thorne?"

Mr. Thorne gave him a look which undeaned him completely for the moment; but he soon remembered his high hopes, and recovering himself quickly, sustained his probable coming dignity by a laugh at Mr. Thorne's expense.

"I never deceive a lady, at any rate," said Mr. Thorne; "especially when the gratification of my own wishes is so strong an inducement to keep me true, as it now is."

Mr. Thorne went on thus awhile with antediluvian grimaces and compliments which he had picked up from Sir Charles Grandison, and the Signora at every grimace and at every bow smiled a little smile and bowed a little bow. Mr. Thorne, however, was kept standing at the foot of the couch, for the new dean sat in the seat of honour near the table. Mr. Arabin the while was standing with his back to the fire, his coat tails under his arms, gazing at her with all his eyes,—not quite in vain, for every now and again a glance came up at him, bright as a meteor out of heaven. "Oh, Mr. Thorne, you promised to let me introduce my little girl to you. Can you spare a moment?—Will you see her now?"

Mr. Thorne assured her that he could, and would see the young lady with the greatest pleasure in life. "Mr. Slope, might I trouble you to ring the bell?" said she; and when Mr. Slope got up she looked at Mr. Thorne and pointed to the chair. Mr. Thorne, however, was much too slow to understand her, and Mr. Slope would have recovered his seat had not the Signora, who never chose to be unsuccessful, somewhat summarily ordered him out of it.

"Oh, Mr. Slope, I must ask you to let Mr. Thorne sit here just for a moment or two. I am sure you will pardon me. We can take a liberty with you this week. Next week, you know, when you move into the dean's house, we shall all be afraid of you."

Mr. Slope, with an air of much indifference, rose from his seat, and, walking into the next room, became greatly interested in Mrs. Stanhope's worsted work.

And then the child was brought in. She was a little girl, about eight years of age, like her mother, only that her enormous eyes were black, and her hair quite jet. Her complexion, too, was very dark, and bespoke her foreign blood. She was dressed in the most outlandish and extravagant way in which clothes could be put on a child's back. She had great bracelets on her naked little arms, a crimson fillet braided with gold round her head, and scarlet shoes with high heels. Her dress was all flounces, and stuck out from her as though the object were to make it lie off horizontally from her little hips. It did not nearly cover her knees; but this was atoned for by a loose pair of drawers, which seemed made throughout of lace. Then she had on pink silk stockings. It was thus that the last of the Neros was habitually dressed at the hour when visitors were wont to call.

"Julia, my love," said the mother,—Julia was ever a favourite name with the ladies of that family;—" Julia, my love, come here. I was telling you about the beautiful party poor mamma went to. This is Mr. Thorne; will you give him a kiss, dearest?"

Julia put up her face to be kissed, as she did to all her mother's visitors; and then Mr. Thorne found that he had got her, and, which was much more terrific to him, all her finery, into his arms. The lace and starch crumpled against his waistcoat and trowsers; the greasy black curls hung upon his cheek, and one of the bracelet clasps scratched his ear. He did not at all know how to hold so magnificent a lady, nor holding her what to do with her. However, he had on other occasions been compelled to fondle little nieces and nephews, and now set about the task in the mode he always had used. "Diddle, diddle; diddle, diddle," said he, putting the child on one knee, and working away with it as though he were turning a knife-grinder's wheel with his foot.

"Mamma, mamma," said Julia, crossly, "I don't want to bo diddle-diddled. Let me go, you naughty old man, you."

Poor Mr. Thorne put the child down quietly on the ground, and drew back his chair; Mr. Slope, who had returned to the pole star that attracted him, laughed aloud; Mr. Arabin winced and shut his eyes; and the Signora pretended not to hear her daughter.

"Go to Aunt Charlotte, lovey," said the mamma, "and ask her if it is not time for you to go out."

But little Miss Julia, though she had not exactly liked the nature of Mr. Thorne's attention, was accustomed to be played with by gentlemen, and did not relish the idea of being sent so soon to her aunt. "Julia, go when I tell you, my dear." But Julia still went pouting about the room. "Charlotte, do come and take her," said the Signora. "She must go out; and the days get so short now." And thus ended the much-talked-of interview between Mr Thorne and the last of the Neros.

Mr. Thorne recovered from the child's crossness sooner than from Mr. Slope's laughter. He could put up with being called an old man by an infant, but he did not like to be laughed at by the bishop's chaplain, even though that chaplain was about to become a dean. He said nothing, but he showed plainly enough that he was angry.

The Signora was ready enough to avenge him. "Mr. Slope," said she, "I hear that you are triumphing on all sides."

"How so?" said he, smiling. He did not dislike being talked to about the deanery, though, of course, he strongly denied the imputation.

"You.carry the day both in love and war." Mr. Slope hereupon did not look quite so satisfied as he had done.

"Mr. Arabin," continued the Signora, "don't you think Mr. Slope is a very lucky man?"

"Not more so than he deserves, I am sure," said Mr. Arabin.

"Only think, Mr. Thorne, he is to be our new dean. Of course we all know that."

"Indeed, Signora," said Mr. Slope, "we all know nothing about it. I can assure you I myself"

"He *is* to be the new dean. There is no manner of doubt of it, Mr. Thorne." »

"Hum!" said Mr. Thorne.

'' Passing over the heads of old men like my father and Archdeacon Grantly. "

"Oh,—oh!" said Mr. Slope.

"The archdeacon would not accept it," said Mr. Arabin; whereupon Mr. Slope smiled abominably, and said, as plainly as a look could speak, that the grapes were sour.

"Going over all our heads," continued the Signora; "for, of course, I consider myself one of the chapter."

"If I am ever dean," said Mr. Slope—" that is, we? I ever to become so, I should glory in such a canoness."

"Oh, Mr. Slope, stop; I haven't half done. There is another canoness for you to glory in. Mr. Slope is not only to have the deanery, but a wife to put in it." Mr. Slope again looked disconcerted. "A wife with a large fortune, too. It never rains but it pours, does it, Mr. Thorne?"

"No, never," said Mr. Thorne, who did not quite relish talking about Mr. Slope and his affairs.

"When will it be, Mr. Slope?"

"When will what be?" said he.

"Oh! We know when the affair of the dean will be. A week will settle that. The new hat, I have no doubt, has been already ordered. But when will the marriage come off?"

"Do you mean mine or Mr. Arabin's?" said he, striving to be facetious.

"Well, just then I meant yours; though, perhaps, after all, Mr. Arabin's may be first. But we know nothing of him. He is too close for any of us. Now all is open and above board with you;—which, by the bye, Mr. Arabin, I beg to tell you I like much the best. He who runs can read that Mr. Slope is a favoured lover. Come, Mr. Slope, when is the widow to be made Mrs. Dean?"

To Mr. Arabin this badinage was peculiarly painful; and yet he could not tear himself away and leave it. He believed,—still believed with that sort of belief which the fear of a thing engenders,—that Mrs. Bold would probably become the wife of Mr. Slope. Of Mr. Slope's little adventure in the garden he knew nothing. For aught he knew Mr. Slope might have had an adventure of quite a different character.-He might have thrown himself at the widow's feet, been accepted, and then returned to town a jolly, thriving wooer. The Signora's jokes were bitter enough to Mr. Slope, but they were quite as bitter to Mr. Arabin. He still stood leaning against the fire-place, fumbling with his hands in his trowsers pockets.

"Come, come, Mr. Slope, don't be so bashful," continued the Signora. "We all know that you proposed to the lady the other day at Ullathorne. Tell us with what words she accepted you. Was it with a simple 'yes,' or was it with two 'no, no's ' which make an affirmative? Or did silence give consent? Or did she speak out with that spirit which so well becomes a widow, and say openly, 'By my troth, sir, you shall make me Mrs. Slope as soon as it is your pleasure to do so?"

Mr. Slope had seldom in his life felt himself less at his ease. There sat Mr. Thorne, laughing silently. There stood his old antagonist, Mr. Arabin, gazing at him with all his eyes. There round the door between the two rooms were clustered a little group of people, including Miss Stanhope and the Rev. Messrs. Gray and Green, all listening to his discomfiture. He knew that it depended solely on his own wit whether or no he could throw the joke back upon the lady. He knew that it stood him to do so if he possibly could; but he had not a word. "'Tis conscience that makes cowards of us all." He felt on his cheek the sharp points of Eleanor's fingers, and did not know who might have seen the blow, who might have told the tale to this pestilent woman who trok such delight in jeering him. He stood there, therefore, red as a carbuncle and mute as a fish; grinning just sufficiently to show his teeth; an object of pity.

But the Signora had no pity. She knew nothing of mercy. Her present object was to put Mr. Slope down, and she

va» determined to do it thoroughly, now that she had him in her power. "What, Mr. Slope, no answer? Why it can't possibly be that the woman has been fool enough to refuse you? She can't surely be looking out after a bishop. But I see how it is, Mr. Slope. Widows are proverbially cautious. You should have let her alone till the new hat was on your head;—till you could show her the key of the deanery."

"Signora," said he at last, trying to speak in a tone of dignified reproach, "you really permit yourself to talk on solemn subjects in a very improper way. "

"Solemn subjects,—what solemn subject? Surely a dean's hat is not such a solemn subject."

"I have no aspirations such as those you impute to me. Perhaps you will drop the subject."

"Oh certainly, Mr. Slope; but one word first. Go to her again with the prime minister's letter in your pocket. I'll wager my shawl to your shovel she does not refuse you then."

"I must say, Signora, that I think you are speaking of the lady in a very unjustifiable manner."

"And one other piece of advice, Mr. Slope; I'll only offer you one other;" and then she commenced singing—

"It's gude to be merry and wise, Mr. Slope;
It's gude to be honest and true;
It's gude to be off with the old love,—Mr. Slope,
Before you are on with the new.
Ha, ha, ha!"

And the Signora, throwing herself back on her sofa, laughed merrily. She little recked how those who heard her would, in their own imaginations, fill up the little history of Mr. Slope's first love. She little cared that some among them might attribute to her the honour of his earlier admiration. She was tired of Mr. Slope and wanted to get rid of him. She had ground for anger with him, and she chose to be revenged.

How Mr. Slope got out of that room he never himself knew. He did succeed ultimately, and probably with some assistance, in getting his hat and escaping into the air. At last his love for the Signora was cured. "Whenever he again thought of her in his dreams, it was not as of an angel with azure wings. He connected her rather with fire and brimstone, and though he could still believe her to be a spirit, he banished her entirely out of heaven, and found a place for her among the infernal gods. When he weighed in the balance, as he not seldom did, the two women to whom he had attached himself in Barchester, the pre-eminent place in his soul's hatred wan usually allotted to the Signora.

CHAPTER XLVII. THE DEAN ELECT.

During the entire next week Barchester was ignorant who was to be its new dean on Sunday morning. Mr. Slope was decidedly the favourite; but he did not show himself in the cathedral and then he sank a point or two in the betting. On Monday he got a scolding from the bishop in the hearing of the servants, and down he went till nobody would have him at any price; but on Tuesday he received a letter, in an official cover, marked private, by which he fully recovered his place in the public favour. On Wednesday, he was said to be ill, and that did not look well; but on Thursday morning he went down to the railway station with a very jaunty air; and when it was ascertained that he had taken a first-class ticket for London, there was no longer any room for doubt on the matter.

While matters were in this state of ferment at Barchester, there was not much mental comfort at Plumstead. Our friend the archdeacon had many grounds for inward grief. He was much displeased at the result of Dr. Gwynne's diplomatic mission to the palace, and did not even scruple to say to his wife that had he gone himself he would have managed the affair much better. His wife did not agree with him, but that did not mend the matter.

Mr. Quiverful's appointment to the hospital was, however, a fait accompli, and Mr. Harding's acquiescence in that appointment was not less so. Nothing would induce Mr. Harding to make a public appeal against the bishop; and the Master of Lazarus quite approved of his not doing so.

"I don't know what has come to the Master," said the archdeacon over and over again. "He used to be ready enough to stand up for his order."

"My dear archdeacon," Mrs. Grantly would say in reply, "what is the use of always fighting? I really think the Master is right." The Master, however, had taken steps of his own, of which neither the archdeacon nor his wife knew anything.

Then Mr. Slope's successes were henbane to Dr. Grantly; and Mrs. Bold's improprieties were as bad. 'What would be all the world to Archdeacon Grantly if Mr. Slope should become Dean of Barchester and marry his wife's sister! He talked of it, and talked of it till he was nearly ill. Mrs. Grantly almost wished that the marriage were done and over, so that she might hear no more about it.

And there was yet another ground of misery which cut him to the quick, nearly as closely as either of the others. That paragon of a clergyman whom he had bestowed upon St. Ewold's, that college friend of whom he had boasted so loudly, that ecclesiastical knight before whose lance Mr. Slope was to fall and bite the dust, that worthy bulwark of the church as it should be, that honoured representative of Oxford's best spirit, was,—so at least his wife had told him half a dozen times,—misconducting himself!

Nothing had been seen of Mr. Arabin at Plumstead for the last week, but a good deal had, unfortunately, been heard of him. As soon as Mrs. Grantly had found herself alone with the archdeacon, on the evening of the Ullathorne party, she had expressed herself very forcibly as to Mr. Arabin's conduct on that occasion. He had, she declared, looked and acted and talked very unlike a decent parish clergyman. At first the archdeacon had laughed at this, and assured her that she need not trouble herself;—that Mr. Arabin would be found to be quite safe. But by degrees he began to find that his wife's eyes had been sharper than his own. Other people coupled the Signora's name with that of Mr. Arabin. The meagre little prebendary who lived in the close, told him to a nioety how often Mr. Arabin had visited at Dr. Stanhope's, and how long he had remained on the occasion of each visit. He had ashed after Mr. Arabin at the cathedral library, and an officious little vicar choral had offered to go and see whether he could be found at Dr. Stanhope's. Humour, when she has contrived to sound the first note on her trumpet, soon makes a loud peal audible enough. It was too clear that Mr. Arabin had succumbed to the Italian woman, and that the archdeacon's credit would suffer fearfully if something were not done to rescue the brand from the burning. Besides, to give the archdeacon his due, he was really attached to Mr. Arabin, and grieved greatly at his backsliding.

They were sitting, talking over their sorrows, in the drawingroom before dinner on the day after Mr. Slope's departure for London; and on this occasion Mrs. Grantly spoke out her mind freely. She had opinions of her own about parish clergymen, and now thought it right to give vent to them. "If you would have been led by me, archdeacon, you would never have put a bachelor into St. Ewold's."

"But, my dear, you don't mean to say that all bachelor clergymen misbehave themselves."

"I don't know that clergymen are so much better than other men," said Mrs. Grantly. "It's all very well with a curate whom you have under your own eye, and whom you can get rid of if he persists in improprieties."

"But Mr. Arabin was a fellow, and couldn't have had a wife."

"Then I would have found some one who could."

"But, my dear, are fellows never to get livings?"

"Yes, to be sure they are; when they get engaged. I never would put a young man into a living unless he were married, or engaged to be married. Now here is Mr. Arabin. The whole responsibility lies upon you."

"There is not at this moment a clergyman in all Oxford more respected for morals and conduct than Arabin."

"Oh, Oxford!" said the lady, with a sneer. "What men choose to do at Oxford, nobody ever hears of. A man may do very well at Oxford who would bring disgrace on a parish; and, to tell you the truth, it seems to me that Mr. Arabin is just such a man."

The archdeacon groaned deeply, but he had no further answer to make.

"You really must speak to him, archdeacon. Only think what the Thornea will say if they hear that their parish clergyman spends his whole time philandering with this woman."

The archdeacon groaned again. He was a courageous man, and knew well enough how to rebuke the younger clergymen of the diocese, when necessary. But there was that about Mr. Arabin which made the doctor feel that it would be very difficult to rebuke him with good effect.

"You can advise him to find a wife for himself, and he will understand well enough what that means," said Mrs. Grantly.

The archdeacon had nothing for it but groaning. There was Mr. Slope; he was going to be made dean; he was going to take a wife; he was about to achieve respectability and wealth, an excellent family mansion, and a family carriage; he would soon be among the comfortable elite of the ecclesiastical world of Barchester; whereas his own protege, the true scion of the true church, by whom he had sworn, would be still but a poor vicar, and that with a very indifferent character for moral conduct! It might be all very well recommending Mr. Arabin to marry, but how would Mr. Arabin when married support a wife!

Things were ordering themselves thus in Plumstead drawingroom when Dr. and Mrs. Grantly were disturbed in their-'sweet discourse by the quick rattle of a carriage and pair of horses on the gravel sweep. The sound was not that of visitors, whose private carriages are generally brought up to country-house doors with demure propriety, but betokened rather the advent of some person or persons who were in a hurry to reach the house, and had no intention of immediately leaving it. Guests invited to stay a week, and who were conscious of arriving after the first dinner bell, would probably approach in such a manner. So might arrive an attorE9y with the news of a granduncle's death, or a son fiom college with all the fresh honours of a double first. No one would have had himself driven up to the door of a country house in such a manner who had the slightest doubt of his own right to force an entry.

"Who is it?" said Mrs. Grantly, looking at her husband.

"Who on earth can it be?" said the archdeacon to his wife. He then quietly got up and stood with the drawing-room door open in liia hand. "Why, it's your father!"

It was indeed Mr. Harding, and Mr. Harding alone. He had come by himself in a post-chaise with a couple of horses from Barchester, arriving almost after dark, and evidently full of news. His visits had usually been made in the quietest manner; he had rarely presumed to come without notice, and had always been driven up in a modest old green fly, with one horse, that hardly made itself heard as it crawled up to the hall door.

"Good gracious, Warden, is it you?" said the archdeacon, forgetting in his surprise the events of the last few years. "But come in; nothing the matter, I hope."

"We are very glad you are come, papa," said his daughter. I'll go and get your room ready at once."

"I an't warden, archdeacon," said Mr. Harding. "Mr. Quiverful is warden."

"Oh, I know; I know," said the archdeacon, petulantly. "I forgot all about it at the moment. Is anything the matter?"

"Don't go this moment, Susan," said Mr. Harding; "I have something to tell you."

"The dinner bell will ring in five minutes," said she.

"Will it," said Mr. Harding. "Then, perhaps, I had better wait." He was big with news which he had come to tell, but which he knew could not be told without much discussion. He had hurried away to Plumstead as fast as two horses could bring him; and now, finding himself there, he was willing to accept the reprieve which dinner would give him.

"If you have anything of moment to tell us," said the archdeacon, "pray let us hear it at once. Has Eleanor gone off?"

"No, she has not," said Mr. Harding, with a look of great displeasure.

"Has Slope been made dean?" "No he has not; but—"

"But what?" said the archdeacon, who was becoming very impatient.

"They have—"

"They have what?" said the archdeacon.

"They have offered it to me," said Mr. Harding, with a modesty which almost prevented his speaking.

"Good heavens!" said the archdeacon, and sank back exhausted in an easy-chair.

"My dear, dear father," said Mrs. Grantly, and threw her arms round her father's neck.

"So I thought I had better come out and consult with you at once," said Mr. Harding.

"Consult!" shouted the archdeacon. "But, my dear Harding, I congratulate you with my whole heart;—with my whole heart; I do indeed. I never heard anything in my life that gave me so much pleasure;" and he got hold of both his father-in-law's hands, and shook them as though he were going to shake them off, and walked round and round the room, twirling a copy of the Jupiter over his head to show his extreme exultation.

"But—" began Mr. Harding.

'' But me no buts,'' said the archdeacon. '' I never was so happy in my life. It was just the proper thing to do. Upon my honour I'll never say another.word against Lord the longest day I have to live."

"That's Dr. Gwynne's doing, you may be sure," said Mrs. Grantly, who greatly liked the Master of Lazarus, he being an orderly married man with a large family.

"I suppose it is," said the archdeacon.

"Oh, papa, I am so truly delighted!" said Mrs. Grantly, getting up and kissing her father.

"But, my dear," said Mr. Harding.— It was all in vain that he strove to speak; nobody would listen to him.

"Well, Mr. Dean," said the archdeacon, triumphing; "the deanery gardens will be some consolation for the hospital elms. Well, poor Quiverful! I won't begrudge him his good fortune any-longer."

"No, indeed," said Mrs. Grantly. "Poor woman, she has fourteen children. I am sure I am very glad they have got it." "So am I," said Mr. Harding.

"I would give twenty pounds," said the archdeacon, "to see how Mr. Slope will look when he hears it." The idea of Mr. Slope's discomfiture formed no small part of the archdeacon's pleasure.

At last Mr. Harding was allowed to go up-stairs and wash hit hands, having, in fact, said very little of all that he had come out to Plumstead on purpose to say. Nor could anything more be said till the servants were gone after dinner. The joy of Dr. Grantly was so uncontrollable that he could not refrain from calling his father-in-law Mr. Dean before the men; and therefore it was soon matter of discussion in the lower regions how Mr. Harding, instead of his daughter's future husband, was to be the new dean, and various were the opinions on the matter. The cook and butler, who were advanced in years, thought that it was just as it should be but the footman and lady's maid, who were younger, thought it was a great shame that Mr. Slope should lose his chance.

"He's a mean chap all the same," said the footman; "and it an't along of him that I says so. But I always did admire the missus's sister; and she'd well become the situation."

While these were the ideas downstairs, a very great difference of opinion existed above. As soon as the cloth was drawn and the wine on the table, Mr. Harding made for himself an opportunity of speaking. It was, however, with much inward troubling that he said:—

"It's very kind of Lord, very kind, and I feel it deeply, most deeply. I am, I must confess, gratified by the offer. " "I should think so," said the archdeacon. "But, all the same, I am afraid that I can't accept it." The decanter almost fell from the archdeacon's hand upon 111'Vol. ir. z table; and the start he made was so great as to make his-wife jump up from her chair. Not accept the deanship! If it really ended in this, there would no longer be any doubt that his fatherin-law was demented. The question now was whether a clergyman with low rank, and preferment amounting to less than 200?. a year, should accept high rank, 1200?. a year, and one of the most desirable positions which his profession had to afford!

"What!" said the archdeaoon, gasping for breath, and staring at his guest as though the violence of his emotion had almost thrown him into a fit. "What!"

"I do not find myself fit for new duties," urged Mr. Harding.

"New duties! what duties?" said the archdeacon, with unintended sarcasm.

"Oh, papa," said Mrs. Grantly, "nothing can be easier than what a dean has to do. Surely you are more active than Dr. Trefoil."

"He won't have half as much to do as he has at present," said Dr. Grantly.

"Did you see what the Jupiter said the other day about young men?"

"Yes; and I saw that the Jupiter said all that it could to induce the appointment of Mr. Slope. Perhaps you would wish to see Mr. Slope made dean."

Mr. Harding made no reply to this rebuke, though he felt it strongly. He had not come over to Plumstead to have further contention with his son-in-law about Mr. Slope, so he allowed it to pass by. "I know I cannot make you understand my feeling," he said, "for we have been cast in different moulds. I may wish that I had your spirit and energy and power of combating; but I have not. Every day that is added to my life increases my wish for peace and rest."

"And where on earth can a man have peace and rest if not in a deanery?" said the archdeacon.

"People will say that. 1 am too old for

it."

"Good heavens! people! what people? What need you care for anj-people?"

"But I think myself I am too old for any new place."

"Dear papa," said Mrs. Grantly, "men ten years older than you are appointed to new situations day after day."

"My dear," said he, "it is impossible that I should make you understand my feelings, nor do I pretend to any great virtue in the matter. The truth is I want the force of character which might enable me to stand against the spirit of the times. The call on all sides now is for young men, and I have not the nerve to put myself in opposition to the demand. Were the Jupiter, when it hears of my appointment, to write article after article, setting forth my incompetency, I am sure it would cost me my reason. I ought to be able to bear with such things, you will say. Well, my dear, I own that I ought. But I feel my weakness, and I know that I can't. And, to tell you the truth, I know no more than a child what the dean has to do."

"Pshaw!" exclaimed the archdeacon.

"Don't be angry with me, archdeacon. Don't let us quarrel about it, Susan. If you knew how keenly I feel the necessity of having to disoblige you in this matter, you would not be angry with me."

This was a dreadful blow to Dr. Grantly. Nothing could possibly have suited him better than having Mr. Harding in the deanery. Though he had never looked down on Mr. Harding on account of his recent poverty, he did fully recognise the satisfaction of having those belonging to him in comfortable positions. It would be much more suitable that Mr. Harding should be dean of Barchester than vicar of St. Cuthbert's and precentor to boot. And then the great discomfiture of that arch enemy of all that was respectable in Barchester, of that new low-church clerical parvenu that had fallen amongst them, that alone would be worth more, almost, than the situation itself. It was frightful to think that such unhoped-for good fortune should be marred by the absurd crotchets and unwholesome hallucinations by which Mr. Harding allowed himself to be led astray. To have the cup so near his lips and then to lose the drinking of it, was more than Dr. Grantly could endure.

And yet it appeared as though he would have to endure it. In vain he threatened and in vain he coaxed. Mr. Harding did not indeed speak with perfect decision of refusing the proffered glory, but he would not speak with anything like decision of accepting it. When pressed again and again, he would again and again allege that he was wholly unfitted to new duties. It was in vain that the archdeacon tried to insinuate, though he could not plainly declare, that there were no new duties to perform. It was in vain he hinted that in all cases of difficulty he, the archdeacon, was willing and able to guide a weak-minded dean. Mr. Harding seemed to have a foolish idea, not only that there were new duties to do, but that no one should accept the place who was not himself prepared to do them.

The conference ended in an understanding that Mr. Harding should at once acknowledge the letter he had received from the minister's private secretary, and should beg that he might be allowed two days to make up his mind; and that during those two iays the matter should be considered.

On the following morning the archdeacon was to drive Mr Harding back to Barchester.

CHAPTER XLVIII. HISS THORNE SHOWS HER TALENT AT MATCH-MAKHfO.

On Mr. Harding's return to Barchester from Plumstead, which was effected by him in due course in company with the archdeacon, more tidings of a surprising nature met him. He was, during the journey, subjected to such a weight of unanswerable argument, all of which went to prove that it was his bounden duty not to interfere with the paternal government that was so anxious to make him a dean, that when he arrived at the chemist's door in High Street, he hardly knew which way to turn himself in the matter, But, perplexed as he was, he was doomed to further perplexity. He

found a note there from his daughter begging him most urgently to come to her immediately. But we must again go bac) a little in our story.

Miss Thorne had not been slow to hear the rumours respecting Mr. Arabin which had so much disturbed the happiness of Mrs. Grantly. And she, also, was unhappy to think that her parish clergyman should be accused of worshipping a strange goddess. She, also, was of opinion, that rectors and vicars should all be married, and with that good-natured energy which was characteristic of her, she put her wits to work to find a fitting match for Mr. Arabin. Mrs. Grantly, in this difficulty, could think of no better remedy than a lecture from the archdeacon. Miss Thorne thought that a young lady, marriageable, and with a dowry, might be of more efficacy. In looking through the catalogue of her unmarried friends, who might possibly be in want of a husband, and might also be fit for such promotion as a country parsonage affords, she could think of no one more eligible than Mrs. Bold; and, consequently, losing no time, she went into Barchester on the day of Mr. Slope's discomfiture, the same day that her brother had had his interesting interview with the last of the Neros, and invited Mrs. Bold to bring her nurse and baby to Ullathorne and make them a protracted visit.

Miss Thorne suggested a month or two, intending to use her influence afterwards in prolonging it so as to last out the winter, in order that Mr. Arabin might have an opportunity of becoming fairly intimate with his intended bride. "We'll have Mr. Arabin too," said Miss Thorne to herself; "and before the spring they'll know each other; and in twelve or eighteen months' time, if all goes well, Mrs. Bold will be domiciled at St. Ewold's;" and then the kind-hearted lady gave herself some not undeserved praise for her match-making genius.

Eleanor was taken a little by surprise, but the matter ended in her promising to go to Ullathorne for at any rate a week or two; and on the day previous to that on which her father drove out to Plum-

stead, she had had herself driven out to Ullathorne.

Miss Thorne would not perplex her with her embryo lord on that same evening, thinking that she would allow her a few hours to make herself at home; but on the following morning Mr. Arabin arrived. "And now," said Miss Thorne to herself, "I must contrive to throw them in each other's way." That same day, after dinner, Eleanor, with an assumed air of dignity which she could not maintain, with tears that she could not suppress, with a flutter which she could not conquer, and a joy which she could not hide, told Miss Thorne that she was engaged to marry Mr. Arabin, and that it behoved her to get back home to Barchester as quick as she could.

To say simply that Miss Thorne was rejoiced at the success of the scheme would give a very faint idea of her feelings on the occasion. My readers may probably have dreamt before now that they have had before them some terribly long walk to accomplish, some journey of twenty or thirty miles, an amount of labour frightful to anticipate, and that immediately on starting they have ingeniously found some accommodating short cut which has brought them without fatigue to their work's end in five minutes. Miss Thome's waking feelings were somewhat of the same nature. My readers may perhaps have had to do with children, and may on some occasion have promised to their young charges some great gratification intended to come off, perhaps at the end of the winter, or at the beginning of summer. The impatient juveniles, however, will not wait, and clamorously demand their treat before they go to bed. Miss Thome had a sort of feeling that her children wero equally unreasonable. She was like an inexperienced gunner, who has ill calculated the length of the train that he has laid. The gunpowder exploded much too soon, and poor Miss Thome felt that she was blown up by the strength of her own petar.

Miss Thorne had had lovers of her own, but they had been gentlemen of old-fashioned and deliberate habits.

Miss Thorne's heart also had not always been hard, though she was still a virgin spinster; but it had never yielded in this way at the first assault. She had intended to bring together a middle-aged studious clergyman, and a discreet matron who might possibly be induced to marry again; and in doing so she had thrown fire among tinder. Well, it was all as it should be, but she did perhaps feel a little put out by the precipitancy of her own success; and perhaps a little vexed at the readiness of Mrs. Bold to be wooed.

She said, however, nothing about it to any one, and ascribed it all to the altered manners of the new age. Their mothers and grandmothers were perhaps a little more deliberate; but it was admitted on all sides that things were conducted very differently now than in former times. For aught Miss Thorne knew of the matter, a couple of hours might be quite sufficient under the new regime to complete that for which she in her ignorance had allotted twelve months.

But we must not pass over the wooing so cavalierly. It has been told, with perhaps tedious accuracy, how Eleanor disposed of two of her lovers at Ullathorne; and it must also be told with equal accuracy, and if possible with less tedium, how she encountered Mr. Arabin.

It cannot be denied that when Eleanor accepted Miss Thorne's invitation she remembered that Ullathorne was in the parish of St. Ewold's. Since her interview with the Signora she had done little else than think about Mr. Arabin, and the appeal that had been made to her. She could not bring herself to believe or try to bring herself to believe, that what she had been told was untrue. Think of it how she would, she could not but accept it as a fact that Mr. Arabin was fond of her; and then when she went further, and asked herself the question, she could not but accept it as a fact also that she was fond of him. If it were destined for her to be the partner of his hopes and sorrows, to whom could she look for friendship so properly as to Miss Thorne? This invitation was like an ordained step towards the fulfilment of her destiny, and when she also heard that Mr. Arabin was expected to be at Ullathorne on the following day, it seemed as though all the world were conspiring in her favour. Well, did she not deserve it? In that affair of Mr. Slope, had not all the world conspired against her?

She could not, however, make herself easy and at home. "When in the evening after dinner Miss Thorne expatiated on the excellence of Mr. Arabin's qualities, and hinted that any little rumour which might be ill-naturedly spread abroad concerning him really meant nothing, Mrs. Bold found herself unable to answer. "When Miss Thorne went a little further and declared that she did not know a prettier vicarage-house in the county than St. Ewold's, Mrs. Bold, remembering the projected bow-window and the projected priestess, still held her tongue; though her ears tingled with the conviction that all' the world knew that she was in love with Mr. Arabin. Well; what would that matter if they could only meet and tell each other what each now longed to tell?

And they did meet. Mr. Arabin came early in the day, and found the two ladies together at work in the drawing-room. Miss Thorne, who had she known all the truth would have vanished into air at once, had no conception that her immediate absence would be a blessing, and remained chatting with them till luncheon-time. Mr. Arabin could talk about nothing but the Signora Neroni's beauty, would discuss no people but the Stanhopes. This was very distressing to Eleanor, and not very satisfactory to Miss Thorne. But yet there was evidence of innocence in his open avowal of admiration.

And then they had lunch, and then Mr. Arabin went out on parish duty, and Eleanor and Miss Thorne were left to take a walk together.

"Do you think the Signora Neroni is so lovely as people say?" Eleanor asked as they were coming home.

"She is very beautiful certainly, very beautiful," Miss Thorne answered; "but I do not know that any one considers her lovely. She is a woman all men would like to look at; but few I imagine would be glad to take her to their hearths, even were she unmarried and not afflicted as she is." There was some little comfort in this. Eleanor made the most of it till she got back to the house. She was then left alone in the drawing-room, and just as it was getting dark Mr. Arabin came in.

It was a beautiful afternoon in the beginning of October, and Eleanor was sitting in the window to get the advantage of the last daylight for her novel. There was a fire in the comfortable room, but the weather was not cold enough to make it attractive; and as she could see the sun set from where she sat she was not very attentive to her book.

Mr. Arabin when he entered stood awhile with his back to the fire in his usual way, merely uttering a few common-place remarks about the beauty of the weather, while he plucked up courage for more interesting converse. It cannot probably be said that he had esolved then and there to make an offer to Eleanor. Men we relieve seldom make such resolves. Mr. Slope and Mr. Stanhope lad done so, it is true; but gentlemen generally propose without any absolutely defined determination as to their doing so. Such was now the case with Mr. Arabia "It is a lovely sunset," said Eleanor, answering hirn on tlie dreadfully trite subject which he had chosen.

Mr. Arabin could not see the sunset from the hearth-rug, so he had to go close to her. "Very lovely," said he, standing modestly so far away from her as to avoid touching the flounces of her dress. Then it appeared that he had nothing further to say; so after gazing for a moment in silence at the brightness of the setting sun, he returned to the fire.

Eleanor found that it was quite impossible for herself to commence a conversation. In the first place she could find nothing to say. Words which were generally plenty enough with her, would not come to her relief. And, moreover, do what she would, she could hardly prevent herself from crying.

"Do you like UUathorne?" said Mr. Arabin, speaking from the safely distant position which he had assumed on the hearthrug

"Yes, indeed, very much!"

"I don't mean Mr. and Miss Thorne. I know you like them; but the style of the house. There is something about old-fashioned mansions, built as this is, and old-fashioned gardens, that to me is especially delightful.''

"I like everything old-fashioned," said Eleanor. "Old-fashioned things are so much the honestest."

"I don't know about that," said Mr. Arabin, gently laughing. "That is an opinion on which very much may be said on eithei side. It is strange how widely the world is divided on a subject which so nearly concerns us all, and which is so close beneath our eyes. Some think that we are quickly progressing towards perfection, while others imagine that virtue is disappearing from the earth."

"And you, Mr. Arabin, what do you think?" said Eleanor! She felt somewhat surprised at the tone which his conversation was taking, and yet she was relieved at his saying something which enabled herself to speak without showing her own emotion.

"What do I think, Mrs. Bold?" and then he rumbled his money with his hands in his trowsers pockets, and looked and spoke very little like a thriving lover. "It is the bane of my life that on important subjects I acquire no fixed opinion. I think, and think, and go on thinking; and yet my thoughts are running ever in different directions. I hardly know whether or no we do lean more confidently than our fathers did on those high hopes to which we profess to aspire."

"I think the world grows more worldly every day," said Eleanor.

"That is because you see more of it than when you were younger. But we should hardly judge by what we see;— we see so very very little." There was then a pause for a while, during which Mr. Arabin continued to turn over his shillings and halfcrowns. "If ie believe in Scripture we can hardly think that mankind in general will now be allowed to retrograde."

Eleanor, whose mind was certainly engaged otherwise than on the general state of mankind, made no answer to this. She felt thoroughly dissatisfied with herself. She could not force her thoughts away from the topic on which the Signora had spoken to her in so strange a way, and yet she knew that she could not converse with Mr. Arabin in an unrestrained natural tone till she did so. She was most anxious not to show to him any special emotion, and yet she felt that if he looked at her he would at once see that she was not at ease.

But he did not look at her. Instead of doing so he left the fireplace and began walking up and down the room. Eleanor took up her book resolutely; but she could not read, for there was a tear in her eye, and do what she would it fell on her cheek. When Mr. Arabin's back was turned to her she wiped it away; but another was soon coursing down her face in its place. They would come; not a deluge of tears that would have betrayed her at once, but one by one, single monitors. Mr. Arabin did not observe her closely, and they passed unseen.

Mr. Arabin, thus pacing up and down the room, took four or five turns before he spoke another word, and Eleanor sat equally silent with her face bent over her book. She was afraid that her tears would get the better of her, and was preparing for an escape from the room, when Mr. Arabin in his walk stood opposite to her. He did not come close up, but stood exactly on the spot to which his course brought him, and thon, with his hands under his coat tails, thus made his confession.

"Mrs. Bold," said he, "I owe you retribution for a great offence of which I have been guilty towards you." Eleanor's heart beat so that she could not trust herself to say that he had never been, guilty of any offence. So Mr. Arabin thus went on.

"I have thought much of it since, and I am now aware that I was wholly unwarranted in putting to you a question which I ones asked you. It was indelicate on my part, and perhaps unmanly. No intimacy which may exist between myself and your connection, Dr. Grantly, could justify it. Nor could the acquaintance which existed between our-selves." This word acquaintance struck cold on Eleanor's heart. Was this to be her doom after all? "I therefore think it right to beg your pardon in a humble spirit, and I now do so."

What was Eleanor to say to him? She could not say much, because she was crying, and yet she must say something. She was most anxious to say that something graciously, kindly, and yet not in such a manner as to betray herself. She had never felt herself so much at a loss for words. "Indeed I took no offence, Mr. Arabin."

"Oh, but you did! And had you not done so, you would not have been yourself. You were as right to be offended as I was wrong so to offend you. I have not forgiven myself, but I hope to hear that you forgive me."

She was now past speaking calmly, though she still continued to hide her tears, and Mr. Arabin, after pausing a moment in vain for her reply, was walking off towards the door. She felt that she could not allow him to go unanswered without grievously sinning against all charity; so, rising from her seat, she gently touched Ma arm and said: "Oh, Mr. Arabin, do not go till I speak to you! I do forgive you. You know that I forgive you."

He took the hand that had so gently touched his arm, and then gazed into her face as if he would peruse there, as though written in a bock, the whole future destiny of his life; and as he did so, there was a sober sad seriousness in his own countenance, which Eleanor found herself unable to sustain. She could only look down upon the carpet, let her tears trickle as they would, and leave hei hand within his.

It was but for a minute that they stood so, but the duration of that minute was sufficient to make it ever memorable to them both. Eleanor was sure now that she was loved. No words, be their eloquence what it might, could be more impressive than that eager, melancholy gaze.

'Why did he look so into her eyes? Why did he not speak to her? Could it be that he looked for her to make the first sign?

And he, though he knew but little of women, even he knew that he was loved. He had only to ask and it would be all his own, that inexpressible loveliness, those ever speaking but yet now mu eyes, that feminine brightness and eager loving spirit which had so attracted him since first he had encountered it at St. Ewold's. It might, must all be his own now. On no other supposition was it possible that she should allow her hand to remain thus clasped within his own. He had only to ask. Ah! but that was the difficulty. Did a minute suffice for all this? Nay, perhaps it might be more than a minute.

"Mrs. Bold —" at last he said, and then stopped himself.

If he could not speak, how was she to do so? He had called her by her name, the same name that any merest stranger would have used! She withdrew her hand from his, and moved as though to return to her seat. "Eleanor!" he then said, in his softest tone, as though the courage of a lover were as yet but half assumed, as though he were still afraid of giving offence by the freedom which he took. She looked slowly, gently, almost piteously up into his face. There was at any rate no anger there to deter him. "Eleanor!" he again exclaimed; and in a moment he had her clasped to his bosom. How this was done, whether the doing was with him or her, whether she had flown thither conquered by the tenderness of his voice, or he with a violence not likely to give offence had drawn her to his breast, neither of them knew. Nor can I declare. There was now that sympathy between them which hardly admitted of individual motion. They were one and the same,—one flesh,—one spirit,—one life.

"Eleanor, my own Eleanor, my own, my wife!" She ventured to look up at him through her tears, and he, bowing his face down over hers, pressed his lips upon her brow, his virgin lips, which, since a beard first grew upon his chin, had never yet tasted the luxury of a woman's cheek.

She had been told that her yea must be yea, or her nay, nay; but she was called on for neither the one nor the other. She told Miss Thorne that she was engaged to Mr. Arabin, but no such words had passed between them, no promises had been asked or given.

"Oh, let me go," said she; "let me go now. I am too happy to remain,—let me go that I may be alone." He did not try to hinder her; he did not repeat the kiss; he did not press another on her lips. He might have done so had he been so minded. She was now all his own. He took his arm from round her waist, his arm that was trembling with a new delight, and let her go. She fled like a roe to her own chamber, and then, having turned the bolt, she enjoyed the full luxury of her love. She idolised, almost worshipped this man who had so meekly begged her pardon. And he was now her own. Oh, how she wept and cried and laughed, as the hopes and fears and miseries of the last few weeks passed in remembrance through her mind.

Mr. Slope! That any one should have dared to think that she who had been chosen by him could possibly have mated herself with Mr. Slope! That they should have dared to tell him, also, and subject her bright happiness to such needless risk! And then she smiled with joy as she thought of all the comforts that she could give Mm;—not that he eared for comforts, but that it would be so delicious for her to give.

She got up and rang for her maid that she might tell her little boy of his new father; and in her own way she did tell him. She desired her maid to leave her, in order that she might be alone with her child; and then, while he lay sprawling on the bed, she poured forth the praises, all unmeaning to him, of the man she had selected to guard his infancy.

She could not be happy, however, till she had made Mr. Arabin take the child to himself, and thus, as it were, adopt him as his own. The moment the idea struck her she took the baby up in her arms, and, opening her door, ran quickly down to the drawingroom. She at once found, by his step still pacing on the floor, that he was there; and a glance within the room told her that he was alone. She hesitated a moment, and then hurried in with her precious charge.

Mr. Arabin met her in the middle of the room. "There," said she, breathless with her haste; "there, take him;—take him and love him."

Mr. Arabin took the little fellow from her, and kissing him again and again, prayed God to bless him. "He shall be all as my own —all as my own," said he. Eleanor, as she stooped to take back her child, kissed the hand that held him, and then rushed back with her treasure to her chamber.

It was thus that Mr. Harding's younger daughter was won for the second time. At dinner neither she nor Mr. Arabin were very bright, but their silence occasioned no remark. In the drawingroom, as we have before said, she told Miss Thome what had occurred. The next morning she returned to Barchester, and Mr. Arabin went over with his budget of news to the archdeacon. As Doctor Grantly was not there he could only satisfy himself by telling Mrs. Grantly how that he intended himself the honour of becoming her brother-in-law. In the ecstasy of her joy at hearing such tidings, Mrs Grantly vouchsafed him a warmer welcome than any he had yet received from Eleanor.

"Good heavens! " she exclaimed;—it was the general exclamation of the rectory. "Poor Eleanor! Dear Eleanor! What a monstrous injustice has been done her!—Well, it shall all be made up now." And then she thought of the Signora. "What lies people tell," she said to herself.

But people in this matter had told no lies at all.

CHAPTER XLIX. THE BELZEBUB COLT.

When Miss Thome left the dining-room, Eleanor had formed no intention of revealing to her what had occurred; but when she was seated beside her hostess on the sofa the secret dropped from her almost unawares. Eleanor was but a bad hypocrite, and she found herself quite unable to continue talking about Mr. Arabin as though he were a stranger, while her heart was full of him. When Miss Thorne, pursuing her own scheme with discreet zeal, asked the young widow whether, in her opinion, it would not be a good thing for Mr. Arabin to get married, she had nothing for it but to confess the truth. "I suppose it would," said Eleanor, rather sheepishly. Whereupon Miss Thome amplified on the idea. "Oh, Miss Thome," said Eleanor, "he is going to be married. I am engaged to him."

Now Miss Thorne knew very well that there had been no such engagement when she had been walking with Mrs. Bold in the morning. She had also heard enough to be tolerably sure that there had been no preliminaries to such an engagement. She was, therefore, as we have before described, taken a little by surprise. But, nevertheless, she embraced her guest, and cordially congratulated her.

Eleanor had no opportunity of speaking another word to Mr. Arabin that evening, except such words as all the world might hear; and these, as may be supposed, were few enough. Miss Thome did her best to leave them in privacy; but Mr. Thorne. who knew nothing of what had occurred, and another guest, a friend of his, entirely interfered with her good intentions. So poor

Vol. n. A A

Eleanor had to go to bed without one sign of affection. Her state, nevertheless, was not to be pitied.

The next morning she was up early. It was probable, she thought, that by going down a little before the usual hour of breakfast, she might find Mr. Arabin alone in the dining-roon. Might it riot be that he also would calculate that an interview would thus be possible? Thus thinking, Eleanor was dressed a full hour before the time fixed in the Ullathorne household for morning prayers. She did not at once go down. She was afraid to seem to be too anxious to meet her lover; though, heaven knows, her anxiety was intense enough. She therefore sat herself down at her window, and repeatedly looking at her watch, nursed her child till she thought she might venture forth.

When she found herself at the dining-room door, she stood a moment, hesitating to turn the handle; but when she heard Mr. Thome's voice inside she hesitated no longer. Her object was defeated, and she might now go in as soon as she liked without the slightest imputation on her delicacy. Mr. Thorne and Mr. Arabin were standing on the hearthrug, discussing the merits of the Belzebub colt; or rather, Mr. Thorne was discussing, and Mr. Arabin was listening. That interesting animal had rubbed the stump of his tail against the wall of his stable, and occasioned much uneasiness to the Ullathorne master of the horse. Had Eleanor but waited another minute, Mr. Thorne would have been in the stables.

Mr. Thorne, when he saw his lady guest, repressed his anxiety. The Belzebub colt must do without him. And so the three stood, saying little or nothing to each other, till at last the master of the house, finding that he could no longer bear his present state of suspense respecting his favourite young steed, made an elaborate apology to Mrs Bold, and escaped. As he shut the door behind him, Eleanor almost wished that he had remained. It was not that she was afraid of Mr. Arabin, but she hardly yet knew how to address him.

He, however, soon relieved her from her embarrassment. He came up to her, and taking both her hands in his, he said; "So, Eleanor, you and I are to be man and wife. Is it so?"

She looked up into his face, and her lips formed themselves into a single syllable. She uttered no sound, but he could read the affirmative plainly in her face.

"It is a great trust," said he; "a very great trust."

"It is;—it is," said Eleanor, not exactly taking what he had said in the sense that he had meant. "It is a very, very great trust, and I will do my utmost to deserve it."

"And I also will do my utmost to deserve it," said Mr. Arabin, very solemnly. And then, winding his arm round her waist, he stood there gazing at the fire, and she with her head leaning on his shoulder, stood by him, well satisfied with her position. They neither of them spoke, or found any want of speaking. All that was needful for them to say had been said. The yea, yea, had been spoken by Eleanor in her own way,—and that way had been perfectly satisfactory to Mr. Arabin.

And now it remained to them each to enjoy the assurance of the other's love. How great that luxury is! How far it surpasses any other pleasure which God has allowed to his creatures! And to a woman's heart how doubly delightful!

When the ivy has found its tower, when the delicate creeper has found its strong wall, we know how the parasite plants grow and prosper. They were not created to stretch forth their branches alone, and endure without protection the summer's sun and the winter's storm. Alone they but spread themselves on the ground, and cower unseen in the dingy shade. But when they have found their firm supporters, how wonderful is their beauty; how all pervading and victorious! What is the turret without its ivy, or the high garden-wall without the jasmine which gives it its beauty and fragrance? The hedge without the honeysuckle is but a hedge.

There is a feeling still half existing, but now half conquered by the force of human nature, that a woman should be ashamed of her love till the husband's right to her compels her to acknowledge it. We would fain preach a different doctrine. A woman should glory in her love; but on that account let her take the more care that it be such as to justify her glory.

Eleanor did glory in hers, and she felt, and had cause to feel, that it deserved to be held as glorious. She could have stood there for hours with his arm round her, had fate and Mr. Thorne permitted it. Each moment she crept nearer to his bosom, and felt more and more certain that there was her home. What now to her was the archdeacon's arrogance, her sister's coldness, or her dear father's weakness? What need she care for the duplicity of such friends as Charlotte Stanhope? She had found the strong shield that should guard her from all wrongs, the trusty pilot that should henceforward guide her through the shoals and rocks. She would give up the heavy burden of her independence, and once more assume the position of a woman and the duties of a trusting and loving wife.

And he, too, stood there fully satisfied with his place. They were both looking intently on the fire, as though they could read there their future fate, till at last Eleanor turned her face towards his. "How sad you are," she said, smiling; and indeed his face was, if not sad, at least serious. "How sad you are, love!"

"Sad," said he, looking down at her; "no, certainly not sad." Her sweet loving eyes were turned towards him, and she smiled softly as he answered her. The temptation was too strong even for the demure propriety of Mr. Arabin, and, bending over her, he pressed his lips to hers. Immediately after this, Mr. Thorne appeared, and they were both delighted to hear that the tail of the Belzebub colt was not materially injured.

It had been Mr. Harding's intention to hurry over to Ullathorne as soon as possible after his return to Barchester, in order to secure the support of his daughter in his meditated revolt against the archdeacon as touching the deanery; but he was spared the additional journey by hearing that Mrs. Bold had returned unexpectedly home. As soon as he had read her note, he started off, and found her waiting for him in her own house.

How much each of them had to tell the other, and how certain each was that the story which he or she had to tell would astonish the other!

"My dear, I am so anxious to see you," said Mr. Harding, kissing his daughter.

"Oh, papa, I have so much to tell you!" said the daughter, returning the embrace.

"My dear, they have offered me the deanery!" said Mr. Harding, anticipating by the suddenness of the revelation the tidings which Eleanor had to give him.

"Oh, papa," said she, forgetting her own love and happiness in her joy at the surprising news; "oh, papa; can it be possible? Dear papa, how thoroughly, thoroughly happy, that makes me!"

"But, my dear, I think it best to refuse it." "Oh, papa!"

" I am sure you will agree with me, Eleanor, when I explain it to you. You know, my dear, how old I am. If I live, I"

"But, papa, I must tell you about myself." "Well, my dear."

"I do so wonder how you'll take it." "Take what?"

"If you don't rejoice at it,—if it doesn't make you happy, if you don't encourage me, I shall break my heart."

"If that be the case, Nelly, I certainly will encourage you."

"But I fear you won't. I do so fear you won't. And yet you can't but think I am the most fortunate woman living on God's earth."

"Are you, dearest? Then I certainly will rejoice with you. Come, Nelly, come to me; and tell me what it is." "I am going"

He led her to the sofa, and seating himself beside her, took both her hands in his. "You are going to be married, Nelly. Is not that it?"

"Yes," she said, faintly. "That is if you will approve; and then she blushed as she remembered the promise which she had so lately volunteered to him, and which she had so utterly forgotten in making her engagement with Mr. Arabin.

Mr. Harding thought for a moment who the man could be whom he was to be called upon to welcome as his son-in-law. A week since he would have had no doubt whom to name. In that case he would have been prepared to give his sanction, although he would have done so with a heavy heart. Now he knew that at any rate it would not be Mr. Slope, though he was perfectly at a loss to guess who could possibly have filled the place. For a moment he thought that the man might be Bertie Stanhope, and his very soul sank within him.

"Well, Nelly?"

"Oh, papa, promise to me that, for my sake, you will love him." "Come, Nelly, come; tell me who it is." "But will you love him, papa?"

"Dearest, I must love any one that you love." Then she turned her face to his, and whispered into his ear the name of Mr. Arabin.

No man that she could have named could have more surprised or more delighted him. Had he looked round the world for a son-in-law to his taste he could have selected no one whom he would have preferred to Mr. Arabin. He was a clergyman; he held a living in the neighbourhood; he was of a set to which all Mr. Harding's own partialities most closely adhered; he was the great friend of Dr. Grantly; and he was, moreover, a man of whom Mr. Harding knew nothing but what he approved. Nevertheless, his surprise was so great as to prevent the immediate expression of his joy. He had never thought of Mr. Arabin in connection with his daughter. He had never imagined that they had any feeling in common. He had feared that his daughter had been made hostile to clergymen of Mr. Arabin's stamp by her intolerance of the archdeacon's pretensions. Had he been put to wish, he might have wished for Mr. Arabin for a son-in-law; but had he been put to guess, the name would never have occurred to him.

"Mr. Arabin!" he exclaimed; "impossible!"

" Oh, papa, for heaven's sake don't say anything against him! If you love me, don't say anything against him. Oh, papa, it's done, and musn't be undone;—oh, papa!" Fickle Eleanor! where was the promise that she would make no choice for herself without her father's approval? She had chosen, and now demanded his acquiescence. "Oh, papa, isn't he good? isn't he noble? isn't he religious, highminded, everything that a good man possibly can be?" and she clung to her father, beseeching him for his consent.

"My Nelly, my child, my own daughter! He is! he is noble and good and highminded; he is all that a woman can love and a man admire. He shall be my son, my own son. He shall be as close to my heart as you are. My Nelly, my child, my happy. happy child!"

We need not pursue the interview any further. By degrees they returned to the subject of the new promotion. Eleanor tried to prove to him, as the Grantlys had done, that his age could be no bar to his being a very excellent dean; but those arguments had now even less weight on him than before. He said little or nothing, but sat meditative. Every now and then he would kiss his daughter, and say "yes," or "no," or "very true," or "well, my dear, I can't quite agree with you there," but he could not be got to enter sharply into the question of "to be, or not to be" dean of Barchester. Of her and her happiness, of Mr. Arabin and his virtues, he would talk as much as Eleanor desired; and, to tell the truth, that was not a little; but about the deanery he would now say nothing further. He had got a new idea into his head. Why should not Mr. Arabin be the new dean?

CHAPTER L. THE ARCHDEACON IS SATIS-FIED WITH THE STATE OF AFFAIRS.

The archdeacon, in his journey into Barchester, had been assured by Mr. Harding that all their prognostications about Mr. Slope and Eleanor-were groundless. Mr. Harding, however, had found it very difficult to shake his son-in-law's faith in his own acuteness. The matter had, to Dr. Grantly, been so plainly corroborated by such patent evidence, borne out by such endless circumstances, that he at first refused to take as true the positive statement which Mr. Harding made to him of Eleanor's own disavowal of the impeachment. But at last he yielded in a qualified way. He brought himself to admit that he would at the present regard his past convictions as a mistake; but in doing this he so guarded himself, that if, at any future time, Eleanor should come forth to the world as Mrs. Slope, he might still be able to say; "There, I told you so. Eemember what you said and what I said; and remember also for' coming years, that I was right in this matter,—as in all others."

He carried, however, his concession so far as to bring himself to undertake to call at Eleanor's house, and he did call accordingly, while the father and daughter were yet in the middle of their conference. Mr. Harding had had so much to hear and to say that he had for-

gotten to advertise Eleanor of the hon-our that awaited her, and she heard her brother-in-law's voice in the hall, while she was quite unprepared to see him.

"There's the archdeacon," she said, springing up.

"Yes, my dear. He told me to tell you that he would come and see you; but, to tell the truth, I had forgotten all about it. "

Eleanor fled away, regardless of all her father's entreatiea. She could not now, in the first hours of her joy, bring herself to bear all the archdeacon's re-tractions, apologies, and congratula-tions. He would have so much to say, and would be so tedious in saying it! Consequently, the archdeacon, when he was shown into the drawing-room, found no one there but Mr. Harding.

"You must excuse Eleanor," said Mr. Harding.

"Is anything the matter? " asked the doctor, who at once anticipated that the whole truth about Mr. Slope had at last come out.

"Well, something is the matter. I wonder now whether you will be much surprised?"

The archdeacon saw by his father-in-law's manner that after all he had noth-ing to tell him about Mr. Slope. "No," said he, "certainly not;—nothing will ever surprise me again." Very many men now-a-days, besides the archdea-con, adopt or affect to adopt the nil ad-mirari doctrine; but nevertheless, to judge from their appearance, they are just as subject to sudden emotions as their grandfathers and grandmothers were before them.

"What do you think Mr. Arabin has done?"

"Mr. Arabin! It's nothing about that daughter of Stanhope's, I hope?"

"No, not that woman," said Mr. Hard-ing, enjoying his joke in his sleeve.

"Not that woman! Is he going to do anything about any woman? Why can't you speak out, if you have anything to say? There's nothing I hate so much as these sort of mysteries."

"There shall be no mystery with you, archdeacon; though, of course, it must go no further at present."

"Well."

"Except Susan. You must promise me you'll tell no one else."

"Nonsense!" exclaimed the archdea-con, who was becoming angry in his suspense. "You can't have any secret about Mr. Arabin."

"Only this;—that he and Eleanor are engaged."

It was quite clear to see, by the archdeacon's face, that he did not be-lieve a word of it. "Mr. Arabin! It's im-possible."

"Eleanor, at any rate, has just now told me so." "It's impossible," repeated the archdeacon.

"Well, I can't say I think it impossi-ble. It certainly took me by surprise; but that does not make it impossible." "She must be mistaken."

Mr. Harding assured him that there was no mistake; that he would find, on returning home, that Mr. Arabin had been at Plumstead with the express ob-ject of making the same declaration, that even Miss Thorne knew all about it; and that, in fact, the thing was as clearly settled as any such arrangement between a lady and a gentleman could well be.

"Good heavens!" said the archdea-con, walking up and down Eleanor's drawing-room. "Good heavens! Good heavens!"

Now, these exclamations certainly betokened faith. Mr. Harding properly gathered from it that, at last, Dr. Grantly did believe the fact. The first utterance clearly evinced a certain amount of dis-taste at the information he had received; the second, simply indicated surprise; in the tone of the third, Mr. Harding fan-cied that he could catch a certain gleam of satisfaction.

The archdeacon had truly expressed the workings of his mind. He could not but be disgusted to find how utterly astray he had been in all his anticipa-tions. Had he only been lucky enough to have suggested this marriage himself when he first brought Mr. Arabin into the country, his character for judgment and wisdom would have received an ad-dition which would have classed him at any rate next to Solomon. And why had he not done so? Might he not have foreseen that Mr. Arabin would want a wife in his parsonage? He had foreseen that Eleanor would want a husband; but should he not also have perceived that Mr. Arabin was a man much more likely to attract her than Mr. Slope? The archdeacon found that he had been at fault, and of course could not immediately get over hia discomfiture.

Then his surprise was intense. How sly this pair of young turtle doves had been with him. How egregiously they had hoaxed him. He had preached to Eleanor against her fancied attachment to Mr. Slope, at the very time that she was in love with his own protege, Mr. Arabin; and had absolutely taken that same Mr. Arabin into his confidence with reference to his dread of Mr. Slope's alliance. It was very natural that the archdeacon should feel surprise.

But there was also great ground for satisfaction. Looting at the match by itself, it was the very thing to help the doctor out of his difficulties. In the first place, the assurance that he should never have Mr. Slope for his brother-in-law, was in itself a great comfort. Then Mr. Arabin was, of all men, the one with whom it would best suit him to be so intimately connected. But the crowning comfort was the blow which this marriage would give to Mr. Slope. He had now certainly lost his wife; rumour was beginning to whisper that he might possibly lose his position in the palace; and if Mr. Harding would only be true, the great danger of all would be surmounted. In such case it might be expected that Mr. Slope would own himself vanquished and take himself altogether away from Barchester. And so the archdeacon would again be able to breathe pure air.

"Well, well," said he. "Good heavens! good heavens!" And the tone of the fifth exclamation made Mr. Harding fully aware that content was reigning in the archdeacon's bosom.

And then slowly, gradually, and craftily Mr. Harding propounded his own new scheme. Why should not Mr. Arabin be the new dean?

Slowly, gradually, and thoughtfully Dr. Grantly fell into his father-in-law's views. Much as he liked Mr. Arabin, sincere as was his admiration for that gentleman's ecclesiastical abilities, he would not have sanctioned a measure which would rob his fatherin-law of his fairly-earned promotion, were it at all practicable to induce his father-in-law to accept the promotion which he had earned. But the archdeacon had, on a former occasion, received proof of the obstinacy with which Mr. Harding could adhere to his own views in opposition to the advice of all his friends. He knew tolerably well that nothing would induce the meek, mild man before him to take the high place offered to him, if he thought it wrong to do so. Knowing this, he also said to himself more than once; "Why should not Mr. Arabin be Dean of Barchester?" It was at last arranged between them that they would together start to London by the earliest train on the following morning, making a little detour to Oxford on their journey. Dr. Gwynne's counsels, they imagined, might perhaps be of assistance to them.

These matters settled, the archdeacon hurried off, that he might return to Plumstead and prepare for his journey. The day was extremely fine, and he had come into the city in an open gig. As he was driving up the High Street he encountered Mr. Slope at a crossing. Had he not pulled up rather sharply he would have run over him. The two had never spoken to each other since they had met on a memorable occasion in the bishop's study. They did not speak now; but they looked each other full in the face, and Mr. Slope's countenance was as impudent, as triumphant, as defiant as ever. Had Dr. Grantly not known to the contrary, he would have imagined that his enemy had won the deanship, the wife, and all the rich honours, for which he had been striving. As it was, he had lost everything that he had in the world, and had just received his conge from the bishop.

In leaving the town the archdeacon drove by the well-remembered entrance of Hiram's hospital. There, at the gate, was a large, untidy, farmer's wagon, laden with untidy-looking furniture; and there, inspecting the arrival, was good Mrs. Quiverful,—not dressed in her Sunday best,—not very clean in her apparel,—not graceful as to her bonnet and shawl; or, indeed, with many feminine charms as to her whole appearance. She was busy at domestic work in her new house, and had just ventured out, expecting to see no one on the arrival of the family chattels. The archdeacon was down upon her before she knew where she was.

Her acquaintance with Dr. Grantly or his family was very slight indeed. The archdeacon, as a matter of course, knew every clergyman in the archdeaconry,—it may almost be said in the diocese,—and had some acquaintance, more or less intimate, with their wives and families. With Mr. Quiverful he had been concerned on various matters of business; but of Mrs. Q. he had seen very little. Now, however, he was in too gracious a mood to pass her by unnoticed. The Quiverfuls, one and all, had looked for the bitterest hostility from Dr. Grantly. They knew his anxiety that Mr. Harding should return to his old home at the hospital, and they did not know that a new home had been offered to him at the deanery. Mrs. Quiverful was therefore not a little surprised and not a little rejoiced also, at the tone in which she was addressed.

"How do you do, Mrs. Quiverful?—how do you do?" said he, stretching his left hand out of the gig, as he spoke to her. "I am very glad to see you employed in so pleasant and useful a manner; very glad indeed."

Mrs. Quiverful thanked him, and shook hands with him, and looked into his face suspiciously. She was not sure whether the congratulations and kindness were or were not ironical.

"Pray tell Mr. Quiverful from me," he continued, "that I am rejoiced at his appointment. It's a comfortable place, Mrs. Quiverful, and a comfortable house, and I am very glad to see you in it. Good-bye;—good-bye." And he drove on, leaving the lady well pleased and astonished at his good-nature. On the whole things were going well with the archdeacon, and he could afford to be charitable to Mrs. Quiverful. He looked forth from his gig smilingly on all the world, and forgave every one in Barchester their sins, excepting only Mrs. Proudie and Mr. Slope. Had he seen the bishop, he would have felt inclined to pa,t even him kindly on the head.

He determined to go home by St. Ewold's. This would take him some three miles out of his way; but he felt that he could not leave Plumstead comfortably without saying one word of good fellowship to Mr. Arabin. When he reached the parsonage the vicar was still out; but, from what he had heard, he did not doubt but that he would meet him on the road between their two houses. He was right in this, for about halfway home, at a narrow turn, he came upon Mr. Arabin, who was on horseback.

"Well, well; well, well;" said the archdeacon, loudly, joyously, and with supreme good humour; "well, well; well, well; so, after all, we have no further cause to fear Mr. Slope."

"I hear from Mrs. Grantly that they have offered the deanery to Mr. Harding," said the other.

"Mr. Slope has lost more than the deanery, I find," and then the archdeacon laughed jocosely. "Come, come, Arabin, you have kept your secret well enough. I know all about it now."

"I have had no secret, archdeacon," said the other with a quiet smile. "None at all,—not for a day. It was only yesterday that I knew my own good fortune, and to-day I went over to Plumstead to ask your approval. From what Mrs. Grantly has said to me, I am led to hope that I shall have it."

"With all my heart; with all my heart," said the archdeacon cordially, holding his friend fast by the hand. "It's just as I would have it. She is an excellent young woman; she will not come to you empty-handed; and I think she will make you a good wife. If she does her duty by you as her sister does by me, you'll be a happy man; that's all I can say." And as he finished speaking, a tear might have been observed in each of the

archdeacon's eyes. Mr. Arabin warmly returned the archdeacon's grasp, but he said little. His heart was too full for speaking, and he could not express the gratitude which he felt. Dr. Grantly understood him as well as though he had spoken for an hour.

"And mind, Arabin," said he, "no one but myself shall tie the knot. We'll get Eleanor out to Plumstead, and it shall come oft there. I'll make Susan stir herself, and we'll do it in style. I must be off to London to-morrow on special business. Harding goes with me. But I'll be back before your bride has got her wedding dress ready." And so they parted.

On his journey home the archdeacon occupied his mind with preparations for the marriage festivities. He made a great resolve that he would atone to Eleanor for all the injury he had done her by the munificence of his future treatment. He would show her what was the difference in his eyes between a Slope and an Arabin. On one other thing also he decided with a firm mind. If the affair of the dean should not be settled in Mr. Arabin's favour, nothing: should prevent him putting a new front and bow-window to the dining-room at St. Ewold's parsonage.

"So we're sold after all, Sue," said he to his wife, accosting her with a kiss as soon as he entered his house. He did not call his wife Sue above twice or thrice in a year, and these occasions were great high days.

"Eleanor has had more sense than we gave her credit for," said Mrs. Grantly. And there was great content in Plumstead rectory that evening; and Mrs. Grantly promised her husband that she would now open her heart, and take Mr. Arabia into it. Hitherto she had declined to do Bo. CHAPTER II.

ME. SLOPE BIDS FAREWELL TO THE PALACE AND ITS INHABITANTS.

We must now take leave of Mr. Slope, and of the bishop also, and of Mrs. Proudie. These leave-takings in novels are as disagreeable as they are in real life;—not so sad, indeed, for they want the reality of sadness; but quite as perplexing, and generally less satisfactory.

What novelist, what Fielding, what Scott, what George Sand, or Thackeray, or Dumas, can impart an interest to the last chapter of his fictitious history? Promises of two children and superhuman happiness are of no avail, nor assurance of extreme respectability carried to an age far exceeding that usually allotted to mortals. The sorrows of our heroes and heroines, they are your delight, oh public! their sorrows, or their sins, or their absurdities; not their virtues, good sense, and consequent rewards. When we begin to tint our final pages with couleur de rose, as in accordance with fixed rule we must do, we altogether extinguish our own powers of pleasing. When we become dull we offend your intellect; and we must become dull or we should offend your taste. A late writer, wishing to sustain his interest to the last page, hung his hero at the end of the third volume. The consequence was, that no one would read his novel. And who can apportion out and dovetail his incidents, dialogues, characters, and descriptive morsels, so as to fit them all exactly into 564 pages, without either compressing them unnaturally, or extending them artificially at the end of his labour? Do I not myself know that I am at this moment in want of a dozen pages, and that I am sick with cudgelling my brains to find them? And then when everything is done, the kindest-hearted critic of them all invariably twits us with the incompetency and lameness of our conclusion. We have either become idle and neglected it, or tedious and overlaboured it. It is insipid or unnatural, overstrained or imbecile. It means nothing, or attempts too much. The last scene of all, as all last scenes we fear must be,

"Js second childishness, and mere oblivion,
Sans teeth, sans eyes, sans taste, sans everything."

1 can only say that if some critic, who thoroughly knows his work, and has laboured on it till experience has made him perfect, will write the last fifty pages of a novel in the way they should be written, I, for one, will in future do my best to copy the example. Guided by

my own lights only, I confess that I despair of success.

For the last week or ten days, Mr. Slope had seen nothing of Mrs. Proudie, and very little of the bishop. He still lived in the palace, and still went through his usual routine work; but the confidential doings of the diocese had passed into other hands. He had seen this clearly, and marked it well; but it had not much disturbed him. He had indulged in other hopes till the bishop's affairs had become dull to him, and he was moreover aware that, as regarded the diocese, Mrs. Proudie had checkmated him. It has been explained, in the beginning of these pages, how three or four were contending together as to who, in fact, should be bishop of Barchester. Each of these had now admitted to himself,— or boasted to herself,— that Mrs. Proudie was victorious in the struggle. They had gone through a competitive examination of considerable severity, and she had come forth the winner, facile princeps. Mr. Slope had, for a moment, run her hard, but it was only for a moment. It had become, as it were, acknowledged that Hiram's hospital should be the testing point between them, and now Mr. Quiverful was already in the hospital, the proof of Mrs. Proudie's skill and courage.

All this did not break down Mr. Slope's spirit, because he had VOL. II. B B other hopes. But, alas, at last there came to him a note from his friend Sir Nicholas, informing him that the deanship was disposed of. Let us give Mr. Slope his due. He did not lie prostrate under this blow, or give himself up to vain lamentations; he did not henceforward despair of life, and call upon gods above and gods: below to carry him off. He sat himself down in his chair, counted / out what monies he had in hand for present purposes, and what others were coming in to him, bethought himself as to the best I sphere for his future exertions, and at once wrote off a letter to a rich sugar-refiner's wife in Baker Street, who, as he well knew, was much given to the entertainment and encouragement of serious young evangelioal olergymen. He was again, he said, "up-

on the world, having found the air of a cathedral town, and the very nature of cathedral services, uncongenial to his spirit; " and then he sat awhile, making firm resolves as to his manner of parting from the bishop, and also as to his future conduct. i

'At last he rose, and twitched his manlle blue,
To-morrow to fresh woods and pastures uew."

Having received a formal command to wait upon the bishop, ho rose and proceeded to obey it. He rang the bell and desired the servant to inform his master that if it suited his lordship, he, Mr. Slope, was ready to wait upon him. The servant, who well understood that Mr. Slope was no longer in the ascendant, brought back a message, saying that "his lordship desired that Mr. Slope would attend him immediately in his study." Mr. Slope waited about ten minutes more to prove his independence, and then he went into the bishop's room. There, as he had expected, he found Mrs. Proudie, i together with her husband.

"Hum, ha,—Mr. Slope, pray take a chair," said the gentleman bishop.

"Pray be seated, Mr. Slope," said the lady bishop.

"Thank ye, thank ye," said Mr. Slope, and walking round to the fire, he threw himself into one of the arm-chairs that graced the hearth-rug.

"Mr. Slope," said the bishop, "it has become necessary that I should speak to you definitively on a matter that has for some time been pressing itself on my attention."

"May I ask whether the subject is in any way connected with myself?" said Mr. Slope.

"It is so,—certainly;—yes, it certainly is connected with yournelf, Mr. Slope."

"Then, my lord, if I may be allowed to express a wish, I would prefer that no discussion on the subject should take place between us in the presence of a third person."

"Don't alarm yourself, Mr. Slope," said Mrs. Proudie; "no discussion is at all necessary. The bishop merely in-

tends to expreas his own wishes."

"I merely intend, Mr. Slope, to express my own wishes;—no discussion will be at all necessary," said the bishop, reiterating his wife's words.

"That is more, my lord, than we any of us can be sure of," said Mr. Slope; "I cannot, however, force Mrs. Proudie to leave the room; nor can I refuse to remain here if it be your lordship's wish that I should do so."

"It is his lordship's wish, certainly," said Mrs. Proudie.

"Mr. Slope," began the bishop, in a solemn, serious voice, "it grieves me to have to find fault. It grieves me much to have to find fault with a clergyman;— but especially so with a clergyman in your position."

"Why, what have I done amiss, my lord?" demanded Mr. Slope, boldly.

"What have you done amiss, Mr. Slope?" said Mrs. Proudie, standing erect before the culpri, and raising that terrible forefinger. "Do you dare to ask the bishop what you have done amiss? Does not your conscience"

"Mrs. Proudie, pray let it be understood, once for all, that I will have no words with you."

"Ah, sir, but you will have words," said she; "you must have words. Why have you had so many words with that Signora Neroni? Why have you disgraced yourself, you a clergyman too, by constantly consorting with such a woman as that,—with a married woman,—with one altogether unfit for a clergyman's society?"

"At any rate, I was introduced to her in your drawing-room," retorted Mr. Slope.

"And shamefully you behaved there," said Mrs. Proudie; "most shamefully. I was wrong to allow you to remain in the house a day after what I then saw. I should have insisted on your instant dismissal."

"I have yet to learn, Mrs. Proudie, that you have the power to insist either on my going from hence or on my staying here."

"What!" said the lady; "I am not to have the privilege of saying who shall and who shall not frequent my own drawingroom! I am not to save my servants and dependents from having their morals corrupted by improper conduct! I am not to save my own daughters from impurity! I will let you see, Mr. Slope, whether I have the power or whether I have not. You will have the goodness to understand that you no longer fill any situation about the bishop; and as your room will be immediately wanted in the palace for another chaplain, I must ask you to provide yourself with apartments as soon as may be convenient to you."

"My lord," said Mr. Slope, appealing to the bishop, and so turning his back completely on the lady, "will you permit me to a-k that I may have from your own lips any decision that you may have come to on this matter?"

"Certainly, Mr. Slope; certainly," said the bishop; "that is but reasonable. Well, my decision is that you had better look for some other preferment. For the situation which you have lately held I do not think that you are well suited."

"And what, my lord, has been my fault?"

"That Signora Neroni is one fault," said Mrs. Proudie; "and a very abominable fault she is;—very abominable and very disgraceful. Fie, Mr. Slope, fie! You an evangelical clergyman indeed!"

"My lord, I desire to know for what fault I am turned out of your lordship's house."

"You hear what Mrs. Proudie says," said the bishop.

"When I publish the history of this transaction, my lord, as I decidedly shall do in my own vindication, I presume you will not wish me to state that you have discarded me at your wife's bidding;—because she has objected to my being acquainted with another lady, the daughter of one of the prebendaries of the chapter?"

"You may publish what you please, sir," said Mrs. Proudie. "But you will not be insane enough to publish any of your doings in Barchester. Do you think I have not heard of your kneelings at that creature's feet,—that is if she has any feet,—and of your constant slobbering over her hand? I advise you to beware, Mr. Slope, of what you do and

say. Clergymen have been unfrocked for less than what you have been guilty of."

"My lord, if this goes on I shall be obliged to indict this woman, —Mrs. Proudie I mean,—for defamation of character."

"I think, Mr. Slope, you had better now retire," said the bishop. '' I will enclose to you a cheque for any balance that may be due to you; and, under the present circumstances, it will of course be better for all parties that you should leave the palace at the earliest possible moment. I will allow you for your journey back to London, and for your maintenance in Barchester for a week from this date."

"If, however, you wish to remain in this neighbourhood," said Mrs. Proudie, "and will solemnly pledge yourself never again to see that woman, and will promise also to be more circumspect in your conduct, the bishop will mention your name to Mr. Quiverful, who now wants a curate at Puddingdale. The house is, I imagine, quite sufficient for your requirements, and there will moreover be a stipend of fifty pounds a year. "

"May God forgive you, madam, for the manner in which you have treated me," said Mr. Slope, looking at her with a very heavenly look; "and remember this, madam, that you yourself may still have a fall;" and he looked at her with a very worldly look. "As to the bishop, I pity him!" And so saying, Mr. Slope left the room. Thus ended the intimacy of the Bishop of BarChester with his first confidential chaplain.

Mrs. Proudie was right in this; namely, that Mr. Slope was not insane enough to publish to the world any of his doings in Barchester. He did not trouble his friend Mr. Towers with any written statement of the iniquity of Mrs. Proudie, or the imbecility of her husband. He was aware that it would be wise in him to drop for the future all allusions to his doings in the cathedral city. Soon after the interview just recorded, he left Barchester, shaking the dust off his feet as he entered the railway carriage; and he gave no longing

lingering look after the cathedral towers as the train hurried him quickly out of their sight.

It is well known that the family of the Slopes never starve. They always fall on their feet like cats, and let them fall where they will, they live on the fat of the land. Our Mr. Slope did so. On his return to town he found that the sugar-refiner had died, and that his widow was inconsolable;—or, in other words, was in want of consolation. Mr. Slope consoled her, and soon found himself settled with much comfort in the house in Baker Street. He possessed himself, also, before long, of a church in the vicinity of the New Road, and became known to fame as one of the most eloquent preachers and pious clergymen in that part of the metropolis. There let us leave him.

Of the bishop and his wife very little further need be said. From that time forth nothing material occurred to interrupt the even course of their domestic harmony. Very speedily, a further vacancy on the bench of bishops gave to Dr. Proudie the seat in the House of Lords, for which he at first so anxiously longed. But by thia time he had become a wiser man. He did certainly take Ids seat, and occasionally registered a vote in favour of Government views on ecclesiastical matters. But he had thoroughly learnt that his proper sphere of action lay in close contiguity to Mrs. Proudie's wardrobe. He never again aspired to disobey, or seemed even to 'wish for autocratic diocesan authority. If ever he thought of freedom, he did so, as men think of the millennium,—as of a good time which may be coming but which nobody expects to come in their day. Mrs. Proudie might be said still to bloom, and was, at any rate, strong; and the bishop had no reason to apprehend that he would be speedily visited with the sorrows of a widower's life.

He is still Bishop of Barchester. He has so graced that throne, that the Government has been averse to translate him, even to higher dignities. There may he remain, under safe pupilage, till the new-fangled manners of the age have discovered him to be superannuated and bestowed on him a pension. As for Mrs.

Proudie, our prayers for her are that she may live for ever.

CHAPTER LIT. THE HEW DEAN TAKES POSSESSION OF THE DEANERY, AND THE NEW WARDEN OF THE HOSPITAL.

Mb. Harding and the archdeacon together made their way to Oxford, and there, by dint of cunning argument, they induced the Master of Lazarus also to ask himself this momentous question: "Why should not Mr. Arabin be Dean of Barchester?" He of course, for a while tried his hand at persuading Mr. Harding that he was foolish, over-scrupulous, self-willed, and weak-minded; but he tried in vain. If Mr. Harding would not give way to Dr. Grantly, it was not likely he would give way to Dr. Gwynne; more especially now that so admirable a scheme as that of inducting Mr. Arabin into the deanery had been set on foot. When the master found that his eloquence was vain, and heard also that Mr. Arabin was about to become Mr. Harding's son-in-law, he confessed that he also would, under such circumstances, be glad to see his old friend and protege, the fellow of his college, placed in the comfortable position that was going a-begging.

'' It might be the means, you know, Master, of keeping Mr. Slope out," said the archdeacon with grave caution.

"He has no more chance of it," said the master, "than our college chaplain. I know more about it than that."

Mrs. Grantly had been right in her surmise. It was the Master of Lazarus who had been instrumental in representing in high places the claims which Mr. Harding had upon the Government, and he now consented to use his best endeavours towards getting the offer transferred to Mr. Arabin. The three of them went on to London together, and there they remained a week, to the great disgust of Mrs. Grantly, and most probably also of Mrs. Gwynne. The minister was out of town in one direction, and his private secretary in another. The clerks who remained could do nothing in such a matter as this, and all was difficulty and confusion. The two doctors seemed

to have plenty to do. They bustled here and they bustled there, and complained at their club in the evenings that they had been driven off their legs; but Mr. Harding had no occupation. Once or twice he suggested that he might perhaps return to Barchester. His request, however, was peremptorily refused, and he had nothing for it but to while away his time in Westminster Abbey. „

At length an answer from the great man came. The Master of Lazarus had made his proposition through the Bishop of Belgravia. Now this bishop, though but newly gifted with his diocesan honours, was a man of much weight in the clerico-political world. He was, if not as pious, at any rate as wise as St. Paul, and had been with so much effect all things to all men, that though he was great among the dons of Oxford, he had been selected for the most favourite seat on the bench by a Whig Prime Minister. To him Dr. Gwynne had made known his wishes and his arguments, and the bishop had made them known to the Marquis of Kensington Gore. The marquis, who was Lord High Steward of the Pantry Board, and who by most men was supposed to hold the highest office out of the Cabinet, trafficked much in affairs of this kind. He not only suggested the arrangement to the minister over a cup of coffee, standing on a drawing-room rug in Windsor Castle, but he also favourably mentioned Mr. Arabin's name in the ear of a distinguished person.

And so the matter was arranged. The answer of the great man came, and Mr. Arabin was made Dean of Barchester. The three clergymen who had come up to town on this important mission dined together with great glee on the day on which the news reached them. In a silent, decent, clerical manner, they toasted Mr. Arabin with full bumpers of claret. The satisfaction of all of them was supreme. The Master of Lazarus had been successful in his attempt, and success is dear to us all. The archdeacon had trampled upon Mr. Slope, and had lifted to high honours the young1 clergyman whom he had ind iced to quit the retirement and comfort of the uni-

versity. So at least the archdeacon thought;—though, to speak sooth, not he, but circumstances, had trampled on Mr. Slope. But the satisfaction of Mr. Harding was, of all, perhaps, the most complete. He laid aside his usual melancholy manner, and brought forth little quiet jokes from the inmost mirth of his heart; he poked his fun at the archdeacon about Mr. Slope's marriage, and quizzed him for his improper love for Mrs. Proudie. On the following day they all returned to Barchester.

It was arranged that Mr. Arabin should know nothing of what had been done till he received the "minister's letter from the hands of his embryo father-in-law. In order that no time might be lost, a message had been sent to lrn by the preceding night's post, begging him to be at the deanery at the hour that the train from London arrived. There was nothing in this which surprised Mr. Arabin. It had somehow got about through all Barchester that Mr. Harding was the new dean, and all Barchester was prepared to welcome him with pealing bells and full hearts. Mr. Slope had certainly had a party; there had certainly been those in Barchester who were prepared to congratulate him on his promotion with assumed sincerity; but even his own party was not broken-hearted by his failure. The inhabitants of the city, even the high-souled ecstatic young ladies of thirty-five, had begun to comprehend that their welfare, and the welfare of the place, was connected in some mysterious manner with daily chants and bi-weekly anthems. The expenditure of the palace had not added much to the popularity of the bishop's side of the question; and, on the whole, there was a strong reaction. When it became known to all the world that Mr. Harding was to be the new dean, all the world rejoiced heartily.

Mr. Arabin, we have said, was not surprised at the summons which called him to the deanery. He had not as yet seen Mr. Harding since Eleanor had accepted him, nor had he seen him since tie had learnt his future father-in-law's preferment. There was nothing more natural, more necessary, than that they should meet each other at the earliest possible moment. Mr. Arabin was waiting in the deanery parlour when Mr. Harding and Dr. Grantly were driven up from the station.

There was some excitement in the bosoms of them all, as they met and shook hands;—by far too much to enable either of them to begin his story and tell it in a proper equable style of narrative. Mr. Harding was some minutes quite dumbfounded, and Mr. Arabin could only talk in short, spasmodic sentences about his love and good fortune. He slipped in, as best he could, some sort of congratulation about the deanship, and then went on with his hopes and fears,—hopes that he might be received as a son and fears that he hardly deserved such good fortune. Then he went back to the dean; it was the most thoroughly satisfactory appointment, he said, of which he had ever heard.

"But! but! but "said Mr. Harding; and then failing to get any further, he looked imploringly at the archdeacon.

"The truth is, Arabin," said the doctor, "that, after all, you are not destined to be son-in-law to a dean. Nor am I either; more's the pity."

Mr. Arabin looked at him for explanation. "Is not Mr. Harding to be the new dean?"

"It appears not," said the archdeacon. Mr. Arabin's face fell a little, and he looked from one to the other. It was plainly to be seen from them both that there was no cause of unhappiness in the matter, at least not of unhappiness to them; but there was as yet no elucidation of the mystery.

"Think how old I am," said Mr. Harding, imploringly.

"Fiddlestick!" said the archdeacon.

"That's all very well, but it won't make a young man of me," said Mr. Harding.

"And who is to be dean?" asked Mr. Arabin.

"Yes; that's the question," said the archdeacon. "Come, Mr. Precentor, since you obstinately refuse to be anything else, let us know who is to be the man. He has got the nomination in his pocket."

With eyes brim full of tears, Mr. Harding pulled out the letter and handed it to his future son-in-law. He tried to make a little speech, but failed altogether. Having given up the document, he turned round to th« wall, feigning to blow his nose, and then sat himself down on the old dean's dingy horse-hair sofa. Here we find it necessary to bring our account of the interview to an end.

Nor can we pretend to describe the rapture with which Mr. Harding was received by his daughter. She wept with grief and wept with joy! with grief that her father should, in his old age, still be without that rank and worldly position which, according to her ideas, he had so well earned; and with joy in that he, her darling father, should have bestowed on that other dear one the good things of which he himself would not open his hand to take possession. And here Mr. Harding again showed his weakness. In the midst of this exposal of their loves and reciprocal affection, he found himself unable to resist the entreaties of all parties that the lodgings in the High Street should be given up. Eleanor would not live in the deanery, she said, unless her father lived there also. Mr. Arabin would not be dean, unless Mr. Harding would be co-dean with him The archdeacon declared that his father-in-law should not have his own way in everything, and Mrs. Grantly carried him off to Plumstead, that he might remain there till Mr. and Mrs. Arabin were in a state to receive him in their own mansion.

Pressed by such arguments as these, what could a weak old man do but yield?

But there was yet another task which it behoved Mr. Harding to do before he could allow himself to be at rest. Little has been said in these pages of the state of those remaining old men who had lived under his sway at the hospital. But not on this account must it be presumed that he had forgotten them, or that in their state of anarchy and in their want of due government he had omitted to visit them. He visited them constantly, and had latterly given them to understand that they would soon be re-

quired to subscribe their adherence to a new master. There were now but five of them, one of them having been but quite lately carried to his rest,—but five of the full number, which had hitherto been twelve, and which was now to be raised to twenty-four, including women. Of these old Bunce, who for many years had been the favourite of the late warden, was one; and Abel Handy, who had been the humble means of driving that warden from his home, was another.

Mr. Harding now resolved that he himself would introduce the new warden to the hospital. He felt that many circumstances might conspire to make the men receive Mr. Quiverful with aversion and disrespect. He felt also that Mr. Quiverful might himself feel some qualms of conscience if he entered the hospital with an idea that he did so in hostility to his predecessor. Mr. Harding therefore determined to walk in, arm in arm with Mr. Quiverful, and to ask from these men their respectful obedience to their new master.

On returning to Barchester he found that Mr. Quiverful had not yet slept in the hospital house, or entered on his new duties. He accordingly made known to that gentleman his wishes, and his proposition was not rejected.

It was a bright clear morning, though in November, that Mr. Harding and Mr. Quiverful, arm in arm, walked through the hospital gate. It was one trait in our old friend's character that he did nothing with parade. He omitted, even in the more important doings of his life, that sort of parade by which most of us deem it necessary to grace our important doings. We have housewarmings, christenings, and gala days; we keep, if not our own birthdays, those of our children; we are apt to fuss ourselves if called upon to change our residences, and have, almost all of us, our little state occasions. Mr. Harding had no state occasions. When he left his old house, he went forth from it with the same quiet composure as though he were merely taking his daily walk; and now that he re-entered it with another warden under his wing, he did so with the same quiet step and calm demeanour. He was a little less upright than he had been five years; nay, it was now nearly six years ago; he walked perhaps a little slower; his footfall was perhaps a thought less firm; otherwise one might have said that he was merely returning with a friend under his arm.

This friendliness was everything to Mr. Quiverful. To him, even in his poverty, the thought that he was supplanting a brother clergyman so kind and courteous as Mr. Harding, had been very bitter. Under his circumstances it had been impossible for him to refuse the proffered boon; he could not reject the bread that was offered to his children, or refuse to ease the heavy burden that had so long oppressed that poor wife of his. Nevertheless, it had been very grievous to him to think that in going to the hospital he might encounter the ill will of his brethren in the diocese. All this Mr. Harding had fully comprehended. It was for such feelings as these, for the nice comprehension of such motives, that his heart and intellect were peculiarly fitted. In most matters of worldly import the archdeacon set down his father-in-law as little' better than a fool. And perhaps he was right. But in some other matters, equally important if they be rightly judged, Mr. Harding, had he been so minded, might with as much propriety have set down his son-in-law for a fool. Few men, however, are constituted as was Mr. Harding. He had that nice appreciation of the feelings of others which belongs of right exclusively to women.

Arm in arm they walked into the inner quadrangle of the building, and there the five old men met them. Mr. Harding shook hands with them all, and then Mr. Quiverful did the same. With Bunce Mr. Harding shook hands twice, and Mr. Quiverful was about to repeat the same ceremony, but the old man gave him no encouragement.

"I am very glad to know that at last you have a new warden," said Mr. Harding in a very cheery voice.

"We be very old for any change," said one of them; "but we do suppose it be all for the best."

"Certainly,—certainly it is for the best," said Mr. Harding. "You will again have a clergyman of your own church under the same roof with you, and a very excellent clergyman you will have.

It is a great satisfaction to me to know that so good a man is coming to take care of you, and that it is no stranger, but a friend of my own, who will allow me from time to time to come in and see you."

"We be very thankful to your reverence," said another of them.

"I need not tell you, my good friends," said Mr. Quiverful, "how extremely grateful I am to Mr. Harding for his kindness ti me;—I must say his uncalled for, unexpected kindness."

"He be always very kind," said a third.

"What I can do to fill the void which he left here, I will do. For your sake and my own I will do so, and especially for his sake. But to you who have known him, I can never be the same wellloved friend and father that he has been."

"No, sir, no," said old Bunce, who hitherto had held his peace; "no one can be that. Not if the new bishop sent a hangel to us out of heaven. We doesn't doubt you'll do your best, sir; but you'll not be like the old master; not to us old ones."

"Fie, Bunce, fie! how dare you talk in that way?" said Mr. Harding; but as he scolded the old man he still held him by his arm, and pressed it with warm affection.

There was no getting up any enthusiasm in the matter. How could five old men tottering away to their final resting-place be enthusiastic on the reception of a stranger? What could Mr. Quiverful be to them, or they to Mr. Quiverful? Had Mr. Harding indeed come back to them, some last flicker of joyous light might have shone forth on their aged cheeks; but it was in vain to bid them rejoice because Mr. Quiverful was about to move his fourteen children from Puddingdale into the hospital house. In reality they did no doubt receive advantage, spiritual as well as corporal; but this they could neither anticipate nor acknowledge.

It was a dull affair enough, this introduction of Mr. Quiverful; but still it had its effect. The good which Mr. Harding intended did not fall to the ground. All the Barchester world, including the five old bedesmen, treated Mr. Quiverful with the more respect, because Mr. Harding had thus walked in arm in arm with him, on his first entrance to his duties.

And here in their new abode we will leave Mr. and Mrs. Quiverful and their fourteen children. May they enjoy the good things which Providence has at length given to them I CHAPTER Lin.
CONCLUSION.

The end of a novel, like the end of a children's dinner-party, must be made up of sweetmeats and sugar-plums. There is now nothing else to be told but the gala doings of Mr. Arabin's marriage, nothing more to be described than the wedding dresses, no further dialogue to be recorded than that which took place between the archdeacon who married them, and Mr. Arabin and Eleanor who were married. "Wilt thou have this woman to thy wedded wife," and "wilt thou have this man to thy wedded husband, to live together according to God's ordinance?" Mr. Arabin and Eleanor each answered, "I will." We have no doubt that they will keep their promises;—the more especially as the Signora Neroni had left Barchester before the ceremony was performed.

Mrs. Bold had been somewhat more than two years a widow before she was married to her second husband, and little Johnnie was then able with due assistance to walk on his own legs into the drawing-room to receive the salutations of the assembled guests. Mr. Harding gave away the bride, the archdeacon performed the service, and the-two Miss Grantlys, who were joined in their labours by other young ladies of the neighbourhood, performed the duties of bridesmaids with equal diligence and grace. Mrs. Grantly superintended the breakfasts and bouquets, and Mary Bold distributed the cards and cake. The archdeacon's three sons had also come home for the occasion. The eldest was great with learning. being regarded by all who knew him as a certain future double first. The second, however, bore the palm on this occasion, bang vot.. n. c o resplendent in a new uniform. The third was just entering the university, and was probably the proudest of the three.

But the most remarkable feature in the whole occasion was the excessive liberality oi the archdeacon. He literally made presents to everybody. As Mr. Arabin had already moved out of the parsonage of St. Ewold's, that scheme of elongating the diningroom was of course abandoned j but he would have refurnished the whole deanery had he been allowed. He sent down a magnificent piano by Erard, gave Mr. Arabin a cob which any dean in the land might have been proud to bestride, and made a special present to Eleanor of a new pony chair that had gained a prize in the Exhibition. Nor did he even stay his hand here; he bought a set of cameos for his wife, and a sapphire bracelet for Miss Bold; showered pearls and work-boxes on his daughters, and to each of his sons he presented a cheque for *20l*. On Mr. Harding he bestowed a magnificent violoncello with all the new-fashioned arrangements and expensive additions, which, on account of these novelties, that gentleman could never use with satisfaction to hia audience or pleasure to himself.

Those who knew the archdeacon well, perfectly understood the cause of his extravagance. 'Twas thus that he sang his song of triumph over Mr. Slope. This was his paean, his hymn of thanksgiving, his loud oration. He had girded himself with his sword, and gone forth to the war. Now he was returning from the field laden with the spoils of the foe. The cob and the cameos, the violoncello and the pianoforte, were all as it were trophies reft from the tent of his now conquered enemy.

The Arabins after their marriage went abroad for a couple of months, according to the custom in such matters now duly established, and then commenced their deanery life under good auspices. And nothing can be more pleasant than the present arrangement of ecclesiastical affairs in Barchester. The titular bishop never interfered, and Mrs. Proudie not often. Her sphere is more" extended, more noble, and more suited to her ambition than that of a cathedral city. As long as she can do what she pleases with the diocese, she is willing to leave the dean and chapter to themselves. Mr. Slope tried his hand at subverting the old-established customs of the close, and from his failure she has learnt experience. The burly chancellor and the meagre little prebendary are not teased by any application respecting Sabbath-day schools, the dean is left to his own dominions, and the intercourse between Mrs. Proudie and Mrs. Arabin is confined to a yearly dinner given by each to the other. At these dinners Dr. Grantly will not take a part; but he never fails to ask for and receive a full account of all that Mrs. Proudie either does or says.

His ecclesiastical authority has been greatly shorn since the palmy days in which he reigned supreme as mayor of the palace to his father, but nevertheless such authority as is now left to him he can enjoy without interference. He can walk down the High Street of Barchester without feeling that those who see him are comparing his claims with those of Mr. Slope. The intercourse between Plumstead and the deanery is of the most constant and familiar description. Since Eleanor has been married to a clergy man, and especially to a dignitary of the church, Mrs. Grantly has found many more points of sympathy with her sister; and on a coming occasion, which is much looked forward to by all parties, she intends to spend a month or two at the deanery. She never thought of spending a month in Barchester when little Johnny Bold was born!

The two sisters do not quite agree on matters of church doctrine, though their differences are of the most amicable description. Mrs. Arabin's church is two degrees higher than that of Mrs. Grantly. This may seem strange to those who will remember that Eleanor was once accused of partiality to Mr. Slope; but it is no less the fact. She likes her husband's silken vest, she likes his adherence to the rubric, she specially likes the eloquent philosophy of his sermons, and she likes the red letters in her own prayer-book. It must not be presumed that she has a taste for candles, or that she is at all astray about the real presence; but she has an inkling tnat way. She sent a handsome subscription towards certain very heavy ecclesiastical legal expenses which have lately been incurred in Bath, her name of course not appearing; she assumes a smile of gentle ridicule when the Archbishop of Canterbury is named, and she has put up a memorial window in the cathedral.

Mrs. Grantly, who belongs to the high and dry church, the high church as it was some fifty years since, before tracts were written and young clergymen took upon themselves the highly meritorious duty of cleaning churches, rather laughs at her sister. She shrugs her shoulders, and tells Miss Thorne that she supposes Eleanor will have an oratory in the deanery before she has done. But she is not on that account a whit displeased. A few high church vagaries do not, she thinks, sit amiss on the shoulders of a young dean's wife. It shows at any rate that her heart is in the subject; and it shows moreover that she is removed, wide as the poles asunder, from that cesspool of abomination in which it was once suspected that she would wallow and grovel. Anathema maranatha! Let anything else be held as blessed, so that that be well cursed. Welcome kneelings and bowings, welcome matins and complines, welcome bell, book, and candle, so that Mr. Slope's dirty surplices and ceremonial Sabbaths be held in due execration!

If it be essentially and absolutely necessary to choose between the two, we are inclined to agree with Mrs. Grantly that the bell, book, and candle are the lesser evil of the two. Let it however be understood that no such necessity is admitted in these pages.

Dr. Arabin,—we suppose he must have become a doctor when he became a dean,—is more moderate and less outspoken on doctrinal points than his wife, as indeed in his station it behoves him to be. He is a studious, thoughtful, haid-working man. He lives constantly at the deanery, and preaohes nearly every Sunday. His time is spent in sifting and editing old ecclesiastical literature, and in producing the same articles new. At Oxford he is generally regarded as the most promising clerical ornament of the age. He and his wife live together in perfect mutual confidence. There is but one secret in her bosom which he has not shared. He has never yet learned how Mr. Slope had his ears boxed

The Stanhopes soon found that Mr. Slope's power need no longer operate to keep them from the delight of their Italian villa. Before Eleanor's marriage they had all migrated back to the shores of Como. They had not been resettled long before the Signora received from Mrs. Arabin a very pretty though very short epistle, in which she was informed of the fate of the writer. This letter was answered by another, bright, charming, and witty, as the Signora's letters always were; and so ended the friendship between Eleanor and the Stanhopes.

One word of Mr. Harding, and we have done.

He is still Precentor of Barchester, and still pastor of the little church of St. Cuthbert's. In spite of what he has so often said himself, he is not even yet an old man. He does such duties as fall to his lot well and concientiously, and is thankful that he has never been tempted to assume others for which he might be less fitted.

The Author now leaves him in the hands of his readers;—not as a hero, not as a man to be admired and talked of, not as a man who should be toasted at public dinners and spoken of with conventional absurdity as a perfect divine, but as a good man without guile, believing humbly in the religion which he has striven to teach, and guided by the precepts which he has striven to learn.

END OP VOL. 11. MUMTID BY J. S. VIRTUE AND CO., LIMITED, CITY ROAD, LONDON.

Lightning Source UK Ltd.
Milton Keynes UK
UKOW06f2221201114

241949UK00011B/416/P